KEY MATHS

▶ **David Baker**
The Anthony Gell School, Wirksworth

▶ **Jim Griffith**
The Bishop of Hereford's Bluecoat School, Hereford

▶ **Paul Hogan**
St. Wilfrid's Church of England High School, Blackburn

▶ **Chris Humble**
Gillotts School, Henley-on-Thames

▶ **Barbara Job**
Christleton County High School, Chester

▶ **Peter Sherran**
Weston Road High School, Stafford

Series Editor: **Paul Hogan**

First published in 1998 by
Stanley Thornes (Publishers) Ltd
Second edition published in 2001 by
Nelson Thornes Ltd
Delta Place
27 Bath Road
CHELTENHAM
GL53 7TH
United Kingdom

01   02   03   04   05   /   10   9   8   7   6   5   4   3   2

A catalogue record for this book is available from the British Library.

ISBN 0-7487-6203-5

Illustrations by Maltings Partnership, Peters and Zabransky, Oxford Illustrators, Clinton Banbury
Page make-up by Tech Set Ltd

Printed and bound in China by Midas

Acknowledgements
The publishers thank the following for permission to reproduce copyright material:
Allied Carpets: 468; Colorsport: 67 (S. Fraser); Getty Images: 156 (left – Tony Stone Images/
Kristian Hilsen); 327 (top – Tony Stone Images/
AB Wadham, 328 (AB Wadham); Image Bank: 156 (right – Michael Melford); Leslie Garland Picture Library: 107 (top – Kay Lomas), 108, 141 (Kay Lomas); Martyn Chillmaid: 1 (middle), 10, 12, 26, 32, 33, 47, 48, 53, 70, 71, 79 (middle), 85, 93, 301 (bottom), 314 (top), 340, 373, 385, 396, 414, 415, 416, 423, 429 (top right and bottom), 433 (top and middle), 439, 444, 471, 472; National Motor Museum: 307 (top); Skyscan Balloon Photography: 165, 166, 327 (bottom), 338, 433 (bottom), 453; Sporting Pictures: 107 (bottom), 116, 275 (bottom), 292; Rex Features: 305 (Vic Thomasson); Still Pictures: 301 (top – David Hoffman), 302; Stockmarket: 247, 252; Topham Picturepoint: 275 (Press Association), 283, 336, 428.
All other photographs Nelson Thornes Archive.

The publishers have made every effort to contact copyright holders but apologise if any have been overlooked.

Contents

1

1 Solids
Using faces, edges and vertices
Naming prisms
Using the language of angle
Drawing nets of solids

2 Recording experiments
Tallying
Designing tally-tables

3 Sizes of numbers
Understanding place value
Using decimals
Rounding to the nearest 10, 100, 1000

CORE

QUESTIONS

EXTENSION

TEST YOURSELF

1 Solids

Louise has grown some crystals.
She has to write about their shape in a report.

Louise is going to describe this crystal.
The crystal is a cuboid.
She needs some other words for her report.

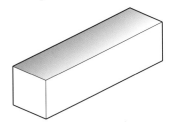

Face	The blue surface is called a **face**. The crystal has 6 faces. They are the top, the bottom and the 4 sides.
Edge	An **edge** is a line where two faces meet. The crystal has 12 edges. There are 4 on the top, 4 on the bottom and 4 vertical ones.
Vertex	A corner where edges meet is called a **vertex**. The plural of vertex is vertices. The crystal has 8 vertices, 4 at the top and 4 at the bottom.

This is how Louise describes the crystal:
'The crystal is a cuboid. It has 6 faces, 12 edges and 8 vertices.'

Exercise 1:1

1 This is how Louise describes this crystal.
Copy it and fill in the missing numbers:
'The crystal is a pyramid.
It has ... faces, ... edges and ... vertices.'

2 Describe each of these crystals. Their names are written by them.

   a Cube

   b Tetrahedron

Prism	A **prism** is a solid which is exactly the same shape and size all the way through.

When you cut a slice through the solid it is the same size and shape.

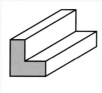 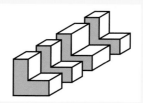

Cross section   The shape of this slice is called the **cross section** of the solid. The shape of the cross section is often used to name the prism.

---

3 Describe each of these prisms. Their names are written by them.
Remember to give the number of faces, edges and vertices.

   a Triangular prism   **b** Hexagonal prism   **c** Pentagonal prism

 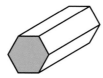 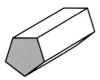

John is describing solids made out of wood.
Some of the solids have curved faces.
He decides to use algebra to cut down on the writing.

This solid is a cone.

It has *2 faces*, the bottom and the curved face.
John writes $f = 2$.
It has 1 *edge*, he writes $e = 1$.
It has 1 *vertex*, he writes $v = 1$.
This is how John describes the solid:
'The solid is a cone, $f = 2$, $e = 1$, $v = 1$.'

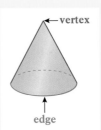

vertex

edge

4 a Which of these solids is a prism?

Square pyramid

Cylinder

Pentagonal pyramid

   b Use algebra to describe each of the solids.

5 a Copy this table.
   b Use your answers to questions **1–4** to fill it in.
 ● **c** Can you find a rule linking f, v and e?
        Use the last column to help you.

Solid	Number of faces, f	Number of vertices, v	Number of edges, e	$f + v$
cube tetrahedron triangular prism hexagonal prism pentagonal prism square pyramid pentagonal pyramid				

6 This solid is called a **sphere**.
  a Write down the values for f, v and e.
  b Does it fit the rule that you found in question **5**?

Plane	A flat surface is called a **plane**.

This shape has all plane faces.

This shape has 1 plane face and 1 curved face.

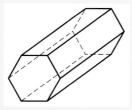 

---

7 Draw a solid which has:
  a 1 curved face and 2 plane faces
  b all plane faces
  c 1 curved face only

Parallel lines	**Parallel lines** never meet. They stay the same distance apart.

Acute angle	Any angle less than 90° is called an **acute angle**.

Obtuse angle	Any angle between 90° and 180° is called an **obtuse angle**.

Reflex angle	Any angle bigger than 180° is called a **reflex angle**.

| **Perpendicular** | 2 lines at right angles to each other are **perpendicular**. | 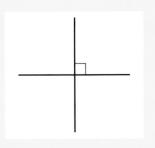 |

Exercise 1:2

The cross sections of these solids are shaded blue.

A    **C** 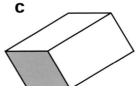   **E**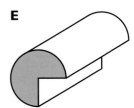

B 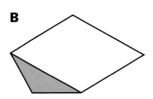   **D** 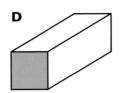   **F**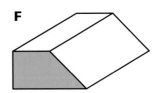

Look at the solids at the start of the exercise.

1 Which of the solids have a cross section that contains:
  a an obtuse angle   **c** a right angle
  b a reflex angle   **d** sides that are parallel?

2 **a** Which of the solids have all plane faces?
  b Which solid has a curved face?

3 Which solid has a cross section that is:
  a a square   **c** a trapezium
  b a parallelogram   **d** part of a circle?

Net

When a solid is opened out and laid flat, the shape that you get is called a **net** of the solid.

This solid   gives   this net.

You can have more than one net for a solid. This is also a net of the same solid.

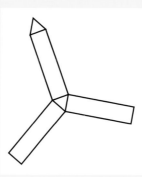

Exercise 1:3

1 Here are some patterns of shapes. Some of them are nets of cubes.
   a Draw the patterns on to squared paper.
   b Cut them out.
   c Fold them up to see if they make a cube.
   d Write down the letters of the ones that make cubes.

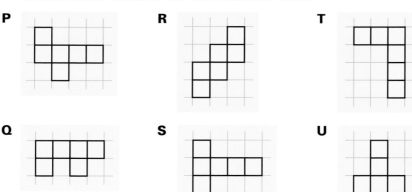

P   R   T

Q   S   U

2 a Copy this net on to 1 cm squared paper.

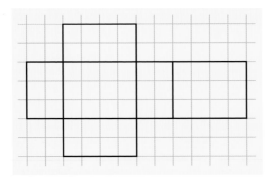

    b Cut out the net. Fold it to make a solid.
    c Write down the name of the solid.
    d The length of the solid is 4 cm.
       Write down the width and the height of the solid.

3 This is a net of a cuboid.
All of the lengths are in centimetres.
Write down the length, width
and height of the cuboid.

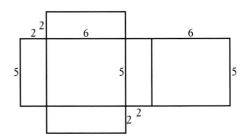

4 a Copy this net.
     Cut it out.
   b Fold it along the lines.
   c Write down the name of
     the solid that it makes.

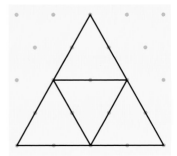

5 Sketch the net of this
square-based pyramid.

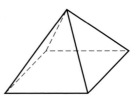

6 Match each solid with its net.

a

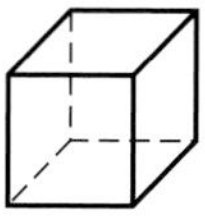

P

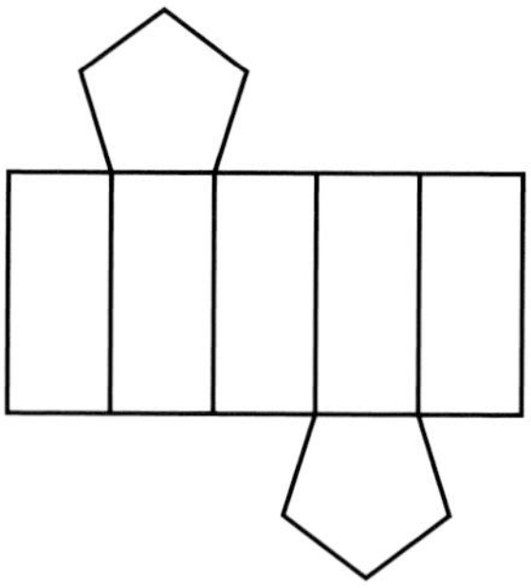

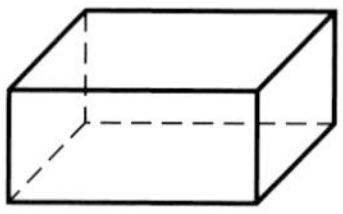

S

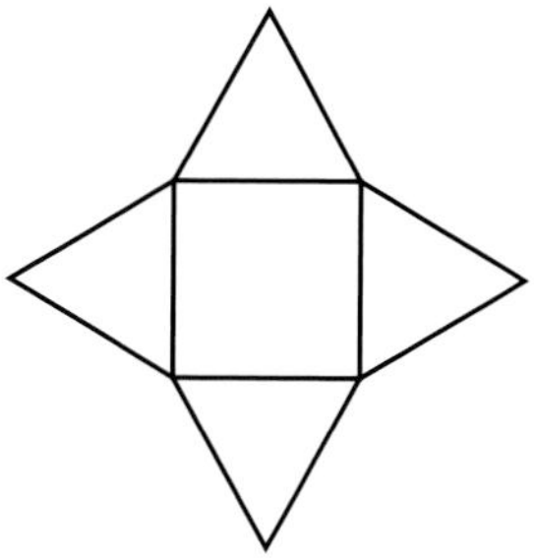

b

c

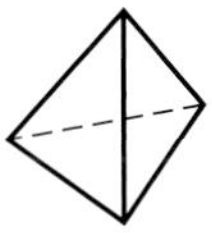

Q

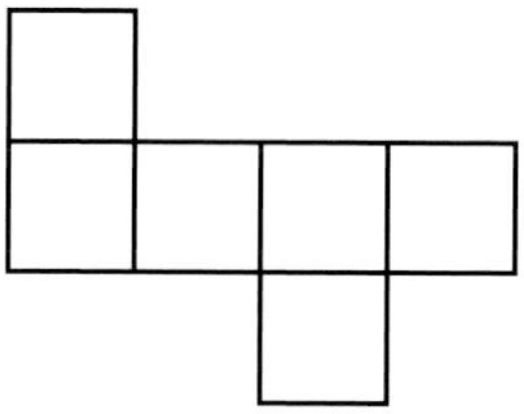

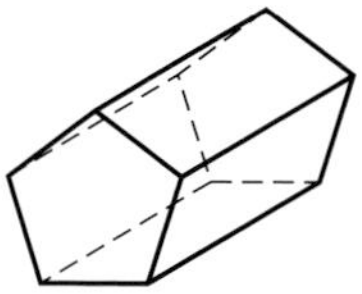

U

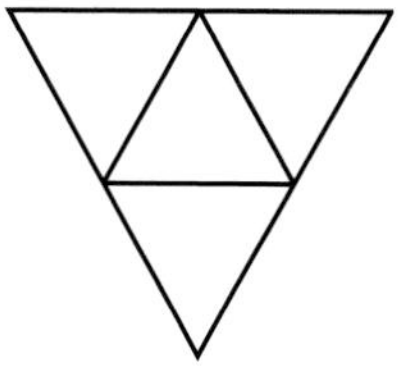

d

e

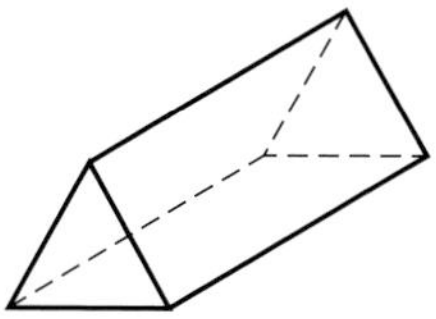

T

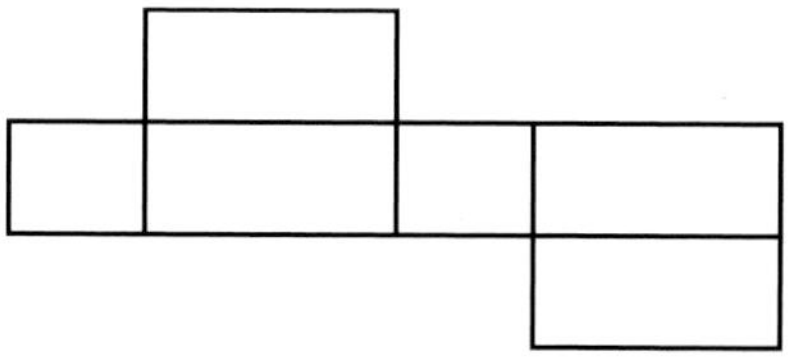

f

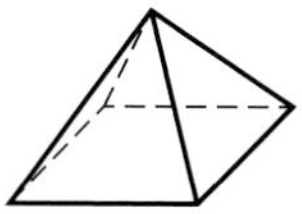

R

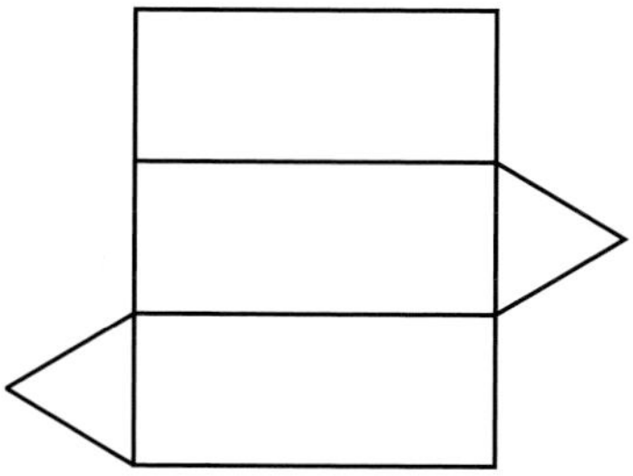

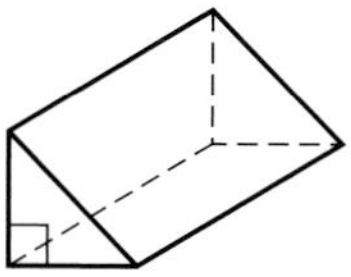

V

g

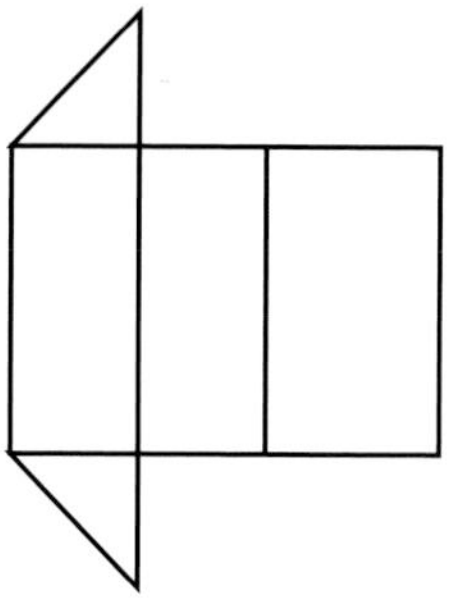

2   Recording experiments

Year 10 are doing some probability experiments.

They are recording their results using a tally-table.

Exercise 1:4

W   You will need Worksheet 1:1 for this exercise.

1   Cut out the net of the dice.

2   Glue the net carefully to make the dice.

3   Cut out the net of the hexagonal prism.

4   Colour the long faces in the colours marked. Colour the three faces that you cannot see in this diagram the same way.

5   Glue the net carefully to make the prism.

You are going to do some experiments with the shapes that you have made. You will need to use a tally-table to record your results.

Tally-marks	**Tally-marks** are always done in groups of five.
	The fifth tally-mark goes across the other 4 like this: ⵜ
	This makes them easier to count.

Exercise 1:5

Write down the number of tally-marks in each of these questions.

1   ⵜ II

2   ⵜ ⵜ III

3   ⵜ ⵜ ⵜ ⵜ I

4   ⵜ ⵜ ⵜ III

5   ⵜ ⵜ ⵜ IIII

6   ⵜ ⵜ ⵜ ⵜ ⵜ ⵜ II

Exercise 1:6

1 **a** Copy this tally-table.

Number	Tally	Total
1		
2		
3		
4		
5		
6		

b Roll a dice 60 times.
Record the number you get each time in your tally-table.

2 **a** Fill in the total column.
b Is the total the same for each number?
c How many times did you expect to get each number?

3 **a** Copy this tally-table.

Colour	Tally	Total
red		
green		
blue		

b Roll your hexagonal prism from Exercise 1:4 60 times.
Record the colour you get each time in your tally-table.

4 **a** Fill in the total column.
b Did you get each colour the same
number of times?
c Did you expect to get equal numbers?
Explain your answer.

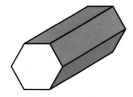

Exercise 1:7

1 Kelly is doing a probability experiment.
She rolls the dice and the prism from Exercise 1:4 together.
She records the number and the colour in a tally-table.

Here is part of her tally-table:

	1	2	3
red green			

a Copy Kelly's table and finish it off.
It must show all the numbers and all the colours.

b Kelly got a red and a $\boxed{\cdot}$ 3 times.

Show this as a tally in your table.

c Kelly got a blue and a $\boxed{\cdot\,}$ 4 times.

Show this as a tally in your table.

d Add these results to your table as tallies:

Green and $\boxed{::}$ twice

Red and $\boxed{::}$ 7 times

Blue and $\boxed{\therefore}$ 5 times

2 a Make another copy of the tally-table.

b Throw your dice and prism 60 times together.
Record each throw in your tally-table.

c Which result did you get most often?

d Which result did you get least often?

Tally-tables are also used to record the results of surveys.

Exercise 1:8

Robbie is doing a computer survey for his GCSE coursework.
He is trying to find out what type of computer pupils in Year 10 own.
Here are his results from 50 Year 10 pupils who own computers.

Computer type	Tally	Total
PC	⅃H ⅃H ⅃H ⅃H	
PlayStation	⅃H ‖	
Nintendo	⅃H ⅃H ⅃H	
Other	⅃H ‖‖	

1 Write down the number of people who own each type of machine.

2 Robbie asked how many computer games each person owned.
The answers ranged from 5 to 72.
Design a tally-table that Robbie could use to put his data in.

3 Robbie then asked how much time each person spent on their computer
on an average day.
The answers ranged from 30 minutes to $3\frac{1}{2}$ hours.
Design a tally-table that Robbie could use to record these results.

4 Robbie asked all the PC owners to give him details of their machines.
Here are some of his results:

	RAM (Mb)	Disk size (Gb)	CD	Printer	Video card	Sound card	Speakers
Chris	16	1	yes	colour	yes	yes	yes
Saadiya	8	1.4	yes	laser	no	no	no
Alison	32	2	yes	none	no	yes	yes
Maggie	16	0.8	no	inkjet	no	yes	no
Ron	32	3	yes	laser	yes	yes	yes

a How many of the PC owners have printers?
b Does Maggie have a video card?
c How much RAM does Alison have?
d Which of the PC owners have sound cards?

3   Sizes of numbers

A supertanker can carry two hundred and sixty-seven million litres of petrol. This number is 267 000 000 litres if you write it in figures.

When you write large numbers you group the digits in 3s from the right with gaps in between.

Look at this number: 461 942
                                              ↑
                            This gap tells you where the thousands start.

The group on the left is the number of thousands.
The number is four hundred and sixty-one thousand, nine hundred and forty-two.

Look at this number: 14 865 293
                                        ↑
                            This gap tells you where the millions start.

This number has an extra group on the left. This is the number of millions.
The number is fourteen million, eight hundred and sixty-five thousand, two hundred and ninety-three.

Exercise 1:9

1   Write these numbers in words.
   a   351 836   **c**   245 870   **e**   7 540 672
   b   87 316   **d**   400 769   **f**   82 649 400

2   Write these numbers in figures.
   a   Three million, two hundred and sixty-five thousand, eight hundred and two.
   b   Three hundred and twenty-six thousand, one hundred and thirty.
   c   Five million, seventy thousand and fifty-one.

3 **a** The Pacific is the largest ocean in the world.
It has an area of 166 241 700 km². Write this number in words.

b The Arctic is the smallest ocean. It has an area of thirteen million, two hundred and twenty-three thousand, seven hundred square kilometres. Write this number in figures.

4 The largest of the world's seas is the South China Sea. It has an area of 2 974 600 km². Write this number in words.

5 Put these numbers in order of size.
Start with the smallest.
a 637   397   372   839
b 45 821   72 498   31 483   56 700
c 4 582 287   375 693   8 483 201   94 573
d 3 684 720   3 825 184   3 285 764   3 926 400

To put decimals in order of size, look at one decimal place at a time.

(1) Look at the numbers before the decimal point first.

94.81 is smaller than 172.34 because **94** is smaller than **172**.

94.81
172.34

(2) If the numbers before the decimal point are the same, then look at the first number after the decimal point.

24.217 is smaller than 24.645 because **2** is smaller than **6**.

24.217
24.645

(3) Sometimes you need to look at the second number after the decimal point.

16.251 is smaller than 16.28 because **5** is smaller than **8**.

16.251
16.28

Exercise 1:10

1 Put these numbers in order of size.
Start with the smallest.
a 2.56   6.41   1.89   **c** 3.257   3.291   3.214
b 14.13   14.81   14.52   **d** 9.35   9.08   9.12

2 These are the lengths, in millimetres, of some crystals.
Put them in order of size. Start with the smallest.

1.57   1.38   1.29   1.72   1.6

3 These are the times that 6 people took to run a cross-country race.
All of the times are in minutes.
Put them in order of size. Start with the fastest time.

     24.6   23.8   25.1   23.2   23.6   22.9

4 These are the number of kilometres cycled by 5 men in one hour.
Put them in order of size, starting with the smallest.

     46.393   45.558   46.923   45.398   46.159

The usual attendance at a Chester City
football match is 2000.

This does not mean that exactly
2000 people come to every game.

The number has been rounded to the
nearest 1000.

You often need to round numbers to a
sensible degree of accuracy.

Rounding to the nearest 10

Examples   **1** Round the number 63 to the nearest 10.

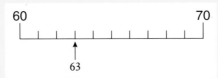

63 is nearer to 60 than 70.
It is rounded to 60 to the nearest 10.

       2 Round the number 85 to the nearest 10.

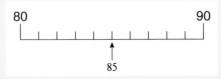

85 is half-way between 80 and 90.
It is rounded to 90 to the nearest 10.

Exercise 1:11

1 Round these numbers to the nearest 10.

a	17	**c**	18	**e**	55	**g**	52	**i**	142
b	84	**d**	46	**f**	79	**h**	99	**j**	237

2 2478 people went to the first match of the 1997/98 season at Chester City.
Write this number to the nearest 10.

3 Paul has done some calculations on a calculator.
These are the calculator displays of his answers.
Round each answer to the nearest 10.

    a *534*   **c** *628*   **e** *3144*

    b *709*   **d** *265*   **f** *79355*

4 These are the number of runs of 6 cricketers.

Name	Score		Name	Score
Lamb	89		Jones	41
Botham	117		Lewis	69
Edwards	65		Lee	5

Write each score to the nearest 10.

Rounding to the nearest 100

Examples

1 Round the number 683 to the nearest 100.

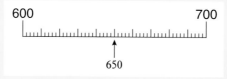

600   700

683

683 is nearer to 700 than 600.
It is rounded to 700 to the nearest 100.

2 Round the number 650 to the nearest 100.

600   700

650

650 is half-way between 600 and 700.
It is rounded to 700 to the nearest 100.

5 Round these numbers to the nearest 100.

a	347	**d**	478	**g**	523	● **j**	4264
b	259	**e**	650	**h**	799	● **k**	1425
c	186	**f**	389	● **i**	999	● **l**	2307

6 2478 people went to the first match of the 1997/98 season at Chester City. Write this number to the nearest 100.

7 76 384 people went to a pop concert. Write this number to the nearest 100.

8 The table has the depth of the deepest caves in 5 countries. Write each depth to the nearest 100 feet.

Depth (ft)	Country
5256	France
4872	Austria
4839	Mexico
4728	Spain
4098	Italy

Rounding to the nearest 1000

Examples

1 Round the number 6125 to the nearest 1000.

6125 is nearer to 6000 than 7000.
It is rounded to 6000 to the nearest 1000.

2 Round the number 4500 to the nearest 1000.

4500 is half-way between 4000 and 5000.
It is rounded to 5000 to the nearest 1000.

9 Round these numbers to the nearest 1000.

a	1473	**d**	3276	**g**	3501	**j**	42 454
b	5694	**e**	5500	**h**	9999	**k**	129 999
c	1256	**f**	7555	**i**	14 251	**l**	412 867

10 These are the attendances at the first matches of the Premier League for the 1997/98 football season.
Write each attendance to the nearest 1000.

Team	Attendance
Barnsley	18 667
Blackburn	23 557
Coventry	22 686
Everton	35 716
Leeds	37 993
Leicester	20 304
Newcastle	36 711
Southampton	15 206
Wimbledon	26 106

11 The table gives the areas of some countries in Europe.

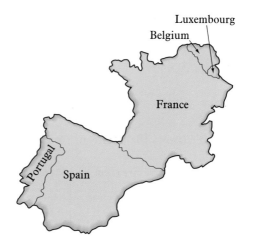

Country	Area (km²)
Belgium	30 513
France	547 026
Luxembourg	2576
Portugal	92 082
Spain	504 782

a Write down the area of each country to the nearest thousand square kilometres.

b Write the countries in order of size. Start with the smallest.

1 Which of these solids are prisms?
Write down their letters.

A    **B**   **C**   **D**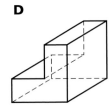

2 Look at this solid.
Write down the number of:

   a vertices   **b** faces   **c** edges

3 Write down the name of each of these angles.
Choose from acute, obtuse, reflex and right.

   a 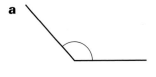   **b** 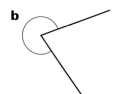   **c**

4 Write down the number of tally-marks in each of these questions.

   a ⩘ ‖‖   **c** ⩘ ‖‖‖   **e** ⩘ ⩘ ⩘ ‖‖

   b ⩘ ⩘ ⩘ ⩘ | **d** ⩘ ⩘ ⩘ ⩘ ⩘   **f** ⩘ ⩘ ⩘ ⩘ ⩘ ‖‖

5 This table shows the details of some of the UK's major reservoirs.

Name	Area (km^2)	Area (miles^2)	Capacity (megalitres)
Rutland Water	12.60	4.86	124 000
Kielder Water	11.00	4.25	199 175
Derwent	4.05	1.56	9478
Loch Bradan	2.09	0.84	20 700
Trawsfynydd	4.78	1.84	32 550
Lough Island	1.05	0.41	7683

   a Which reservoir has the biggest capacity?
   b Which reservoir covers the most area?
   c Which reservoirs cover less than 1 mile^2?
   d Which reservoirs have less than 50 000 megalitres capacity?

6 These are the times that 5 people took to run a cross-country race.
   All the times are in minutes.
   Put them in order of size. Start with the fastest.

   23.9   24.1   22.1   19.2   20.7

7 The highest price ever paid for a diamond is £10 507 143.
   Write this price in words.

8 Sara uses each of the digits 5 8 1 4 to make up a four-digit number.
   For example, she can make 5184.
   a What is the smallest even number that she can make?
   b What is the largest odd number that she can make?
   c What is the smallest odd number that she can make?

9 Write these numbers in words.
   a 325 124   **c** 325 147   **e** 6 245 000
   b 23 148   **d** 200 957   **f** 36 120 001

10 Round these numbers to the nearest 10.
    a 23   **c** 14   **e** 75   **g** 55   **i** 124
    b 97   **d** 28   **f** 92   **h** 120   **j** 547

11 The Royal Family receives money from the 'Civil list'.
    Some of the amounts for 1997 were:

    The Queen   £5 090 230
    The Queen Mother   £   439 520
    The Duke of York   £   169 470

    Round these amounts to the nearest £1000.

12 The lengths of some of Britain's rivers are:

River	Length (km)
Severn	354
Thames	346
Trent	297
Aire	259
Ouse	230
Tyne	118.5

    Round these distances to the nearest 10 km.

1 Look at this solid.
Write down the number of:

a vertices   **b** faces   **c** edges

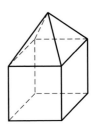

2 Look at these decimals.
Write them in order of size.
Start with the smallest.

     3.26   3.621   3.620   3.266   3.2641

3 These are some of the top films ever shown in the UK.
This list shows how much they took at the box office.
Round each amount to the nearest £100.

Film	Amount
Robin Hood: Prince of Thieves	£19 823 356
Terminator 2: Judgment Day	£18 014 880
The Silence of the Lambs	£17 112 896
Three Men and a Little Lady	£12 967 783
Home Alone	£11 997 997
Dances with Wolves	£10 598 273

4 The daily circulation of some national
newspapers is shown here.
Write these numbers out in full.

Newspaper	Circulation
Daily Express	1.56 million
Daily Mail	1.7 million
Daily Mirror	2.91 million

5 Which of these is a net of this cube?

a

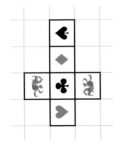

b

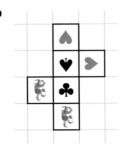

c

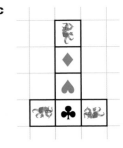

1 **a** Write down the name of this solid.

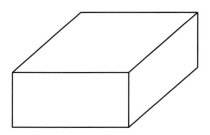

  b Write down the number of:
   (1) vertices
   (2) faces
   (3) edges
  c Sketch a net for the solid.

2 The angle 90° is a right angle.
Write down an angle that is:

  a reflex   **b** acute   **c** obtuse

3 Liam has measured the height of 6 of his friends.
These are the heights in metres.

   1.30   1.37   1.29   1.08   1.45   1.21

Write these heights in order of size.
Start with the tallest.

4 Each net will make a 3-D shape.
Write down the name of each shape and sketch the shape.

  a   **b**

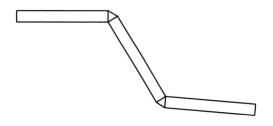

5 Julia is a receptionist. She records the number of phone calls that she answers each hour during one week. This is Julia's data.

7	4	2	6	3	5	1	6	5	7	4	7
5	8	7	3	5	4	7	5	2	8	5	4
3	6	8	4	5	7	5	4	8	3	7	2

a Copy this tally-table.
b Enter Julia's data into the tally-table.

Number of calls	Tally	Total
1		
2		
3		
4		
5		
6		
7		
8		

6 One hundred and forty thousand, seven hundred and nine people visited a National Trust Manor House.
a (1) Write this number in figures.
(2) Write this number to the nearest thousand.

95 082 of the visitors were members of the National Trust.
b (1) Write this number in words.
(2) Write this number to the nearest hundred.

7 The table gives the prices of new cars in August 2000.

Car	Price in £	Price to the nearest £100
Ford Ka	9595	
Nissan Micra	9550	
Peugeot 106	9070	
Rover Mini Cooper	9630	
Vauxhall Corsa	9295	
Fiat Punto	9995	

a Copy the table. Fill in the last column.
b Write down the cars in order of price. Start with the cheapest.

2

1 Drawing shapes
Drawing shapes on isometric paper
Completing part drawn shapes on isometric paper
Drawing missing pieces of shapes
Plans and elevations

2 Grouping data
Getting information
Tallying discrete data
Reading tally-tables
Tallying grouped discrete data

CORE

3 Fractions of an amount
Finding fractions of quantities
Using a calculator to make it easy

4 Sequences
Writing down terms of a sequence
Writing down missing terms
Looking at special sequences
  – odd numbers
  – even numbers
  – multiples
  – square numbers
  – triangle numbers
Playing a sequence game

01 07 22 25 31 47

04 10 25 36 44 47

08 20 27 28 36 41

02 09 19 20 38 49

? ? ? ? ? ?

QUESTIONS

EXTENSION

TEST YOURSELF

1   Drawing shapes

Look at this picture carefully.

Can you see what is wrong with it?

You can use isometric paper to help you draw some 3-D shapes.
But you must remember to use it the right way up. It must show vertical lines.

Example   Copy the cube onto the grid.

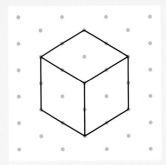

Start at a corner.

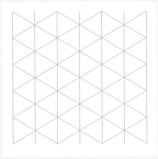

Use the grid this way up.

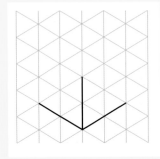

Every line on the grid is in
one of these directions.

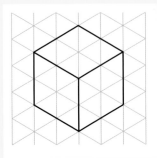

Follow the grid lines to
complete the drawing.

Exercise 2:1

1 Copy these objects onto isometric paper.

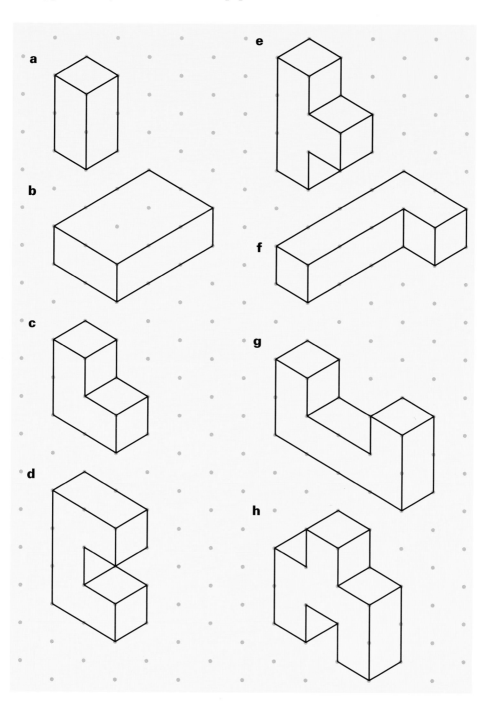

2 Copy and complete each diagram so that it shows a cuboid.

a

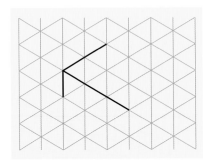

d

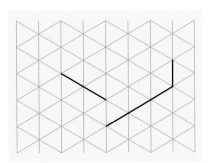

b

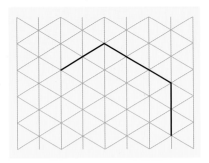

e

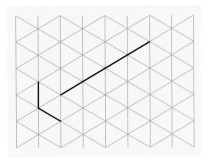

c

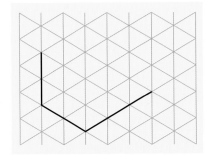

f

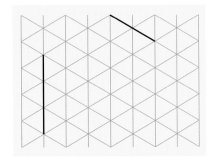

3 Each diagram shows a cuboid with a piece missing.
Draw the missing piece.

a

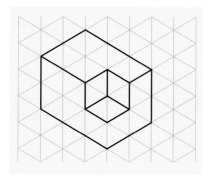

d

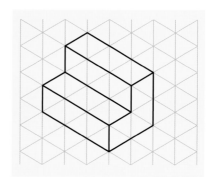

b

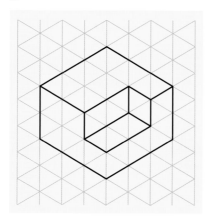

e

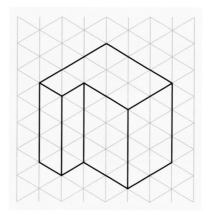

c

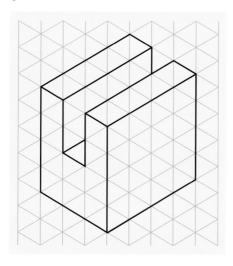

f

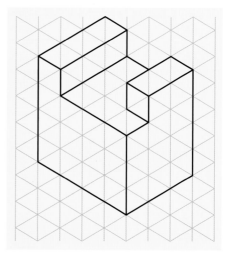

Here is an object made up of cubes.

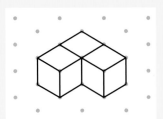

Katie is looking at the object from directly above.
This is what she sees.

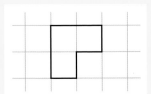

This is called the plan view of the object.

Exercise 2:2

1 Draw the plan view of each of these objects.

a

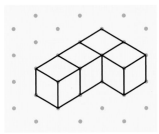

c

b

d

Here is another object.

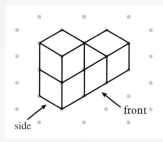

Leah is looking at the object
from the front.
This is what she sees.

Danielle is looking at the object
from the side.
This is what she sees.

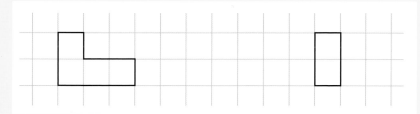

This is called the
front elevation of the object.

This is called the
side elevation of the object.

2 Draw the front elevation of each of these objects.

a 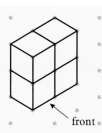 **b**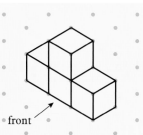

3 Draw the front and side elevations of each of these objects.

a 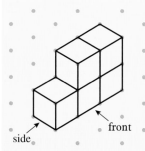 **b**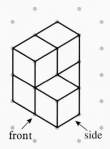

2 Grouping data

John is the salesman at this garage.

He has a list of all the cars for sale.

Rita wants a blue car.

Anna wants an 'S' registration car.

John needs to know how many of each type of car he has.

He needs to organise his data to be able to help people.

Exercise 2:3

W   You will need Worksheet 2:2 for this exercise.

1 **a** Look at the colours of the cars.
Copy this tally-table.
Fill it in.

Colour	Tally	Number of cars
red blue green white grey black silver		

b How many cars has John got altogether?
c Afzal wants a red car.
How many red cars can Afzal choose from?

2 **a** Look at the registration letters of the cars.
Copy this tally-table.
Fill it in.

Registration letter	Tally	Number of cars
J		
K		
L		
M		
N		
P		
R		
S		
T		

b How many 'S' registration cars can Anna choose from?

3 **a** Look at the makes of the cars.
Copy this tally-table.
Fill it in.

Make	Tally	Number of cars
BMW		
Citroën		
Fiat		
Ford		
Mazda		
Nissan		
Renault		
Rover		
Vauxhall		

b Kiavash wants to buy a Ford. How many cars can he choose from?
c James wants to buy a BMW. How many cars can he choose from?
d Abbey wants to buy a Rover. How many cars can she choose from?
e Katie wants to buy a Fiat. How many cars can she choose from?

4 **a** Paul wants to buy a Renault Laguna.
Look at the Renault cars. You need to tally the models.
Copy this tally-table.
Fill it in.

Model	Tally	Number of cars
Clio		
Megane		
Laguna		
Espace		
5		
19		
25		

b How many cars can Paul choose from?
c Eileen wants to buy a Clio. How many cars can she choose from?

5 **a** Javed wants a car that has an R, an S or a T registration.
Look at your tally-table for question **2**.
You can group the information together.
Copy this table.
Fill it in.

Registration letter	Number of cars	
J–L		← Add up the number of J, K and L registration cars for this row.
M–P		← Add up the number of M, N and P registration cars for this row.
R–T		← Add up the number of R, S and T registration cars for this row.

b How many cars can Javed choose from?
c Pardeep wants to buy an M, N or P registration car.
How many cars can he choose from?
d Peter wants to buy an N or P registration car.
This table does not help you find how many cars he can choose from.
Explain why.
e Look at your table from question **2**.
How many cars can Peter choose from?

Grouping data

When you buy a car, you might want to spend between £3000 and £4000.
You can group the data to make it easier to see how many cars are in this price range.
You could use groups that are £1000 wide.
The first two groups would be £0 up to £1000 and £1000 up to £2000.
You have to decide where you are going to put a value of £1000.
You could put it in the £0 up to £1000 or £1000 up to £2000.
Once you decide you must do the same with £2000, £3000 and so on.

Exercise 2:4

You will need Worksheet 2:2 for this exercise.

1 Look at the cost of the cars.
   a How much is the cheapest car?
   b How much is the dearest car?

2 **a** Copy this tally-table.
     Fill it in.
     You need to add more rows to the table to fit in all the prices.

Cost (£)	Tally	Number of cars
2000 up to 3000		
3000 up to 4000		
4000 up to 5000		

   b Brian has £4000 to spend.
     (1) How many cars can he choose from?
     (2) How many cars can he choose from if he spends between £3000 and £4000?
   c Rupert has £12 000 to spend.
     (1) How many cars can he choose from?
     (2) How many cars can he choose from if he spends between £10 000 and £12 000?
   d Jennifer has £18 000 to spend.
     (1) How many cars can she choose from?
     (2) How many cars can she choose from if she spends between £16 000 and £18 000?

3   Fractions of an amount

Most people sleep for about 8 hours a day, so you probably spend about $\frac{1}{3}$ of each day sleeping.

If you live for 75 years, you could spend about 25 years asleep!

To find a fraction of something you will need to divide.

To find	**You**
$\frac{1}{2}$ of something	divide by 2
$\frac{1}{3}$ of something	divide by 3
$\frac{1}{4}$ of something	divide by 4

Example $\frac{1}{4}$ of $12 = 12 \div 4$
                            $= 3$

Exercise 2:5

1 Work out:

a $\frac{1}{2}$ of 16   **f** $\frac{1}{4}$ of 24   **k** $\frac{1}{3}$ of 27

b $\frac{1}{3}$ of 15   **g** $\frac{1}{2}$ of 50   **l** $\frac{1}{8}$ of 24

c $\frac{1}{3}$ of 18   **h** $\frac{1}{5}$ of 20   **m** $\frac{1}{2}$ of 100

d $\frac{1}{4}$ of 20   **i** $\frac{1}{6}$ of 30   **n** $\frac{1}{4}$ of 80

e $\frac{1}{5}$ of 15   **j** $\frac{1}{10}$ of 70   **o** $\frac{1}{3}$ of 75

2 a The petrol tank of a car holds 64 litres. How much petrol is left when it is $\frac{1}{2}$ full?

b The car travels 270 miles on $\frac{1}{2}$ of a tank of fuel. How far could it go on a full tank?

3 There are 24 pupils in Dave's maths group. One third of them are girls.
 a How many girls are in the group?
 b How many boys are there?

4 There are 88 cars in a car park. One quarter of them are red.
 a How many are red?
 b How many are not red?

5 Macduff is half-way between Portnockie and Rosehearty.

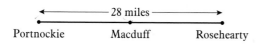

Portnockie   Macduff   Rosehearty

How far is it from Portnockie to Macduff?

Dividing by 2 is easier than dividing by 4.
To divide by 4 you can divide by 2 *twice*.
This is because $4 = 2 \times 2$

Example

Work out $\frac{1}{4}$ of 60.

$\frac{1}{2}$ of $60 = 60 \div 2 = 30$
$\frac{1}{2}$ of $30 = 30 \div 2 = 15$
So, $\frac{1}{4}$ of $60 = 15$

---

6 Find $\frac{1}{4}$ of:
 a 48   **e** 100   **i** 180
 b 84   **f** 120   **j** 108
 c 56   **g** 128   **k** 600
 d 72   **h** 140   **l** 720

7 Chris buys 4 tyres for his car. The total cost is £126.
 How much does each tyre cost?

8 8 people share a cash prize of £420.
 a What fraction of the prize does each person receive?
 b How much is each share worth?

Sometimes division may be difficult to do in your head. **Short division** is a way of breaking the problem into smaller parts.

Example

Find $\frac{1}{3}$ of 174.

First do $17 \div 3$.

$$3\overline{)1\ 7\ 4}$$

This is 5 with 2 left over.

$$\overset{\quad 5}{3\overline{)1\ 7^2 4}}$$

Now do $24 \div 3$.

$$\overset{\quad 5}{3\overline{)1\ 7^2 4}}$$

This is 8.

$$\overset{\quad 5\ 8}{3\overline{)1\ 7^2 4}}$$

So, $\frac{1}{3}$ of 174 is 58.

Exercise 2:6

1 Work out each of these using short division.

a $\frac{1}{3}$ of 162

b $\frac{1}{3}$ of 255

c $\frac{1}{5}$ of 310

d $\frac{1}{5}$ of 465

e $\frac{1}{7}$ of 154

f $\frac{1}{6}$ of 216

g $\frac{1}{9}$ of 279

● **h** $\frac{1}{3}$ of 2424

2 Barbara and Jim did a survey of 295 students.
Only 1 in 5 said that they did regular exercise.
a How many students claimed to do regular exercise?
b How many students claimed not to do regular exercise?

3 Copy the diagram and label the positions of:

a $\frac{1}{3}$ **b** $\frac{1}{4}$ **c** $\frac{1}{6}$

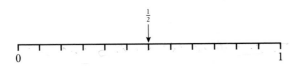

4 Name the labelled point that is closest to:

a $\frac{1}{3}$ **b** $\frac{1}{4}$

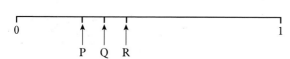

5 **a** Name the labelled point closest to $\frac{1}{3}$ of 500.

   b Use the scale to estimate $\frac{1}{3}$ of 500.

6 Estimate $\frac{1}{4}$ of 599.

• **7** Estimate $\frac{1}{3}$ of 899.

So far you have worked with fractions that have 1 on the top. Other fractions of an amount may be found with one extra step.

To find	You
$\frac{2}{3}$ of something	First find $\frac{1}{3}$ then times by 2.
$\frac{3}{4}$ of something	First find $\frac{1}{4}$ then times by 3.
$\frac{5}{8}$ of something	First find $\frac{1}{8}$ then times by 5.

Example   Find $\frac{2}{3}$ of 12.

First find $\frac{1}{3}$ of 12 $12 \div 3 = 4$

Then times by 2 $4 \times 2 = 8$

So $\frac{2}{3}$ of 12 = 8

Exercise 2:7

1 Work each of these out.

   a $\frac{2}{3}$ of 15   **e** $\frac{3}{5}$ of 30   **i** $\frac{5}{6}$ of 18

   b $\frac{3}{4}$ of 12   **f** $\frac{2}{3}$ of 33   ● **j** $\frac{4}{3}$ of 12

   c $\frac{5}{9}$ of 18   **g** $\frac{5}{8}$ of 24   ● **k** $\frac{7}{4}$ of 20

   d $\frac{3}{4}$ of 20   **h** $\frac{3}{5}$ of 100   ● **l** $\frac{8}{5}$ of 15

2 Find the number of minutes in each of these.

   a $\frac{1}{2}$ h   **e** $\frac{3}{4}$ h

   b $\frac{1}{3}$ h   **f** $\frac{2}{3}$ h

   c $\frac{1}{4}$ h   **g** $\frac{5}{12}$ h

   d $\frac{1}{12}$ h   **h** $\frac{3}{5}$ h

3 A car that is travelling at 60 mph takes 1 min to travel each mile. A motorway sign shows that the next exit is in $\frac{2}{3}$ mile. How long does it take to reach the exit at this speed?

4   **a** $\frac{1}{3}$ of 726 is 243. What is $\frac{2}{3}$ of 726?

     b $\frac{1}{5}$ of a number is 312. What is $\frac{3}{5}$ of the same number?

  ● **c** $\frac{1}{3}$ of a number is 24. What is the number?

5   **a** Copy this rectangle. Measure the sides carefully.

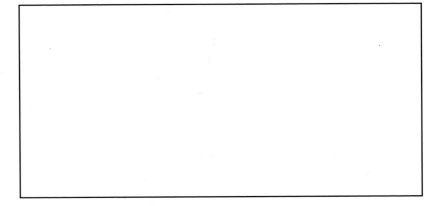

     b Divide your rectangle into three equal vertical strips. You need to measure the positions. Can you find an easier way than measuring straight across?

You can use a calculator to find a fraction of an amount.

Example

Find $\frac{2}{3}$ of 729.

These are the keys that you press:

If your calculator has an $a^{b}/_{c}$ key then you can work it out like this:

Answer: 486

Exercise 2:8

1 Use a calculator to work these out.

  a $\frac{7}{9}$ of 477

  b $\frac{11}{12}$ of 204

  c $\frac{3}{8}$ of 1008

  d $\frac{3}{7}$ of 266

  e $\frac{5}{6}$ of 2322

  f $\frac{4}{17}$ of 816

  g $\frac{23}{24}$ of 576

  h $\frac{19}{33}$ of 1914

2 Julie owns a business.
  With VAT at 17.5% she can claim back $\frac{7}{47}$ of what she pays.
  How much can she claim back on these amounts?

  a £94

  b £141

  c £376

  d £940

  e £846

  f £3337

  g £11 092

  h £110.92

3 A computer costs £1468.75 including VAT.
  The VAT is $\frac{7}{47}$ of this amount.
  a Find the amount of VAT included in the price.
  b Find the price before VAT was added.

4 A mobile phone costs £99.99 including VAT.
  The VAT is $\frac{7}{47}$ of this amount.
  Find the amount of VAT correct to the nearest penny.

4 Sequences

These numbers were worth *millions of pounds*!

| 01 | 07 | 22 | 25 | 31 | 47 |

| 04 | 10 | 25 | 36 | 44 | 47 |

You can find out the results of all of the lottery draws so far.

| 08 | 20 | 27 | 28 | 36 | 41 |

But no-one can use them to predict the results next time, because they do not follow a rule or pattern.

| 02 | 09 | 19 | 20 | 38 | 49 |

| ? | ? | ? | ? | ? | ? |

If only there was a sequence...

Number sequence	A **number sequence** is a list of numbers that follows a rule.
Example	Find the next two numbers in the sequence 7, 12, 17, 22, ..., ...

The rule is **add 5**. You +5 to get each new term.

The next two numbers in the sequence are **27** and **32**.

Exercise 2:9

1 Write down the next three numbers in each sequence.

a
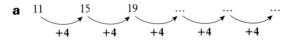

b 20, 27, 34, 41, ..., ..., ...

c 23, 43, 63, 83, ..., ..., ...

d 57   52   47   ...   .
  −5   −5   −5   −5   −5

e 88, 80, 72, 64, ..., ..., ...

f 1000, 990, 980, 970, ..., ..., ...

2 Find the two missing numbers in each of these sequences.

a 5   ...   11   14   ...   20

     +3

b 21, ..., 37, 45, ..., 61
c ..., 52, 56, ..., 64
d 64   ...   56   52   ...   44

     −4

e 76, ..., 64, 58, ..., 46
f ..., 130, 105, ..., 55

Term	Each number in a sequence is called a **term**.
Example	Find the next two terms of the sequence 3, 6, 12, 24, ..., ...

The rule is **multiply by 2**. You ×2 to get each new term.

The next two terms in the sequence are **48** and **96**.

---

3 Find the next two terms in each of these sequences.

a 5   10   20   ...   ...

b 1, 3, 9, ..., ...
c 4, 20, 100, ..., ...
d 17, 170, 1700, ..., ...

4 Find the two missing terms.

a 6   12 ..., ..., 96   **d** 64   32 16, ..., ...,

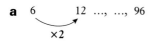

     ×2   ÷2

b 10, ..., 90, 270, ...   **e** 96, 48, ..., ..., 6
c ..., 12, 36, ..., 324   **f** ..., 10 000, 1000, ..., 10

To build a sequence you need the right information.
You need to know:
(1) One of the terms.
(2) The rule to get the next term.

Example

The first term of a sequence is 11.
The rule is add 4.
Write down the first five terms of the sequence.

Each new term is 4 more than the previous term.

The first five terms are: 11, 15, 19, 23, 27.

Exercise 2:10

1 Write down the first five terms of each of these sequences.
  a First term: 3   rule: add 6
  b First term: 10   rule: multiply by 2
  c First term: 30   rule: subtract 4

2 Write down the first five terms of each of these sequences.
  a Third term: 19   rule: add 5
  b Third term: 128   rule: divide by 2

3 Find the rule for each sequence.
  a 16, 19, 22, 25   **c** 16, 13, 10, 7   **e** 16, 32, 64, 128
  b 41, 61, 81, 101   **d** 76, 66, 56, 46   **f** 5, 15, 45, 135

4 The first term of a sequence is 4.
The rule for finding the next term is 'multiply by 2 and add 3'.
Write down the first four terms.

Some sequences are so important that they have special names.

Odd numbers

The **odd numbers** are 1, 3, 5, 7, 9, ...

Even numbers

The **even numbers** are 2, 4, 6, 8, 10, ...
These are the numbers in the 2 times table.

Multiples

The **multiples** of 3 are the 3 times table: 3, 6, 9, 12, 15, ...
The **multiples** of 5 are the 5 times table: 5, 10, 15, 20, 25, ...

Exercise 2:11

1 List the even numbers between 31 and 49.

2 List the odd numbers between 120 and 140.

3 Write down if each of these numbers is a multiple of 3.
    a 18   **b** 22   **c** 37   **d** 42

4 Write down if each of these numbers is a multiple of 5.
    a 12   **b** 15   **c** 740   **d** 503

5 Look at these numbers.
    Write down the numbers that are:
    a odd   **b** multiples of 7   ● **c** multiples of 3 and even

       20   23   31   35   42

       16   9   24   86   124

       32   66   56   48   210

       63   83   84   94   777

Some special sequences can be made from shapes.

Square numbers The **square numbers** are 1, 4, 9, 16, 25, …

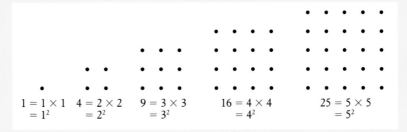

$$1 = 1 \times 1 \quad 4 = 2 \times 2 \quad 9 = 3 \times 3 \quad 16 = 4 \times 4 \quad 25 = 5 \times 5$$
$$= 1^2 \qquad\quad = 2^2 \qquad\quad = 3^2 \qquad\qquad = 4^2 \qquad\qquad = 5^2$$

Triangle numbers The **triangle numbers** are 1, 3, 6, 10, …

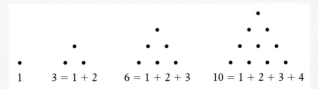

$$1 \qquad 3 = 1 + 2 \qquad 6 = 1 + 2 + 3 \qquad 10 = 1 + 2 + 3 + 4$$

6 **a** List the square numbers that are between 30 and 60.
  b Draw a square pattern for each of these numbers.

7 Which of these are square numbers?
  a 63 **b** 64 **c** 79 **d** 144

8 **a** Show 15 and 21 as triangular patterns of dots.
  b Copy these. Fill in the spaces.
    (1) $15 = 1 + 2 + \ldots + \ldots + \ldots$
    (2) $21 = 1 + 2 + \ldots + \ldots + \ldots + \ldots$

9 **a** Write down the triangle numbers that are between 25 and 40.
  b Show each of these numbers as a triangular pattern.

● **10** **a** Copy this: $\quad\quad 1 = 1^2$
    Fill in the spaces. $1 + 3 = 4 = 2^2$
      $1 + 3 + 5 = \ldots = 3^2$
      $1 + \ldots + \ldots + 7 = 16 = \ldots$
      $1 + \ldots + \ldots + \ldots + \ldots = \ldots = 5^2$
  b What do the first ten odd numbers add up to?

Sequence game

This is a game for two players.

You need 1 dice between you.

You need to make a score sheet like this one.

Score on dice	Running total	Player 1 score	Player 2 score

You take it in turns to roll the dice and add the score to the running total.

You score points for recognising special numbers in the running total.

Running total	Number of points
even	1
multiple of 3	2
multiple of 5	3
triangle number	4
square number	5

So if the running total on your turn is 9 then you score:

2 points if you say that it is a multiple of 3
5 points if you say that it is a square number
If you say both of these then you score $2 + 5 = 7$ points.

When you have had your turn, your opponent can claim any points that you missed.

If you make a mistake, then you score no points on that turn.

The winner is the first player to score 15 points *or* the player with the highest score when the running total reaches 100.

1 Copy these objects on to isometric paper.

a

b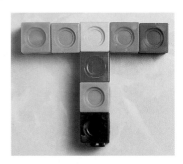

2 Draw the front elevation of each of these objects:

a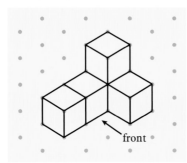

b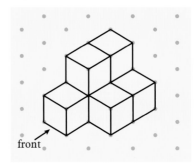

3 20 families were asked how many lottery tickets they bought for each draw. Here are the results.

2 0 3 3 0 3 2 4 2 1
1 4 6 2 3 1 2 1 2 1

a Draw a tally-table to show the results.
b How many families bought less than 2 tickets?

4 When a shop sells a CD they keep $\frac{1}{5}$ of the cost for themselves.
A CD is sold for £13.50. How much does the shop keep?

5 **a** What fraction of this shape is coloured?

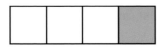

b Copy this. Colour in $\frac{2}{5}$ of the shape.

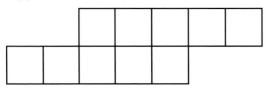

6 Do each of these using short division.

    a $\frac{1}{7}$ of 126   **b** $\frac{1}{3}$ of 186

7 Use a calculator to work these out.

    a $\frac{5}{9}$ of 486   **c** $\frac{5}{6}$ of 2328

    b $\frac{7}{12}$ of 216   **d** $\frac{11}{17}$ of 833

8 A hi-fi costs £1535.96 including VAT.

The VAT is $\frac{7}{47}$ of this amount.

    a Find the amount of VAT included in the price.

    b Find the price before VAT was added.

9 For each sequence:

    (1) Write down the next three numbers.

    (2) Write down the rule.

    a 12, 16, 20, 24, …, …, …

    b 21, 26, 31, 36, …, …, …

10 Find the next two terms in each of these sequences.

    a 2, 4, 8, …, …

    b 2, 6, 18, …, …

11 The first term of a sequence is 4.

The rule for finding the next term is 'multiply by 2 and add 1'.

    a Write down the first four terms.

    b Ray uses the same rule but he starts with a different number.
Ray's second term is 11. What is his starting number?

12 Barry is thinking of a number.

His number is between 10 and 20.

It is odd. It is a multiple of 3.

What number is Barry thinking of?

13 Look at these numbers:

    3 4 5 6 7 8 9

Write down the numbers that are

    a even

    b multiples of 4

    c square

    d triangle

1 **a** Draw this cuboid on isometric paper.

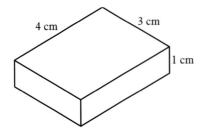

4 cm   3 cm

1 cm

b Draw a cuboid that has all its sides twice as long as the ones in part **a**.

2 30 pupils took a Science test.
Here are their results:

```
24  24  35  54  31  37  65  21  24  46
11  13  17  23  43  24  35  34  23  32
56  53  42  35  67  56  65  12  24  23
```

Draw a grouped frequency table to show these results. You need to choose sensible groups.

3 These are the balls used in the National Lottery.
a Write down the numbers that are:
(1) even
(2) multiples of 7
(3) square
(4) triangle
b John picks his numbers like this:

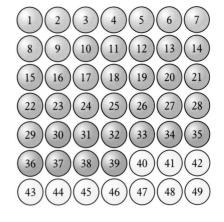

He chooses the numbers that are multiples of 3 and 7.
He chooses the square numbers that are bigger than 20.
He chooses the odd number that is a square number and a triangle number.

What are John's six numbers?

4 The rule for a sequence is:
'Start with 1, 2, 3, then add the previous three terms to get the next term each time.'
a Write down the first six terms of the sequence.
b The first term is 1 which is odd. The next term is 2 which is even. The next term is 3 which is odd. Does this pattern of odd and even carry on? Can you see why?

1   Draw the front and side elevations of each of these objects:

a
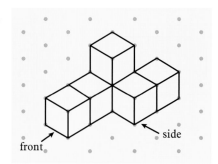

b
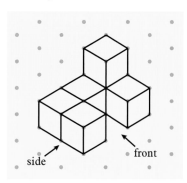

2   John works in a car park.
He records the time spent by cars in the car park.
These are his times in minutes.

45	12	75	83	49	87	92	60	48	42
75	96	82	76	46	25	53	58	77	93
67	35	72	31	37	48	19	73	33	28
67	83	25	36	65	18	70	38	93	54

a   Copy this tally-table.
Fill it in.

Time (minutes)	Tally	Total
0 to 20 21 to 40 41 to 60 61 to 80 81 to 100		

b   How many cars stayed more than 40 minutes?

3   A primary school has 420 pupils.

a $\frac{1}{3}$ have brown hair.
How many pupils have brown hair?

b $\frac{3}{4}$ are right handed.
How many pupils are right handed?

51

4 Work out each of these.
Give your answers in pence.

    a $\frac{1}{4}$ of £1   **c** $\frac{3}{5}$ of £1   **e** $\frac{1}{6}$ of £9

    b $\frac{3}{4}$ of £1   **d** $\frac{7}{10}$ of £3   **f** $\frac{2}{7}$ of £1.40

5   **a** $\frac{1}{3}$ of a number is 12. What is the number?

    b $\frac{2}{5}$ of a number is 24. What is the number?

6 Write down the next two terms in each of these sequences.
    a 3 9 15 21   ...   ...
    b 2 6 18 54   ...   ...

7   **a** The rule for a sequence is 'multiply by 10 and subtract 20'.
      The first term is 4.
      Write down the second and third terms.
    b Write down the first 5 triangle numbers.

8 Look at these patterns of dots.

    a Draw the next two patterns.
    b Copy this table. Fill it in.

Pattern number	1	2	3	4	5
Number of dots					

    c Describe the rule for the numbers in the bottom line of your table.

3

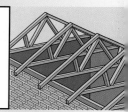

CORE

QUESTIONS

EXTENSION

TEST YOURSELF

1 Zooming in

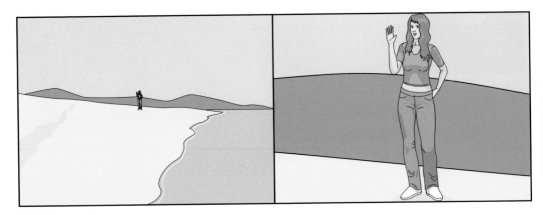

These are pictures of Jenny.
The picture on the right is what you see through a telescope.
This picture has been **magnified**.
It is 10 times bigger than the picture on the left.

Multiply by 10	To **multiply by 10**, move all the digits **one** column to the left.
	This makes a number 10 times bigger.
	You can use columns to help you.
	Put the names of each column across your page.
	Then fill in the numbers in the right place.

Examples   **1** Work out 27×10

HTh TTh Th   H   T   U . t   h

27 is **2** tens
and **7** units

        2   7 . 27×10
    2   7   0 . $= 270$

Fill in any spaces before the decimal point with 0s

2 Work out 31.53×10

HTh TTh Th   H   T   U . t   h

31.53 is **3** tens,
1 unit, **5** tenths
and **3** hundredths

        3   1 . 5   3 31.53×10
    3   1   5 . 3 $= 315.3$

Exercise 3:1

1 Copy this. Fill it in.

HTh	TTh	Th	H	T	U .	t	h	

a   8   9 . 89×10

×10 ×10

...   . $= ...$

b   2   2 . 7 22.7×10

×10 ×10 ×10

...   . $= ...$

c   6 . 4   2 6.42×10

×10 ×10 ×10

...   . $= ...$

d   3   1   7   4 . 2   4 3174.24×10

×10 ×10 ×10 ×10 ×10 ×10

...   . $= ...$

e   5   0   4   2 . 1 5042.1×10

×10 ×10 ×10 ×10 ×10

...   . $= ...$

2 Multiply each of these numbers by 10.
You might want to draw columns to help you.

    a 3   **c** 25.2   **e** 2567   **g** 21 439.34
    b 83   **d** 235.14   **f** 3200.1   ● **h** 243 128.2

Multiply by 100 To **multiply by 100**, move all the digits **two** columns to the left.
This makes a number 100 times bigger.
You can use the columns to help you again.

Example Work out 63.2×100

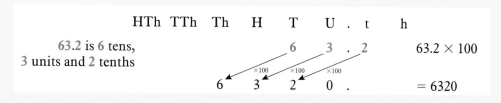

HTh	TTh	Th	H	T	U .	t	h

63.2 is **6** tens,   6   3 . 2 63.2×100
3 units and **2** tenths

×100 ×100 ×100

6   3   2   0 . $= 6320$

Exercise 3:2

1 Copy this. Fill it in.

HTh	TTh	Th	H	T	U	.	t	h	
a				2	3	.			23×100
			... ×100	... ×100	...	.	...		$= ...$
b			4	2	6	.			426×100
		... ×100	... ×100	... ×100	...	.	...		$= ...$
c				5	9	.	4		59.4×100
		...	... ×100	... ×100	... ×100	.	...		$= ...$
d			2	4	0	.	4	3	240.43×100
	...	... ×100	... ×100	... ×100	... ×100	. ×100	...		$= ...$
e	8	0	0	1	.	3			8001.3×100
... ×100	... ×100	... ×100	... ×100	... ×100	...	.			$= ...$

2 Multiply each of these numbers by 100.
   You might want to draw columns to help you.
   a 2   **c** 87.2   **e** 217.34   **g** 7429.1
   b 39   **d** 116.1   **f** 3601   ● **h** 43 135.14

Multiply by 1000 To **multiply by 1000**, move all the digits **three** columns to the left.
This makes a number 1000 times bigger.
You can use the columns to help you again.

Example   Work out 28.1×1000

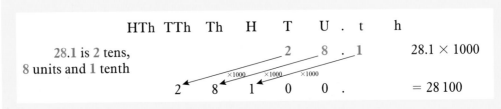

	HTh	TTh	Th	H	T	U	.	t	h	
28.1 is **2** tens,					2	8	.	1		28.1×1000
8 units and **1** tenth		2	8	1 ×1000	0 ×1000	0 ×1000	.			$= 28\,100$

Exercise 3:3

1 Copy this. Fill it in.

HTh	TTh	Th	H	T	U	.	t	h	
a					3	.			3×1000
	...	...	...	...	.				$= ...$
b			2	5	.	3			25.3×1000
	...	...	...	...	...	.			$= ...$
c		7	3	1	.	2	4		731.24×1000
	...	...	...	...	...	...	.		$= ...$

2 Multiply each of these numbers by 1000.
You might want to draw columns to help you.
a 5   **c** 36.3   **e** 207.25   **g** 400.1
b 16   **d** 106.1   **f** 620.24   • **h** 3475.12

3 To change centimetres into millimetres you multiply by 10.
Change these lengths into millimetres.
a 3 cm   **b** 24 cm   **c** 25.2 cm   **d** 56.3 cm

4 To change metres into centimetres you multiply by 100.
Change these lengths into centimetres.
a 2 m   **b** 13 m   **c** 212.2 m   **d** 539.13 m

5 To change kilometres into metres you multiply by 1000.
Change these lengths into metres.
a 3 km   **b** 36 km   **c** 73.8 km   **d** 289.05 km

• **6** To change metres squared into centimetres squared you multiply by 10 000.
a How many columns do you have to move the digits?
b Change these areas into centimetres squared:
(1) 6 m^2 (2) 7 m^2 (3) 12.2 m^2 (4) 34.25 m^2

2 Polygons

This is a picture of some roof trusses. Roof trusses are made by joining triangles. Triangles have three sides. Structures that are made from triangles are very strong.
Roof trusses have to be very strong to support a roof.

There are lots of different types of triangles.

Equilateral triangle	An **equilateral triangle** has three equal sides.	
Isosceles triangle	An **isosceles triangle** has two equal sides. Both of these triangles are isosceles.	
Scalene triangle	A **scalene triangle** has no equal sides.	
Right-angled triangle	A **right-angled triangle** has a right angle. A right angle is 90°. The sides can be any length.	

Exercise 3:4

1 What type of triangle is each of these?

a  **b**   **c**   **d**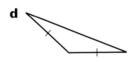

Look at this triangle. Its corners are labelled A, B, and C.
It is called triangle ABC.

The red side is called **AB**.
The blue side is called **BC**.
The green side is called **AC**.

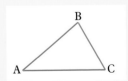

It does not matter which order you use for the letters. BA is the same as AB.

2 Use a ruler to measure the sides of this triangle.
Copy this and fill it in.

Side AB = ... cm
Side BC = ... cm
Side AC = ... cm
The triangle has ... equal sides.
It is an ... triangle.

3 **a** Copy the table.

Triangle	Equilateral	Isosceles	Scalene	Right-angled	Reason
ABC DEF GHI JKL MNO PQR			✓	✓	no equal sides

b For each triangle:
(1) Measure the sides with a ruler. Give your answers in millimetres.
(2) Decide what type of triangle it is. Put a tick in the right column.
You may need to tick more than one column.
(3) Give a reason for your answer. Write it in the table.
Triangle ABC has been done for you.

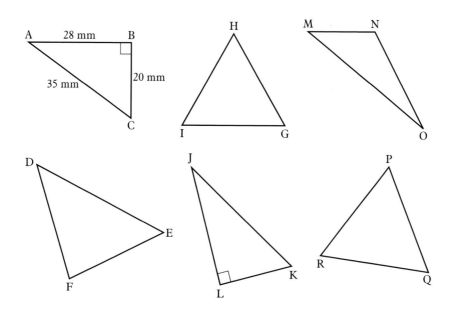

3

Polygon

A **polygon** is a shape with straight sides.
Some polygons have special names.
A polygon with **3** sides is called a **triangle**.
A polygon with **4** sides is called a **quadrilateral**.
These are all quadrilaterals.

A polygon with 5 sides is called a **pentagon**.
These are all pentagons.

A polygon with **6** sides is called a **hexagon**.
A polygon with **7** sides is called a **heptagon**.
A polygon with **8** sides is called an **octagon**.

Exercise 3:5

1 Write down the name of each of these polygons.

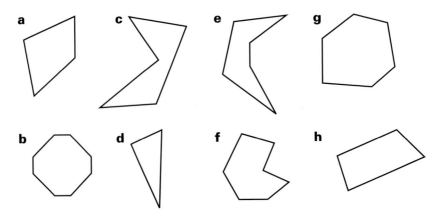

These circles have 12 points equally spaced around their edges.
You can use them to draw polygons.

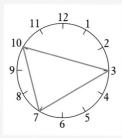

Join the points:
$3 \rightarrow 7 \rightarrow 10 \rightarrow 3$
to get a triangle.

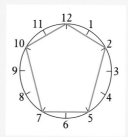

Join the points:
$2 \rightarrow 5 \rightarrow 7 \rightarrow 10 \rightarrow 12 \rightarrow 2$
to get a pentagon.

W You will need Worksheet 3:6 for questions **2** and **3**.

2 For each part:
(1) Join the points.
(2) Write the name of the polygon underneath the clock face.
 a $3 \rightarrow 6 \rightarrow 8 \rightarrow 3$
 b $1 \rightarrow 3 \rightarrow 4 \rightarrow 5 \rightarrow 6 \rightarrow 1$
 c $2 \rightarrow 3 \rightarrow 6 \rightarrow 8 \rightarrow 9 \rightarrow 11 \rightarrow 12 \rightarrow 2$
 d $10 \rightarrow 12 \rightarrow 2 \rightarrow 6 \rightarrow 10$
 e centre $\rightarrow 10 \rightarrow 8 \rightarrow 6 \rightarrow 4 \rightarrow 2 \rightarrow$ centre
 f $5 \rightarrow 4 \rightarrow 2 \rightarrow 1 \rightarrow 11 \rightarrow 10 \rightarrow 8 \rightarrow 7 \rightarrow 5$

3 For each part:
(1) Draw the polygon on a clock face.
(2) Write down the points that you joined underneath the polygon.
 a quadrilateral   **d** pentagon
 b triangle   **e** hexagon
 c octagon   **f** heptagon

4 Write down the name of each of the coloured polygons.

a   **b**   **c**   **d**   **e**

The hexagon ABCDEF has its corners labelled A, B, C, D, E and F.

Diagonal

A line that joins two corners is called a **diagonal**.
An edge does not count as a diagonal.

There are three diagonals that start from A.
AC, AD AE.
They are all shown in red.

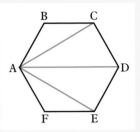

Exercise 3:6

1 Write down the letter names of the diagonals in each of these polygons. Remember that AC is the same as CA, so do not write each diagonal more than once.

a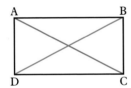

b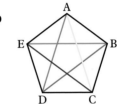

2 For each part:
   (1) Copy the diagram.
   (2) Draw all the diagonals that start from A.
       Write them down.
   (3) Draw all the diagonals that start from B.
       Write them down.
   (4) Carry on until you have written down all the diagonals.
       Do not write CA because it is the same as AC.

a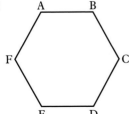

b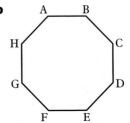

Interior angle	An **interior angle** is the angle inside a shape where two sides meet. The red angles are all interior angles.	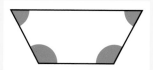
Exterior angle	To find an **exterior angle**: (1) Make one side longer. (2) Mark the angle between your line and the next side. (3) This is the exterior angle. The blue angles are all exterior angles.	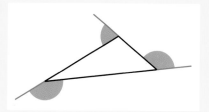

Exercise 3:7

1 a Write down the colour of the interior angle in shape **A**.
  b Write down the colour of the exterior angle in shape **B**.

A 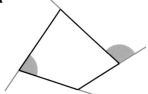 **B**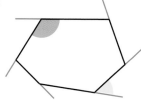

2 a Draw a pentagon.
  b Make the sides longer like the ones shown in question **1**.
  c Colour all the interior angles red.
  d Colour all the exterior angles blue.

3 a Draw an octagon.
  b Make the sides longer like the ones shown in question **1**.
  c How many interior angles are there?
  d Colour all the interior angles red.
  e How many exterior angles are there?
  f Colour all the exterior angles blue.

3 Up and down

This is a photo of Mount Everest.
The summit of Mount Everest is
8848 m above sea level.

When people climb a mountain they do
it in stages.
They start from Base Camp. Then they
make camps on the way up the
mountain.
They can add the heights each day to
see how far they've climbed.

Adding without a calculator

When you add numbers together you put the digits in columns.

Examples　**1**　Work out 335 + 43.

```
H T U
3 3 5
+   4 3
─────
3 7 8
```

Add each column to get the answer.

2　Work out 6336 + 249.

```
Th H T U
  6 3 3 6
+   2 4 9
─────────
        5
        1
```

First add the 6 and 9 to get 15.
Put the 5 in the units column and carry the 1.

```
Th H T U
  6 3 3 6
+   2 4 9
─────────
  6 5 8 5
      1
```

Now add the 3, the 4 and the 1 that you carried.
This gives 8. Put the 8 in the tens column.
Add the other columns to get the answer.

Exercise 3:8

1 This table shows the heights in metres that a mountain team climb each day. They start at sea level.

Day	Height (m)
1	604
2	282
3	119
4	161
5	117
6	79
7	103
8	78
9	19
10	34

a How far have they climbed after the first 2 days?

b How far do they climb during days 3 and 4?

c How far do they climb during days 5 and 6?

d How far do they climb during days 7 and 8?

e How far do they climb during days 9 and 10?

f How far have they climbed after the first 4 days?

g How far have they climbed after the first 6 days?

h They reach the top at the end of day 10.
How high is the mountain?

2 This is a cricket score book showing the batting scores of Jim, Paul, Dave and Leroy.

a How many runs has Jim scored?

b How many runs has Paul scored?

c How many runs has Dave scored?

d How many runs has Leroy scored?

e How many runs has the team got so far?
The rest of the team score
42, 18, 22, 18, 0, 11 and 1.

f What is the final team total?

Jim	Paul	Dave	Leroy
3	2	1	2
1	4	1	2
2	1	1	1
3	6	3	4
1	4	2	1
2	1	1	2
4	2	4	1
6	6		1
4	2		1
4	2		2
3	1		2
2	3		2
1	1		2
1	4		3
6	1		2
	4		2
	6		4
	6		

Subtracting without a calculator

When you subtract numbers put the digits in columns again.

Example

Work out 542 − 334.

```
  H  T  U
  5  ³4̷ ¹2
−  3  3  4
─────────
         8
```

You can't take 4 from 2. Take 1 from the column on the left. The 4 becomes 3 and the 2 becomes 12. Now do 12 − 4 = 8 and put the 8 in the units column.

```
  H  T  U
  5  ³4̷ ¹2
−  3  3  4
─────────
  2  0  8
```

Now subtract the other columns to get the answer.

Exercise 3:9

This is a diagram of the camps on Everest.
This table shows you the height of each camp above sea level.

Camp	Height above sea level (m)
Base	1260
A	3278
B	5738
C	7634

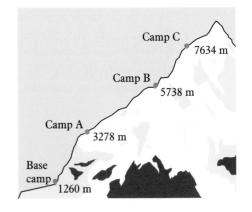

1 How far is it between:
  a Base Camp and Camp A
  b Camp A and Camp B
  c Camp B and Camp C
  d Base Camp and Camp C?

2 The top of Everest is 8848 m above sea level.
How much further is it from Camp C to the top of Everest?

The photo shows a swimming relay race.

The times for each swimmer are added to get the time for the whole team.

You need to be able to add and subtract decimal numbers.

Adding decimals without a calculator

You set out additions of decimals in columns as you do for whole number questions.

Make sure that you put the decimal points underneath each other.

Examples

1 Work out 3.35 + 4.3

```
  U   t h
  3 . 3 5
+ 4 . 3 0  ←   You can fill the gap with a 0.
  ───────      Add each column to get the answer.
  7 . 6 5      Put the decimal point in the answer.
  ───────
```

2 Work out 63.36 + 24.9

```
  T U   t h        First add the 6 and the 0. The 0 is there to
  6 3 . 3 6        fill the gap.
+ 2 4 . 9 0
  ─────────
      .   6
  ─────────
```

```
  T U   t h        Now add the 3 and the 9.
  6 3 . 3 6        The answer is 12. Put the 2 in the column
+ 2 4 . 9 0        and carry the 1.
  ─────────
      . 2 6
  ─────────
    1
```

```
  T U   t h        Now add the 3, the 4 and the 1 that you
  6 3 . 3 6        carried.
+ 2 4 . 9 0        The answer is 8.
  ─────────
    8 . 2 6
  ─────────
    1
```

```
  T U   t h        Finally, add the 6 and the 2.
  6 3 . 3 6
+ 2 4 . 9 0
  ─────────
  8 8 . 2 6
  ─────────
    1
```

3

Exercise 3:10

1 Work these out.

a   3.54
   +2.40
   ‾‾‾‾

b   6.47
   +1.92
   ‾‾‾‾

c   4.26
   +3.55
   ‾‾‾‾

d   62.56
   +28.2   ← You can fill the
   ‾‾‾‾   space with a 0.

e   45.5
   +76.38
   ‾‾‾‾

f   76.25
   + 9.66
   ‾‾‾‾

2 These are the times in seconds for a 4 × 50 m swimming relay team.

   Kerry   34.65 s   Pinky   34.1 s   Josie   33.18 s   Kay   33.1 s

a What is the total of Kerry and Pinky's times?
b What is the total of Kerry, Pinky and Josie's times?
c What is the total time for the team?

3 The table shows the times in seconds for all the swimmers in a 4 × 100 m relay race.

	Swimmer 1	Swimmer 2	Swimmer 3	Swimmer 4
Team A	65.3	66.1	67.23	64.23
Team B	64.4	64.82	64.9	63.13
Team C	64.86	64.27	65.21	64.11
Team D	64.69	66	66.13	64.17

a Work out the total time for each team.
b Which team won?
c Which team came last?

Subtracting decimals without a calculator

Set out subtractions in columns as you do whole number questions.
Make sure that you put the decimal points underneath each other.

Examples **1** Work out 57.73 − 23.31

```
  T U   t h
  5 7 . 7 3        Subtract each column to get the answer.
− 2 3 . 3 1
  ─────────
  3 4 . 4 2
```

2 Work out 54.25 − 33.44

```
  T U   t h       First do 5 − 4.
  5 4 . 2 5
− 3 3 . 4 4
  ─────────
      .   1
```

```
  T U   t h       You can't take 4 from 2. Take 1 from the
  5 ³4̸ .¹2 5       column on the left. The 4 becomes 3 and the
− 3 3 . 4 4        2 becomes 12. Now do 12 − 4.
  ─────────
      . 8 1
```

```
  T U   t h       Now do 3 − 3 and 5 − 3 to finish the
  5 ³4̸ .¹2 5       question.
− 3 3 . 4 4
  ─────────
  2 0 . 8 1
```

Exercise 3:11

1 Work these out.

a
```
  46.53
− 15.21
  ─────
```

d
```
  53.12
−  2.61
  ─────
```

b
```
  62.3    ←  You can fill the
− 41.75      space with a 0.
  ─────
```

e
```
  26.6
−  7.76
  ─────
```

c
```
  36.39
−  2.87
  ─────
```

f
```
  175.5
−   7.64
  ─────
```

2   The table shows the times in seconds for 4 teams in a 4 × 100 m relay race.

	Team 1	Team 2	Team 3	Team 4
Time	262.86	258.25	258.45	260.99

a   How many seconds are there between the winning team and the team that came last?

b   How many seconds are there between the winning team and the team that came second?

c   How many seconds are there between the team that came second and the team that came third?

Game: dicey

This is a game for 2 players.
You need a coin and two 10-sided dice.

The coin tells you to add or subtract:

  heads = add   tails = subtract

The dice tell you the number to use.
One of them is for the **whole number** part.
The other is the **decimal** part.
You decide at the start of the game which of your dice is for each part.

In this picture, the red dice is for whole numbers. The green dice is the decimal part.
So this picture tells you to **add 3.4**

Start from 90. Take it in turns to throw the coin and roll the dice.
The winner is the first person to reach a number that is bigger than 100.

You might have dice that are numbered 1 to 10.
If your dice are like this, count the 10 as a 0.

4 Getting information

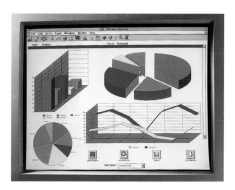

You can get a lot of information from tables, but graphs and charts show it in a more eye-catching way.

Bar-chart A **bar-chart** is a diagram made up of bars.

The height of each bar shows you how many of each type you have.

This is a bar-chart showing the favourite colour of 24 pupils.
The chart shows you that 4 pupils chose the colour yellow.
The most popular colour is black because the black bar is the highest.

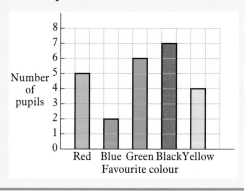

Exercise 3:12

1 Sam has done a survey. He asked his friends if they have a part-time job.

The bar-chart shows his results.

a How many of Sam's friends do a gardening job?

b Which is the most popular job?

c How many friends were in Sam's survey?

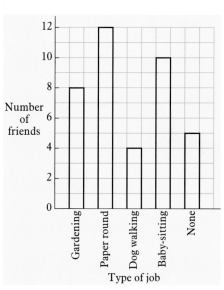

2 The bar-chart shows the type of music in Andrew's collection of CDs.

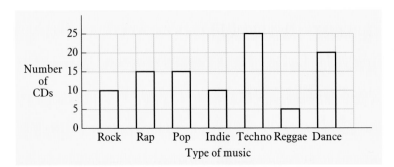

a What kind of music does Andrew like best?
b Write down the number of CDs of each type.
  Start with the smallest number.
● **c** Andrew forgot to include his collection of Jungle CDs on the graph.
  He has 105 CDs altogether. How many Jungle CDs does he have?

3 Emily and Ruth went to the Canary Islands for their holiday. The temperature at their favourite beach was recorded at noon each day for 7 days. The vertical line graph shows the results.

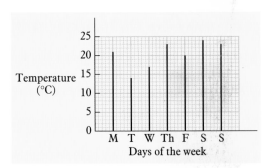

a Which day was the hottest?
b Which day was the coldest?
c Which days had a temperature more than 22 °C?
d Which 2 days had the same temperature?

| Pictogram | A **pictogram** is a diagram which uses pictures instead of bars. A pictogram must always have a key to show what each picture represents. |

If 🧍 represents 2 pupils, then ⸳ represents 1 pupil.

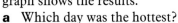 represents 2 + 2 + 2 + 1 = 7 pupils.

4 Tom and Veena make clocks for their school 'Young Enterprise Company'.
The pictogram shows the clocks that they made from September to December.

September	☉ ☉ ◖
October	☉ ◹
November	☉ ☉ ☉ ◔
December	☉ ◖

Key: ☉ represents 4 clocks

a How many clocks does ◖ represent?

b How many clocks does ☉ ◔ represent?

c How many clocks were made in September?

d In which month did they make 6 clocks?

e How many clocks did they make altogether?

5 This pictogram shows how many bicycles can be carried by 4 airlines.

Airways	🚲 🚲 🚲
Beeways	🚲 🚲 🚲
Safeways	🚲
Crossways	🚲

Key: 🚲 represents 30 bicycles

a Which airline can carry the most bicycles?

b What is the largest number of bicycles it can carry?

c How many bicycles can be carried by Airways?

d How many more bicycles can Airways carry than Safeways?

e How many bicycles can be carried by Crossways?
Why is this a difficult question to answer?

1   This vertical line graph shows the temperature every hour between 9 a.m. and 9 p.m.

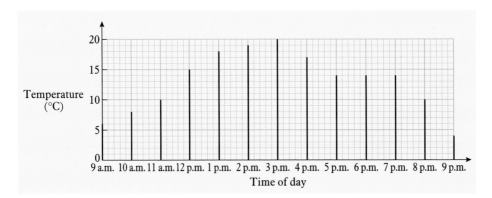

a What is the highest temperature?
b Write down the time when the temperature is highest.
c Is the temperature rising or falling between 9 a.m. and 3 p.m.?
d What is happening to the temperature between 3 p.m. and 5 p.m.?
e What time does the temperature reach 10 °C?
f What is happening to the temperature between 5 p.m. and 7 p.m.?

2 Multiply each of these numbers by 10.
   a 3   **b** 56.1   **c** 27.85   **d** 7462.24

3 Multiply each of these numbers by 100.
   a 8   **b** 29.2   **c** 78.23   **d** 4937.13

4 Multiply each of these numbers by 1000.
   a 6   **b** 68.5   **c** 93.62   **d** 764.06

5 Christopher was repairing a stained-glass window. He noticed that the 4 coloured pieces of glass were in the shape of triangles.

What type of triangle is each piece of glass?

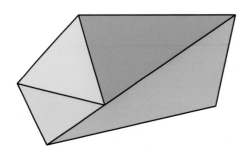

6 This table shows the distances that are ridden in the Tour de France on the first 6 days of the competition.

Day	Distance (km)
1	142
2	146
3	149
4	146
5	201
6	79

a How far have competitors cycled after day 2?
b How far have competitors cycled after day 3?
c How far have competitors cycled after day 4?
d How far have competitors cycled after day 5?
e How far have competitors cycled after day 6?
f The Tour de France covers a total distance of 3267 km.
How much further do the cyclists have to go at the end of day 6?

7 The table shows the times in seconds for the swimmers in a 4 × 50 m relay race.

	Swimmer 1	Swimmer 2	Swimmer 3	Swimmer 4
Team A	32.3	33.1	32.23	34.23
Team B	31.4	32.82	33.9	34.13

a Work out the total time for each team.
b Which team won?
c How many seconds are there between the two teams?
d What is the fastest individual time?
e What is the slowest individual time?
f How many seconds are there between these two times?

8 Write down the names of these coloured polygons.

a   **b**   **c**   **d**   **e**

1 The numbers in ( ) and ( ) add together to give ▢ like this:

(13.2)——[28.3]——(15.1)

Fill in the missing numbers.

a (22.7)——▢——(43.3)

c (16.24)——[125.7]——( )

b ( )——[36.3]——(12.4)

d (−2.8)——▢——(−4.6)

2 This is a diagram of a roof truss for a house.

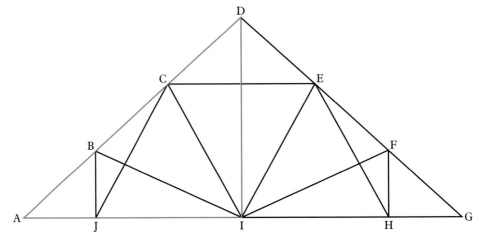

  a Copy the table.
  b For each triangle:
    (1) Measure the sides   (2) Fill in the table.
        in millimetres.   Put a tick in the right
                                    column(s) in the table.

Triangle	Length (mm)	Equilateral	Isosceles	Scalene	Right-angled
ADI	AD = 80 DI = 53 IA = 60				
DIF	DI = ... IF = ... FD = ...				
CID	CI = ... ID = ... DC = ...				
EIH	EI = ... IH = ... HE = ...				

1 Copy these. Fill in the missing numbers.

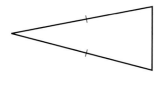

  a 23.5 × 10 = ...
  b 45 × ... = 4500
  c 0.3 × ... = 3
  d 21.5 × 1000 = ...

  e 0.04 × 10 = ...
  f 40.625 × 100 = ...
  g 762 + 509 = ...
  h 407 − 267 = ...

2 Write down the name of each of these shapes.

a

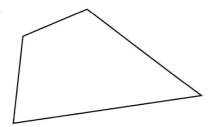

c

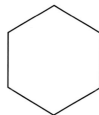

b

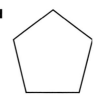

d

3 The map shows the distances between junctions on a motorway.
The distances are in kilometres.

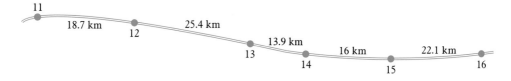

  a Find the total distance between junctions 11 and 16.
  b A service station is between junctions 12 and 13. It is 8.7 km from junction 12.
  How far is it from junction 13?
  c John joined the motorway at junction 11.
  He travels 64 km. How far is he from junction 15?

77

4 These are the amounts that Martin paid for his lunch for 5 days one week.

£4.68   £3.71   £5.06   £2.65   £4.30

Find the total amount he spent on lunches.

5 Harry carries out a survey into the distances travelled by shoppers in a town car park. The diagram shows his data.

Less than 5 miles

Between 5 and 10 miles

 represents 25 cars

Over 10 miles

a Write down the name given to this type of diagram.
b How many people travelled less than 5 miles?
c How many cars were in Harry's survey?

 6 A superstore is selling mountain bikes for £89.99
The bar-chart shows the number of bikes sold during one week.

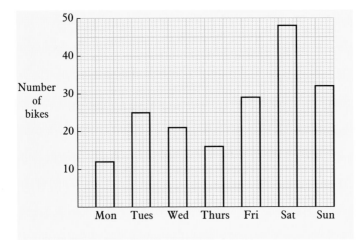

a Write down the number of bikes sold on Wednesday.
b Find the total number of bikes sold during the week.
c How much money was taken for bikes on Sunday?
d On which day were most bikes sold?
Why do you think this is so?

4

1 Identical shapes
Defining congruence
Looking at congruence
Looking at quadrilaterals

2 Presenting data
Reading from different charts
Drawing bar-charts
Drawing pictograms
Drawing frequency polygons

CORE

3 Remember this!
Learning your 9 times table using your fingers
Learning the 10, 5 and 2 times tables
Learning the other tables up to 10×10

4 Reading graphs
Reading heights and weights of babies
Using conversion graphs
Reading and drawing travel graphs

QUESTIONS

EXTENSION

TEST YOURSELF

CORE

1 Identical shapes

These twins are said to be identical.

There may be very small differences but most people can't tell them apart.

In maths, if two shapes are identical they are called congruent.

Congruent	Two shapes are **congruent** if they are identical.
	They have to be the same **size** and the same **shape**.

Exercise 4:1

1 Look at these shapes.

Which shapes are congruent? Write down their letters in pairs.

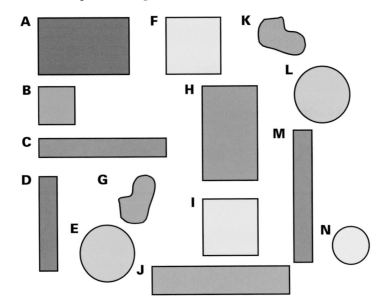

Exercise 4:2

1 Look at these triangles.

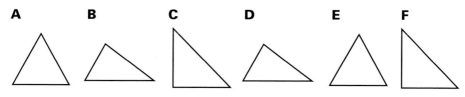

A   B   C   D   E   F

Which triangles are congruent to each other?
Write down their letters in pairs.

2 A triangle with all of its sides the same length is called an **equilateral** triangle.
Copy this. Fill it in.

Triangles ... and ... are both equilateral triangles.

3 A triangle with two of its sides the same length is called an **isosceles** triangle.
Copy this. Fill it in.

Triangles ... and ... are both isosceles triangles.

4 A triangle with all of its sides different lengths is called a **scalene** triangle.
Copy this. Fill it in.

Triangles ... and ... are both scalene triangles.

5 Which of the triangles are right-angled?
Write down their letters.

Exercise 4:3

You will need 9 dot paper for this exercise.

You can draw 8 different triangles on a 9 dot grid.
Here are 3 of them.

A   B   C

1 Copy these triangles.

2 Draw the other 5 triangles. They must all be different.

3 Letter your triangles **A, B, C, D, E, F, G,** and **H**.

4 a Copy this table.

Triangle	Equilateral	Isosceles	Scalene	Right-angled
A		✓		
B		✓		✓
C				
D				
E				
F				
G				
H				

b Fill in the rest of the table.

Quadrilateral   A shape with 4 straight sides is a **quadrilateral**.

These are all quadrilaterals.

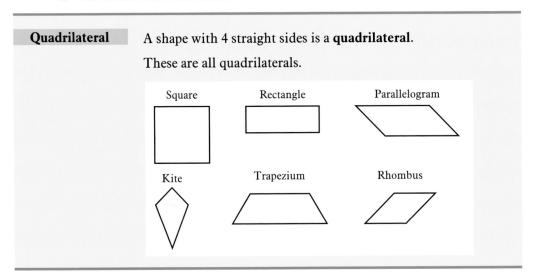

Exercise 4:4

You will need 9 dot paper for this exercise.

You can draw 16 different quadrilaterals on a 9 dot grid.
Here are some of them.

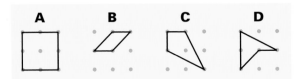

1 Draw as many quadrilaterals as you can.
Make sure that they are all different.

2 Label your shapes with letters.
Start with E.

3 Copy this table.

Shape	square	rectangle	rhombus	parallelogram	kite	others
Letters						

4 Write the letters of your shapes in the right places in your table.

Exercise 4:5

 You will need Worksheet 4:1 for this exercise.

On the worksheet there are 7 shape cards.
There are also 7 description cards and 7 name cards.

Cut out all 3 sets of cards.

Match the shape with the description, and the name.
Stick the cards into your book.

Here is an example.

	Rectangle	Corners are right angles. Opposite sides are the same length.

Shapes do not have to be drawn the same way round to be congruent.

These kites are **all** congruent.
The kite is **rotated** through 90° clockwise each time to make each new picture.
The middle dot is held still. This point is called the **centre of rotation**.

Exercise 4:6

1 a Copy this diagram on to dotty paper.

b When the rectangle is rotated through 90°
clockwise it looks like this.

The middle dot is held still.

Copy this diagram on to dotty paper.

c Draw the shape after it has been rotated by another 90° clockwise.

d Rotate the rectangle through another 90° clockwise.
Draw the new shape.

2 a Draw this triangle on dotty paper.

b When this shape is rotated through 90°
clockwise it looks like this.
Copy this diagram on to dotty paper.

c Draw the shape after it has been rotated
by another 90° clockwise.

d Rotate the triangle through another 90° clockwise.
Draw the new shape.

3 a Draw this shape on dotty paper.

b Rotate the shape through 90° three times.
Draw the new shape at each stage as you did
in question **2**.

You can also use congruent shapes to make tessellation patterns.

| **Tessellation** | A **tessellation** pattern is made by repeating the same shape over and over again.
There are **no gaps** in a tessellation. |

This is a tessellation made from right-angled triangles.

Exercise 4:7

1 **a** Copy this shape on to dotty paper.
   b Repeat the shape over and over again to
          make a tessellation pattern.

2 Use this shape to make a tessellation pattern.

3 Will this shape make a tessellation pattern?

4 Barbara thinks that all triangles will make a tessellation pattern.
   Try some different triangles and see if they tessellate.
   You could cut triangles out of card and draw round them.

5 Maggie thinks Barbara is right about the triangles.
   She also thinks that any quadrilateral will tessellate.

   Do you agree with Maggie?
   Try some different shapes to check.

2 Presenting data

Ian Hatem is the Headteacher of Adeney School. He is preparing a report for parents on the Key Stage 3 results in Maths, English and Science.

He has to report separately on boys' and girls' results. He has to decide which diagrams are best to make the results clear to the parents.

Here are some of the diagrams he has produced so far.

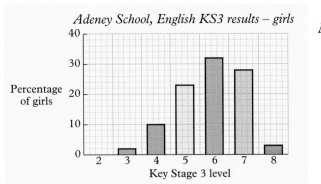

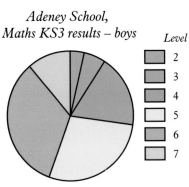

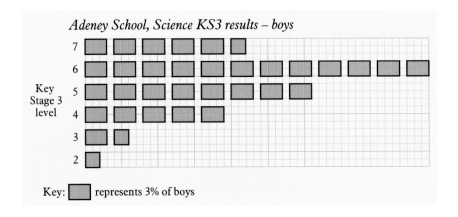

Exercise 4:8

1 Look at the bar-chart.
   a What percentage of girls gained level 5?
   b What percentage of girls gained level 4?
   c What percentage of girls gained a level 6 or higher?

2 Look at the pie-chart.
   a Which level is most common?
   b Which level is least common? How can you tell?
   c Did more or less than a quarter of the boys gain a level 4?

3 Look at the pictogram.
   a What percentage of the boys does ▨ stand for?
   b What percentage of boys gained level 6 in their test?
   c What percentage of boys gained level 3?

4 Look at all 3 diagrams.
Which diagram is the easiest to read the percentages from?

5 Here are the boys' results in Maths at Bishop's School.

Level	2	3	4	5	6	7	8
Percentage	4	6	18	28	32	12	0

   a Copy these axes on to graph paper.

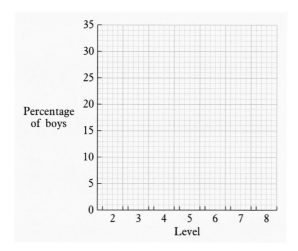

   b Draw a bar-chart to show these results.
      Remember the gaps between the bars.
   c Don't forget a title and labels.

6 Here are the girls' results in Maths at Bishop's School.

Level	2	3	4	5	6	7	8
Percentage	5	8	20	32	25	10	0

   a Copy the axes that you used in question **5**.
   b Draw a bar-chart of these results.

You can also use pictograms to display data.
A pictogram can look more interesting than a bar-chart.
It is sometimes difficult to read accurately.

Pictogram

A **pictogram** is a diagram which uses pictures.
All the pictures must be the same size.
They must be lined up underneath each other.

A pictogram must have a **key** to show what each picture represents. Here is an example of a key.

Key: ⚇ represents 2 students.

With this key ⚇ represents 1 student.

and ⚇⚇⚇ represents 2 + 2 + 1 = 5 students.

Exercise 4:9

1 Here are the boys' results in English at Bishop's School.

Level	2	3	4	5	6	7	8
Percentage	4	8	16	28	28	12	4

   a Choose a symbol for your pictogram.
      Let it represent 4% of the boys.
   b Draw a pictogram of the English results.

2 These are the girls' results in English at Bishop's School.

Level	2	3	4	5	6	7	8
Percentage	0	12	16	28	16	20	8

Draw a pictogram of these results.

Instead of a bar-chart or pictogram, you can draw a frequency polygon.

Here are the girls' English results that you used in the last exercise.

Level	2	3	4	5	6	7	8
Percentage (%)	0	12	16	28	16	20	8

To draw a frequency polygon:

(1) Mark the levels along the bottom axis.

(2) Plot the 'percentage' values at the right height.

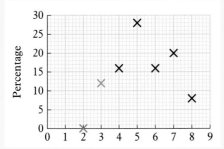

(3) Join the points with **straight** lines.

(4) Add a title and labels.

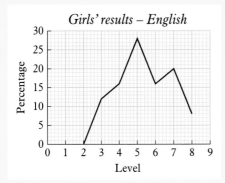

This is the completed frequency polygon.

Exercise 4:10

1 Copy the frequency polygon on the last page.
Don't forget the title and labels.

2 Here are the boys' English results.

Level	2	3	4	5	6	7	8
Percentage	4	8	16	28	28	12	4

a Copy the axes from question **1**.
b Draw a frequency polygon for the boys' results.

3 The Science results have not been tallied yet.
Here are the boys' results.

```
5  2  6  5  4  5  5  7  3
5  5  6  5  4  7  6  6  3
4  5  4  4  5  6  5  4  7
4  5  6  2  4  5  5  6  5
7  6  6  5  7  4  6  5  2
6  5  6  5  4
```

a Copy this table.

Level	Tally	Total
2		
3		
4		
5		
6		
7		

b Tally the results into this table.
c Draw a frequency polygon of these results.

1. Hatem!!!

Anne Alise, the Head of the Maths Department, is looking at the results in more detail.
She is not just looking at the levels. She is looking at the scores the pupils got in the test.

Here are the boys' scores. They have been grouped.

Score	0–9	10–19	20–29	30–39	40–49
Number of pupils	3	10	8	14	18

Score	50–59	60–69	70–79	80–89	90–99
Number of pupils	16	17	9	3	2

To draw a frequency polygon of this data:

(1) Put the groups along the bottom axis.
This is the same as you would do for a bar-chart.

(2) Put the 'percentage' values at the right height.
Plot them in the middle of each group.

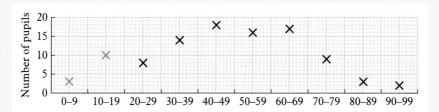

(3) Join the points with **straight** lines.

(4) Add a title and labels.

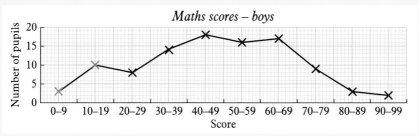

This is the completed frequency polygon.

Exercise 4:11

1   Copy the frequency polygon on the last page.
Remember that the points go in the middle of each group.

2   These are the girls' results.

Score	0–9	10–19	20–29	30–39	40–49
Number of pupils	2	7	6	14	19

Score	50–59	60–69	70–79	80–89	90–99
Number of pupils	20	13	8	7	4

  a   Draw a frequency polygon over the top of the one that you drew in
question **1**. Use a different colour if you can.

● **b**   What are the main differences between the two graphs?

3   Howard records the number of runs scored by each member of his
cricket team.
Here are his results for the first five matches of the season.

Number of runs	0–9	10–19	20–29	30–39	40–49	50–59	60–69
Number of times	7	9	14	12	6	4	3

  a   Draw a frequency polygon to show this data.
Don't forget to plot the points in the middle of the groups.

  b   Here are the results for the last five matches of the season.

Number of runs	0–9	10–19	20–29	30–39	40–49	50–59	60–69
Number of times	3	4	16	14	9	6	3

Plot a second frequency polygon over the top of the first one.
Use a different colour if you can.

  c   Would you say that the team has improved?
Explain your answer.

3 Remember this!

You have to know your times tables up to 10 times 10.

It is much better to know them than to have to work them out every time you need them.

Jenny is doing 9×3 in this picture.

There is a great way to remember how to do your 9 times table.

9 times table

Start by holding your hands up in front of you.

Then each of your fingers needs a number.

Starting from the left you think of your fingers as 1, 2, 3, up to 10.

If you want to work out 9×3 like Jenny, you bend finger number 3 down like this.

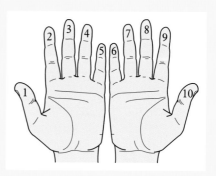

You now have 2 fingers before the folded finger.

You have 7 fingers after the folded finger.

This tells you that $9 \times 3 = 27$

This works for the rest of the 9 times table.

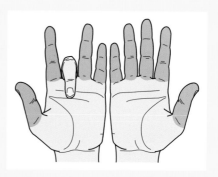

2, 5 and 10 times tables

The 10 times table is easy to remember.

All you have to do is add a 0 to the number.

So $10 \times 3 = 30$ $\qquad$ $10 \times 6 = 60$

There is a nice pattern in the 5 times table.

All the answers end in 0 or 5.

This makes it an easy pattern to remember.

$5 \times 1 = 5$	$5 \times 6 = 30$
$5 \times 2 = 10$	$5 \times 7 = 35$
$5 \times 3 = 15$	$5 \times 8 = 40$
$5 \times 4 = 20$	$5 \times 9 = 45$
$5 \times 5 = 25$	$5 \times 10 = 50$

The numbers in the 2 times table are all the **even** numbers.

You should know the even numbers
2, 4, 6, 8, ...

$2 \times 1 = 2$	$2 \times 6 = 12$
$2 \times 2 = 4$	$2 \times 7 = 14$
$2 \times 3 = 6$	$2 \times 8 = 16$
$2 \times 4 = 8$	$2 \times 9 = 18$
$2 \times 5 = 10$	$2 \times 10 = 20$

This should help you to remember the
2 times table.

Exercise 4:12

1 Write out the 9 times table.
You can use any method that you know to help you.

2 **a** Write out the 10 times table.
b Write out the 2 times table.
c Write out the 5 times table.

3 **a** Work out 1×4.
b Work out 1×7.
c Write out the 1 times table.
d Explain why the 1 times table is so easy to remember.

So far you have looked at the tables for 1, 2, 5, 9 and 10.
That's half of them done!

The rest are not as easy to remember.
But you can learn them and it is worth the effort.

You will have drawn a **table square** before.
You don't need the whole square.
This is because 8×5 is the same as 5×8.

×	1	2	3	4	5
1					
2					
3					
4					
5					

So you only need to remember the ones with the smaller number first.

Exercise 4:13

1 Copy this grid.

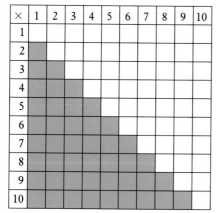

×	1	2	3	4	5	6	7	8	9	10
1										
2										
3										
4										
5										
6										
7										
8										
9										
10										

   a Fill in the 1 times table in the first row.
   b Fill in the 2 times table in the second row.
   You don't need to fill in 2×1 because this is the same as 1×2.
   c Fill in the 5 times row.
   You only need to fill in 5×5, 5×6, 5×7, 5×8, 5×9, and 5×10.
   d Fill in the other rows.
   You can use a table square to help you.
   e When you get to the 10 times row you only need to fill in 10×10.
   Explain why.

2 You need two 10-sided dice in this question.
Roll the dice.
Multiply the two numbers together in your head.
Try to do it without looking at your grid.
You can check your answers using the grid.

You can do this with a friend and see who can
get 10 right first.

4   **Reading graphs**

This is a picture of Tina and Jonathan.

Jonathan is 6 months old.

Tina needs to know if Jonathan is about the right weight and height for his age.

She can get the information that she needs from a graph.

This is a graph that Tina can use to check Jonathan's weight.
The curve shows the average weights for baby boys.

Tina knows that Jonathan is 6 months old.
She starts at 6 months on the age axis.

She draws a line **up** to the curve.
Then she draws a line **across** to the weight axis.
She can now read off the weight.

Jonathan should weigh about 8 kg.

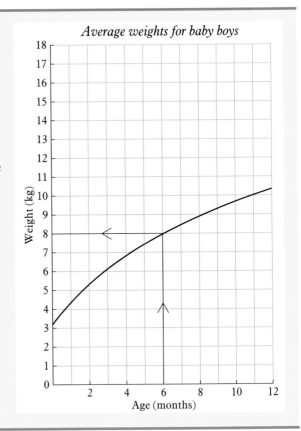

Average weights for baby boys

Exercise 4:14

1   Use the graph to write down how much Jonathan should weigh when he is:

    a   7 months old   **b**   8 months old   **c**   1 year old

2 This graph shows the average heights for baby boys.

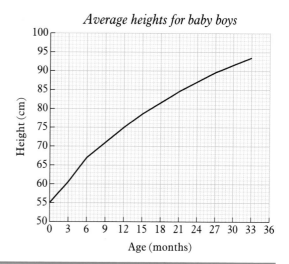

Average heights for baby boys

  a Use the graph to write down how tall Jonathan should be at 6 months.
  b Use the graph to write down how tall he should be when he is:
   (1) 6 months old
   (2) 9 months old
   (3) 1 year old
   (4) 2 years old
   (5) 3 years old

Conversion graph   A **conversion graph** is a graph that you can use to change from one unit to another.

Conversion graphs are always straight lines.

This graph lets you convert from miles into kilometres. To change miles into kilometres you go up to the line and then across.

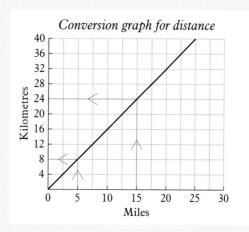

Conversion graph for distance

Example   Convert 15 miles into kilometres.
Follow the blue lines on the graph.
15 miles is 24 km.

Exercise 4:15

1 Convert 5 miles into kilometres.
   Use the red lines on the conversion graph.

2 a Convert 20 miles into kilometres.
   b How can you use the graph to convert from kilometres into miles?
      Copy this to help you. Fill it in.
         Start from the ... axis.
         Go across to the line.
         Then go ... to the ... axis.
   c Convert 16 km into miles.
 ● **d** Convert 36 km into miles.

3 This is a conversion graph for converting temperatures in Celsius (°C) into Fahrenheit (°F).

  a Convert these temperatures into Fahrenheit.
  (1) 0 °C
  (2) 10 °C
  (3) 20 °C
  (4) 30 °C

  b How can you use the graph to convert temperatures from Fahrenheit into Celsius?

  c Convert these temperatures into Celsius.
  (1) 41 °F
  (2) 59 °F
  (3) 77 °F
  ● (4) 70 °F

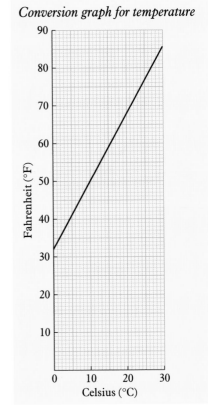

Conversion graph for temperature

4 Jaswinder is going on holiday to the USA. He needs to exchange his money into dollars ($).

  £1 will buy $1.60

  He is going to draw a conversion graph to help him convert his money.

  a How many dollars can he buy for £10?
  b How many dollars can he buy for £20?
  c Copy these axes.
  d Use your answers to parts **a** and **b** to plot 2 points on the conversion graph.
  One point is (10, …).
  The other is (20, …).
  Your graph should also go through (0, 0), because £0 buys $0.
  e Join the points with a straight line.
  f Use your graph to convert £35 into dollars.

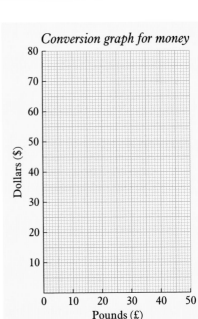

Conversion graph for money

Travel graphs

Travel graphs are used to show distance and time.

They show you the distance that something has moved away from a starting point.

Time always goes on the horizontal axis.

This graph shows Paul's journey to school.

School is
3 km from
home.
So the distance
axis goes up
to 3 km.

He starts from home here.

He gets
to school
here.

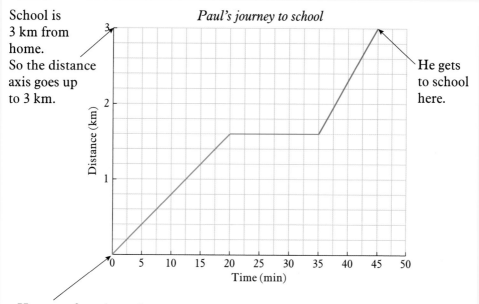

This is the first part of Paul's journey.

The graph is sloping upwards.
This means that Paul is walking away
from his house.

He walks **1.6 km** in **20 min**.

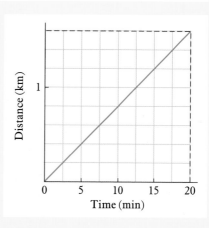

The next part of the graph looks like this.

The graph is horizontal.
This means that Paul is not moving.
His distance away from home is staying at 1.6 km.
He has stopped somewhere for 15 min.

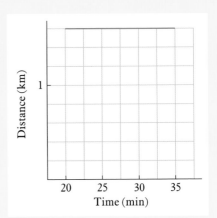

The last part of the graph looks like this.

This part is sloping upwards again so Paul is moving away from his house.
He gets to school after **45 min**.
He travels the last **1.4 km** in **10 min**.
He is going faster in this part.
The line is steeper than in the first part.

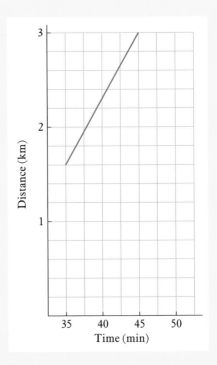

Exercise 4:16

1 This is a graph of Anne's journey from home to school.

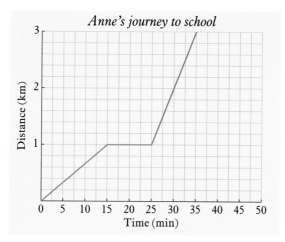

Anne's journey to school

She starts by walking from her home to the bus stop.
a How far is the bus stop from her house?
Anne has to wait at the bus stop for her bus.
b How long does she have to wait?
Anne then catches the bus.
c How far does the bus travel to get Anne to school?
d How long does the bus journey take?

2 Copy the axes on to squared paper.
The Patel family are travelling on the
motorway in their car.

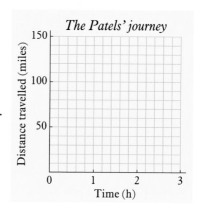

The Patels' journey

a They travel at 60 mph.
   How far do they travel in one hour?
   Plot this point on your graph.
b They continue at 60 mph for another 30 min.
   (1) How far do they travel in 30 min?
   (2) How far have they travelled altogether?
   (3) Plot this point on your graph.
   (4) Draw the line for the first part of the
        journey.
c The Patels stop for coffee for 30 min.
   Draw this on your graph.
d They continue for 1 more hour.
   They are now 120 miles from home.
   (1) Plot the point they have reached on your graph.
   (2) Draw a line for this part of the journey.
e What was their speed after they stopped for coffee?

1 Write down the name of each of these shapes.

a

c

e

b

d

f

2 The number of people dying from solvent abuse in the UK from 1987 to 1994 is shown in the table.
The figures have been rounded to the nearest 10.

Year	1987	1988	1989	1990	1991	1992	1993	1994
Number of people	120	140	110	150	120	80	70	60

a Copy these axes.
b Draw a frequency polygon to show this data.
c What is happening to the number of deaths each year?

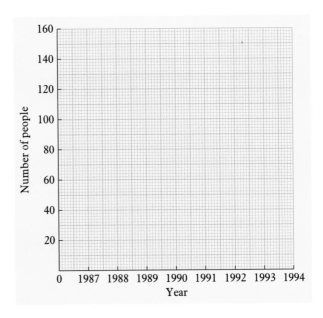

3 The number of pupils per teacher in different types of school is shown opposite.

Draw a pictogram to show this data. Remember to include a title and a key.

Type of school	Pupils per teacher
Nursery	22
Primary	22
Secondary	16
Private	10

4 Jenny asked the 30 members of 10T how many children there are in their families. These are her results.

```
2  3  1  2  4  2  1  2  3  4
4  1  2  4  1  2  1  2  1  5
3  4  2  2  3  1  4  2  1  1
```

a Draw a tally-table for this data.

b Draw a pictogram to show this data.

c Explain why there are no families with 0 children.

5 This is a graph for converting inches into centimetres.

a Convert these into centimetres.
  (1) 6 in
  (2) 2 in

b Convert these into inches.
  (1) 10 cm
  (2) 6 cm

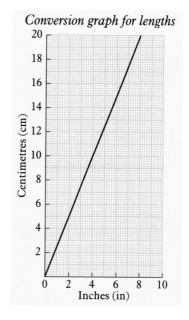

Conversion graph for lengths

6 This is a graph showing Mrs Holland's day out from Manchester.

Mrs Holland stopped at a service station for a short break.

a What time did she stop?

b How long did she spend there?

c What does the graph tell you that Mrs Holland was doing between 2.30 p.m. and 5.00 p.m.?

d What time did Mrs Holland set off to come home to Manchester?

e How long did the return journey take her?

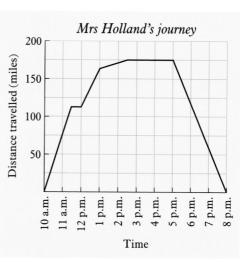

Mrs Holland's journey

1 Sajid says that these two shapes are congruent because they are both red rectangles.

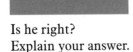 

Is he right?
Explain your answer.

2 This table shows the exchange rate for Spanish pesetas and English pounds.

English pounds (£)	1	2	3	4
Spanish pesetas (pta)	200	400	600	800

a Copy these axes.
Draw a conversion graph.
b Continue your graph to the edge of the scale.
c Use your graph to work out the cost of these items in pounds.
  (1) A toy donkey costing 800 pta.
  (2) A picture of Madrid costing 500 pta.
d How many pesetas would you get for £3.50?

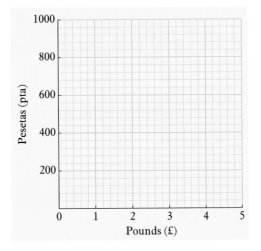

3 Mr Green left his home to go to a friend's house.
He drove for 1 hour at 70 mph.
He stopped for lunch for 30 min.
After lunch he carried on driving for 45 min at 60 mph.
Then he drove for 30 min at 70 mph and arrived at his friend's house.

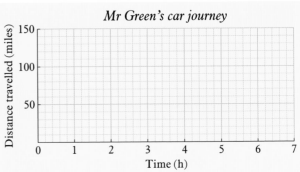

a Copy these axes. Draw a graph to show Mr Green's journey so far.
b How far away from home is Mr Green now?
c Mr Green stays at his friend's for 1 hour.
Then he returns home at 50 mph.
Show this information on your graph.
d How long has Mr Green been away from home?

1 The rectangle on the left is reflected in the dashed line to give the rectangle on the right.
The two rectangles are congruent.
Explain what this means.

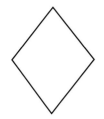

2 Write down the name of each quadrilateral.

a

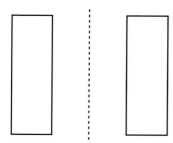

c

e

b

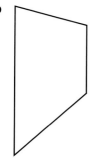

d

f

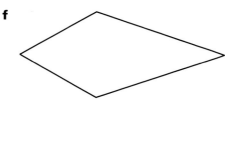

3 Nigel has recorded the number of aces he served in each of his last 40 tennis matches. The table shows his data.

Number of aces	0	1	2	3	4	5
Number of matches	5	3	8	11	9	4

Draw a bar chart to show this data.

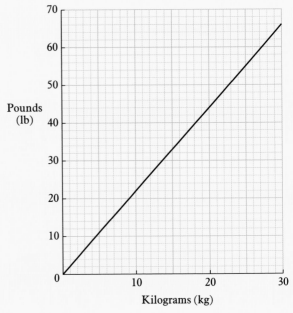

4 This is a conversion graph for converting kilograms (kg) into pounds (lb).
Convert:
a 15 kg into lb
b 48 lb into kg

5 Lorna leaves home and cycles to the local supermarket. She stops to buy some milk. She then cycles to the Post Office to post a letter.
She then cycles home by the same route. She stops to talk to a friend on the way home.

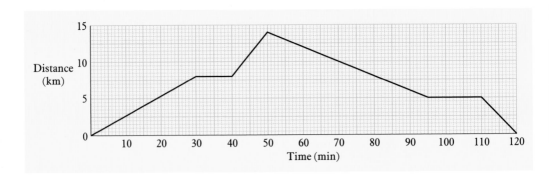

a How far is it from Lorna's home to the supermarket?
b How long did Lorna stay in the supermarket?
c How far is it from the supermarket to the Post Office?
d How long did Lorna stop to talk to her friend?
e How far from home was she when she talked to her friend?
f Lorna left home at 11:20. When did she get back home?

5

1 Symmetry
Counting lines of symmetry
Completing patterns with symmetry
Drawing reflections in a line of symmetry

2 Probability
Looking at probability
Deciding if it's fair

CORE

3 Linking parts
Looking at percentages, decimals and fractions
Working out one number as a percentage of another
Ordering percentages, decimals and fractions

4 Formulas
Substituting into formulas written in words
Substituting into formulas written in algebra
Finding a formula

QUESTIONS

EXTENSION

TEST YOURSELF

1   Symmetry

This lady is performing a joke made famous by Harry Worth.

He was famous for standing by a shop window and looking as though he had both legs off the ground!

Comedy was so much easier then!

Line of symmetry

A **line of symmetry** divides a shape into two identical halves.
Each part is a reflection of the other.
If you fold a shape along this line, each part fits exactly on top of the other.

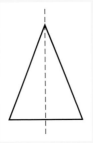

This isosceles triangle has one line of symmetry.
You draw a line of symmetry with a dashed line.

Exercise 5:1

1   How many lines of symmetry does each of these shapes have?

a

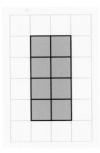

b

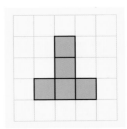

2 Copy these shapes on to squared paper.
Mark on all the lines of symmetry.

a

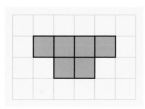

c

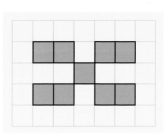

b

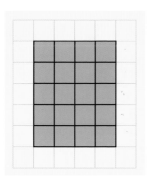

d

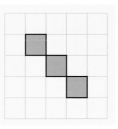

Example   Complete this pattern so that the
red line is a line of symmetry.

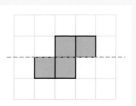

You need to shade in the squares
that complete the pattern.
There are two squares needed.
This is the completed pattern.

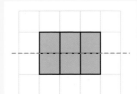

3 Copy these shapes on to squared paper.
Shade in two more squares so that the **red** line is a line of symmetry.

a

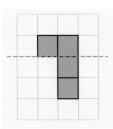

c

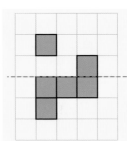

b

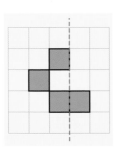

d

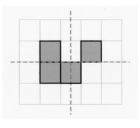

4 Copy these shapes on to squared paper.
Shade in two more squares so that the **red** line and the **blue** line are both
lines of symmetry.

a

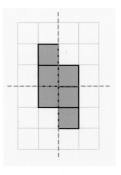

c

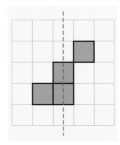

b

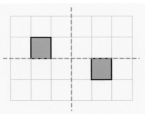

d

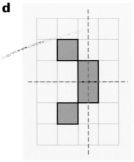

Example   Draw the reflection of the shape in the red line.

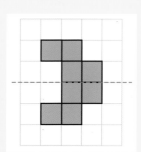

You need to draw what you would see in a mirror if you put a mirror on the red line.
You can use a mirror to help you.
This is the completed picture.
The red line is a line of symmetry.

5   Copy these shapes on to squared paper.
Draw the reflection of each shape in the line of symmetry.

a

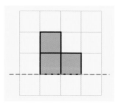

d

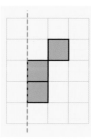

b

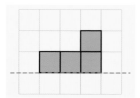

e

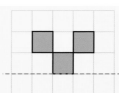

c

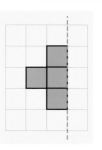

● **f**

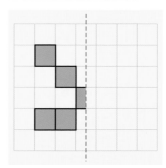

2   Probability

Roy Sullivan is the only known person to be struck by lightning seven times!
He was first struck in 1942.
The last strike took place while he was fishing in 1977.

Probability

Probability tells you how likely something is to happen.

Probabilities are often shown on a scale with 'impossible' at one end and 'certain' at the other.

This is a probability scale:

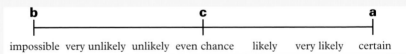

These probabilities are shown on the scale.
a The Sun will rise tomorrow.
b Ice will be found on the Sun.
c The Sun will shine on the first day of spring.

Exercise 5:2

For questions **1–3**, draw a probability scale.
Mark on it points **a**, **b**, and **c** to show how likely you think each one is.

1   **a**   You will be struck by lightning tomorrow.
      b   You will drink something tomorrow.
      c   You will eat chips tomorrow.

2 **a** A £1 ticket will win the jackpot in the National Lottery.
   b A £1 ticket will win £10 in the National Lottery.
   c A ticket will not win anything in the National Lottery.

3 **a** There will be at least one car in the
       school car park next Monday.
   b There will be a Rolls-Royce in the
       school car park next Monday.
   c A car will break down in the school
       car park next Monday.

Numbers are used to measure probability more accurately.
A probability scale often has numbers on it instead of words.
An event that is impossible has a probability of 0.
An event that is certain has a probability of 1.

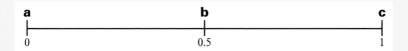

These probabilities are shown on the scale.
a Great Britain will sink into the sea tomorrow.
b If I toss a coin it will land tail up.
c It will be sunny tomorrow in the Arizona desert.

The value of probability can only be between 0 and 1.

For questions **4–6**, draw a probability scale with numbers.
Mark on it points **a**, **b** and **c** to show how likely you think each one is.

4 **a** It will snow in Scotland in January.
   b It will snow in Greece in August.
   c It will snow in Wales in April.

5 **a** The score will be an even number when an ordinary dice is rolled.
   b The score will be a six when an ordinary dice is rolled.
   c The score will be an eight when an ordinary dice is rolled.

6 **a** The school bus will be late
next Thursday.
b The school bus will be on time
next Thursday.
c The school bus will not turn
up next Thursday.

7 **a** Write down two things that have a probability close to 1.
b Write down two things that have a probability of 0.
c Write down two things that have a probability of 0.5

8 John says that the probability of Liverpool winning the cup is 1.5
Explain what is wrong with his value for the probability.

9 Lucy says that the probability of her passing her music exam is −0.5
Explain what is wrong with her value for the probability.

10 This fair dice is rolled.
Write down whether the following
statements are true or false.
a The probability of getting a 2 is about 0.5
b The probability of getting a 7 is about 0.3
c The probability of getting an even number
is about 0.5
d The probability of getting a number less than 6
is about 0.8

● **11** A fair coin is tossed.
Write down whether the following
statements are true or false.
a There is a 50% chance of getting a head.
b The chance of getting a head on two
tosses is about 0.9
c The chance of getting a head or a tail is 1.
d The chance of getting a tail on two tosses
is about 1.2

You can use probability to decide whether something is fair or not.

Example   Julia and Peter are deciding who is going to eat the last Rolo.

They are going to use this spinner.
Julia will eat it if the spinner lands on blue.
Peter will eat it if the spinner lands on yellow.
Why is this unfair?

There are more blue sections on the spinner than yellow.
There is a greater chance it will land on a blue section.
Julia has a better chance of getting the last Rolo!

Exercise 5:3

1   Katy and Laura have just one ticket for the football match.
They decide to roll a dice to see who gets the ticket.
Katy gets the ticket if the dice shows a 1, 2, 3 or 4.
Laura gets the ticket if the dice shows a 5 or 6.
Is this fair? Explain your answer.

2   Both David and Penel want the
last slice of chocolate fudge cake.
They both toss a coin.
If both the coins show heads then
Penel gets the cake. Otherwise
David gets to eat the cake.
Who is more likely to win?
Explain your answer.

3   Sam and Liam are playing a game with a dice.
They take turns to roll the dice.
If the dice shows an even number Liam writes it down.
If the dice shows an odd number Sam writes it down.
The winner is the first person whose numbers add up to 30.
Explain why the game is unfair.

3 Linking parts

Henman
Points won on first serve 80%.
Points won on second serve 40%.

The percentages show that Henman is winning twice as many points when his first serve is in.
Percentages are a good way of showing information like this.

Percentages are another way of writing fractions.

Sharon has scored $\frac{68}{100}$ in a test.

This means she scored 68 marks out of 100.

The fraction $\frac{68}{100}$ can be written 68%.

68% means 68 out of 100.

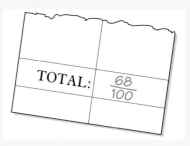

TOTAL: $\frac{68}{100}$

Exercise 5:4

1 Copy these and fill in the missing numbers.
  a 27% means 27 out of …
  b 32% means … out of 100.
  c 19% means … out of …
  d 78% means … out of …

2 Copy these and fill in the missing numbers.

  a $39\% = \dfrac{39}{\cdots}$ **c** $13\% = \dfrac{\cdots}{\cdots}$

  b $81\% = \dfrac{\cdots}{\cdots}$ **d** $7\% = \dfrac{\cdots}{\cdots}$

3   Write these percentages as fractions out of 100.
    a 91%   **c** 73%   **e** 3%
    b 23%   **d** 19%   **f** 1%

4   Chris scored 79 out of 100 in a test.
What percentage is this?

5   100 people in a supermarket were asked if they had bought eggs.
41 said 'yes'. What percentage is this?

6   100 people were asked if they owned a computer. 57 said 'yes'.
    a   What percentage is this?
    b   What percentage did not own a computer?

7   A box contains 100 apples.
23 apples are bad.
    a   What percentage of apples are bad?
    b   What percentage of apples are not bad?

Percentages always add up to 100%.

Example   Jane has completed 75% of her training course.
What percentage of the course does she still have to do?

100% − 75% = 25%

She still has to complete 25%.

---

8   In a box of disks 5% were faulty.
What percentage were not faulty?

9   In a survey, 72% of tennis players
were suffering from some type of
injury.
What percentage were not suffering
from injury?

10   Mia has spent 60% of her clothes allowance.
What percentage does she have left?

Other fractions can be changed to percentages.

Ian got 32 out of 50 in his test.

To change this to a percentage you have to make it out of 100.

32 out of 50

is the same as $\Big|$ ×2 $\qquad$ $\Big|$ ×2

64 out of 100

32 out of 50 is the same as 64%.

Exercise 5:5

1 Change these marks to percentages.
- **a** 40 out of 50
- **b** 22 out of 50
- **c** $\frac{30}{50}$
- **d** $\frac{15}{50}$

2 Carla says that 16 out of 50 pupils eat chips every day.
What percentage is this?

3 Richard has won 38 out of his last 50 matches.
What percentage is this?

Example

4 out of every 10 people eat fruit every day.
What percentage is this?

To change this to a percentage you have to make it out of 100.

4 out of 10

is the same as $\Big|$ ×10 $\qquad$ $\Big|$ ×10

40 out of 100

4 out of 10 is the same as 40%.

4 Change these marks to percentages.

   a 1 out of 10   **c** $\frac{5}{10}$

   b 8 out of 10   **d** $\frac{9}{10}$

5 In Newtown, 7 out of 10 households have more than one TV.
What percentage is this?

Example   Change each of these to percentages.

      a 6 out of 20   **b** 20 out of 25

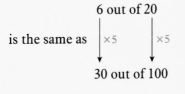

6 out of 20

is the same as $\times 5$ $\times 5$

30 out of 100

20 out of 25

is the same as $\times 4$ $\times 4$

80 out of 100

6 out of 20 is the same as 30%.   20 out of 25 is the same as 80%.

---

6 Change these marks to percentages.

   a 16 out of 20   **c** $\frac{14}{20}$

   b 12 out of 20   **d** $\frac{10}{20}$

7 Change these marks to percentages.

   a 22 out of 25   **c** $\frac{8}{25}$

   b 11 out of 25   **d** $\frac{10}{25}$

8 Sally has bought a CD.
7 out of 20 tracks have been on other CDs.
What percentage is this?

9 Tom won £25 in a raffle.
He has spent £15.
What percentage is this?

Exercise 5:6

1 What percentage of each of these diagrams is coloured?

a 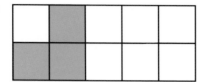 **b**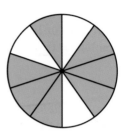

2 Change these fractions to percentages.

a $\frac{3}{10}$ **b** $\frac{7}{25}$ **c** $\frac{21}{50}$ **d** $\frac{13}{20}$

3 Change these fractions to percentages.

a $\frac{1}{2}$ **b** $\frac{1}{4}$ **c** $\frac{3}{4}$

4 What percentage of each of these diagrams is coloured?

a **b** **c**

5 A special offer pack of toffees
contains 25% extra free.
What is this percentage as a fraction?

6 A new size box contains 20% more than the old size.
What is this percentage as a fraction?

7 What fraction of each of these diagrams is coloured?

a 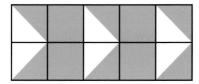   b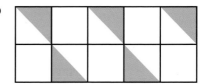

Changing fractions to decimals

You can use a calculator to change a fraction to a decimal.

Example   Change $\frac{3}{5}$ to a decimal.

Key in: **3** **÷** **5** **=**

$\frac{3}{5} = 0.6$

Exercise 5:7

1 Change these fractions to decimals.
  a $\frac{1}{2}$ **b** $\frac{1}{4}$ **c** $\frac{1}{8}$ **d** $\frac{3}{4}$

2 Change these fractions to decimals.
  a $\frac{5}{8}$ **b** $\frac{2}{5}$ **c** $\frac{3}{8}$ **d** $\frac{7}{10}$

3 What decimal of each of these diagrams is coloured?

a    c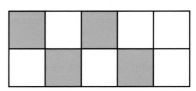

b   d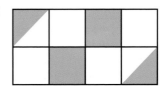

Changing decimals to percentages

To change a decimal to a percentage you multiply by 100.

Example   Change 0.37 to a percentage.

$$0.37 = 0.37 \times 100\%$$
$$= 37\%$$

4 Change these decimals to percentages.
  a 0.25   **c** 0.3   **e** 0.08
  b 0.75   **d** 0.01   **f** 1.5

5 Change these decimals to percentages.
  a 0.53   **c** 0.19   **e** 0.4
  b 0.28   **d** 0.06   **f** 2.45

Changing percentages to decimals

To change a percentage to a decimal you divide by 100.

Example   Change 69% to a decimal.

$$69\% = 69 \div 100 = 0.69$$

6 Change these percentages to decimals.
  a 46%   **c** 89%   **e** 7%   **g** 125%
  b 23%   **d** 45%   **f** 10%   **h** 250%

7 Copy and complete this table.

Fraction	Decimal	Percentage
$\frac{1}{2}$	0.5	50%
...	0.25	...
...	...	75%
$\frac{1}{5}$	...	...

8 Copy and complete this table.

Fraction	Decimal	Percentage
$\frac{3}{10}$	...	...
$\frac{4}{25}$	...	...
$\frac{7}{20}$	...	...
$\frac{1}{8}$	...	...

9 **a** Draw a line about 8 cm long.
   Mark a point about 0.4 of the way along the line.
   b Draw another line about 8 cm long.
   Mark a point about 60% of the way along the line.
   c Draw another line about 8 cm long.
   Mark a point about $\frac{4}{5}$ of the way along the line.

10 Match the pairs of cards that show the same amount.

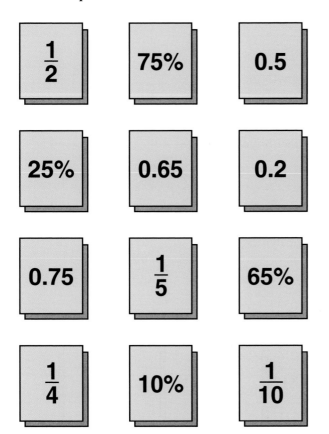

Example

List these in order. Start with the smallest.

$\frac{3}{4}$ 60% 0.8

Change each one to a percentage.

$$\frac{3}{4} = 3 \div 4 = 0.75$$
$$0.75 = 0.75 \times 100\%$$
$$= 75\%$$
$$0.8 = 0.8 \times 100\%$$
$$= 80\%$$

The order is: 60% 75% 80%
 60% $\frac{3}{4}$ 0.8

11 List these in order. Start with the smallest.
$\frac{1}{4}$ 0.23 21%

12 List these in order. Start with the smallest.
$\frac{2}{5}$ 43% 0.39%

13 List these in order. Start with the smallest.
$\frac{3}{8}$ 0.4 $\frac{7}{20}$ 43% $\frac{36}{100}$

14 Put $<$ or $>$ signs between these pairs of numbers.
Remember: $<$ means 'less than'
 $>$ means 'greater than'

a 0.7 56% **c** 45% 0.25
b $\frac{3}{5}$ 0.7 **d** $\frac{35}{100}$ 0.4

15 Put these cards in order. Start with the smallest.

$\frac{4}{5}$ **0.9**   **85%** $\frac{3}{4}$

Changing decimals to fractions

You can change decimals back to fractions by thinking about the column headings.

Example   Write these decimals as fractions.

a 0.6   **b** 0.43   **c** 0.173

a H T U . t h th
        0 . 6

The 6 is in the tenths column so $0.6 = \frac{6}{10}$

b H T U . t h th
        0 . 4 3

The 4 is in the tenths column and the 3 is in the hundredths column. You can think of this as 43 hundredths.
This means that $0.43 = \frac{43}{100}$

c H T U . t h th
        0 . 1 7 3

This is the same as 173 thousandths.
This means that $0.173 = \frac{173}{1000}$

Look at the answers to the example. $0.6\ \ \ = \frac{6}{10}$

$0.43\ \ = \frac{43}{100}$

$0.173 = \frac{173}{1000}$

Notice that the number of 0s in the number on the bottom of the fraction is the same as the number of digits after the decimal point.

Exercise 5:8

1 Write these decimals as fractions.

a 0.4	**e** 0.41	**i** 0.324	**m** 0.24
b 0.7	**f** 0.63	**j** 0.154	**n** 0.005
c 0.1	**g** 0.59	**k** 0.057	**o** 0.308
d 0.9	**h** 0.05	**l** 0.009	**p** 0.1241

4 Formulas

There is a formula that gives the length of a skid.
The length of the skid depends on the speed of the car.
The formula is: $L = 0.02S^2$
L is the length of the skid in metres.
S is the speed of the car in miles per hour.

Example

A car is travelling at 60 miles per hour.
Find the length of the skid for this speed.

$L = 0.02S^2$
$\quad = 0.02 \times S^2$ $\qquad S^2$ means $S \times S$.
$\quad = 0.02 \times 60 \times 60$
$\quad = 72$

The car would skid 72 m.

Exercise 5:9

1 Use the formula above to find the length of the skid if the speed is:
   a 30 miles per hour   **c** 10 miles per hour
   b 50 miles per hour   **d** 80 miles per hour

2 Rod works on a farm.
   This is a formula to work out how much he is paid:

   Wages in pounds = number of hours worked $\times$ 6

   a How much does Rod get for 8 hours work?
   Copy this and fill in the missing numbers.

   Wages in pounds = ... $\times$ 6
   $\qquad\qquad\qquad\quad = ...$

   Rod gets £...
   b How much does Rod get for 10 hours work?

You can also work backwards using a formula.

Example

Rod gets £30. How many hours has he worked?

Wages in pounds = number of hours worked × 6
| 30 | = | ? | × 6 |
| 30 | = | 5 | × 6 |

Rod has worked for 5 hours.

---

3 Use the formula above to find the hours Rod has worked if he gets:
   a £18   **b** £42   **c** £54

4 The cost of hiring a boat is £2 per hour, therefore:
   Cost of hire in pounds = number of hours × 2
  a Find the cost of hiring the boat for:
    (1) 1 hour
    (2) 3 hours
    (3) 7 hours
  b Lisa pays £8 to hire the boat.
    How many hours does she have the boat?
  c Jim goes out fishing in the boat.
    He pays £10. How many hours is Jim fishing?

5 Pritesh uses this formula to estimate the distance around the outside of circles:
   Distance = 3 × diameter
  a Find the distance around a circle with diameter:
    (1) 5 cm
    (2) 7 cm
    (3) 12 cm
  b The distance around the outside of this crater is 1200 m. Use the formula to find the diameter.

Sometimes formulas have two parts.

Example

This formula is used to find the cost, in pounds, to service a boiler:

Cost = 30 + 12 × number of hours worked

a How much will a 3 hour service cost?
b A service cost £54. How long did it take?

a   Cost = 30 + 12 × 3
        = 30 + 36
        = £66

b   54 = 30 + 12 × ?   The inverse of +30 is −30.
        54 − 30 = 12 × ?   You subtract 30 from both sides.
           24 = 12 × ?   12 × 2 = 24
The number of hours is 2.

Exercise 5:10

1 This formula gives the cost, in pounds, of servicing a washing machine:

Cost = 25 + 10 × number of hours worked

a How much will a 2 hour service cost?
b A service cost £55. How long did it take?

2 This formula gives the cost, in pounds, of hiring a mini tractor:

Cost = £10 delivery charge + £8 for each day of hire

a Find the cost of hire for:
  (1) 2 days
  (2) 6 days
b Carl paid £42 to hire the tractor.
  How many days did he have the tractor?

3 David has to pay to park his car in town.
This is the way the amount he has to pay is worked out:

£2 for 3 hours then 50 p for each extra hour

a How much does David pay to park for:
  (1) 4 hours
  (2) 2 hours
  (3) 8 hours?
b David paid £3 on Tuesday. How long did he park?

Sometimes **letters** are used in formulas instead of words.

Example This formula gives the cost, C, in pence of an advert in the local paper:

$$C = 200 + 10n$$

where n is the number of words.

a Find the cost of an advert with 16 words.
b Jean's advert costs 450 p.
How many words are there in Jean's advert?

a $\quad C = 200 + 10n$ $\qquad\qquad$ $10n$ means $10 \times n$
$\quad = 200 + 10 \times 16$
$\quad = 200 + 160$
$\quad = 360$
The advert cost 360 pence.

b $\qquad 450 = 200 + 10 \times ?$ $\quad$ The inverse of $+200$ is -200.
$450 - 200 = 10 \times ?$ $\qquad$ Subtract 200 from both sides.
$\qquad 250 = 10 \times ?$ $\qquad$ $250 = 10 \times 25$
So $\qquad ? = 25$
There are 25 words in Jean's advert.

Exercise 5:11

1 This formula gives the cost, C, in pence of an advert in the local paper:
$$C = 200 + 10n$$
where n is the number of words.
a Michael's advert has 35 words.
Find the cost of Michael's advert.
b Sue's advert costs 640 p.
How many words are there in Sue's advert?

2 Rhian is using the formula $D = ST$ in her Physics lesson.
D is the distance in metres.
S is the speed in metres per second.
T is the time in seconds.
a Find the distance when the speed is 15 m/s and the time is 20 seconds.
Remember: ST means $S \times T$.
b Rhian is told that the distance is 300 m when the speed is 60 m/s.
Use the formula to find the time.

3 The time to cook a large turkey is given by the formula:

$$T = 20p + 30$$

T is the time in minutes.
p is the weight of the turkey in pounds.

a A turkey weighs 16 pounds. How long should it be cooked?
b Mark's turkey will take 270 minutes to cook. Find the weight of Mark's turkey.

4 The perimeter of a rectangle is given by the formula:

$$p = 2l + 2w$$

p is the length of the perimeter in centimetres.
l and w are the length and width in centimetres.
Find the perimeter when:
a $l = 4\,\text{cm}$ and $w = 6\,\text{cm}$ **b** $l = 15\,\text{cm}$ and $w = 20\,\text{cm}$

In coursework you sometimes have to **write your own** formula.

Example

A puppy is 14 cm tall when it is born. It grows 5 cm every *month* until it is fully grown.
Write a formula for the *h*eight of the puppy.

The formula is for the *h*eight, so it starts $h =$
The height is: $14 + 5 \times$ the number of *months*
The formula is: $h = 14 + 5m$
where h is the height and m is the number of months.

Exercise 5:12

Write formulas for each of these.
Use the red letters and numbers.

1 The *t*otal money raised in a sponsored walk at £2 for each *m*ile.

2 The *t*otal weight of a number of *b*oxes when each box weighs 5 kg.

3 The *n*umber of tins of dog food needed by dogs who eat 6 tins each *w*eek.

4 The *w*ages earned by someone who gets paid £5 per *h*our.

5 The number of *s*ticks in a pattern of squares is 5 plus 4 × the *n*umber of squares.

6 The number of *d*ots in a pattern is 7 plus 3 × the number of the *p*attern.

7 The total *l*ength of a car 5 m long and a *c*aravan.

8 The *d*istance left on a 300 mile journey after travelling a number of *m*iles.

9 The *m*oney received by each of 3 winners when a *p*rize is shared equally between them.

10 The *t*otal cost of a meal for *f*ood and *d*rink.

Exercise 5:13

1 The rule for changing kilometres into miles is:

> To find the number of *m*iles you multiply the number of *k*m by 5 and divide the answer by 8.

    a Write a formula for this rule. Use the red letters and numbers.
    b Use your formula to change 160 km into miles.

2 The *c*ost of hiring a car is:

> £25 + £15 per *d*ay

    a Write a formula for this rule.
    Use the red letters and numbers.
    b Use your formula to find the cost of hiring a car for 4 days.

3 Matthew's *w*age is made up of £20 plus £5 for each *c*omputer he sells.
    a Write a formula for this rule. Use the red letters and numbers.
    b Use your formula to find Matthew's wage when he sells 7 computers.

4 To change degrees Celsius (°C) to degrees *F*ahrenheit (°F) you can multiply the *C*elsius temperature by 2 and then add 30.
    a Write a formula for this rule. Use the red letters and numbers.
    b Use your formula to find 25 °C in degrees Fahrenheit.

1 Copy these shapes on to squared paper.
Mark on all the lines of symmetry.

a

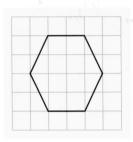

b

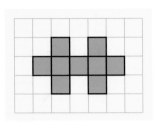

2 Copy these shapes on to squared paper.
Shade in two more squares so that the **red** line is a line of symmetry.

a

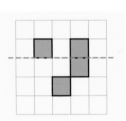

b

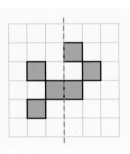

3 Copy these shapes on to squared paper.
Draw the reflection of each shape so that the **red** line is a line of symmetry.

a

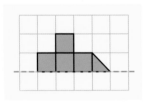

b

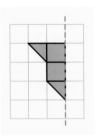

4 Draw a probability scale like this one.

Mark on it points **a**, **b** and **c** to show how likely you think each one is.
  a It will rain tomorrow.
  b Tuesday will follow Monday.
  c All your teachers will be absent on Friday.

5 Jenny spins the spinner.
Write down whether the following
statements are true or false.
   a The probability of getting a green
      is about 0.6
   b The probability of getting a blue
      is about 0.5
   c Getting a red is twice as likely as
      getting a blue.
   d The probability of getting a
      yellow is about 0.1

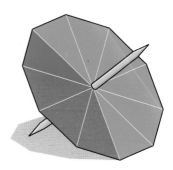

6 Alice says that the probability that she will get a car for her
birthday is 1.8
Explain what is wrong with her probability.

7 Sue and Ian have to decide who is going to
weed the garden.
They are going to use this spinner to
decide.
If it lands on an even number, Sue has to
do the weeding, otherwise Ian will have to
do the weeding.
Is this fair?
Explain your answer.

8 Penny scored 68 out of 100 in her exam.
What percentage is this?

9 **a** Draw a line about 8 cm long.
      Mark a point 0.6 of the way along the line.
   b Draw another line about 8 cm long.
      Mark a point 40% of the way along the line.
   c Draw another line about 8 cm long.
      Mark a point $\frac{1}{3}$ of the way along the line.

10 A box contains 50 oranges.
   7 oranges are bad.
   a What percentage of oranges are bad?
   b What percentage of oranges are not bad?

11 The table shows the percentage of homes with telephones and washing machines in different years.

Year	1960	1970	1980	1990
Households with a telephone	10%	39%	72%	95%
Households with a washing machine	35%	53%	75%	92%

a What percentage of households had a telephone in 1960?

b Estimate the year that the percentage of telephones overtook the percentage of washing machines.

c In 1990, what percentage of households did not have a telephone?

d In 1980, what fraction of households did not have a washing machine?

12 Copy and complete this table.

Fraction	Decimal	Percentage
$\frac{1}{2}$	...	...
...	0.7	...
...	...	75%
$\frac{2}{5}$	...	...

13 Here is a list of fractions, percentages and decimals:

53%   0.5 $\frac{3}{4}$ 45%   0.55 $\frac{5}{8}$

Rewrite them in order of size. Start with the smallest.

14 This formula gives the cost of hiring a paint sprayer:

Cost in pounds $= 4 \times$ number of days

a Find the cost of hiring the sprayer for:
(1) 1 day   (2) 3 days   (3) 6 days

b Jack paid £20 to hire the sprayer.
How many days did he hire the sprayer?

15 The North West Electricity Board, NORWEB, charges customers 6 pence per unit of electricity that they use. They also charge a fixed charge of £8.

a How much is the fixed charge in pence?

b How much does it cost for u units of electricity in pence?

c Write down a formula for C, the total cost of the electricity.

1 Copy these shapes on to squared paper.
Use the **red** lines of symmetry to complete each picture.

a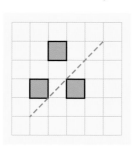

b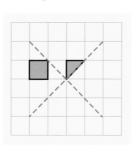

2 Mary bought two raffle tickets. She won a prize with one of them.
Mary says the chance of her winning a raffle prize must have been 0.5
Explain why she is wrong.

3 Either a male or a female will win the lottery. So the probability a man
will win is 0.5
What is wrong with this?

4 A shop gives 15 p in the pound discount.
What percentage is this?

5 **a** Jim sleeps for 6 hours in every 24 hours.
What percentage is this?
b If Jim lives to be 80, how many years of his life will he have spent
sleeping?

6 This formula tells you what size fuse to use:

$$F = \frac{P}{240}$$

where F is the size of the fuse in amps
and P is the power in watts.
a What size fuse is needed for Sonya's hairdryer?
The power of her hairdryer is 1200 watts.
b Jill's heater uses a 13 amp fuse.
What is the power of Jill's heater?

7 David is using the formula $v = u + at$ in his Physics lesson.
He knows that $u = 20$, $a = 5$ and $t = 7$
Use the formula to find v.

1 Complete the pattern so that the two **red** lines are lines of symmetry.

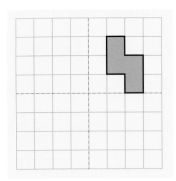

2 Sam and Gemma use this spinner to decide who takes the dog for a walk. Sam has to walk the dog if it lands on a multiple of 4, otherwise Gemma walks the dog. Is this fair? Explain your answer.

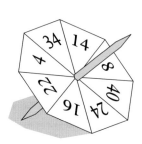

3 Write:
  a $\frac{33}{100}$ as a percentage
  b 16 out of 25 as a percentage
  c $\frac{3}{5}$ as a decimal
  d 0.57 as a fraction
  e 0.35 as a percentage
  f 81% as a decimal

4 Rachid works 7 hours of overtime.
He uses this formula to work out his overtime pay:
  Overtime pay in £ = 4.75 × number of hours of overtime

  a Work out Rachid's overtime pay.
    Rachid uses this formula to work out his total pay:
      Total pay = basic pay + overtime pay
    His basic pay is £145.
  b Work out his total pay.

5 The cost, £C, of an electrician's home visit is worked out using the formula:

  $C = 30 + 0.25n$

Where n is the number of minutes the visit lasts.

  a Find the cost of a visit that lasts 50 minutes.
  b Another visit costs £35. How long did this visit last?

6

1 Multiplying
Multiplying without a calculator
  – whole numbers
  – decimals
  – two decimals

2 Line graphs
Deciding what type of data you've got
Reading and drawing line graphs for continuous data
Reading and drawing vertical line graphs for discrete data

CORE

3 Dividing
Dividing without a calculator
  – with whole numbers
  – with decimals
Multiplying and dividing with a calculator
Multiplying and dividing by numbers between 0 and 1

4 More symmetry
Looking at regular polygons
Using rotational symmetry
Using planes of symmetry in 3D
Making and drawing 3D symmetrical shapes with cubes

"Pollygone Mummy"

QUESTIONS

EXTENSION

TEST YOURSELF

1 Multiplying

Melvin is collecting his money.
He needs to work out the cost of any
number of pints.
A pint of milk costs 34 p.
He doesn't know his 34 times table!

You need to be able to work out
multiplications like this without using
your calculator.
If you know your tables up to 10×10 then
you can do any multiplication.

Multiplying without using a calculator

When you want to multiply two quite large numbers together you
need to do it in stages.

Example   Work out 123×23.

First do 123×3.

$$
\begin{array}{r}
1\ 2\ 3 \\
\times \quad\ 3 \\
\hline
3\ 6\ 9
\end{array}
$$

$123 \times 3 = 369$

Now do 123×20.
Do this by doing 123×2 and then multiply by 10.
This works because $20 = 2 \times 10$.

123×2

$$
\begin{array}{r}
1\ 2\ 3 \\
\times \quad\ 2 \\
\hline
2\ 4\ 6
\end{array}
$$
$246 \times 10 = 2460$

$123 \times 20 = 2460$

Now add the two parts together.

$$
\begin{array}{r}
3\ 6\ 9 \\
+\ 2\ 4\ 6\ 0 \\
\hline
2\ 8\ 2\ 9 \\
\scriptstyle 1
\end{array}
$$

So $123 \times 23 = 2829$.

Usually you write the working out like this:

$$
\begin{array}{r}
1\ 2\ 3 \\
\times\quad 2\ 3 \\
\hline
3\ 6\ 9 \\
2\ 4\ 6\ 0 \\
\hline
2\ 8\ 2\ 9 \\
{}_1
\end{array}
$$

If you have carries in the multiplication, write them very small so that you don't count them twice.

Example   Work out 234 × 24

$$
\begin{array}{r}
2\ 3\ 4 \\
\times\quad\ 2\ 4 \\
\hline
{}_1 9\ {}_1 3\ 6 \\
4\ 6\ 8\ 0 \\
\hline
5\ 6\ 1\ 6 \\
{}_1\ \ {}_1
\end{array}
$$

There are no carries on this line.

4 × 4 = 16
Put the 6 under the 4 and carry the 1.
4 × 3 = 12, add the 1 to get 13.
Put the 3 under the 2 and carry the 1.
4 × 2 = 8, add the 1 to get 9. Put the 9 in the next column.

So 234 × 24 = 5616.

Exercise 6:1

Work these out.
Show all your working.

1 **a**
$$
\begin{array}{r}
2\ 1\ 4 \\
\times\quad 2\ 4 \\
\hline
\end{array}
$$

c
$$
\begin{array}{r}
3\ 5\ 5 \\
\times\quad 4\ 3 \\
\hline
\end{array}
$$

e
$$
\begin{array}{r}
1\ 0\ 7 \\
\times\quad 3\ 8 \\
\hline
\end{array}
$$

b
$$
\begin{array}{r}
3\ 4\ 5 \\
\times\quad 3\ 2 \\
\hline
\end{array}
$$

d
$$
\begin{array}{r}
3\ 6\ 7 \\
\times\quad 5\ 7 \\
\hline
\end{array}
$$

f
$$
\begin{array}{r}
9\ 2 \\
\times\ 1\ 7 \\
\hline
\end{array}
$$

2 **a** 125 × 43   **c** 264 × 36   **e** 724 × 24
   b 294 × 56   **d** 835 × 12   **f** 75 × 28

3 **a** Melvin sells 247 pints of milk each day.
      Each pint costs 34 p.
      How much money does Melvin make each day?
   b Mrs Holmes buys 23 pints a week.
      How much does she have to pay each week?
   c How much does it cost for 10 pints of milk?
   d How much does it cost for 50 pints of milk?
      Use your answer to part **c** to help you do this.
   e Melvin wants to know how much 55 pints cost.
      Write down a quick way for Melvin to work this out.

Multiplying decimals without a calculator

You need to set these out like you do whole number questions.

Example   Work out 4.73×5

$$
\begin{array}{r}
4\,.\,7\ 3 \\
\times \quad\quad 5 \\
\hline
5 \\
\scriptstyle 1
\end{array}
$$

Start with 5×3. The answer is 15.
Put the 5 in the column and carry the 1.

$$
\begin{array}{r}
4\,.\,7\ 3 \\
\times \quad\quad 5 \\
\hline
.\,6\ 5 \\
\scriptstyle 3 \quad\ \scriptstyle 1
\end{array}
$$

Now do 5×7. The answer is 35.
Add the 1 to get 36.
Put the 6 in the column and carry the 3.
Put the decimal point in.

$$
\begin{array}{r}
4\,.\,7\ 3 \\
\times \quad\quad 5 \\
\hline
2\ 3\,.\,6\ 5 \\
\scriptstyle 3 \quad\ \scriptstyle 1
\end{array}
$$

Finally do 5×4. The answer is 20.
Add the 3 to get 23.
Put the 3 in the column and put the 2 in the next column.

So $4.73 \times 5 = 23.65$

Exercise 6:2

Work these out.
Show all your working.

1 **a**
$$
\begin{array}{r}
2\,.\,4\ 2 \\
\times \quad\quad 3 \\
\hline
\end{array}
$$

b
$$
\begin{array}{r}
2\,.\,5\ 8 \\
\times \quad\quad 2 \\
\hline
\end{array}
$$

c
$$
\begin{array}{r}
4\,.\,5\ 8 \\
\times \quad\quad 6 \\
\hline
\end{array}
$$

2 **a** 3.44×2
    b 7.66×3
    c 2.39×4

    d 1.26×5
    e 4.3×4
    f 38.3×3

    g 22.4×6
    h 3.05×9
 • **i** 157.06×8

3 CDs cost £8.49 in a sale.
How much would you pay for 6 CDs?

4 Clare pays £2.80 to travel through the Mersey tunnel every day. How much does she pay each week from Monday to Friday?

You sometimes need to use long multiplication with decimals. This works like normal long multiplication.

Example   Work out 3.76 × 24.

Start with 3.76 × 4.

```
    3 . 7 6
×         4
  1 5 . 0 4
    3   2
```

Now do 3.76 × 20. Do this by multiplying by 2 first.

```
    3 . 7 6
×         2
    7 . 5 2
    1   1
```

Now multiply by 10.   7.52 × 10 = 75.2

Now add the two answers together. Fill in missing spaces with zeros.

```
    7 5 . 2 0
  + 1 5 . 0 4
    9 0 . 2 4
      1
```

Usually the working looks like this.

```
    3 . 7 6
×       2 4
  1 ₃5 .₂0 4
 ₁7 ₁5 . 2 0
    9 0 . 2 4
      1
```

So 3.76 × 24 = 90.24

Exercise 6:3

Work these out.
Show all your working.

1
a 4.74 × 35	**d** 6.78 × 13	**g** 14.31 × 23
b 3.95 × 15	**e** 5.05 × 37	**h** 42.56 × 71
c 3.36 × 24	**f** 7.25 × 16	● **i** 245.28 × 26

2 Elizabeth sells coats on a market stall.
Each coat costs £26.95
One day she sells 13 coats.
How much money does she get?

3 Stephen sells sweets.
A large bag of sweets costs £1.79
He sells 58 bags of sweets.
How much money does he get?

4 Debbie does face painting at a school fete.
She paints a face for £1.75
How much does she get if she paints 34 faces?

5 David sells CDs and tapes.
He sells CDs for £6.95 each.
He sells tapes for £3.45 each.
  a He sells 26 CDs.
    How much does he get?
  b He sells 42 tapes.
    How much does he get?
  c How much money does he get altogether?

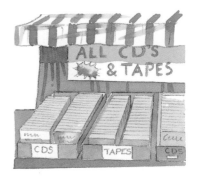

6 Warren is buying crisps for a party.
He buys 24 boxes.
Each box costs £4.39
Each box contains 48 bags.
  a How much does he pay altogether?
  b How many bags of crisps does he buy?

7 Chalk is packed in boxes.
Miss Huddleston buys 120 boxes.
A box costs £0.37
How much money does she spend?

Multiplying two decimals

Exercise 6:4

1 **a** Copy these questions.

$0.3 \times 0.4 = \ldots$	$0.2 \times 0.6 = \ldots$
$0.4 \times 0.7 = \ldots$	$0.34 \times 0.2 = \ldots$
$0.02 \times 0.65 = \ldots$	$0.006 \times 0.005 = \ldots$

   b Work out the answers to the questions on your calculator.
   Write each answer down.

Look at your answers to question **1**.
The number of digits after the decimal point in the answer is the same as the number of digits after the decimal point in the question.
$0.3 \times 0.4 = 0.12$

If there are two digits after the decimal points in the question (shown in red) then there will be two digits after the decimal point in the answer (shown in blue).
You can use this fact to do decimal multiplications without a calculator.

Example   Work out 0.04×0.05

0.04×0.05

Ignore all the 0s and work out $4 \times 5 = 20$.
There are 4 digits after the decimal points in the question.
This means that there must be 4 in the answer.

So $0.04 \times 0.05 = 0.0020$

So the final answer is 0.002 as you don't need the last 0 any more.

---

2 Work these out. Do not use your calculator.

a	0.4×0.3	**e**	0.42×0.3	**i**	0.03×0.02
b	0.7×0.5	**f**	0.32×0.2	**j**	0.05×0.07
c	0.1×0.1	**g**	0.1×0.78	**k**	0.06×0.08
d	0.9×0.7	**h**	0.4×0.21	**l**	0.009×0.1

3 Work these out. Do not use your calculator.

a	0.004×0.0004	**e**	0.0002×0.000031
b	0.0004×0.0006	**f**	0.032×0.00002
c	0.0001×0.0001	**g**	0.00001×0.7898
d	0.0006×0.0007	**h**	$0.000043 \times 0.0000003$

2 Line graphs

When you draw graphs you usually plot some points. Then you join the points together.

Sometimes you can't do this. The lines in between the points may not have a meaning.

This happens a lot in statistics. If you are plotting data about numbers of people you can't join the points. You can't have 2.8 people for example!

Discrete data	When data can only take certain individual values they are called **discrete data**. Numbers of people is discrete data. You can't have 2.8 people.
Continuous data	When data can have any number value in a certain range they are called **continuous data**. The lengths of worms is continuous data. A worm can be 2.8 cm long. It can be *any* length between 2 cm and 3 cm.

Exercise 6:5

1 Write down if each of these types of data is discrete or continuous.

a Number of cans of Coke

b Temperature

c Marks in a test

d Time

e Volume

f Height

g Weight

h Shoe sizes

i Length

j Number of CDs

k Area

l Number of friends you have

Peter is recording the number of people in a queue in a supermarket between 12:00 and 13:00.
He wants to draw a graph to show his results.

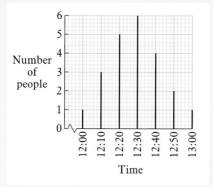

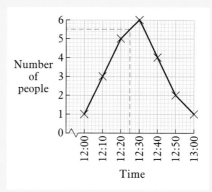

This type of graph is called a **vertical line graph**. This is like a bar-chart where the bars are just lines. You can draw graphs like this for discrete data.
So Peter can draw this type of graph.

This type of graph is called a **line graph**. You join the points together with lines. You can only draw this type of graph for continuous data. The number of people is discrete data, so Peter cannot draw this type of graph. This graph shows that there were 5.5 people in the queue at 12:25!

You can only draw a line graph for continuous data.
If you have discrete data you can draw a vertical line graph.

2 Write down whether you would draw a line graph or a vertical line graph to show each of these.

    a The number of bicycles sold each month by a shop.

    b The number of Smarties in 30 tubes.

    c The temperature of a cup of coffee as it cools down.

    d The number of people on a train during a journey.

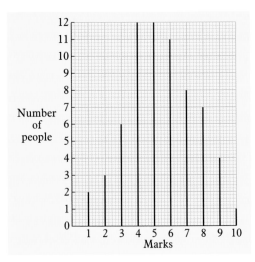

3 This graph is a vertical line graph showing the results of a test.
  a How many people scored 8?
  b How many people scored 3?
  c How many people took the test altogether?
  d Why can't you join the points and draw a line graph for these data?

4 Here is a line graph showing the temperature in London over a 24-hour period. The temperature is recorded every hour.

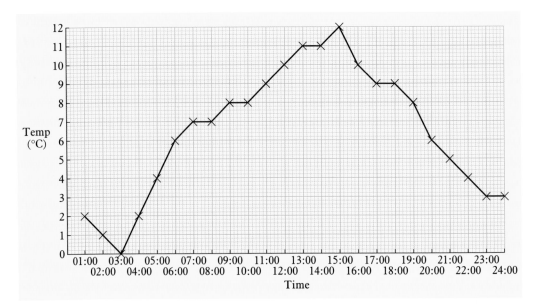

  a What is the temperature at 12:00?
  b What is the temperature at 14:00?
  c What is happening to the temperature between 15:00 and 22:00?
  d There are two times where the temperature is 6 °C.
     Write down both times.
  e Use the graph to estimate the temperature at 04:30.
     Why is this temperature only an estimate?

5 A music shop records the number
of CD sales over a week.
Here are the results.

Day	Number of CDs
Mon	16
Tue	23
Wed	14
Thu	17
Fri	27
Sat	63

a Draw a vertical line graph to show the sales.

b Why do you think most sales are made on a Saturday?

6 Mr Holmes has oil-fired central
heating. He records the amount of
oil left in the tank every hour one
cold afternoon.
Here are his results.

Time	Oil left (litres)
1 p.m.	155
2 p.m.	148
3 p.m.	140
4 p.m.	132
5 p.m.	125

a Draw a line graph to show the amount of oil left in his tank.

b Estimate the volume of oil left in his tank at 3.30 p.m.

3 Dividing

Ben, John, Jennie, Rachel and Emma play the lottery as a syndicate.
They have just won £775.
Ben wants to work out how much each of them wins.
Ben needs to work out £775 ÷ 5.

You need to be able to work out the answer to questions like this without using a calculator.

Dividing without using a calculator

| **Short division** | You have seen **short division** on p 38 in Unit 2. Here is a reminder about how it works. |

Example

Find 785 ÷ 5.

$$5\overline{)7\,^28\ 5}$$
      1

First do **7 ÷ 5**. This is **1** with **2** left over.
Put the **1** above the **7** and carry the **2**.

$$5\overline{)7\,^28\,^35}$$
      1 5

Now do **28 ÷ 5**.
$5 \times 5 = 25$. So **28 ÷ 5** is **5** with **3** left over.
Put the **5** above the **²8** and carry the **3**.

$$5\overline{)7\,^38\,^35}$$
      1 5 7

Now do **35 ÷ 5**.
This is **7**. Put the **7** above the **³5**.

So 785 ÷ 5 = 157.

Exercise 6:6

Work these out.
Show all your working.

1
a 375 ÷ 5	**d** 738 ÷ 9	**g** 784 ÷ 7
b 430 ÷ 5	**e** 336 ÷ 8	**h** 5725 ÷ 5
c 264 ÷ 3	**f** 504 ÷ 3	● **i** 12 225 ÷ 3

2 6 friends win £852 on the lottery.
How much does each of them win?

3 The most people who are allowed
in this lift is 8.
There are 136 people who work on
this floor.
What is the least number of
journeys that are needed if
everyone wants to go down in the
lift?

4 Alice is sharing a bag of sweets
with her friends.
She wants to share a bag of sweets
equally with Sam and Charlene.
The bag contains 81 sweets.
  a How many people are sharing the sweets?
  b How many sweets will each person get?

You sometimes need to use long division.
This happens when you divide by a number that is bigger than 10.

Example Find $375 \div 15$

$15\overline{)3\ 7\ 5}$ First do $37 \div 15$.

You need to know how many times 15 goes into 37.
You need to work out the 15 times table.
  $15 \times 1 = 15$
  $15 \times 2 = 30$
  $15 \times 3 = 45 \leftarrow 45$ is too many, so stop.
  $15 \times 2 = 30$ so $37 \div 15$ is 2 with some left over.
  $37 - 30 = 7$ so $37 \div 15$ is 2 with 7 left over.

$\overset{2}{15\overline{)3\ 7\ {}^{7}5}}$ Put the 2 above the 7 and carry the 7.

$\overset{2}{15\overline{)3\ 7\ {}^{7}5}}$ Now do $75 \div 15$.

You need to carry on the 15 times table. $15 \times 4 = 60$
                                         $15 \times 5 = 75$

$\overset{2\ 5}{15\overline{)3\ 7\ {}^{7}5}}$ So $75 \div 15$ is 5.
                     Put the 5 above the ${}^{7}5$.

So $375 \div 15 = 25$.

Exercise 6:7

1 Work these out.
Show all your working.

a	675 ÷ 15	**d**	378 ÷ 14	**g**	805 ÷ 23
b	576 ÷ 12	**e**	768 ÷ 24	**h**	1400 ÷ 25
c	676 ÷ 13	**f**	918 ÷ 17	**i**	1120 ÷ 32

2 All of the pupils in Years 10 and 11 are going on a coach trip.
There are 264 pupils in Year 10.
There are 242 pupils in Year 11.

  a How many pupils are going on the trip?
    48 pupils can go in each coach.

  b How many coaches are needed?

3 Eileen is talking to primary school children about looking after their teeth.
She gives every child a free toothbrush at the end of her talk.
She has 4 boxes of toothbrushes.
Each box contains 54 toothbrushes.

  a How many toothbrushes does Eileen have?
    Every class that Eileen talks to has 36 children in it.

  b How many classes can she talk to if every child has to get a toothbrush?

4 Graham and his 15 friends are in a lottery syndicate at work.
  a How many people are in the syndicate?
  b How much would each person get if the syndicate won:
    (1) £2032
    (2) £1 503 248?

Dividing decimals without a calculator

Fiona, Diane, Lucy, Charles and Haydn are buying chocolates for a present.
The total cost is £8.75
They want to share the cost equally.
They want to know how much they need to pay.
They need to divide £8.75 by 5.
You need to be able to do questions like this without a calculator too!

Set these out like you do whole number questions.

Example

Work out 8.75 ÷ 5

$$\begin{array}{r} 1\,. \\ 5\overline{)8.\,^37\ 5} \end{array}$$

First do 8 ÷ 5. This is 1 with 3 left over.
Put the 1 above the 8 and carry the 3.
Put the decimal point in.

$$\begin{array}{r} 1\,.\ 7 \\ 5\overline{)8.\,^37\,^25} \end{array}$$

Now do 37 ÷ 5.
5 × 7 = 35. So 37 ÷ 5 is 7 with 2 left over.
Put the 7 above the ³7 and carry the 2.

$$\begin{array}{r} 1\,.\ 7\ 5 \\ 5\overline{)8.\,^37\,^25} \end{array}$$

Now do 25 ÷ 5.
This is 5. Put the 5 above the ²5.

So 8.75 ÷ 5 = 1.75

Exercise 6:8

Work these out.
Show all your working.

1 **a** 7.75 ÷ 5   **c** 5.73 ÷ 3   **e** 7.77 ÷ 3
    b 6.35 ÷ 5   **d** 4.36 ÷ 4   **f** 17.25 ÷ 5

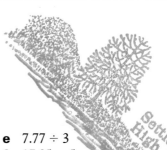

2 A packet of choc ices costs £3.90
    The packet contains 6 choc ices.
    What is the cost of one choc ice?

3 A packet of 7 chicken pieces costs £3.64
    Find the cost of 1 piece of chicken.

4 A box of computer disks costs £2.95
    The box contains 5 disks.
    Find the cost of 1 disk.

5 Pete pays for 6 tickets to the cinema. He pays £14.70
    How much does each ticket cost?

Multiplying and dividing with a calculator

All of the number work that you have done so far is much easier with a calculator. Take care to press the right keys and you can't get it wrong!

Exercise 6:9

1 Work these out using a calculator.

a	125×43	**i**	264×36	**q**	724×24
b	7.66×3	**j**	4.3×4	**r**	3.05×9
c	4.74×35	**k**	6.78×13	**s**	14.31×23
d	3.95×15	**l**	5.05×37	**t**	42.56×71
e	$375 \div 5$	**m**	$738 \div 9$	**u**	$784 \div 7$
f	$430 \div 5$	**n**	$336 \div 8$	**v**	$5725 \div 5$
g	$576 \div 12$	**o**	$768 \div 24$	**w**	$1400 \div 25$
h	$6.35 \div 5$	**p**	$4.36 \div 4$	**x**	$17.25 \div 5$

2 a Work these out using a calculator.

(1) 20×0.3 (3) 20×0.13 (5) 20×0.7
(2) 20×0.4 (4) 20×0.25 (6) 20×0.834

  b In part **a** you are multiplying 20 by decimal numbers.
The answers are all bigger or smaller than 20.
Write down what you notice about all of the answers to part **a**.

3 a Work these out using a calculator.

(1) $20 \div 0.2$ (3) $20 \div 0.5$ (5) $20 \div 0.75$
(2) $20 \div 0.4$ (4) $20 \div 0.25$ (6) $20 \div 0.8$

  b In part **a** you are dividing 20 by decimal numbers.
The answers are all bigger or smaller than 20.
Write down what you notice about all of the answers to part **a**.

4 Jason is working out 40×0.5 on his calculator.
He gets 80 as his answer.
  a Explain how you know that Jason must be wrong.
• **b** What has Jason done on his calculator?

5 Liza is working out $50 \div 0.4$ on her calculator.
She gets 12.5 as her answer.
  a Explain how you know that Liza must be wrong.
• **b** What has Liza done on her calculator?

4 More symmetry

"Pollygone Mummy"

Polly the parrot has escaped from her cage!

Emily's mum is very proud of her daughter.

She thinks that Emily is telling her that the base of the cage is a polygon.

Regular polygon   A **regular polygon** is a polygon with all its sides the same length and all its angles equal.

This is a regular triangle.
It is an equilateral triangle.

This is a regular pentagon.

This is a regular quadrilateral.
It is a square.

This is a regular hexagon.

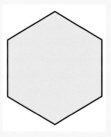

Irregular polygon   A polygon that is not regular is called an **irregular polygon**. All of these shapes are irregular polygons.

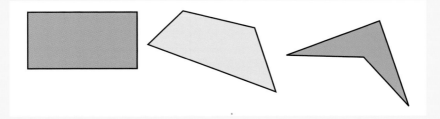

Exercise 6:10

1 Write down if each of these polygons is regular or irregular.
You may need to measure the sides to help you to decide.

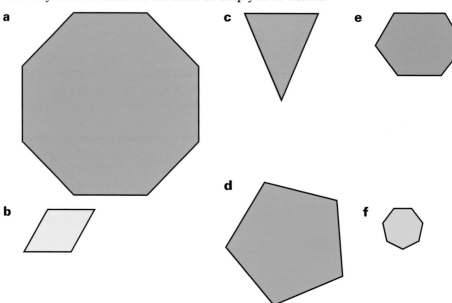

a

c

e

b

d

f

2 Copy these regular polygons.
Draw all the lines of symmetry on each one.

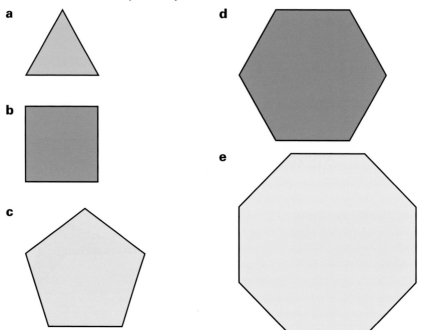

a

b

c

d

e

Regular polygons have rotational symmetry as well as line symmetry.

Rotational symmetry	A shape has **rotational symmetry** if it fits on top of itself more than once as it makes a complete turn.
Order of rotational symmetry	The **order of rotational symmetry** is the number of times that the shape fits on top of itself as it makes a complete turn.
Centre of rotation	The **centre of rotation** is the point that stays still as the shape makes a complete turn.

A shape only has rotational symmetry if it fits on top of itself twice or more as it makes a complete turn.

A shape that fits on top of itself only once has no rotational symmetry.

This shape has no rotational symmetry.

This square has rotational symmetry of order 4 about O. Don't count the starting position.

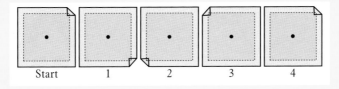

Start   1   2   3   4

Exercise 6:11

Write down the order of rotational symmetry of each of the shapes in questions **1** and **2**.

1   **a**   **b**   **c**   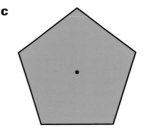

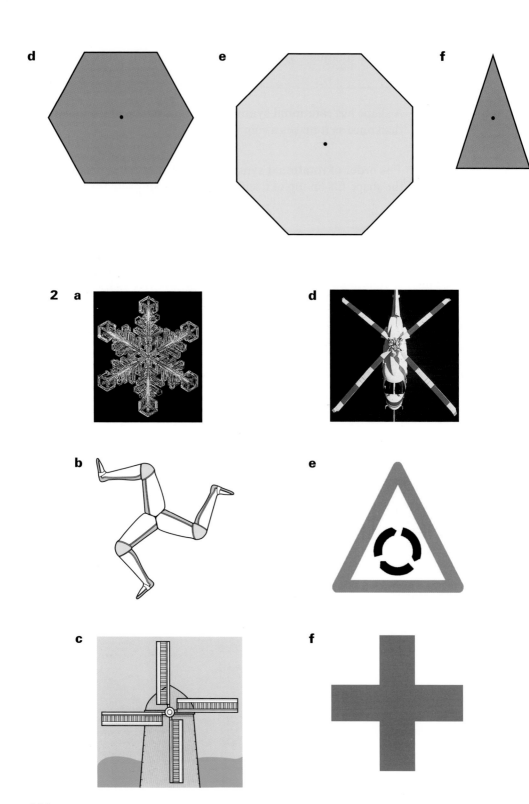

d

e

f

2 **a**

b

c

d

e

f

You can also have symmetry in three dimensions.

Instead of having a mirror line you can now think about putting a whole mirror into the shape.

This is a cuboid.

You can see the three possible places to put a mirror so that the two halves are symmetrical.

When you can put a mirror into a shape like this the mirror is called a plane of symmetry.

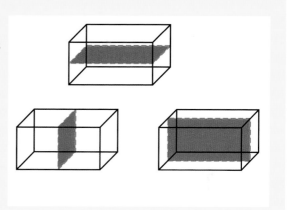

Exercise 6:12

1 How many planes of symmetry does each of these shapes have?

a  b   c

2 How many planes of symmetry does a cube have?

 3 How many planes of symmetry does a sphere have?

This shape is symmetrical about the plane of symmetry.

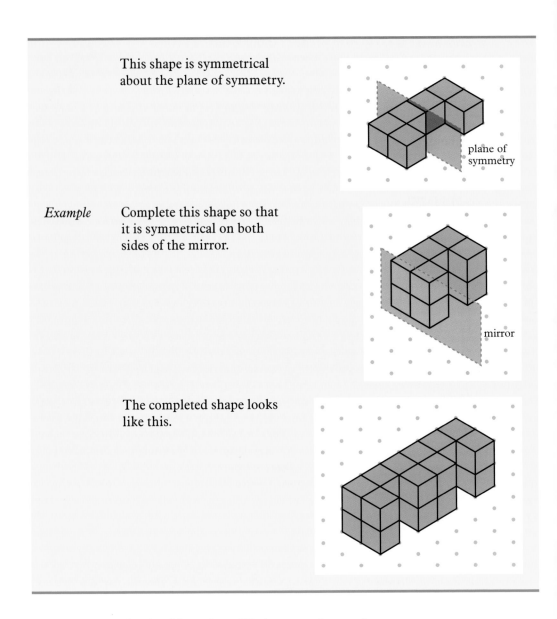

plane of symmetry

Example   Complete this shape so that it is symmetrical on both sides of the mirror.

mirror

The completed shape looks like this.

You need to be able to draw 3D shapes on isometric paper.
You saw this in Unit 2.

Exercise 6:13

Make each of these shapes with cubes.
Complete each shape so that the mirror is a plane of symmetry.
Draw the completed shape on dotty isometric paper.

1

2

3

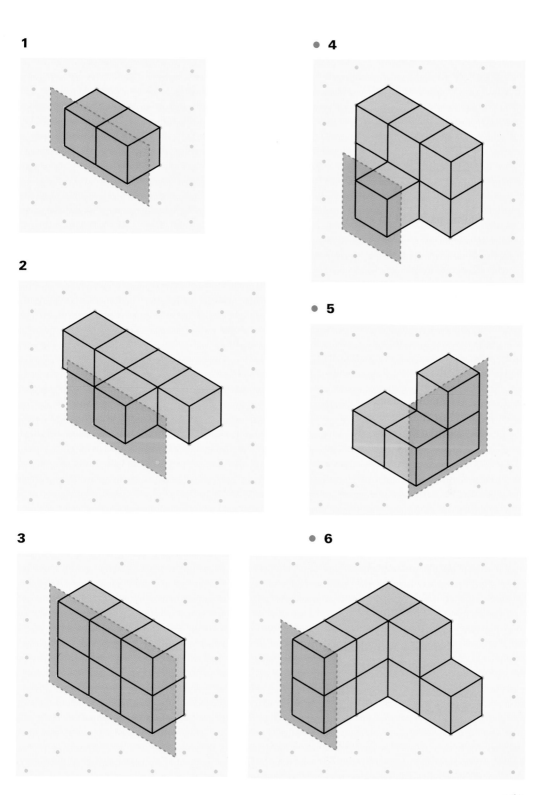

1 Work these out. Show all your working.

a 1 3 6 × 2 4 ─────	**c** 2 4 6 × 5 2 ─────	**e** 3 2 4 × 2 7 ─────
b 1 . 6 2 × 3 ─────	**d** 3 . 2 7 × 2 ─────	**f** 7 . 2 3 × 6 ─────

2 Saima pays £14.95 every month for her travel pass.
   a How much does she pay in 6 months?
   b How much does she pay in a year?

3 Work these out.
   Show all your working.
   a 3.75×15 **c** 4.78×14 **e** 0.6×0.9
   b 2.65×36 **d** 5.05×28 **f** 0.34×0.02

4 **a** This staircase has 14 steps.
      Each step is 19 cm high.
      How high does the staircase rise?
   b How many steps would you need to
      build a staircase that rises 285 cm?

5 Anita has a market stall.
   She sells car sponges for £1.29
   How much money does she
   get if she sells 27 sponges?

6 A music shop records the number of tape sales over a week.
   Here are the results.

Day	Mon	Tue	Wed	Thu	Fri	Sat
Number of tapes	11	13	6	8	14	23

   a Draw a vertical line graph to show the sales.
   b Why wouldn't you draw a line graph to show these data?

7 Paul is ill. His Mum takes his temperature every hour one afternoon. Here are the results.

Time	1 p.m.	2 p.m.	3 p.m.	4 p.m.	5 p.m.
Temperature (°C)	38.5	38.3	38.1	38.0	37.6

a Draw a line graph to show Paul's temperature.
b Estimate his temperature at 4.30 p.m.
c Normal temperature is about 37.4 °C.
Do you think Paul is getting better or worse?

8 Work these out.
Show all your working.
a 285 ÷ 3   **c** 724 ÷ 4   **e** 791 ÷ 7
b 240 ÷ 5   **d** 432 ÷ 8   **f** 6755 ÷ 5

9 Work these out.
Show all your working.
a 330 ÷ 15   **c** 574 ÷ 14   **e** 782 ÷ 23
b 420 ÷ 12   **d** 624 ÷ 24   **f** 1025 ÷ 25

10 A shoe shop stores all of its shoes in boxes.
The width of one box is 24 cm.
Each shelf is 312 cm long.
a How many boxes fit along the shelf?

There are 36 shelves in the storeroom.
Each shelf has 2 rows of boxes on it.
b How many boxes of shoes are on each shelf?
c How many boxes can the shop store altogether?

11 Work these out.
Show all your working.
a 8.25 ÷ 5   **c** 8.43 ÷ 3   **e** 8.76 ÷ 3
b 6.34 ÷ 2   **d** 7.64 ÷ 4   **f** 37.25 ÷ 5

12 Liam is working out 200×0.5 on his calculator.
He gets 1000 as his answer.
   a Explain how you know that Liam must be wrong.
   b How has Liam got his answer on his calculator?

13 Write down if each of these polygons is regular or irregular.
You may need to measure the sides to help you to decide.

   a   **b**    **c**

14 For each of these polygons:
   (1) Write down how many lines of symmetry it has.
   (2) Write down the order of rotational symmetry.

   a 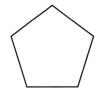   **b**    **c**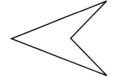

15 How many planes of symmetry does each of these shapes have?

   a   **b** 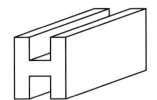   **c**

16 Copy these diagrams on to isometric paper.
Complete them so that the mirror is a plane of symmetry.

   a    **b**    **c**

1 Here is another way of doing long multiplication.
To use this method all you have to be able to do is double a number.

To work out 21 × 35,
start with 1 lot of 35.

Double up on each row.

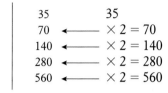

1	35	35
2	70 ←	× 2 = 70
4	140 ←	× 2 = 140
8	280 ←	× 2 = 280
16	560 ←	× 2 = 560

The next row would be 32.

You only want 21 times. 32 is too many so you stop at 16.

Now you need to get 21 by adding numbers in the left-hand column.

$$21 = 1 + 4 + 16$$

Keep the 1, 4 and 16 rows
and cross out the others.

Now add up the numbers
in the right column.
This is the answer!

1	35
2	70
4	140
8	280
16	560
21	735

So 21 × 35 = 735

Use this method to work these out. Show all your working.

a 24 × 36   **c** 12 × 34   **e** 83 × 15
b 35 × 25   **d** 38 × 14   **f** 113 × 25

2 Look at what happens when you try to work out 134 ÷ 5.

$$\begin{array}{r} 2\,6 \quad \text{with a remainder } 4 \\ 5\,\overline{)1\ 3\ ^34} \end{array}$$

Instead of leaving a remainder you can carry on if you add a decimal
point and an extra zero like this.

$$\begin{array}{r} 2\,6\,.\,8 \\ 5\,\overline{)1\ 3\ ^34\,.^40} \end{array}$$

So 134 ÷ 5 = 26.8
Sometimes you might need to add more than one zero.

Work these out. Show all your working.

a 214 ÷ 5   **c** 162 ÷ 4   **e** 202 ÷ 8
b 315 ÷ 2   **d** 318 ÷ 4   **f** 113 ÷ 4

1 Work these out. Show all your working.
    a 7.91 × 4   **c** 0.05 × 0.8
    b 2.47 × 31   **d** 7.12 ÷ 4

2 Jane is taking her son to the seaside for the day.
The coach ticket costs £15.98. Children go half price.
    a Find the cost of a child's ticket.
    b Find the total Jane pays for both tickets.

3 Mrs Job is taking 395 students on a trip to a theme park.
They go by coach. Each coach holds 51 students.
    a How many coaches are needed for the trip?
       Show all your working.
    b The cost for the trip for one student is £17.
       How much will it cost for all 395 students?
       Show all your working.

4 The table shows the numbers of different
vehicles using a stretch of country road in
a 1-hour period.
Draw a vertical line graph to show this
information.

Vehicle	Number
car	22
bus	5
lorry	7
bicycle	11
other	4

5 For each polygon write down:
    (1) How many lines of symmetry it has.
    (2) The order of rotational symmetry.

a
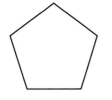

c
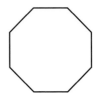

b

d
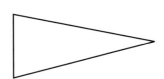

7

1 Get in position
Using co-ordinates in the first quadrant
Doing scale drawings and maps
Drawing triangles with a protractor
Drawing triangles with compasses

2 It all adds up to one
Drawing probability scales
Finding probabilities that add up to 1
Marking probability scales with fractions
Marking probability scales with decimals
and percentages

3 Estimating
Multiplying by 20, 30 etc.
Dividing by 20, 30 etc.
Multiplying by multiples of 100, 1000 etc.
Dividing by multiples of 100, 1000 etc.
Checking answers by working backwards

4 Stem and leaf diagrams
Drawing stem and leaf diagrams

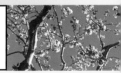

CORE

QUESTIONS

EXTENSION

TEST YOURSELF

1 **Get in position**

This is an aerial view of Alton Towers.

It is a big place!

You need a map to find your way around.

Here is a map of a part of Alton Towers.

You can use co-ordinates to give the positions of each ride.

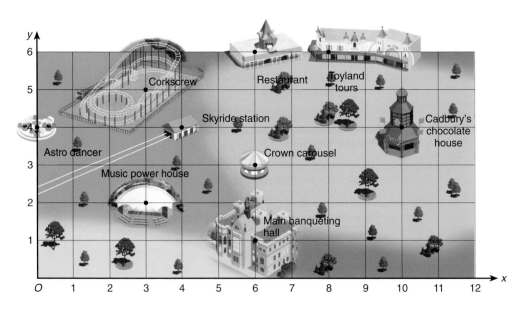

Example   What are the co-ordinates of the Corkscrew?

The Corkscrew is 3 across and 5 up.
Its co-ordinates are (3, 5).

Exercise 7:1

1 Write down the co-ordinates of the following using the map on page 166.
   a Skyride station
   b Cadbury's chocolate house
   c Main banqueting hall
   d Astro dancer
   e Crown carousel
   f Music power house
   g Toyland tours
   h Restaurant

2 Look at this plan of a cricket pitch.
It shows some of the possible positions of the players.

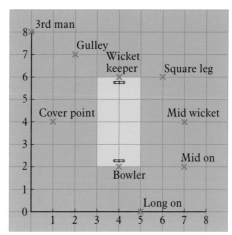

Write down the co-ordinates of these positions.
   a Bowler
   b Cover point
   c Square leg
   d Wicket keeper
   e Mid wicket
   f Mid on
   g Long on
   h 3rd man

3 **a** Draw these axes on squared paper.
   b Plot each of these points on your diagram.
   Mark each one with its letter.

     A (2, 1)   F (3, 4)
     B (9, 1)   G (2, 4)
     C (10, 4)   H (1, 1)
     D (7, 4)   I (2, 1)
     E (7, 8)

   c Join up the points in alphabetical order.

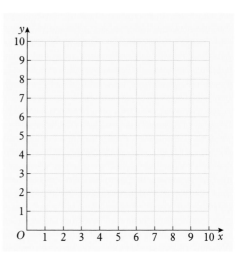

Scales

Most maps are drawn to scale.
This means that you can take measurements from them.

This map of a theme park is drawn to scale.
The scale is   1 cm = 100 m.
This means that every 1 cm on the map represents 100 m
in the park.

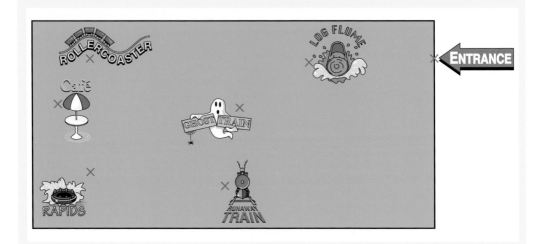

Example

How far is it from the rollercoaster to the log flume?

On the map, the distance is 6 cm.
The scale is   1 cm = 100 m.
So in the park it is 6 × 100 m = 600 m.

1 cm	1 cm	1 cm	1 cm	1 cm	1 cm
100 m	100 m	100 m	100 m	100 m	100 m

Exercise 7:2

Use the above map to answer questions **1–4**.

1 **a** How far is it on the map from the rollercoaster to the runaway train?
   b How far is it in the park from the rollercoaster to the runaway train?

2 a How far is it on the map from the rapids to the café?
  b How far is it in the park?

3 How far is it in the park from the café to the ghost train?

4 William has a day out at the theme park.
  He walks from the entrance to the log flume then to the runaway train.
  He then walks to the rollercoaster.
  How far has William walked altogether?

5 This is a scale drawing of Joe's bedroom.
  1 cm = 1 m

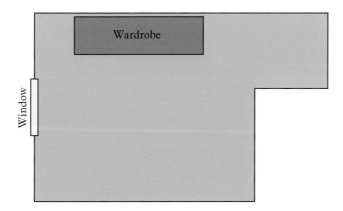

  a How long is the plan of the room?
  b How long is the real room?
  c What is the width of the real room?
  d How wide is Joe's wardrobe?
  e How wide is Joe's window?

6 Mark's bedroom is a rectangle 6 m long and 4 m wide.
  a Draw a scale plan of Mark's bedroom.
    Use a scale of 1 cm = 1 m.
  b Mark has a wardrobe which is 2.5 m long and 1 m wide.
    He also has a desk which is 1.2 m long and 0.8 m wide.
    Mark these in on your diagram.
    It does not matter where you put them.

7   This is part of a Derby street map.
The scale is 4 inches = 1 mile.

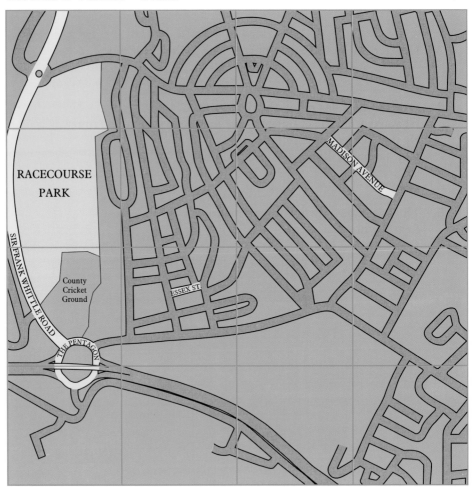

a   What distance does 2 inches on the map represent?
b   What distance does 1 inch represent?
c   About how long is Racecourse Park on the map?
d   About how long is the real Racecourse Park?
e   How long is Madison Avenue on the map?
f   How long is the real Madison Avenue?
g   How long is the real Essex Street?
● **h**   What is the diameter of The Pentagon roundabout?
i   Estimate the length of Sir Frank Whittle Road.
j   The width of this section of map is about 5 inches.
What length does this represent?
● **k**   The map shown is a square.
What area of Derby is shown on the map?

Plans

There are other types of scale drawing.

Lots of people draw **plans** so that they can see what the real thing will look like.

Lizzy is a garden designer. She runs a busy company.

She draws a plan of each garden before she plants it.

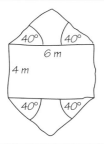

Here is a sketch of one of Lizzy's gardens.

Lizzy wants to draw a scale plan of the garden.

She decides on a scale of 1 cm = 1 m.

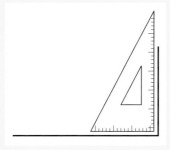

First she draws the rectangular section.

She uses a set square to make sure that the corners are exactly 90°.

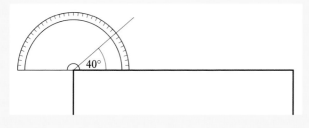

Lizzy uses a protractor to measure the angles of the triangle.

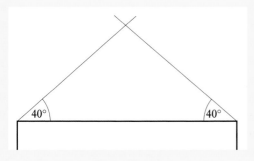

She draws one line from each side. The top of the triangle is where the two lines cross.

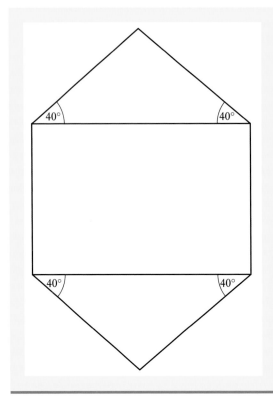

She does the same for the other triangle to finish the plan.

Scale: 1 cm = 1 m

Exercise 7:3

1 Make a copy of Lizzy's plan, shown above. Use a scale of 1 cm = 1 m.

2 Here is a sketch of another garden that Lizzy is designing.
 a Draw the centre line.
 Use a scale of 1 cm = 1 m.
 b Draw the top triangle.
 Use a protractor to measure the angles.
 c Turn your diagram upside down. Draw the other triangle.

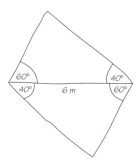

3 This is a sketch of a school playing field.
 a Make a scale drawing of the field.
 Use a scale of 1 cm = 5 m.
 b Measure the sides of your drawing in centimetres.
 c What is the perimeter of your drawing?
 d What is the perimeter of the real field?

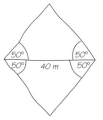

172

4 Lee is building a bird table with a nesting box on top. Here is the sketch that he has made for it.

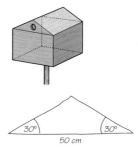

The end pieces look like this.

Make a scale drawing of the end piece. Use a scale of 1 cm = 5 cm.

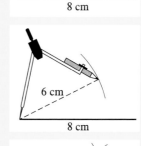

You can also draw triangles using compasses and a ruler. To do this you need to know the length of all three sides.

Example   Draw a triangle with sides 8 cm, 6 cm and 4 cm.

(1) Draw the 8 cm side with a ruler. Leave space above it for the other sides.

(2) Set your compasses to 6 cm. Draw an arc from one end of your line.

(3) Set your compasses to 4 cm. Draw an arc from the other end of your line. The two arcs should cross. This is the third corner of the triangle.

(4) Join the ends of your line to the crossing point.

(5) Do not rub out your construction lines. In an exam, these show your method.

Exercise 7:4

1 Use compasses to draw a triangle with sides 8 cm, 5 cm and 6 cm.

2 Draw an equilateral triangle with sides of 6 cm.

3 Construct each of these shapes.

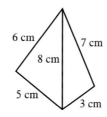

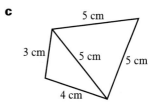

2 It all adds up to one

Moses and Whitney are watching the weather forecast.
The presenter says that the probability of a hurricane is 40%.
Moses is worried.
Whitney is more cheerful.
She says the probability of the hurricane missing them is 60%.

You usually write probabilities as fractions:
40% is $\frac{40}{100}$ and 60% is $\frac{60}{100}$

Probabilities always add up to 1.

Example

Suppose you have 4 Multilink cubes in an envelope.
You have 3 red cubes and 1 blue cube.
The probability of choosing a red cube is $\frac{3}{4}$.
The probability of choosing a blue cube is $\frac{1}{4}$.

You can show this on a probability scale.

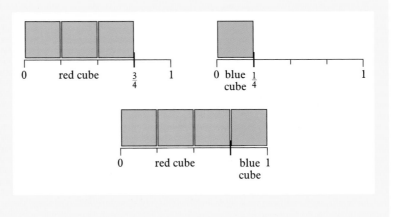

Exercise 7:5

1   You will need some Multilink.
Take 4 red cubes and 1 blue cube.
  a   Copy this probability scale so that the cubes can fit on it like this.
You have 5 cubes so mark your scale in fifths.

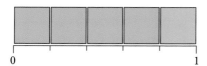

Now put the cubes in an envelope.
  b   What is the probability of picking a red cube?
  c   What is the probability of picking a blue cube?
  d   What do these probabilities add up to?

2   You will need some more Multilink.
Take 5 red cubes and 3 blue cubes.
  a   Copy this probability scale so that the cubes can fit on it like this.
You have 8 cubes so mark your scale in eighths.

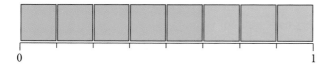

Now put the cubes in an envelope.
  b   What is the probability of picking a red cube?
  c   What is the probability of picking a blue cube?
  d   What do these probabilities add up to?
● **e**   Would it change the probabilities if you put the cubes down like this?

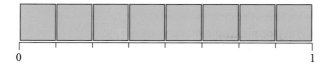

3 You will need some more Multilink.
Take 7 green cubes and 3 yellow cubes.
  a Copy this probability scale so that the cubes can fit on it like this.
  b How many cubes have you got?
  c What fractions is it best to show on your scale?
  d Now mark your scale with these fractions.

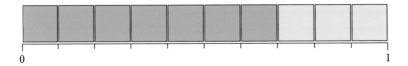

Now put the cubes in an envelope.
  e What is the probability of picking a green cube?
  f What is the probability of picking a yellow cube?
  g What do these probabilities add up to?

4 Take 2 red counters and 3 blue counters.
  a Copy this probability scale so that the counters can fit on it like this.

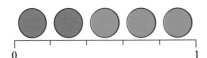

  b How many counters have you got?
  c What fraction is it best to show on your scale?
  d Now mark your scale with these fractions.

Now put the counters in an envelope.
  e What is the probability of picking a red counter?
  f What is the probability of picking a blue counter?
  g What do these probabilities add up to?

5 Take 4 black counters and 3 red counters.
  a Draw a suitable probability scale.
Now put the counters in an envelope.
  b What is the probability of picking a black counter?
  c What is the probability of picking a red counter?
  d What do these probabilities add up to?

You can work out probabilities by just colouring the scale.

You have 4 green cubes and 1 blue cube in an envelope.
There are 5 cubes altogether so you draw a scale using fifths.

The probability that you will pick a green cube is $\frac{4}{5}$.
You can now colour the first $\frac{4}{5}$ of your scale in green.
The rest of the scale must be blue.

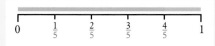

So the probability of blue is $\frac{1}{5}$.
This is also the probability of *not* getting a green.

These probabilities add up to 1
$$\frac{4}{5} + \frac{1}{5} = 1$$

Exercise 7:6

1   You have 4 red cubes and 2 blue cubes in an envelope.
There are 6 cubes altogether so you draw a scale like this:

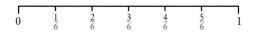

a   What is the probability that you will pick a red cube?
You can now colour that part of your scale in red.
The rest of the scale is blue. Colour this in.

b   What is the probability that you will pick a blue cube?
c   What is the probability that you won't pick a red cube?

d   Copy this.
Fill in the gaps.
The probability of picking a red cube is …
The probability of picking a blue cube is …
The probability of picking a red cube or a blue cube is …

2 Sankha has 3 blue-eyed friends and 7
brown-eyed friends.
He has 10 friends altogether.

a Copy the scale.
Fill in the missing values.

Sankha wants to ring one of his friends at
random.

b What is the probability that Sankha
rings a blue-eyed friend?
Colour that part of your scale in blue.
The rest of the scale is brown.
Colour it in.

c Find the probability that Sankha does not ring a blue-eyed friend.

d Copy this. Fill in the gaps.
The probability that Sankha rings a blue-eyed friend is …
The probability that Sankha rings a brown-eyed friend is …
The probability of ringing either type of friend is …

3 Gemma has 8 red socks and 2 black socks
in a drawer.
She has 10 socks altogether.

a Copy the scale.
Fill in the missing values.

b Gemma picks a sock without looking.
What is the probability that she will
pick a red sock?
Colour that part of your scale in red.
The rest of the scale is black.
Colour it in.

c What is the probability that she will not pick a red sock?

d Copy this. Fill in the gaps.
The probability of picking a red sock is …
The probability of not picking a red sock is …
The probability of picking a red sock or not picking a red sock is …

Probabilities always add up to 1.
We can show this on a probability scale.

Suppose the probability of a hurricane is 40%.
Then the probability of no hurricane is 60%.

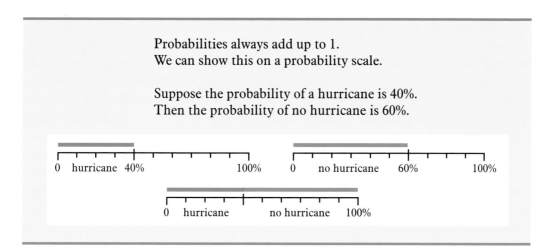

Exercise 7:7

In this exercise draw a probability scale for each question.

1 Zara has lots of nail varnish. 1 out of every 4 bottles is red.
She paints her nails choosing a bottle at random.

What is the probability that she doesn't have red nails?

2 Dennis plays the piano. He gets 9 out of 10 notes right.

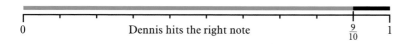

What is the probability that he hits the wrong note?

3 The probability that Gaby will pass her accountancy exam is 0.8.

What is the probability that she will fail?

4 Mr Fish, the weather forecaster, says there's a 20% chance of a storm tomorrow.

0   storm   20%   100%

What is the probability that there is no storm tomorrow?

5 Bella is very lucky at bingo.
The probability she wins when she goes is 0.7
What is the probability that she won't win?

6 Nelson loves watching rugby.
The probability he is at a rugby match on Saturday is 84%.
What is the probability that he won't be there?

7 Steve has a lot of bright ties.
4 out of 5 of his ties are bright.
What is the probability that he wears a dull tie?

8 John likes eating chicken.
3 days out of 4 he eats chicken.
What is the probability that he doesn't eat chicken one day?

9 Rona likes to talk.
Her friend says the probability that Rona is talking is 62%.
What is the probability that Rona isn't talking?

● **10** Paul collects money people have forgotten to pay.
7 people out of every 100 greet Paul with a smile.
a What is the probability that they don't smile?
b Write your probability as a percentage.

● **11** Kevin supports Dartmouth Argyle.
The chance they will win is 0.08
The chance they will draw is 0.66
What is the probability that they won't lose?

3 Estimating

Jas works in a supermarket.
The staff are counting the stock.
The manager needs to estimate the number of apples.
She asks Jas to count the apples.
The apples come in boxes of 96.
Jas is not too hot at his 96 times table!

There is a simple way to multiply by 20.
This is because $20 = 2 \times 10$
You can do it in two parts.
First you multiply by 2, then you multiply by 10.

Examples

1 Find 32×20.

First do
$$\begin{array}{r} 3\ 2 \\ \times\ \ 2 \\ \hline 6\ 4 \end{array}$$
then do 64×10
$= 640$

H	T	U
	6	4
6	4	0

So $32 \times 20 = 640$.

You can use this method with 30, 40, 50, 60, 70 …

2 Find 84×70.

First do
$$\begin{array}{r} 8\ 4 \\ \times\ \ \ 7 \\ \hline 5\ 8\ 8 \\ {\scriptstyle 2} \end{array}$$
then do 588×10
$= 5880$

Th	H	T	U
	5	8	8
5	8	8	0

So $84 \times 70 = 5880$.

Exercise 7:8

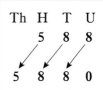

1 Multiply these numbers by 20.
Show your working as in the example.

a 17	**c** 38	**e** 57	**g** 71	**i** 95
b 23	**d** 43	**f** 64	**h** 88	• **j** 360

2 Multiply these numbers by: (1) 30 (2) 40
Show your working as in the example.

a	12	**c**	36	**e**	51	**g**	79	**i**	95
b	23	**d**	44	**f**	68	**h**	82	● **j**	180

3 Multiply these numbers by: (1) 60 (2) 90
Show your working as in the example.

a	13	**c**	37	**e**	56	**g**	77	● **i**	105
b	22	**d**	45	**f**	61	**h**	89	● **j**	987

4 A used-car dealer has 70 cars.
Amy gets £28 for each car she polishes.
How much does Amy earn if she
polishes all of the cars?

5 A premier league player gives £49 to
charity every time he scores a goal.
If he scores 30 goals in a season,
how much does he give to charity?

● **6** Mr Christian has 50 tropical fish. They each cost 37 p a day to feed.
How much does Mr Christian spend on feed in June?

There is a simple way to divide by 20.
This is because $20 = 2 \times 10$
You can do it in two parts.
First you divide by 2, then you divide by 10.

Example Find 320 ÷ 20.

First do
$$\begin{array}{r} 1\ 6\ 0 \\ \hline 2\overline{)3\ {}^12\ 0} \end{array}$$
then 160 ÷ 10
= 16

So 320 ÷ 20 = 16.

---

7 Divide these numbers by: (1) 20 (2) 80
Show your working as in the example.

a	240	**c**	560	**e**	3280	**g**	7680	● **i**	32
b	480	**d**	640	**f**	4240	**h**	8960	● **j**	4.8

There is an easy way to multiply multiples of 10 together.

Example

Work out 40×30.
Do $4 \times 3 = 12$.
Count the zeros. There are two. 40×30
Put these at the end.
So $40 \times 30 = 1200$.

Exercise 7:9

1 Multiply these numbers by: (1) 30   (2) 80
   Show your working as in the example.

a 20	**c** 30	**e** 50	**g** 70	**i** 90
b 10	**d** 40	**f** 60	**h** 80	• **j** 200

The same method can be used for multiples of a hundred and multiples of a thousand.

Examples

Work out **1** 400×30 **2** 600×7000

1 Do $4 \times 3 = 12$
Count the zeros. There are three. 400×30
Put these at the end.
So $400 \times 30 = 12\,000$.

2 Do $6 \times 7 = 42$
Count the zeros. There are five. 600×7000
Put these at the end.
So $600 \times 7000 = 4\,200\,000$.

2 Multiply these numbers by: (1) 400   (2) 6000
   Show your working as in the example.

a 20	**c** 30	**e** 500	**g** 700	**i** 900
b 10	**d** 40	**f** 60	**h** 800	• **j** 5000

• **3** In a race, 20 000 competitors run 40 000 m. How far is this in total:
   a in metres   **b** in kilometres?

There is also an easy way to divide by 10s, 100s or 1000s.

Example Work out $600 \div 30$

Cross **one** zero out on the 30.   This divides the 30 by 10.
Cross **one** zero out on the 600.   This divides the 600 by 10.
Then you have $60\cancel{0} \div 3\cancel{0}$.

Then do $60 \div 3 = 20$ ($6 \div 3 = 2$ and add the 0 that you need).

4   Divide these numbers by: (1) 20   (2) 60
Show your working as in the example.

a	120	**c**	360	**e**	1200	**g**	4800	● **i** 4620
b	180	**d**	600	**f**	2400	**h**	9600	● **j** 9000

Example Work out $80\,000 \div 400$.

Cross **two** zeros out on the 400.   This divides the 400 by 100.
Cross **two** zeros out on the 80 000.   This divides the 80 000 by 100.
Then you have $80\,0\cancel{00} \div 4\cancel{00}$.

Then do $800 \div 4 = 200$ ($8 \div 4 = 2$ and add the 00 that you need).

5   Do these divisions. Show your working as in the example.

a	$40\,000 \div 200$	**c**	$80\,000 \div 200$	● **e** $240\,000 \div 6000$
b	$60\,000 \div 300$	**d**	$90\,000 \div 300$	● **f** $750\,000 \div 500$

You have been multiplying and dividing rounded numbers.
This is very useful for making estimates.

Example Work out 21×32

Calculation: [2] [1] [×] [3] [2] [=]   **Answer:** 672

Estimate: 21 is 20 to the nearest 10.
32 is 30 to the nearest 10.

21×32 is about $20 \times 30 = 600$.
672 is near to 600.
So the answer is probably right.

Exercise 7:10

1   Work these out. Write down the answer and an estimate for each one.
   a 22×23 c 61×42 e 24×28 g 55×34
   b 42×31 d 84×71 f 49×52 h 66×85

2   Work these out. Write down the answer and an estimate for each one.
   a 201×32 c 568×212 e 398×623 • g 2001×6003
   b 273×52 d 800×233 f 300×525 • h 4344×8979

Example   Work out $576 \div 32$.

   Calculation: | 5 | 7 | 6 | ÷ | 3 | 2 | = | **Answer:**   18

   Estimate: 576 is 600 to the nearest 100.
   32 is 30 to the nearest 10.

   $576 \div 32$ is about $600 \div 30 = 20$.
   20 is near to 18.
   So the answer is probably right.

---

3   Work these out. Write down the answer and an estimate for each one.
   a $308 \div 28$ c $468 \div 52$ e $572 \div 26$ • g $3936 \div 82$
   b $399 \div 21$ d $819 \div 39$ f $915 \div 61$ • h $8960 \div 64$

You can also check calculations by working backwards.

If you work out $34 \times 26 = 884$ you can work backwards and check the answer
by doing:
   $884 \div 26$ which would give you 34
   or $884 \div 34$ which should give you 26.

If you work out $672 \div 24 = 28$ you can check this by doing:
   28×24 which should give 672
   or $672 \div 28$ which should give 24.

---

4   Check all of your answers to Questions **1–3** by working backwards.

• 5   Work these out. Write down the answer and an estimate for each one.
   Also check your answers by working backwards.
   a   27 teachers each win £47 659 on the pools. How much is this in total?
   b   2143 people each pay £19 999 for a car. How much is this in total?

4   Stem and leaf diagrams

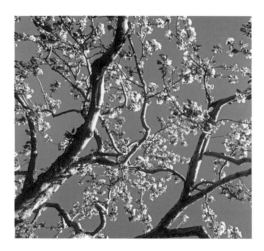

There is another way of showing data.
You split the data values into two parts.
The first is called the stem and the second part is called the leaf.
This is like a branch of this tree, which has its leaves growing out from the stem.

| Stem and leaf diagram | A **stem and leaf diagram** shows the shape of a set of data. It is like a bar chart with the numbers forming the bars. |

Example

These are the times, in minutes, taken by 10 pupils to solve a page of puzzles.

    18   25   23   31   20   19   28   35   22   33

Draw a stem and leaf diagram to show these times.

Each number has a tens digit and a unit digit   e.g.   18, 35.

The tens digits form the stems, the units digits form the leaves.

Stem	Leaf
1	8 9
2	5 3 0 8 2
3	1 5 3

Times taken by pupils to solve puzzles

Now put the leaves (units) in size order.

Stem	Leaf
1	8 9
2	0 2 3 5 8
3	1 3 5

Give your diagram a title and a key.

Key: 2|3 means 23 minutes

Exercise 7:11

1 These are the numbers of beds sold each week by a store during a twelve-week period.

    25   15   30   27   21   17   15   36   29   30   17   22

Draw a stem and leaf diagram to show this data.

2 These are the highest daytime temperatures, in °C, in Adeney during a two-week period in August.

    18   20   19   21   25   17   23
    22   16   17   29   18   24   30

Draw a stem and leaf diagram to show this data.

These are the weekly attendances at a sports club for eight weeks.

    351   169   265   291   304   178   250   265

With larger numbers you need to decide how to split them into a stem and leaves.

Use the hundreds unit for the stem.

Stem	Leaf
1	69 78
2	65 91 50 65
3	51 4

Putting the leaves in order gives the final diagram.

Weekly attendance

Stem	Leaf
1	69 78
2	50 65 65 91
3	4 51

Key: 2|65 means 265

---

3 Dawn has done a survey on the miles travelled by people on an intercity train. These are her results.

    234   189   306   271   165   284   316   166   217   178   305

Draw a stem and leaf diagram to show this data.

4 Rory measures the lengths in centimetres of 20 earthworms. These are his results.

7.5   4.8   3.9   5.1   3.5   4.7   8.2   4.3   6.0   5.7
8.5   4.6   7.7   3.8   4.2   5.4   4.8   6.1   4.2   5.8

Draw a stem and leaf diagram for this data.
Use the units for the stem and the first
decimal place for the leaves.
Don't forget a key.

Stem	Leaf
3	9 8 ...
4	8 ... ...
...	... ...

5 Mr Williams has to write 24 reports for his form.
He recorded the time it took to write each report.
These are his times in minutes.

7.8   6.3   7.2   8.1   6.5   7.0   7.7   6.0   8.4   7.1   6.7   8.9
6.8   7.5   7.2   8.2   8.9   7.1   6.6   7.4   6.5   7.5   7.0   6.8

Draw a stem and leaf diagram to show his results.

6 Tom is testing a machine to check
that it delivers the correct weight
of sweets.
He takes a sample of 20 packets and
weighs them.
These are his results.
The weights are in grams.

248   244   237   240   237
245   240   247   236   249
235   234   246   250   232
238   245   241   239   251

Draw a stem and leaf diagram to show Tom's data.
Use the values 23, 24, ... as the stems.

1 Look at the points on this grid.
Write down the co-ordinates of each point.

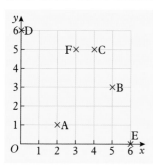

2 This street map uses a scale of 1 cm = 100 m.
  a Estimate the length of the High Street.
  b Estimate the length of the school playing fields.
  c Estimate the length of this journey:
         Start at the school entrance.
         Turn left down School Road.
         Turn right down the High Street.
         Turn left into York Street.
         Stop at the house marked A.

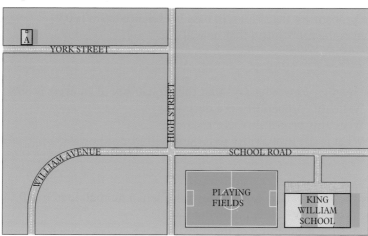

3 Draw a triangle with sides 7 cm, 5 cm and 4 cm.

4 Make an accurate drawing
of this sketch.

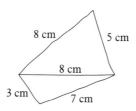

5 Jamie has 5 red cubes and 3 blue cubes in an envelope.
He picks out one cube at random.
  a Copy this scale.

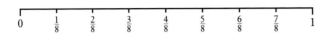

  b What is the probability that he will pick a red cube?
  You can now colour that part of your scale in red.
  The rest of the scale is blue. Colour this in.
  c What is the probability that he will pick a blue cube?
  d Copy and complete.
  The probability of a red cube is ...
  The probability of a blue cube is ...
  The probability of a red cube or a blue cube is ...

6 The probability that Terry will pass his driving test is 0.73
What is the probability that he will fail?

7 The probability that Phil will pass his science exam is 0.91
What is the probability that he will fail?

8 The weather forecaster says that the probability of showers is 30%.
  a Write this probability as a decimal.
  b Write this probability as a fraction.
  c What is the probability that there will be no showers?

9 The probability that Adeney Town FC win a football match is 0.74
The probability of them drawing is 0.21
What is the probability of them losing?

10 Write down the answer and an estimate for each of these.
  a 27 × 21   **b** 52 × 31   **c** 71 × 49   **d** 26 × 39

11 Write down the answer and an estimate for each of these.
  a 546 ÷ 13   **b** 598 ÷ 26   **c** 987 ÷ 21   **d** 2891 ÷ 59

12 The stem and leaf diagram shows the ages, in years, of a group of people.

Ages of people

Stem	Leaf
1	4 7 8 8 9
2	0 1 3 5 5 8
3	4 5 8 9
4	0 2 3 5
5	2 7

Key: 4|2 means 42 years

a What is the age of:
   (1) the youngest
   (2) the eldest?
b How many people are in the group?

13 Rory measures the time for a ball to roll down a track in his Physics lesson. He does this 12 times. This is his data.
The times are to the nearest second.

   24   18   25   31   25   32
   20   19   20   17   36   22

Draw a stem and leaf diagram to show this data.

14 Cara cycles to school each day. She writes down how long each journey takes. She does this for two weeks.
These are her times to the nearest tenth of a minute.

   6.8   8.4   7.3   8.0   7.9   6.2   7.1   7.5   6.8   7.6

Draw a stem and leaf diagram to show this data.
Don't forget to draw a key.

15 Mrs Rice entered 18 students for a piano exam.
These are the marks that they scored.

   105   127   139   108   114   128   140   137   112
   138   126   120   128   130   119   127   132   121

Draw a stem and leaf diagram to show this data.

1 500 children in a primary school each buy one ticket for the school's prize draw.
Andy buys ticket number 357. Brian buys ticket number 210.
  a What is the probability that Brian will win first prize?
  b There are three prizes altogether.
     What is the probability that Andy will win one of the prizes?
  c What is the probability that a ticket number higher than Brian's will win first prize?

2 This is a box made of card.
Ben wants to find the area of the card used.
He knows that to find the area of a rectangle you multiply its length by its width.

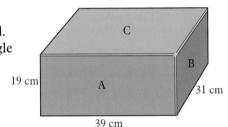

  a Work out an estimate for the area of side A.
  b Work out the exact area of side A.
  c Work out estimates for the areas of sides B and C.
  d Work out the exact areas of sides B and C.
  e Work out the total surface area of the box.

3 A map is drawn to a scale of 1 cm = 2 km.
  a How many centimetres are there in 2 km?
  b What would a distance of 1 mm on the map represent?
  c What length on the map would be needed to represent a distance of 0.4 km?

4 Neil has a box with five new plug fuses in it.
He takes an old fuse out of a plug.
He accidentally drops it into the box of new fuses!
He picks a fuse out of the box at random.
  a What is the probability that the fuse will be a new one?
  b What is the probability that the fuse will be the broken one?

5 MicroElec produces chips for computers.
The probability that a new chip will work properly is 0.6
  a What is the probability that a chip will not work?
  b The company produces 1000 chips a day.
     How many of these chips would you expect to work?

1 a Write down the co-ordinates of the points P, Q and R.

b Copy the axes.

c Plot and label these points on your axes.
A (5, 4)
B (4, 0)
C (0, 2)

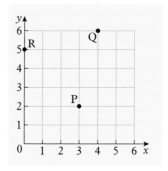

2 This is a plan of the gym at Mia's club. She has used a scale of 1 cm to 2 m. Write down:

a the length of the gym

b the width of the gym.

Mia wants to mark off a rectangle in one corner for 2 rowing machines. The length of the rectangle is 4 m and the width is 3 m. For this rectangle, what will be:

a the length on the plan

b the width on the plan?

Gym

Scale: 1 cm to 2 m

3 Construct each of these triangles.

a

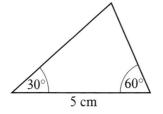

30°   60°
5 cm

b

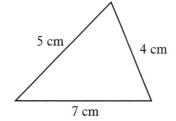

5 cm   4 cm

7 cm

4 The probability that Zara will go to France for her holiday is 0.55
What is the probability that Zara will not go to France for her holiday?

5 Ivan says the probability that he will win his squash match is 67%.
What is the probability that he won't win?

6 There are 8 girls and 5 boys in the school chess club.
One of these is chosen at random to receive a shield.
What is the probability that a girl is chosen?

7 Work these out.

a 14×30	**c** 23×50	**e** $800 \div 20$
b 55×20	**d** 80×300	**f** $60\,000 \div 300$

8 Keith records how long it takes to swim a length of the swimming pool.
These are his results.
They are written to the nearest second.

```
35  28  41  39  32  27  30
44  29  31  38  40  42  36
```

Draw a stem and leaf diagram to show this data.

9 Janine has grown 15 sunflowers.
The diagram shows the heights
of these sunflowers.
  a What is the height of the
  tallest sunflower?
  b Two sunflowers are the
  same height.
  What is this height?

Stem	Leaf
14	3 7 9
15	1 3 6 7
16	0 5 5 8 9
17	1 3 4

Key: 15|3 means 153 cm

8

1 Turning
Clockwise and anticlockwise
Measuring and drawing angles
Using a compass
Finding a bearing

2 Following the trend
Reading information from graphs
Looking for trends

CORE

3 Using percentages
Finding a percentage
Increasing and decreasing by a percentage

Investment Account

Under £500	4.75%	Taxable	£20–
£500–£2499	5.25%	Paid Gross	£100 000
£2500–£9999	5.45%		
£10 000–£24 000	5.6%		
£25 000+	5.75%		

4 Tables and graphs
Working out values in a table
Using values in a table to draw a graph

QUESTIONS

EXTENSION

TEST YOURSELF

1 **Turning**

Kiran and Jenny are orienteering.
They need to be able to use angles to find
their way.

| **Degrees of a turn** | Angles are measured in **degrees**.
A full **turn** is 360°. |

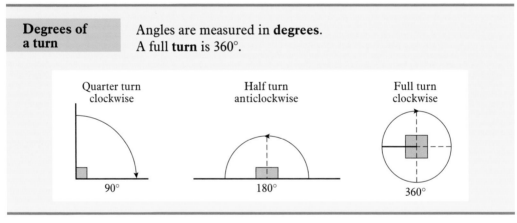

Exercise 8:1

1 Write down how many degrees are in:

    a $\frac{1}{4}$ turn anticlockwise   **b** $\frac{1}{2}$ turn clockwise   **c** 1 turn anticlockwise

2 Write down how many degrees are in:

    a $\frac{3}{4}$ turn anticlockwise   **b** $\frac{3}{4}$ turn clockwise   **c** 2 turns anticlockwise

3 Write down how many degrees are in:

    a   **b**   **c**   **d**   • **e**

Using a protractor	You can use a **protractor** to measure angles.

It has two scales.
It has a clockwise scale on the outside.
It has an anticlockwise scale on the inside.
It also has a cross and a zero line.

You read ∠JKL as **angle** JKL.

To measure ∠JKL:
Put the **cross** on the point of the angle.
The zero line of the protractor goes on one side of the angle.

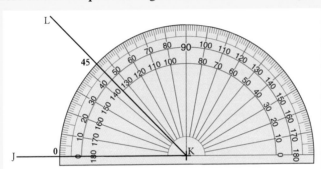

Look for the scale with the zero on one side of the angle.
Use this scale: ∠JKL is 45°.

Exercise 8:2

1   Use the diagram to find the size of these angles.

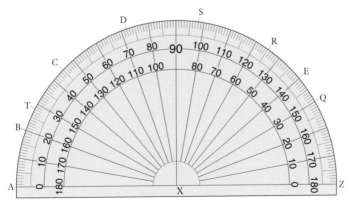

a ∠AXB	**c** ∠AXD	**e** ∠ZXQ	**g** ∠ZXS
b ∠AXC	**d** ∠AXE	**f** ∠ZXR	**h** ∠ZXT

2 For each part in this question:
  (1) Estimate the size of each angle. Make sure your answer is reasonable.
  (2) Measure these angles using a protractor or angle measurer.

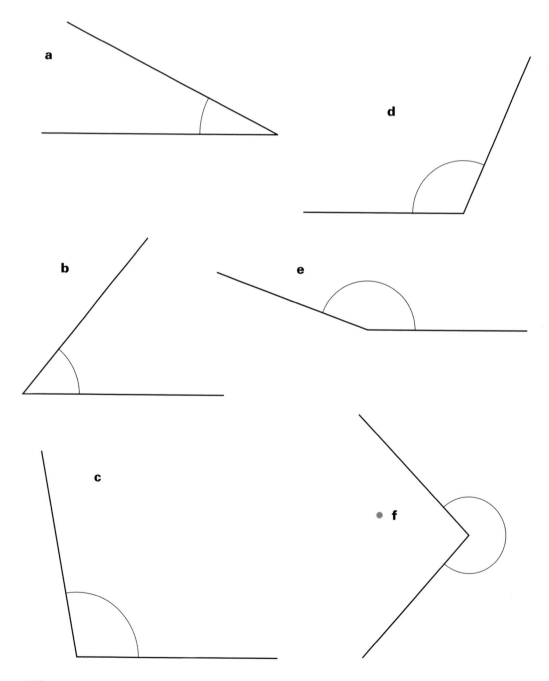

Drawing an angle

To **draw an angle** of 60° at P.

(1) Draw a horizontal line.
(2) Put a small × at P.

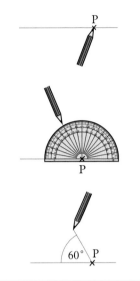

(3) Put the cross of the protractor on the ×. The zero line of the protractor must lie on the horizontal line.
(4) Find **60°** on the clockwise scale.
(5) Make a mark at this point.

(6) Join the × to this mark with a straight line.

(7) Label the angle 60°.

Exercise 8:3

1 Draw these angles.

a 10°	**c** 30°	**e** 50°	**g** 70°
b 20°	**d** 40°	**f** 60°	**h** 80°

2 Draw these angles.

a 15°	**c** 36°	**e** 57°	**g** 71°
b 24°	**d** 43°	**f** 62°	**h** 88°

3 Sally is a window cleaner.
She leans a ladder against a wall.
The angle of the ladder with the ground is 66°.
Draw this angle accurately.

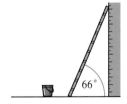

4 Len is a builder.
He puts a roof support at an angle of 37° to the horizontal.
Draw this angle accurately.

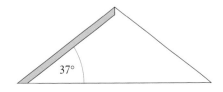

5 Draw these angles.
  a 100°   **c** 135°   **e** 106°   **g** 172°
  b 120°   **d** 143°   **f** 168°   **h** 109°

6 Gerald is unloading his farm trailer.
The tailgate is at an angle of 176°.
Draw this angle accurately.

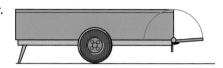

7 Jenny turns her spanner 157°.
Draw this angle accurately.

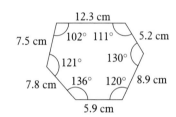

8 Draw the angles and sides in this
hexagon accurately.
If you draw it really well the
sides *will* join up!

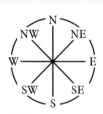

12.3 cm
7.5 cm   102° 111°   5.2 cm
121°   130°
7.8 cm   136°   120° 8.9 cm
5.9 cm

There are 360° in a full turn.
There are **8 points on the compass.**

  $360° \div 8 = 45°$

So there are 45° between each pair of points.
You turn 45° clockwise to go from
N to get to **NE.**

Exercise 8:4

1 Here is a map of Kiran and Jenny's route
through the woods.
In what direction are they going at:
  a A   **c** C   **e** E   **g** G
  b B   **d** D   **f** F   **h** H?

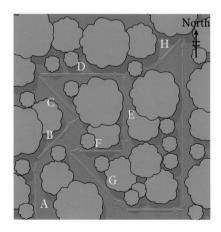

Bearing

A **bearing** is an angle.
It gives a direction from one place to another.
It is always measured clockwise from the North.
It is measured in degrees. Bearings *always* have 3 figures.

Jane faces North.
She turns to look at the tree.
She turns 72° clockwise.

The bearing of the tree
from Jane is 072°.

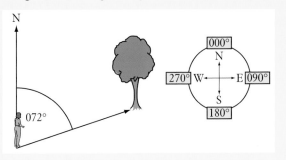

2 Write down the bearing of these places from Jane's house.

a Disco	**c** Leisure centre	**e** KO records	**g** Ice rink	**i** School
b Church	**d** Hairdresser	**f** Clock tower	**h** Boutique	**j** Hope hill

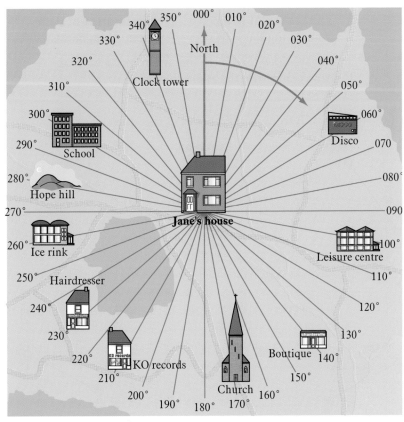

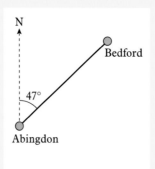

▽   You need Worksheet 8:1.

Finding bearings

You can **find bearings** by turning clockwise from North.

N
47°
Bedford
Abingdon

N
Abingdon
256°
Bath

You are at Abingdon.
You face North.

You turn clockwise until
you are facing Bedford.

The bearing of Bedford
from Abingdon is 047°.

You are at Abingdon.
You face North.

You turn clockwise until
you are facing Bath.

The bearing of Bath
from Abingdon is 256°.

Always draw the North line where you start *from*.
Always measure the angle clockwise.

3 Find the bearing of B from A in each part of this question.

a N
B
24°
A

c N
A
223°
B

e N
A
12°
B

b N
136°
A
B

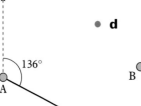

d N
B
24°
A

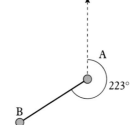

f N
A
63°
B

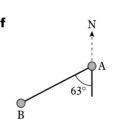

2 Following the trend

A trend shows how something has changed over a period of time. This cartoon shows how fashion has changed over the last 50 years!

You can also talk about trends in jobs or a trend in car design. People use the word 'trendy' to mean up to date.

Graphs are used to show trends in statistics.
This graph shows the trends in work over the last 50 years.
The numbers up the side are people in millions.
The years are along the bottom.
This is sometimes called a time series graph.

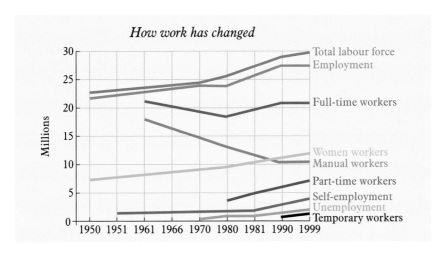

How work has changed

Exercise 8:5

Answer questions **1–4** by reading the information from the graph above.

1   **a**   How many people were working full time in 1961?
      b   How many people were working full time in 1999?

2   **a**   How many manual workers were there in 1961?
      b   How many manual workers were there in 1999?

3 Copy this and fill in the gaps.

> Between 1961 and 1999, the number of full-time workers has ......
> Between 1961 and 1999, the number of manual workers has ......

4 Copy this and fill in the gaps.
Choose from more/less in each case.

> The trend is for .... people to work part-time.
> The trend is for .... people to be self-employed.
> The trend is for .... people to have manual jobs.

5

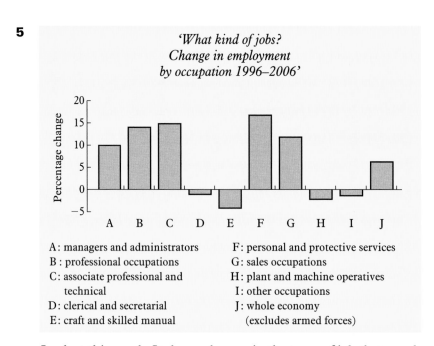

'What kind of jobs?
Change in employment
by occupation 1996–2006'

A: managers and administrators
B: professional occupations
C: associate professional and
   technical
D: clerical and secretarial
E: craft and skilled manual

F: personal and protective services
G: sales occupations
H: plant and machine operatives
I: other occupations
J: whole economy
   (excludes armed forces)

Look at this graph. It shows changes in the types of job that people may
have. The graph is a prediction.
Which type of job is predicted:
a to increase the most
b to decrease the most
- **c** to increase the least
- **d** to increase by 10%?

6 Look at the graph at the top of the next page.
It shows car ownership since 1950.
  a What percentage of families did not have a car in 1950?
  b What percentage of families did not have a car in 1995?
-   **c** Describe the trend in families without a car.

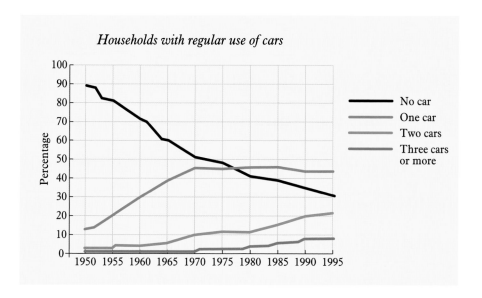

Households with regular use of cars

7 **a** Describe the trend in the number of families with one car.
 b Describe the trend in the number of families with two and three cars.

8 This table shows the number of people who attend different types of churches.
It also predicts the numbers for 2005.
The numbers are in thousands.

	1980	1985	1990	1995	2000	2005
Anglican	968	921	918	839	794	748
Baptist	201	196	198	213	224	230
Methodist	438	421	395	347	313	279

 a Copy these axes onto graph paper.
 b Plot the points to show the number of people who attend an Anglican church in each year.
 c Join the points with straight lines.
 d Plot the points for the number of people who attend the Baptist church **on the same graph**. Join the points.
 e Plot the graph for the Methodist church **on the same graph**.
 f Write a sentence to describe the trend for each type of church.

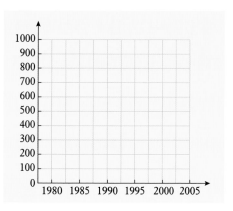

9 This table shows how spending on certain items has changed since 1971.
The numbers in the table come from setting the amounts in 1971 at 100 and
then comparing the amounts in each of the other years to this.
These are called index numbers.

	1971	1981	1986	1991	1996
Food	100	104	109	115	125
Alcohol	100	127	134	132	131
Tobacco	100	89	74	71	59
Recreation	100	142	156	182	206

a Copy these axes onto graph paper.
b Plot the points for Food
on the axes.
Join the points with straight
lines.
c Plot the points for Alcohol
on the same axes.
Join the points with straight
lines.
Use a different colour if you can.
d Plot the points for Tobacco
on your axes.
Join the points with straight
lines.
Use a different colour if you can.
e Draw the graph for Recreation
on your axes.
f Which type of spending has
increased the most?
g Which type of spending has
decreased the most?
Say why you think this is.

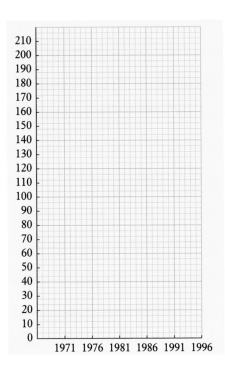

10 This graph shows how the
UK population is expected
to change up to the year 2051.
Write about the trends in
this graph.

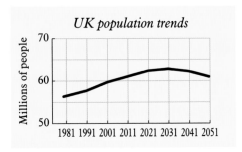

UK population trends

206

3 Using percentages

```
                        Investment Account
            Under £500      4.75%        Taxable          £20–
          £500–£2499        5.25%        Paid Gross       £100 000
         £2500–£9999        5.45%
       £10 000–£24 999      5.6%
            £25,000+        5.75%
```

Katy is putting £80 into a Post Office account. She wants to work out
how much interest she will get in one year.
You can work out how much interest Katy will get.
You use percentages.

**Percentages on
a calculator**   To work out a **percentage on a calculator**:
                    Change the percentage into a decimal by dividing by 100.
                    Multiply by the decimal.

Katy gets 5% interest on her £80.

Key in:

$5\% = 5 \div 100 = 0.05$ `5` `÷` `1` `0` `0` `=`

5% of £80 $= 0.05 \times 80$ `×` `8` `0` `=`

$\qquad = £4.00$

Katy will get £4.00 interest in one year.

Exercise 8:6

1 Change these percentages to decimals.
   a 56%   **c** 7%   **e** 136%
   b 39%   **d** 12.5%   **f** $17\frac{1}{2}\%$

2 Find 20% of £120.   **5** Find 17% of 600 miles.

3 Find 5% of £45.   **6** Find 80% of 340 g.

4 Find 35% of 500 cm.   **7** Find 12.5% of £40.

8 Ken has put £700 into a Post Office account.
The account pays 5.25% interest per year.
Find the interest that Ken gets at the end of the year.

9 Tom pays £4.50 each day to travel into London.
He is told that train fares are going up by 12%.
How much extra will Tom have to pay each day?

10 Rudi has raised £96 for charity.
He decides to give 25% to a local charity.
How much is this?

11 Sue's salary is £7800.
She gets an increase of 4.5%.
How much is her increase?

12 The population of Sorton village is 1540.
The population increases by 5% in one year.
How many more people is this?

You sometimes want to find the final amount.

Examples **1** Paul buys an old car for £450.
He does a lot of work on the car and then sells it.
He makes a profit of 15%. What price did he sell the car at?

You first need to find the profit.
   15% of £450 = 15 ÷ 100 × 450 = £67.50

You now add the £67.50 to £450 because it is a profit.
Selling price = £517.50

If something is decreased or reduced, you still find how much
the amount changes. This change must then be subtracted.

2 Sarah buys a computer game for £52.
She decides to sell the game because she doesn't like it.
She makes a loss of 25%. At what price did Sarah sell the game?

The loss is 25% of £52 = 25 ÷ 100 × 52 = £13

You now take away the £13 from £52 because it is a loss.
Sarah sold the game for £52 − £13 = £39.

Exercise 8:7

1 Satsumas are normally sold in packs of 20.
This special offer pack has 15% more.
How many satsumas are in this pack?

2 Andrew spends £7.60 a week on bus fares.
The fares are going down by 5%.
Find how much he will spend each week after the decrease.

3 Paz wants to buy a jumper which costs £28.
She finds that the shop is reducing the price by 15%.
Find the new price.

4 Don's garage bought a Fiesta for £4800.
They are selling it at a profit of 10%.
Find the new price.

5 A bottle of shampoo contains 250 ml.
A new bottle is designed.
The new bottle contains 8% more.
Find the size of the new bottle.

6 The marked price of a pair of jeans is £54.
Find the sale price.

7 Sanjay gets a rise of 12% on his salary of £6500.
Marita gets a rise of 7% on her salary of £13 500.
a Work out the rise that each person gets.
b Who gets the bigger rise and by how much?

8 Emma has to drive 280 miles in one day.
She stops for lunch when she has driven 70% of the journey.
How many miles does she still have left to drive?

9 The number of jobless in a city area is 5700.
During the summer months the number drops by 5.9%.
Find the new number of jobless people.

4 **Tables and graphs**

Tim is selling CDs.
He has made a table to help him
work out the cost of more than
1 CD.

Example Rita is selling earrings. Each pair of earrings costs £2.40
You can draw a table to show the cost of more than one pair of
earrings.

2 pairs cost **2** × 2.40 = 4.80   You work out the cost of 2, 3
3 pairs cost **3** × 2.40 = 7.20   and 4 pairs of earrings.
4 pairs cost **4** × 2.40 = 9.60   Then put them into a table.

Pairs	1	2	3	4
Cost (£)	2.40	4.80	7.20	9.60

Exercise 8:8

1 Jamie is selling ice cream at the cinema. Each ice cream costs 85 p.
Draw a table to show the cost of up to 4 ice creams.

2 A shop sells cut-price books. Each book costs £2.99
Draw a table to show the cost of up to 5 books.

Example You can use a formula to draw a table.
This formula shows the cost *C*, in pounds, of hiring a boat.

$C = 5h$ *h* is the number of hours

For 1 hour $h = 1$ so $C = 5 \times 1 = 5$
For 2 hours $h = 2$ so $C = 5 \times 2 = 10$
For 3 hours $h = 3$ so $C = 5 \times 3 = 15$
These can now be put in a table.

Hours	1	2	3
Cost (£)	5	10	15

3 Jim runs a cycle repair shop service.
The formula shows the number, N, of bikes that he services.
w is the number of weeks.

$$N = 20w$$

Copy the table.
Fill it in.

w	1	2	3	4	5
N	20				

4 Joy is drawing a graph.
This is the formula she is using:

$$y = 4x$$

Copy the table.
Fill it in.

x	1	2	3	4
y		8		

5 This formula gives the cost, C, in pence, of an advert.
L is the number of lines in the advert.

$$C = 250 + 30L$$

a Find the cost when $L = 4$.
b Copy the table.
Fill it in.

L	1	2	3	4	5
C			340		

6 Louise is using this formula in science:

$$V = 5 + 8t$$

a Find the value of V when $t = 2$.
b Copy the table.
Fill it in.

t	1	2	3	4	5
V					

7 The table is for the formula:

$$y = 4x - 1$$

Copy the table.
Fill it in.

x	1	2	3	4
y			11	

Example   The table is for the formula $y = 2x + 1$.
Jamie is plotting points from the table.

x	1	2	3
y	3	5	7

The top row is the x value.
The bottom row is the y value.

Jamie plots the points $(1, 3)$, $(2, 5)$, $(3, 7)$.
He joins the points with a straight line.
He labels the line $y = 2x + 1$.

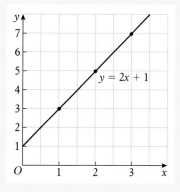

Exercise 8:9

1 The table is for $y = x + 2$.

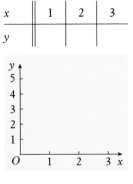

x	1	2	3
y			

a Copy the table.
Fill it in.
b Copy the axes onto squared paper.
c Plot the points from your table.
Join them with a straight line.
d Label the line $y = x + 2$.

2 The table is for $C = 3n - 1$.

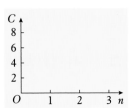

n	1	2	3
C			

a Copy the table.
Fill it in.
b Copy the axes onto squared paper.
c Plot the points from your table.
The first point is (1, 2).
d Join the points with a straight line.
e Label the line $C = 3n - 1$.

3 The table is for $s = 2t + 1$.

t	1	2	3
s			

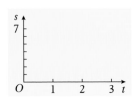

a Copy the table.
Fill it in.
b Copy the axes onto squared paper.
c Plot the points from your table.
d Join the points with a straight line.
e Label the line $s = 2t + 1$.

4 Sarah is going to France with the school.
She finds out that £1 is worth
9 French francs.

Pounds (£)	1	5	10	20
French francs (F)	9			180

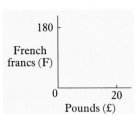

a Copy the table.
Fill it in.
b Copy the axes onto squared paper.
Remember to label the axes.
c Plot the points from your table.
d Join the points with a straight line.
Use the graph to convert:
e £15 to French francs
f 65 French francs to pounds.

5 The table belongs to the straight line drawn.

x	1	2	3
y			

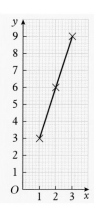

a Copy the table.
Use the graph to fill it in.
b The formula for the line is $y = ...x$
Write down the missing number.

6 The table belongs to the straight line drawn.

n	1	2	3
P			

a Copy the table.
Use the graph to fill it in.
b The formula for the line is $P = ...n + ...$
Copy this formula.
Fill in the missing numbers.

You can get information from your graphs.

Example   The table shows the cost of different numbers of cards.

Number of cards	10	20	30	40
Cost in pence	25	50	75	100

The graph has been drawn from the table.
You can use the graph to find:
a the cost for 25 cards
b how many cards cost 90 p.

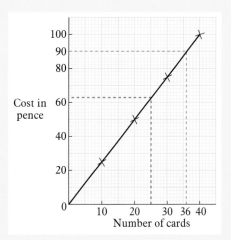

a To find the cost of 25 cards:
Start at 25 on the cards axis.
Draw a dotted line up to the graph.
At the graph draw a dotted line
across to the cost axis. Follow the **red** line.
25 cards cost 63 p.
b To find how many cards cost 90 p
follow the **blue** line.
It must start at 90 on the cost axis.
36 cards cost 90 p.

Exercise 8:10

1 Paul can surf the Internet at his local shop.
The table shows the charge made for the total number of hours used.

Hours used	5	10	20	50	100
Charge (£)	6	12	24	60	120

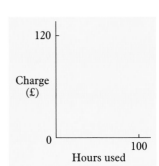

  a Copy the axes.
  b Plot the points from the table.
  c Join them with a straight line.

    Use your graph to find:
  d the charge for 40 h
  e how many hours cost £30.

2 Joanne sells Christmas cards.
She prints the sender's address on the card.
The table shows the charge made for the total number of cards.

Number of cards	10	20	50	100
Charge (£)	13	18	33	58

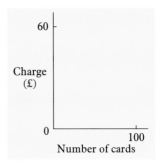

  a Copy the axes.
  b Plot the points from the table.
  c Join them with a straight line.

    Use your graph to find:
  d the charge for 70 cards
  e the number of cards for £53.

3 Anne organises coach trips to London.
The table shows the cost for different numbers of people.

Number of people	10	20	25	40	50
Cost (£)	90	130	150	210	250

  a Use the table to draw a straight line graph.

    Use your graph to find:
  b the cost for 30 people
  c the number of people who can travel for £110.

Sometimes the formulas are written in a different way.

Example   This table is for $x + y = 7$.

x	1	2	3	4
y				

    a Copy the table. Fill it in.
    b Plot the points on a graph. Join them with a straight line.

The formula is $x + y = 7$.
This means that the x number added to the
y number must come to 7.
Write numbers in the y row so that the numbers
add up to 7.

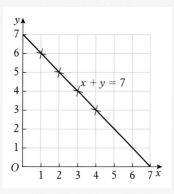

x	1	2	3	4
y	6	5	4	3

Now draw the graph as you have done before.

Exercise 8:11

1 This table is for $x + y = 5$.

x	1	2	3	4
y				

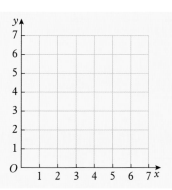

    a Copy the table. Fill it in.
    b Copy the axes onto squared paper.
    c Plot the points from your table. Join
        them with a straight line.
    d Label the line $x + y = 5$.

2 This table is for $x + y = 6$.

x	1	2	3	4
y				

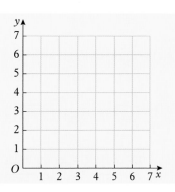

    a Copy the table. Fill it in.
    b Copy the axes onto squared paper.
    c Plot the points from your table. Join
        them with a straight line.
    d Label the line $x + y = 6$.

1   How many degrees are there in each of these?

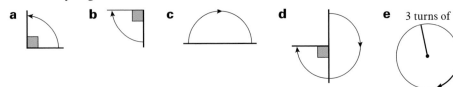

a   **b**   **c**   **d**   **e**   3 turns of

2   **a**   This is a plan of a castle courtyard.
         Measure all the angles.

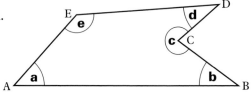

   b   A secret passageway runs under the ground from A to C. Measure ∠BAC.

3   This map shows some buildings in Blaston town centre.

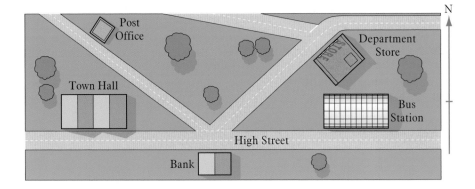

   Karsten walks east down High Street to the Bank.
   a   What building does he pass?
   b   What direction must he take at the bank to go to the Post Office?
   c   What direction must he take at the bank to go to the Department Store?

4 This graph predicts the numbers of people (in millions) in different age groups in the future. Write about the trends shown in this graph.

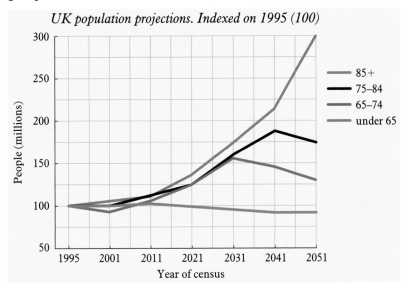

UK population projections. Indexed on 1995 (100)

85+
75–84
65–74
under 65

People (millions)

1995 2001 2011 2021 2031 2041 2051

Year of census

5 **a** Find 60% of £700.
    b Find 14% of 220 km.
    c Find 75% of 1800 m.
    d Find 12.5% of £50.

6 Louise's flat cost her £23 000.
She sells it at a loss of 8.5%. How much does she sell her flat for?

7 A firm employs 350 people. It has to reduce its workforce by 4%.
How many people will be working after the reduction?

8 Penny has ordered some oil for her central heating. It costs £160.
5% VAT has to be added to the cost. Find the total cost of the oil.

9 This table is for the formula $y = 6x + 2$
    a Copy the table.
    b Fill it in.

x	1	2	3	4
y				

10 This table is for $y = 2x - 2$
    a Copy the table.
    Fill it in.

x	1	2	3
y			

    b Copy the axes on to squared paper.
    c Plot the points from your table.
Join them with a straight line.
    d Label the line $y = 2x - 2$

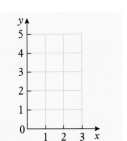

1   Measure the angles on
    the outside of this
    flying saucer.

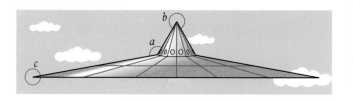

2   Draw this octagon accurately.
    If you draw it really well the sides
    will join up!

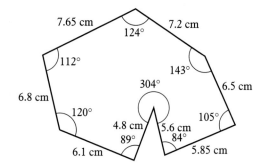

7.65 cm   124°   7.2 cm

112°

143°

6.8 cm   304°   6.5 cm

120°   105°

4.8 cm   5.6 cm

89°   84°

6.1 cm   5.85 cm

3   The towns Antham, Barton and Carrow are all
    8 km from each other.
    The bearing of Barton from Antham is 030°.
    The bearing of Carrow from Barton is 150°.
    a What is the bearing of Carrow from Antham?
    b What is the bearing of Antham from Carrow?

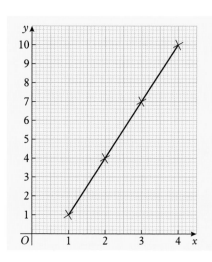

N

Barton 150°

8 km

30° 8 km

Antham   Carrow

4   Gunpowder contains 75% nitre, 15% charcoal and 10% sulphur.
    How many grams of each are needed to make 2 kg of gunpowder?

5   **a** Copy this table.

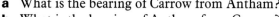

x	1	2	3	4
y				

   b Fill the table in for this line.
   c The formula for this line is:
       $y = \ldots x - \ldots$
    Use your table to find the
    missing numbers.

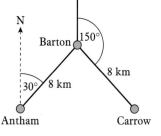

1 Jim stands facing north.
Write down the direction he will be facing when he makes each of the
following turns. He always starts facing north.

a 45° clockwise **c** 135° anticlockwise
b 180° anticlockwise **d** 225° clockwise

2 Find the bearing of R from Q.

a

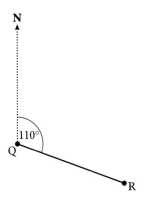

b

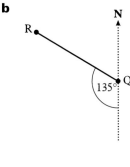

3 The graph shows how the numbers of people using different forms of
transport have changed in the last 50 years.
Write about the trends shown in the graph.

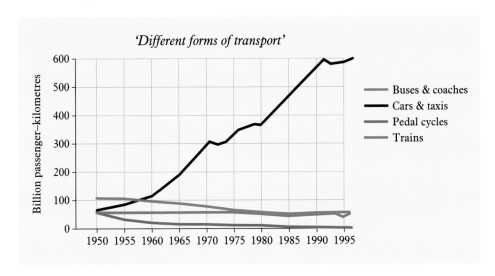

4 The same type of TV is sold in three shops at different prices.

Davies Electricals	Buyrite	Discount TVs
£268	£390	£350
SALE	**SALE** $\frac{1}{3}$ OFF	SALE 25%
5% discount today only	this week!	off this price

a Work out the sale price for each shop.
b Which shop has the best price in the sale?

5 A firm makes chocolate cakes. It is expected that 3% will be faulty.
Today the firm made 864 cakes.
How many would you expect to be faulty?

6 The table is for $t = 5s - 3$.

s	1	2	3	4
t				

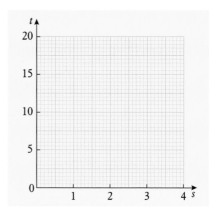

a Copy the table.
 Fill it in.
b Copy the axes.
c Plot the points from your table.
d Join the points with a straight line.
e Label your line.
f Use your graph to find s when $t = 8$.

7 The table is for $x + y = 8$.

x	1	2	3	4
y				

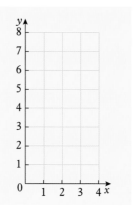

a Copy the table.
 Fill it in.
b Copy the axes.
c Plot the points from your table.
d Join the points with a straight line.
e Label the line $x + y = 8$.

9

1 Measurement
Changing between metric units of length
Finding perimeters
Changing between metric units of weight
Changing between metric units of capacity

2 Pie-charts
Working out the angles in a pie-chart
Drawing pie-charts
Getting information from pie-charts

3 Patterns in number
Looking at some special patterns
Finding patterns in Pascal's Triangle
Finding factors and primes
Finding squares and square roots

4 Finance
Working out the cost of VAT
Working out tax on earnings
Writing change as a percentage

1 Measurement

At the end of the 18th century, French scientists invented a new unit of length. They worked out the distance from the North Pole to the Equator and divided it by 10 million.

They called this distance 1 metre.

The metric system of weights and measures is named after the metre.

In the metric system, 10s, 100s and 1000s of the smaller units make the bigger units.

Length

The metric units of **length** are millimetres (mm), centimetres (cm), metres (m) and kilometres (km).

$$1 \text{ cm} = 10 \text{ mm}$$
$$1 \text{ m} = 100 \text{ cm}$$
$$1 \text{ km} = 1000 \text{ m}$$

Example

Change each of these to the units given.

a 16 cm to millimetres
b 3.7 m to centimetres
c 0.98 km to metres

a There are 10 mm in every centimetre,
so 16 cm = 16 × 10 mm
= 160 mm

b There are 100 cm in every metre,
so 3.7 m = 3.7 × 100 cm
= 370 cm

c There are 1000 m in every kilometre,
so 0.98 km = 0.98 × 1000 m
= 980 m

Exercise 9:1

1 Change each of these to millimetres.
Remember: There are 10 mm in every centimetre.
 a 7 cm   **c** 125 cm   **e** 19.8 cm
 b 32 cm   **d** 163 cm   **f** 0.7 cm

2 Change each of these to centimetres.
Remember: There are 100 cm in every metre.
 a 8 m   **c** 3.9 m   **e** 0.97 m
 b 11 m   **d** 17.6 m   **f** 3.05 m

3 Change each of these to metres.
Remember: There are 1000 m in every kilometre.
 a 8 km   **c** 15 km   **e** 0.36 km
 b 10 km   **d** 2.7 km   **f** 0.04 km

4 Change each of these to millimetres.
 a 2 m   **c** 1.8 m   **e** 0.5 m
 b 11 m   **d** 3.72 m   **f** 0.47 m

Example   Change each of these to the units shown.
 a 400 mm to centimetres
 b 164 cm to metres
 c 7800 m to kilometres

 a Every 10 mm make 1 cm.
 Find how many lots of 10 mm there are in 400 mm.
 400 ÷ 10 = 40 so 400 mm = 40 cm

 b Every 100 cm make 1 m.
 Find how many lots of 100 cm there are in 164 cm.
 164 ÷ 100 = 1.64 so 164 cm = 1.64 m

 c Every 1000 m make 1 km.
 Find how many lots of 1000 m there are in 7800 m.
 7800 ÷ 1000 = 7.8 so 7800 m = 7.8 km

5 Change each of these to centimetres.
Remember: Every 10 mm make 1 cm.

a	300 mm	**c**	910 mm	**e**	45 mm	**g**	9.2 mm
b	260 mm	**d**	508 mm	**f**	7 mm	**h**	0.6 mm

6 Change each of these to metres.
Remember: Every 100 cm make 1 m.

a	600 cm	**c**	230 cm	**e**	96 cm	**g**	10 cm
b	450 cm	**d**	107 cm	**f**	38.5 cm	**h**	9.5 cm

7 Change each of these to kilometres.
Remember: Every 1000 m make 1 km.

a	8000 m	**c**	2060 m	**e**	1008 m	**g**	903 m
b	7400 m	**d**	6043 m	**f**	735 m	**h**	550 m

Exercise 9:2

1 Dave swims 40 lengths of the
swimming pool each day.
The pool is 50 m long.
How many kilometres does Dave
swim each day?

2 The measurements of modern
kitchen units are always given in
millimetres.
Chris needs a unit to fit in a space that
measures 150 cm × 58 cm × 87 cm.
Which of these models should he
choose?

Model A 1600 mm × 500 mm × 870 mm
Model B 1470 mm × 550 mm × 870 mm
Model C 1500 mm × 600 mm × 870 mm

Explain your answer.

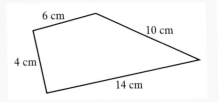

Perimeter	The total distance around the outside of a shape is called the **perimeter**.

The perimeter of this shape is:
   4 cm + 6 cm + 10 cm + 14 cm = 34 cm

Exercise 9:3

1 Find the perimeters of these shapes.

a

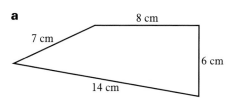

b

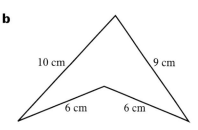

2 Find the perimeters of these shapes.

a

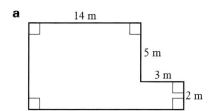

● **b**

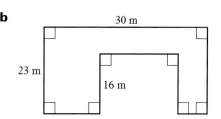

● **3** Find the perimeters of these shapes in centimetres.

a

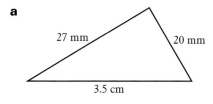

b

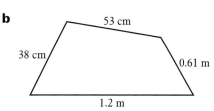

4 Find the perimeter of a regular octagon with sides of length 3.4 cm.

5 The Pentagon is the building that holds the offices of the US defence department. It is the largest office building in the world. Each outside wall is 281 m long.
   a Find the perimeter of the building.
● **b** Give your answer in kilometres.

Weight	You can measure weight in milligrams (mg), grams (g), kilograms (kg) or tonnes (t).

$$1000 \text{ mg} = 1 \text{ g}$$
$$1000 \text{ g} \ = 1 \text{ kg}$$
$$1000 \text{ kg} = 1 \text{ t}$$

Example

Change each of these to the units shown.

a 0.37 t to kilograms **b** 2400 mg to grams

a There are 1000 kg in every tonne
so $0.37 \text{ t} = 0.37 \times 1000 \text{ kg}$
$= 370 \text{ kg}$

b Every 1000 mg make 1 g.
Find how many lots of 1000 mg there are in 2400 mg.
$2400 \div 1000 = 2.4$ so 2400 mg = 2.4 g

Exercise 9:4

1 Change each of these to kilograms.
Remember: Every 1000 g make 1 kg.

a 7000 g	**c** 8450 g	**e** 10 000 g	**g** 960 g
b 3600 g	**d** 4030 g	**f** 750 g	**h** 45 g

2 Change each of these to kilograms.
Remember: There are 1000 kg in every tonne.

a 3 t	**b** 7.12 t	**c** 0.5 t	**d** 0.046 t

• **3** Change each of these to the units shown.

a 25 g to milligrams **c** 8400 kg to tonnes
b 1200 mg to grams **d** 720 kg to tonnes

4 The largest fish ever caught on a
rod and line was a great white shark.
The shark weighed 1537 kg.
Write this weight in tonnes.

• **5** A gudgeon is a small freshwater fish.
The largest gudgeon ever caught weighed 141 g.
Write this weight in kilograms.

Capacity	You can measure capacity in litres (l), centilitres (cl) or millilitres (ml).

$$100 \text{ cl} = 1\,l \qquad\qquad 1000 \text{ ml} = 1\,l$$

Example

Change each of these to the units shown.

a 2.5 l to millilitres   **b** 750 cl to litres

a There are 1000 ml in every litre.
$$\text{so } 2.5\,l = 2.5 \times 1000 \text{ ml}$$
$$= 2500 \text{ ml}$$

b Every 100 cl make 1 l.
Find how many lots of 100 cl there are in 750 cl.
$$750 \div 100 = 7.5 \text{ so } 750 \text{ cl} = 7.5\,l$$

Exercise 9:5

1 Change each of these to millilitres.
Remember: There are 1000 ml in every litre.
a 5 l **c** 2.5 l **e** 3.124 l **g** 0.075 l
b 90 l **d** 4.08 l **f** 0.8 l **h** 0.0304 l

2 Change each of these to litres.
Remember: Every 1000 ml make 1 l.
a 7000 ml   **c** 4350 ml   **e** 250 ml   **g** 50 ml
b 20 000 ml   **d** 1750 ml   **f** 750 ml   **h** 8 ml

3 Change each of these to the units shown.
a 200 cl to litres   **c** 2.5 l to centilitres   ● **e** 850 ml to centilitres
b 550 cl to litres   **d** 0.75 l to centilitres   ● **f** 45 cl to millilitres

4 A 2 l bottle of Ribena makes 66 servings.
Find the number of millilitres in
each serving.
Give your answer to the nearest
whole number.

5 A bottle of milk holds 568 ml.
Len has 50 crates of milk on his milk-float.
Every crate holds 20 bottles.
How many litres of milk are there on
Len's milk-float?

2 Pie-charts

Healthy diet

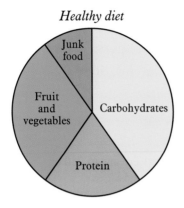

Danny's diet

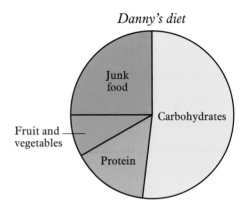

These pie-charts show a healthy diet and what Danny eats.
Junk food includes chocolate and sweets.
Danny should try to eat more fruit and vegetables and less junk food.

You can use pie-charts to compare two sets of data.
The slices of these pie-charts show the different foods.
These slices have to be drawn accurately. You use the angle at the centre of the pie-chart to do this.

Example

120 students were asked what they want to do when they leave school. Here are the results.

Go to university	Go to college	Get a job	Don't know
50	35	25	10

Draw a pie-chart to show this data.

First you need to work out the angles for the pie-chart.
There are 360° to share between the 120 students.
Each student gets $360° \div 120 = 3°$.
Now work out the angle for each slice.

	Number of students	Angle
University	50	$50 \times 3° = 150°$
College	35	$35 \times 3° = 105°$
Job	25	$25 \times 3° = 75°$
Don't know	10	$10 \times 3° = 30°$

Check the angles add up to 360°.
$$150° + 105° + 75° + 30° = 360° \checkmark$$

You can now draw the pie-chart.

(1) Draw a circle. Mark the centre.
Draw a line to the top of the circle.
Draw the first angle (150°).

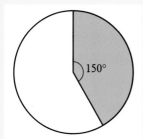

(2) Measure the next angle from the line that you have just drawn (105°).

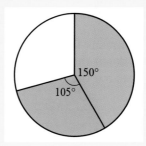

(3) Carry on until you have drawn all the angles.
Label the pie-chart.
You need to label each slice like this.
You also need a title.

What students hope to do when they leave school

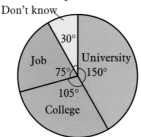

Exercise 9:6

1 A shop sells silk shirts in 4 different colours.
The shop sold 60 of these shirts last week.
These are the numbers of each colour sold.

Colour	black	white	cream	grey
Number	28	9	17	6

a Work out the angle for one shirt: $360° \div ... = ...°$
b Work out the angle for each colour.

Colour	Number of shirts	Angle
black	28	$28 \times ...° = ...$
white	9	$9 \times ...° = ...$
cream	...	$... \times ...° = ...$
grey	...	$... \times ...° = ...$

c Check that your angles add up to 360°.
d Draw a pie-chart to show the data. Label your pie-chart.

2 Sita is doing a survey on the vegetables eaten by students for their lunch. Each student chose one vegetable. These are the results of her survey.

Type of vegetable	chips	peas	baked potato	baked beans
Number of students	21	5	8	6

a How many students did she ask in her survey?
b Work out the angle for one student.
c Work out the angle for each type of vegetable.

Type	Number of students	Angle
chips	...	...
peas	...	...
baked potato	...	...
baked beans	...	...

d Draw a pie-chart to show the data. Label your pie-chart.

3 The table shows the amount of each type of fuel sold by a garage in one week.

Type of fuel	leaded petrol	unleaded petrol	diesel
Amount (thousands of litres)	35	45	20

a How many thousands of litres of fuel did the garage sell?
b Work out the angle for one thousand litres, $360° ÷ ... = ...°$
c Work out the angle for each type of fuel.

Type of fuel	Amount (thousands of litres)	Angle
leaded petrol	...	...
unleaded petrol	...	...
diesel	...	...

d Draw a pie-chart to show the data. Label your pie-chart.

4 Mary earns £120 per week.
This is how she spends her money.

Where spent	rent	food	clothes	bus fares	other
Amount	£50	£30	£20	£10	£10

Draw a pie-chart to show how Mary spends her wages.

Example   Philip did a survey of
720 students at his school.
One of the questions he
asked was how they got to
school. The pie-chart shows
his results.
  a How many students
    travelled to school by:
    (1) bus
    (2) car?
  b What fraction of students
    walk to school?

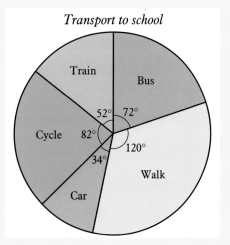

Transport to school

a (1) In this pie-chart, 360° show all 720 students,
     so 1° is 720 ÷ 360 = 2 students
     The bus part of the pie-chart has an angle of 72°.
     The number of students that come by bus is 72 × 2 = 144.
   (2) The car part of the pie-chart has an angle of 34°.
     The number of students that come by car is 34 × 2 = 68.
b The walk part of the pie-chart has an angle of 120°.
   The total angle is 360°.

   The fraction of students that walk to school is $\dfrac{120}{360} = \dfrac{1}{3}$

Exercise 9:7

1 A firm surveyed 360 people.
They wanted to find what type
of heating they used.
The pie-chart shows the results.
  a Copy this and fill it in.
    360° shows all ... people.
      1° is ... person.

How many people use:
  b solid fuel
  c oil
  d gas
  e electricity?

Type of heating

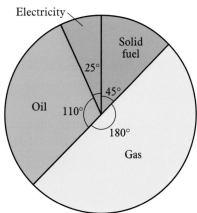

2 This pie-chart shows the results of a survey.

The survey is on the type of books that people read.

a What is the angle of the romance part of the pie-chart?

b What fraction of the people read romances?

What fraction of the people read:
c thrillers
d science fiction
e other?

Books read

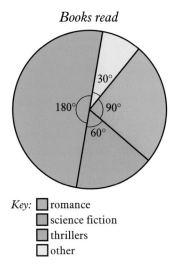

Key: ☐ romance
☐ science fiction
☐ thrillers
☐ other

3 This pie-chart shows the crowd attending a rally.

a Measure the angle for each section of the pie-chart.

b Write down the fraction of the crowd that was:
(1) women
(2) children.

c 720 people attended the rally. How many of these were women?

Rally attendance

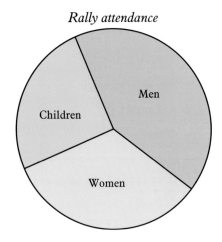

4 Louise, Sam and Fatima deliver 180 newspapers between them each day.

The pie-chart shows the amount that each girl delivered yesterday.

Work out how many papers each girl delivered.

Newspapers delivered

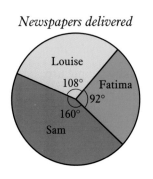

3 Patterns in number

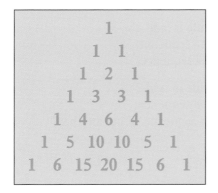

Pascal was a French mathematician. He knew how important and useful patterns in number can be.
The picture shows numbers in the shape of a triangle.
The numbers follow a rule.
This pattern of numbers is called Pascal's Triangle.

This is the rule for finding the numbers in Pascal's Triangle.
Each number is found by adding the pair of numbers in the row above it.

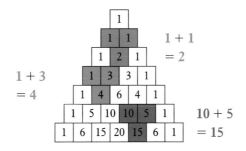

Exercise 9:8

1 a Copy Pascal's Triangle.
   b Add three more rows to your triangle.

You have already used rules to get number patterns.

Example   The first term of a sequence is 7.
The rule is 'add 7'.
You can work out more terms of the sequence using the rule.

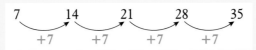

The first five terms of the sequence are 7, 14, 21, 28, 35
This sequence gives the multiples of 7.

2 The first term of a sequence is 3. The rule is 'add 3'.
  a Write down the first five terms of the sequence.
  b Write down the special name for this sequence.

3 The first term of a sequence is 1. The rule is 'add 2'.
  a Write down the first five terms of the sequence.
  b Write down the special name for this sequence.

4 The first term of a sequence is 2. The rule is 'add 2'.
  a Write down the first five terms of the sequence.
  b There are two special names for this sequence. What are they?

5 The first three triangle numbers are 1, 3, 6
  Write down the next two triangle numbers.

6 The first three square numbers are 1, 4, 9
  Write down the next two square numbers.

Write down the first 14 rows of Pascal's Triangle on a large sheet of paper.

Two parallelograms have been drawn.
The numbers inside the parallelograms
add up to 5 and to 9.
One of the numbers outside each
parallelogram can help you find this
sum quickly. Can you see which
number it is?

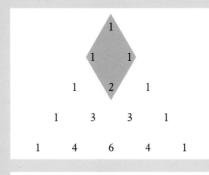

Draw more parallelograms and find the
sum of the numbers inside.
Each parallelogram must start at the *top*
of Pascal's Triangle.
Is there always a number that helps you
to find the sum quickly?

There are more special number patterns
in Pascal's Triangle.
Write down any that you can find.
Use diagrams to show where you
found each pattern.

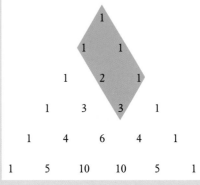

| **Factor** | A number that divides exactly into another number is called a **factor**. Factors are always whole numbers. |

To find the factors of 8:
Look at all the pairs of numbers that multiply to give 8.

$8 = 1 \times 8$
$8 = 2 \times 4$ The factors of 8 are 1, 2, 4 and 8.

To find the factors of 12:
Look at all the pairs of numbers that multiply to give 12.

$12 = 1 \times 12$
$12 = 2 \times 6$
$12 = 3 \times 4$ The factors of 12 are 1, 2, 3, 4, 6 and 12.

Exercise 9:9

1 Write down the factors of each of these:

   a 6   **c** 10   **e** 16   **g** 24
   b 7   **d** 9   **f** 20   **h** 30

| **Prime numbers** | **Prime numbers** have exactly two factors, themselves and 1. |

$17 = 1 \times 17$ No other two numbers multiply to give 17.
17 is a prime number.

The first six prime numbers are: 2, 3, 5, 7, 11, 13

1 is *not* a prime number. It only has one factor, 1 itself.
The first prime number is 2. It is the only *even* prime number.
All other even numbers have 2 as a factor.

2 Write down all the factors of:
   a 15   **b** 17   **c** 19   **d** 21   **e** 23

3 Which numbers in question **2** are prime numbers?

4 Look at the numbers: 20, 21, 22, 23, 24, 25, 26, 27, 28, 29, 30
   Write down the numbers that are:
   a prime   **b** factors of 100   **c** multiples of 6

5 Find these numbers using the clues.

    a It is a factor of 28 and it is an odd prime number.

    b It is a factor of 11 and it is not a prime number.

6   **a** Write down the factors of 6.

    b Write down the factors of 9.

    c Look at your answers to parts **a** and **b**.
      Write down the factors that are in both lists.

Common factor	If two or more numbers have the same factor then this factor is called a **common factor**.
Example	Write down the common factors of 12 and 18. The factors of 12 are 1, 2, 3, 4, 6 and 12. The factors of 18 are 1, 2, 3, 6, 9 and 18. The common factors of 12 and 18 are 1, 2, 3 and 6.
Highest common factor	The largest of the common factors is called the **highest common factor**. The highest common factor of 12 and 18 is 6.

---

7   **a** Write down the factors of 16.

    b Write down the factors of 24.

    c Write down the common factors of 16 and 24.

    d Write down the highest common factor of 16 and 24.

8   **a** Write down the factors of 14.

    b Write down the factors of 42.

    c Write down the common factors of 14 and 42.

    d Write down the highest common factor of 14 and 42.

9 Work out the highest common factor of:

    a 12 and 16   **e** 6 and 42

    b 14 and 28   **f** 7 and 21

    c 10 and 25   **g** 12 and 36

    d 12 and 30   **h** 13 and 39

10   **a**   Write down the common factors of 3 and 7.
       b   Write down the common factors of 13 and 19.
  ●   **c**   What is the highest common factor of two prime numbers?

Square numbers   You can find the **square numbers** by doing these multiplications.

The 1st square number is found by doing: $1 \times 1 = 1$
The 2nd square number is found by doing: $2 \times 2 = 4$
The 3rd square number is found by doing: $3 \times 3 = 9$
The 4th square number is found by doing: $4 \times 4 = 16$

You can use the x^2 key on your calculator to work out square numbers.

The square of 5 is written 5^2, which you read as 5 squared. To find 5^2:

Key in:

Answer: 25
So $5^2 = 25$.

Exercise 9:10

1   Use the x^2 key on your calculator to work out:

    a 6^2 **c** 12^2 **e** 15^2 **g** 21^2
    b 11^2 **d** 13^2 **f** 19^2 **h** 47^2

2   **a**   Use the x^2 key on your calculator to work out:

       (1) 20^2 (2) 30^2 (3) 60^2 (4) 80^2

    b   Without using your calculator, write down:

       (1) 40^2 (2) 50^2 (3) 70^2 (4) 90^2

3   **a**   Use the x^2 key on your calculator to work out:

       (1) 0.2^2 (2) 0.3^2 (3) 0.4^2 (4) 0.5^2

    b   Without using your calculator, write down:

       (1) 0.6^2 (2) 0.7^2 (3) 0.8^2 (4) 0.9^2

Square root

There is a key on the calculator.

This is called the **square root** key.

This key undoes the effect of using the key.

To find the square root of 196:

Key in:

Answer: 14

So the square root of 196 is 14. You can write the square root of 196 as √196.
So √196 = 14.

What you are doing is finding the missing number in ... × ... = 196
Both spaces must have the same number.

$$14 \times 14 = 196$$

4 Use your calculator to find the square root of:
a 289 **b** 169 **c** 529 **d** 361

5 Find:
a √576 **b** √324 **c** √144 **d** √1681

6 Use your calculator to find the square root of:
a 0.01 **b** 0.04 **c** 0.25 **d** 0.49

7 Without using your calculator, write down the square root of:
a 0.09 **b** 0.16 **c** 0.36 **d** 0.81

Use your calculator to check your answers.

4 Finance

You pay income tax on money that you earn.

VAT is a different kind of tax.
You pay VAT on things that you buy.

VAT stands for **V**alue **A**dded **T**ax.

Example

Colin has to pay VAT on a garage bill of £68.
VAT is charged at 17.5%.
a How much VAT does Colin pay?
b What is the total bill?

a Colin pays 17.5% of £68 in VAT.
You can do this on your calculator.

Key in: **1 7 . 5 ÷ 1 0 0 × 6 8 =**

This is what your calculator displays: $\boxed{11.9}$

You need 2 dp in your answer to
show the number of pence. = £11.90

Colin pays £11.90 in VAT.

b The total bill is £68 + £11.90 = £79.90

Exercise 9:11

VAT is 17.5% in this exercise.

1 Find the VAT on each of these amounts.
  a £72   **c** £134   **e** £814
  b £38   **d** £232   **f** £9760

2 Find the total cost of each of these.
  a £146 + VAT   **c** £2012 + VAT
  b £98 + VAT   **d** £37.20 + VAT

3 Paul wants to buy a new computer.
He sees the same model in two different shops.

| Shop A | Shop B |

Which shop gives the lower price? Explain your answer.

4 It costs a builder £58 000 to build a house.
He wants to make a profit of 30% when he
sells it.

  a How many pounds profit does the
    builder make?

  b Find the total of: cost + profit.

  c He has to add VAT on to this price.
    Work out the VAT on your answer to
    part **b**.

  d What is the price of the house
    including VAT?

Tax allowance	You can earn a certain amount of money before you start to pay tax. This amount is called your **tax allowance**.
Taxable income	You take your tax allowance from what you earn to find your **taxable income**.
Example	Andy earns £8420 in one year. His tax allowance is £4000. What is his taxable income?

Earnings	£8420
− Tax allowance	£4000
Taxable income	£4420

Exercise 9:12

1 Copy and complete these.

a
Earnings	£8140
− Tax allowance	£5680
Taxable income	...

b
Earnings	£7250
− Tax allowance	£3980
Taxable income	...

2 Copy and complete these.

a
Earnings	£5230
− Tax allowance	£3875
Taxable income	...

c
Earnings	...
− Tax allowance	£3980
Taxable income	£1645

b
Earnings	£6496
− Tax allowance	...
Taxable income	£2671

d
Earnings	£9735
− Tax allowance	...
Taxable income	£4675

Income tax

There are three rates of **income tax**: 10%, 22% and 40%.
The amount of tax that you pay depends on your taxable income.

Example

Denise earned £7560 last year.
Her tax allowance was £4200.
She paid tax at the 10% rate.
How much did she pay?

First you find her taxable income.

$$\begin{array}{r} £ \\ 7560 \\ -4200 \\ \hline 3360 \end{array}$$

Her taxable income was £3360.
She paid 10% of this in tax.

10% of £3360 = £336

Key in: `1` `0` `÷` `1` `0` `0` `×` `3` `3` `6` `0` `=`

Denise paid £336 in tax.

---

3 Copy the table. Fill in the last two columns.

Name	Earnings	Tax allowance	Taxable income	Tax paid at 10%
Karen	£6842	£4010		
Jo	£5237	£3995		
Noel	£7320	£4689		
Simon	£6107	£4256		
Kath	£11 986	£7482		

4 Steph and Sally both earn the same amount.
Steph has a tax allowance of £4780. Sally has a tax allowance of £5620.
Who pays more tax? Explain your answer.

| **Percentage change** | You always work out a **percentage change** using the starting value. |

$$\text{Percentage change} = \frac{\text{actual change}}{\text{starting value}} \times 100\%$$

The change can be an increase or a decrease.

Example The price of a coat goes up from £35 to £42. Find the percentage increase.

The actual increase is £42 − £35 = £7
The starting price was £35.

$$\text{Percentage increase} = \frac{\text{actual increase}}{\text{starting price}} \times 100\%$$

$$= \frac{7}{35} \times 100\%$$

Key in:

7 ÷ 3 5 × 1 0 0 =

$$= 20\%$$

Exercise 9:13

1 Susie does a paper round.
She is given a rise in pay.
She was paid £2.25 an hour.
Her new pay is £2.61 an hour.
Find the percentage increase in her pay.

2 Jack and Jill bought their house for £56 000.
It is now worth £70 000.
What is the percentage increase in its value?

| **Percentage profit** | **Percentage profit** is a special kind of percentage increase. |

$$\text{Percentage profit} = \frac{\text{actual profit}}{\text{cost price}} \times 100\%$$

Actual profit is the actual increase.
Cost price is the starting price.

3 Copy the table. Fill in the spaces.

Item	Cost price	Selling price	Actual profit	% profit
watch	£16	£24		
necklace	£12	£15		
discman	£60	£75		
dishwasher	£125	£175		

Example Find the percentage reduction when a shirt is reduced from £25 to £17.

$$\text{Percentage reduction} = \frac{\text{actual reduction}}{\text{starting value}} \times 100\%$$

$$= \frac{8}{25} \times 100\%$$

Key in:

8 ÷ 2 5 × 1 0 0 =

$$= 32\%$$

4 Copy the table. Fill in the spaces.

Item	Normal price	Sale price	Actual reduction	% reduction
bracelet	£30	£24		
earrings	£36	£27		
clock	£125	£109		
watch	£50	£43		

Percentage loss **Percentage loss** is a special kind of percentage reduction.

$$\text{Percentage loss} = \frac{\text{actual loss}}{\text{starting value}} \times 100\%$$

5 Copy the table. Fill in the spaces.

Item	Cost price	Selling price	Actual loss	% loss
record player	£20	£15		
camcorder	£100	£80		
vase	£40	£30		
kettle	£20	£17		

1 Change each of these to the units shown.
   a 3 m to centimetres   **d** 37 mm to centimetres
   b 8 cm to millimetres   **e** 123 cm to metres
   c 7 km to metres   **f** 6300 m to kilometres

2 Find the perimeter of a regular octagon with sides of length 5 cm.

3 Change each of these to the units shown.
   a 764 mg to grams   **b** 1260 g to kilograms   **c** 2.4 t to kilograms

4 Change each of these to the units shown.
   a 3000 ml to litres   **b** 6.2 l to centilitres   **c** 450 cl to litres

5 The table shows the amount of the different ingredients of a digestive biscuit.

Type of ingredient	protein	carbohydrate	sugar	fat	fibre
Percentage	10%	50%	15%	20%	5%

   a Work out the angle for 1% ready to draw a pie-chart.
   b Work out the angle for each ingredient.
   c Draw a pie-chart to show the data. Label your pie-chart.
   d What fraction of the biscuit is sugar?
   e A packet of digestive biscuits weighs 400 g.
      How much sugar is there in a packet of digestive biscuits?

6 Write down the factors of:
   a 5   **b** 14   **c** 18   **d** 4

7 Write down the first six prime numbers.

8 Use your calculator to work out:
   a 14^2 **b** 23^2 **c** 35^2 **d** 41^2

9 Use your calculator to find:
   a $\sqrt{64}$ **b** $\sqrt{1444}$ **c** $\sqrt{1369}$ **d** $\sqrt{676}$

10 A midi system costs £468 + VAT. The rate of VAT is 17.5%.
   a How much is the VAT?
   b What is the total cost of the midi system?

11 Simon earns £7465 in one year. He has a tax allowance of £4280.
   a How much taxable income does Simon have?
   b Simon pays tax at the 10% rate. How much tax does he pay?

1 Add these together. Give your answer in metres.
64 cm, 1.3 m, 127 cm, 4 m

2 How much heavier is 8.4 kg than 900 g? Give your answer in kilograms.

3 Grange Girl Guides have raised some
money for charities.
The pie-chart shows how they split the
money that they raised.
  a They gave £40 to the RSPCA.
    How much did they raise altogether?
  b How much money did they give to
    each of the other charities?

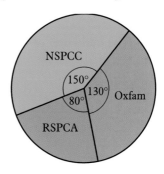

4 **a** Find two triangle numbers that add up to 36.
  b Find two prime numbers that add up to 36.

5 The square root of 21 lies between two whole numbers.
What are these numbers?

6 Choose a number larger than 1.
  a Find the square root of your number.
  b Find the square root of your answer to part **a**.
  c Find the square root of your answer to part **b**.
  d Write down what happens if you carry on like this.
  e What happens if you start with a number between 0 and 1?

7 Ben earns £14 760 in one year.
He has a tax allowance of £5700.
Ben pays tax at the 10% rate on the
first £1500 of his taxable income.
He pays tax at the 22% rate on the
rest.
  a What is Ben's taxable income?
  b How much tax does he pay at
    the 10% rate?
  c How much of Ben's income is
    taxed at 22%?
  d How much tax does Ben pay at the 22% rate?
  e How much tax does Ben pay altogether?

8 Bob buys a trailer for £160. He sells it for £195.
  a How much profit does he make?
  b Find his percentage profit correct to 1 dp.

1 Change each of these to the units shown.
    a 12.7 m to cm.
    b 59 mm to cm.
    c 3.2 kg to g.
    d 4700 mg to g.
    e 2.5 *l* to ml.
    f 67 000 cl to *l*.

2 Find the perimeter of this shape in cm.

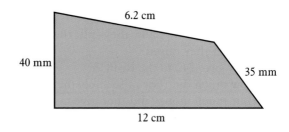

3 This was one of the questions on a questionnaire.

Which of these types of food do you like best?

French ☐   Italian ☐   Chinese ☐   Indian ☐

465 people were surveyed.
The pie-chart shows the results.
    a What percentage chose Italian?
    b How many chose French?
    c What fraction chose Chinese?

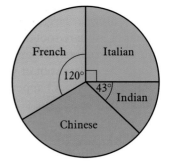

4 Work out the highest common factor of 48 and 90.

5 Write down the value of:
    a 7^2 **b** $\sqrt{81}$

6 Write down the first six prime numbers.

7 Edward bought his bike for £282.89
He sold it for £215.
Find the percentage loss.

8 The cost of a garage bill is £178.
VAT is charged at 17.5%.
Find the total bill.

10

1 Transformations
Reflecting shapes
Using negative numbers in co-ordinates
Turning shapes

2 Averages
Finding the mean by adding and dividing
Finding the most common item of data
Finding the one in the middle

3 Fractions
Looking at fractions
Adding and subtracting fractions
Cancelling fractions
Using a calculator

4 Finding a formula
Using formulas
Finding the formula for a times table sequence
Formulas with two parts
Finding formulas for patterns with shapes

CORE

QUESTIONS

EXTENSION

TEST YOURSELF

1 Transformations

Alice can see her reflection in the mirror.

You have already reflected shapes made up of squares in mirror lines. You can reflect any shape in a mirror line.

Example   Reflect this shape in the dotted line.

Find the reflection of each corner of the shape and then join them up.

You can use tracing paper to check your reflection. Trace the shape, its reflection and the dotted line.
Fold the tracing paper on the dotted line. The reflection fits exactly on top of the shape.

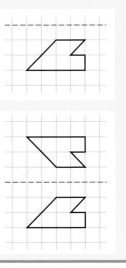

Exercise 10:1

1   Copy these shapes on to squared paper.
Draw the reflection of each shape in the dotted line.

a

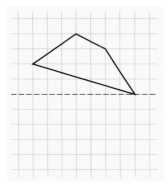

b

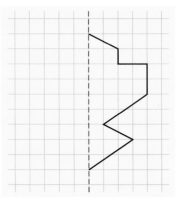

You have used co-ordinates to mark points on a grid.
Negative numbers can also be used on the axes.

The **co-ordinates** of the
point A are $(2, -3)$.

The first number is the
x co-ordinate.
It tells you where to go on the
horizontal axis.

The second number is the
y co-ordinate.
It tells you where to go on the
vertical axis.

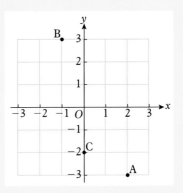

The co-ordinates of B are $(-1, 3)$.
The co-ordinates of C are $(0, -2)$.

2 a Write down the co-ordinates
of the points marked.
  b Join the points J and D.
Mark the point in the
middle of this line.
Write down its co-ordinates.
  c Join the points A and F.
Write down the co-ordinates of
the mid-point of this line
  d Find the mid-point of the line
joining points N and I.

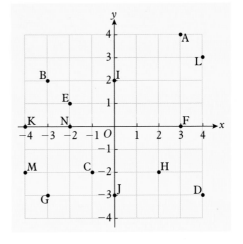

3 a Copy these axes and the shape
on to squared paper.
  b Reflect the shape in the y axis.
  c What are the new co-ordinates
of P, Q and R?

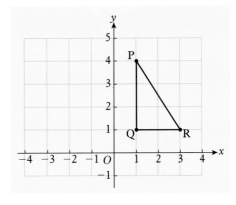

4 **a** Copy these axes and the shape onto squared paper.
  b Reflect the shape in the *x* axis.
  c What are the new co-ordinates of D, E, F and G?
  d Write down the co-ordinates of the mid-point of the line joining the old point D to the new point D.

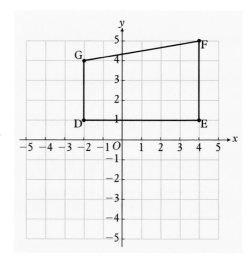

5 **a** Copy these axes and the shape onto squared paper.
  b Draw and label the line *y* = 2.
  c Reflect the shape in the line *y* = 2.
  d What are the new co-ordinates of A, B, C and D?

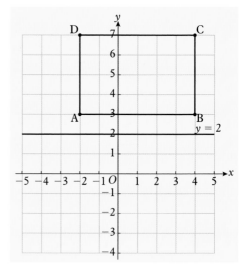

Rotation

A **rotation** turns a shape about a fixed point. This point is called the centre of rotation.

When you describe a rotation you must give these three things:
• the angle
• the direction (clockwise or anticlockwise)
• the centre.

In the diagram, A is rotated **90° clockwise** about the point (0, 0) to D.

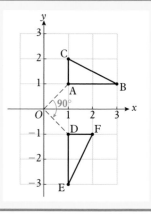

Exercise 10:2

1   You are going to draw the new position of C after a rotation of 90°
    clockwise about (0, 0).

    a   Copy the diagram.

    b   Put a piece of tracing paper on
    the diagram. Trace the shape C
    and the red cross at the point
    (0, 0).

    c   Put the point of your pencil on
    (0, 0) to hold the tracing paper
    firmly in place.

    d   Turn the tracing paper through
    90° clockwise. Use the cross at
    (0, 0) to help you.

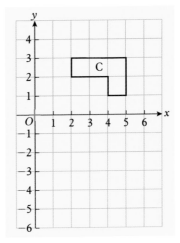

    e   Copy the new position of C on to your axes. Label it D.
    You have rotated C 90° clockwise about the point (0, 0).

2   **a**   Copy the diagram.
    b   Rotate S 90° anticlockwise
    about (0, 0).
    Label the new position T.
    Use tracing paper to help you.

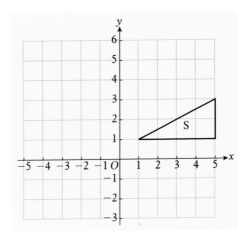

2 Averages

During most Formula 1 races, cars make at least one pit stop to change the tyres. Mechanics have been known to change all four tyres in less than 5 seconds!

Mean

To find the **mean** of a set of data:
(1) Find the total of all the data values.
(2) Divide the total by the number of data values.

Example

These are the times, in seconds, that a team of mechanics took to change the tyres during 5 pit stops. Find the mean time.

7.3   8.2   7.9   9.6   7.5

The total is: $7.3 + 8.2 + 7.9 + 9.6 + 7.5 = 40.5$ s.
The mean is: $40.5 \div 5 = 8.1$ s.

Exercise 10:3

1 These are the times, in seconds, of three different teams of mechanics.
Find the mean time for each team.
  a Williams   7.6   8.3   7.9   9.2   7.8   8.6   8.0
  b Lotus   8.3   9.0   8.1   7.8
  c McLaren   6.1   7.9   7.0   6.3   8.2

Use your means to write down:
  d the fastest team
  e the slowest team.

2 These are the number of wins per make of car.

Make of car	Ferrari	McLaren	Lotus	Williams	Brabham	Tyrrell
Number of wins	104	104	79	78	35	23

    a Find the mean number of wins.
    b Write down the make of car whose number of wins is closest to the mean.
    c Write down the make of car whose number of wins is furthest from the mean.

3 These are the number of fastest laps per make of car.

Make of car	Ferrari	McLaren	Lotus	Williams	Brabham	Tyrrell
Number of fastest laps	119	69	71	83	40	20

Find the mean number of fastest laps.

Mode   The **mode** is the most common or most popular data value.
It is sometimes called the **modal value**.

Example   These are the highest numbers of wins in a season for different drivers.

Driver	Andretti	Mansell	Hunt	Senna	Ascari	Prost	Schumacher
Number of wins	6	9	6	7	6	7	8

What is the modal number of wins?

6 is the most common number of wins.
The modal number of wins is 6.

---

4 These are the numbers of most consecutive wins for different drivers.

Driver	Mansell	Senna	Lauda	Moss	Fangio	Prost	Hill	Brabham
Number of wins	5	4	3	3	4	4	3	4

What is the modal number of consecutive wins?

5   These are the numbers of wins over several seasons for different drivers.

Driver	Mansell	Senna	Lauda	Fangio	Prost	Hill	Brabham
Number of wins	9	8	5	6	7	5	5

What is the modal number of wins?

6   The bar-chart shows the ages of Jason's favourite racing drivers.
What is the modal age?

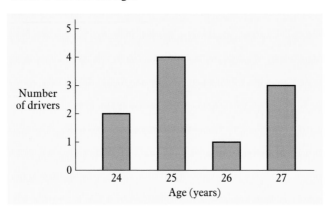

7   The table shows the number of wins per driver in Formula 1 races
during the 1997 season.

Driver	Coulthard	Villeneuve	Frentzen	Schumacher	Berger	Hakkinen
Number of wins	2	7	1	5	1	1

What is the modal number of wins?

Median   To find the median you put all the data values in order of size.
The **median** is then the middle value.

Example   These are the numbers of Grands Prix entered by different drivers.

Driver	Lauda	Bonnier	Fittipaldi	Mansell	Brabham	Surtees	Berger
Number of wins	171	102	144	185	126	111	163

Find the median number of Grands Prix entered.

Write the numbers in order. Start with the smallest.

102   111   126   144   163   171   185

Find the middle number. It is 144.

The median number is 144.

Sometimes there are *two* numbers in the middle.
For example, find the median of:

32   41   43   46   50   57   63   67

There are two numbers in the middle: 46 and 50
To find the median:
(1) Add the two middle numbers together.
(2) Divide the answer by 2.

46 + 50 = 96   96 ÷ 2 = 48

The median is 48.

Exercise 10:4

1 These are the number of fastest laps per make of car.

Make of car	Williams	Benetton	Lotus	Maserati	Ferrari
Number of laps	83	25	71	15	119

Find the median number of fastest laps.

2 These are the pit stop times of three different teams of mechanics.
Find the median time for each team.
a Williams   7.6   8.3   7.9   9.2   7.8   8.6   8.0
b Lotus   8.3   9.0   8.1   7.8
c McLaren   6.1   7.9   7.0   6.3   8.2

3 These are the lengths, in miles, of some Grand Prix circuits.

Circuit	Spa	Monza	Silverstone	Monaco	Imola	Montreal	Hockenheim
Length	4.350	3.604	3.142	2.068	3.042	2.765	4.234

Find the median length of these circuits.

3 Fractions

Jane is doing some school exams.
She is reading a sheet of instructions.

It says:

Paper 1	$\frac{3}{4}$ hour
Paper 2	$\frac{3}{4}$ hour
Paper 3	$\frac{1}{2}$ hour

Jane is puzzled.
She is trying to work out how long before
the end of the exam.
Jane wishes she had worked harder on
fractions!

Alf is a chef.
He is looking at a pack of soup.
A pack contains 4 cartons.

Here are 4 cartons of soup:
This is one whole pack.

Here is 1 carton of soup:
This is $\frac{1}{4}$ of a pack.

Alf says there are $1\frac{1}{4}$ packs here altogether.

Exercise 10:5

Copy the diagrams.
You are working in Alf's kitchen.

1 For each part: (1) Write down how many cartons of soup there are.
(2) Write down how many packs of soup there are.

a   **b**   **c**   **d**

<table>
<tr><td>

'Top heavy' fractions

</td><td>

Look at the fraction $\frac{9}{4}$

The top number is bigger than the bottom.
The fraction is **'top heavy'**.

Look at Alf's packs of soup.
Nine quarters make two
wholes and one quarter: $\frac{9}{4} = 2\frac{1}{4}$

</td></tr>
</table>

2 Write each of these diagrams as:
   (1) a top heavy fraction
   (2) a whole number and a fraction.

a    **c**   **e**

b   **d**   **•f**

Look at these cartons of soup.

  is the same number of cartons as

so half a pack   is the same as   two quarter packs

You can write: $\frac{1}{2}$ $=$ $\frac{2}{4}$

These are called **equivalent** fractions.
They are the **same** fraction shown in different ways.

Look at this tray of strawberries in Alf's kitchen.

There are 8 cartons in a tray,
so each carton is $\frac{1}{8}$ of the tray.

   is the same number of cartons as

so half a tray   is the same as   four lots of one eighth of a tray.

You can write: $\frac{1}{2} = \frac{4}{8}$

3 Copy these. Fill them in.

a $\dfrac{}{2} = \dfrac{}{4}$

b $\dfrac{}{4} = \dfrac{}{8}$

c  $\dfrac{}{4} = \dfrac{}{8}$

d  $\dfrac{}{2} = \dfrac{}{4}$

4 Amy delivers bottles of salad cream to Alf.
Bottles of salad cream are in packs of 16. Copy these. Fill them in.

a $\dfrac{}{2} = \dfrac{}{16}$

c $\dfrac{}{8} = \dfrac{}{16}$

b $\dfrac{}{4} = \dfrac{}{16}$

d 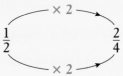 $\dfrac{}{8} = \dfrac{}{16}$

You can **make equivalent fractions** by multiplying.
To change $\frac{1}{2}$ into quarters, you need to make the bottom number 4.

$$\frac{1}{2} \quad\xrightarrow{\times 2}\quad \frac{}{4}$$

You **multiply** the bottom **by 2** to get 4.

$$\frac{1}{2} \quad\xrightarrow{\times 2}\quad \frac{2}{4}$$

Then you **multiply** the top **by 2** to get 2.

To change $\frac{3}{4}$ into sixteenths, you need to make the bottom number 16.

$$\frac{3}{4} \quad\xrightarrow{\times 4}\quad \frac{}{16}$$

You **multiply** the bottom **by 4** to get 16.

$$\frac{3}{4} \quad\xrightarrow{\times 4}\quad \frac{12}{16}$$

Then you **multiply** the top **by 4** to get 12.

You always multiply the top and bottom **by the same number**.

Exercise 10:6

1 Change these fractions into eighths. Show your working.

a

b

c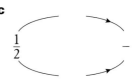

2 Change these fractions into sixteenths. Show your working.

a $\frac{1}{8}$ **c** $\frac{3}{8}$ **e** $\frac{5}{8}$ **g** $\frac{7}{8}$

b $\frac{1}{4}$ **d** $\frac{3}{4}$ **f** $\frac{1}{2}$ **● h** $1\frac{1}{2}$

Adding fractions

To **add fractions**, the bottom numbers must be the same.
Alf knows this when he collects together different packs.

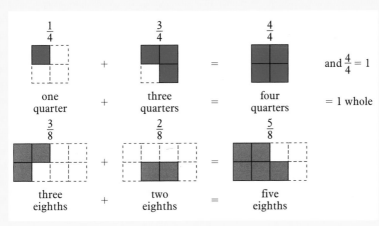

Exercise 10:7

1 Work these out:

a $\frac{1}{4} + \frac{2}{4}$ **b** $\frac{2}{8} + \frac{3}{8}$ **c** $\frac{1}{8} + \frac{4}{8}$ **d** $\frac{5}{8} + \frac{2}{8}$

2 Work these out:

a $\frac{6}{8} + \frac{1}{8}$ **b** $\frac{3}{8} + \frac{4}{8}$ **c** $\frac{2}{4} + \frac{3}{4}$ **d** $\frac{4}{8} + \frac{5}{8}$

3 Work these out:

a $\frac{3}{8} + \frac{7}{8}$ **b** $\frac{3}{16} + \frac{4}{16}$ ● **c** $\frac{3}{16} + \frac{14}{16}$ ● **d** $\frac{3}{8} + \frac{5}{8} + \frac{7}{8}$

Subtracting fractions

You can **subtract fractions** in the same way that you add fractions.

So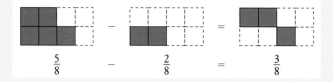

          $\frac{5}{8}$ $-$ $\frac{2}{8}$ $=$ $\frac{3}{8}$

4 Work these out:

a $\frac{3}{4} - \frac{2}{4}$ **b** $\frac{5}{8} - \frac{4}{8}$ **c** $\frac{5}{16} - \frac{4}{16}$ **d** $\frac{9}{16} - \frac{2}{16}$

5 Work these out:

a $\frac{13}{16} - \frac{2}{16}$ **b** $\frac{15}{16} - \frac{12}{16}$ ● **c** $\frac{19}{16} - \frac{11}{16}$ ● **d** $\frac{3}{8} - \frac{5}{8} + \frac{7}{8}$

Sometimes the bottom numbers in fractions are different.
To add or subtract these fractions you must make the bottom numbers the same.

Example   Find   **a** $\frac{3}{4} + \frac{1}{2}$ **b** $\frac{7}{8} - \frac{3}{4}$

     a You need to change $\frac{1}{2}$ into quarters.

         So $\frac{3}{4} + \frac{1}{2} = \frac{3}{4} + \frac{2}{4}$

               $= \frac{5}{4}$ and this is $1\frac{1}{4}$

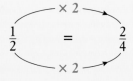

     b You need to change $\frac{3}{4}$ into eighths.

         So $\frac{7}{8} - \frac{3}{4} = \frac{7}{8} - \frac{6}{8}$

               $= \frac{1}{8}$

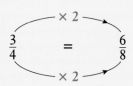

Exercise 10:8

1 Work these out:

a $\frac{1}{4} + \frac{1}{2}$ c $\frac{5}{8} + \frac{1}{4}$ e $\frac{5}{16} + \frac{1}{8}$ g $\frac{11}{16} + \frac{1}{2}$

b $\frac{3}{4} + \frac{1}{8}$ d $\frac{3}{4} + \frac{7}{8}$ f $\frac{9}{16} + \frac{3}{4}$ h $\frac{15}{16} + \frac{3}{4}$

2 Work these out:

a $\frac{1}{2} - \frac{1}{4}$ c $\frac{3}{8} - \frac{1}{4}$ e $\frac{15}{16} - \frac{3}{8}$ • g $\frac{11}{16} - \frac{1}{2} + \frac{3}{4}$

b $\frac{3}{4} - \frac{1}{8}$ d $\frac{7}{8} - \frac{1}{2}$ f $\frac{13}{16} - \frac{3}{4}$ • h $\frac{5}{16} - \frac{3}{4} + \frac{7}{8}$

Adding fractions with whole numbers

To work out: $1\frac{3}{4} + 2\frac{7}{8}$

First add the whole numbers: $1 + 2 = 3$

Then add the fractions: $\qquad \frac{3}{4} + \frac{7}{8} = \frac{6}{8} + \frac{7}{8}$

$$= \frac{13}{8} = 1\frac{5}{8}$$

Now add your two answers together: $\quad 3 + 1\frac{5}{8} = 4\frac{5}{8}$

3 Work these out:

a $1\frac{1}{4} + \frac{1}{2}$ c $4\frac{3}{8} + 5\frac{7}{8}$ e $5\frac{5}{16} + 1\frac{3}{4}$ • g $8\frac{3}{4} + 4\frac{11}{16}$

b $2\frac{3}{4} + 3\frac{1}{8}$ d $2\frac{1}{16} + 6\frac{7}{8}$ f $1\frac{1}{2} + 4\frac{9}{16}$ • h $27\frac{7}{8} + 14\frac{15}{16}$

Subtracting fractions with whole numbers

To work out: $2\frac{3}{4} - 1\frac{7}{8}$

First write the fractions as top heavy fractions: $2\frac{3}{4} = \frac{11}{4}$ and $1\frac{7}{8} = \frac{15}{8}$

Then change $\frac{11}{4}$ into eighths:

Finally, subtract: $\frac{11}{4} - \frac{15}{8} = \frac{22}{8} - \frac{15}{8}$

$$= \frac{7}{8}$$

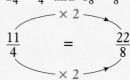

4 Work these out:

a $1\frac{1}{4} - \frac{1}{8}$ c $4\frac{3}{8} - 3\frac{1}{4}$ e $2\frac{1}{16} - 1\frac{3}{8}$ • g $6 - 2\frac{7}{8}$

b $2\frac{1}{4} - 1\frac{1}{8}$ d $1\frac{11}{16} - 1\frac{3}{8}$ f $5\frac{1}{2} - 1\frac{9}{16}$ • h $10\frac{7}{8} - 4\frac{15}{16}$

• **5** Laura has baked two large Christmas cakes. Each cake has 16 slices.
She gives $\frac{11}{16}$ of a cake to one aunt and $\frac{3}{4}$ of a cake to another.
How much is left for Laura and her family to share?

Cancelling fractions

You can cancel fractions by dividing.
You need to look at the top and bottom of a fraction.
If you can divide both by the same whole number you can cancel.
You can change $\frac{2}{4}$ into halves if you divide the top and bottom by 2.

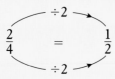

You can change $\frac{12}{16}$ into quarters if you divide the top and bottom by 4.

You divide by 4 because this is the *biggest* number that goes into both the top and the bottom.

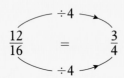

You must always divide the top and bottom by the same number.

Exercise 10:9

For each of questions **1** and **2**
  a Copy the diagrams. Complete the diagram on the right.
  b Cancel the fraction down.

1

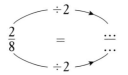

2

3 Cancel these fractions down.

a $\frac{3}{9}$ **c** $\frac{15}{20}$ **e** $\frac{12}{15}$ **g** $\frac{8}{20}$ **i** $\frac{14}{21}$

b $\frac{6}{9}$ **d** $\frac{2}{10}$ **f** $\frac{7}{14}$ **h** $\frac{16}{20}$ **j** $\frac{20}{30}$

Cancelling fractions with a calculator

You can cancel fractions using the $a^{b/c}$ button on a calculator.

To cancel $\frac{6}{10}$ you press $\boxed{6}$ $\boxed{a^{b/c}}$ $\boxed{1}$ $\boxed{0}$ $\boxed{=}$

The display shows $\boxed{\text{3⌐5}}$ or $\boxed{\text{3⌐5}}$. This means $\frac{3}{5}$.

Exercise 10:10

1 Cancel these fractions. Use your calculator to check your answers.

a $\frac{2}{4}$	**e** $\frac{4}{8}$	**i** $\frac{2}{6}$	**m** $\frac{4}{12}$
b $\frac{3}{6}$	**f** $\frac{5}{10}$	**j** $\frac{3}{9}$	**n** $\frac{5}{15}$
c $\frac{2}{8}$	**g** $\frac{2}{10}$	**k** $\frac{8}{24}$	**o** $\frac{56}{72}$
d $\frac{6}{8}$	**h** $\frac{4}{24}$	**l** $\frac{5}{35}$	**p** $\frac{12}{56}$

You can use your fractions button to do more difficult questions.
Do questions **2** to **5** with your calculator.

2 Work these out:

a $\frac{1}{6} + \frac{1}{3}$	**c** $\frac{4}{15} + \frac{1}{3}$	**e** $\frac{2}{7} + \frac{1}{5}$	**g** $\frac{11}{12} + \frac{1}{3}$
b $\frac{1}{6} + \frac{1}{2}$	**d** $\frac{3}{4} + \frac{1}{12}$	**f** $\frac{8}{9} + \frac{3}{5}$	**h** $\frac{13}{20} + \frac{3}{5}$

3 Work these out:

a $\frac{1}{2} - \frac{1}{6}$	**c** $\frac{5}{12} - \frac{1}{4}$	**e** $\frac{5}{7} - \frac{3}{5}$	**g** $\frac{11}{20} - \frac{2}{5} + \frac{3}{4}$
b $\frac{3}{5} - \frac{1}{10}$	**d** $\frac{5}{6} - \frac{1}{3}$	**f** $\frac{13}{20} - \frac{2}{5}$	**h** $\frac{5}{6} - \frac{7}{12} + \frac{1}{4}$

4 Work these out:

a $1\frac{1}{3} + 1\frac{1}{2}$	**c** $4\frac{2}{5} + 5\frac{1}{10}$	**e** $1\frac{1}{5} - \frac{3}{10}$	**g** $4\frac{1}{6} - 3\frac{1}{2}$
b $2\frac{3}{4} + 3\frac{1}{12}$	**d** $2\frac{3}{10} + 6\frac{1}{5}$	**f** $2\frac{1}{4} - 1\frac{1}{8}$	**h** $2\frac{11}{20} - 1\frac{3}{4}$

5 A newspaper goes out of business.

$\frac{2}{5}$ of the land it stands on is given to a school as playing fields.

$\frac{1}{3}$ of the land it stands on is sold to use to build a retirement home.

How much of the land is left to be used as a park?

4 Finding a formula

The numbers of blocks in the pillars give the sequence:

3, 4, 5, 6, 7, 8, …

Sequences are often found in investigations.
You can find formulas for sequences.

Look at the sequence: 2, 4, 6, 8… . These are the multiples of 2.

Term number	1	2	3	4	
Multiples of 2	2	4	6	8	…

Here is a formula to work out the multiples of 2.
The formula is: $m = 2n$ m is the multiple.
n is the term number.

The value of the multiple of two depends on the term number.

Example   Find the multiple in the 2 times table for:
   a   term number 5   **b**   term number 8

a Term number 5 is the 5th term.   **b** Term number 8 is the 8th term.
You put $n = 5$ in the formula.   You put $n = 8$ in the formula.
So: $m = 2 \times 5 = 10$ So: $m = 2 \times 8 = 16$
The 5th term is 10.   The 8th term is 16.

Exercise 10:11

1   The formula for the 2 times table is: $m = 2n$
Find the multiple in the 2 times table for term number:
   a 6   **b** 7   **c** 9   **d** 10

2 The formula for the 3 times table is: $m = 3n$
Find the multiple in the 3 times table for term number:
a 1   **b** 2   **c** 3   **d** 4
e Write down the rule for the 3 times table.

3 The formula for the 4 times table is: $m = 4n$
Find these terms in the 4 times table:
a 3rd term (term number 3)   **b** 5th term   **c** 10th term
d Write down the rule for the 4 times table.

4 **a** Write down a formula for the 5 times table, $m = ...n$
Find these terms in the 5 times table:
b 2nd term   **c** 3rd term   **d** 5th term   **e** 9th term

Finding a formula for a sequence of numbers

Look at the sequence: 7, 14, 21, 28, ...
You can find the formula for a sequence of numbers.
You need to write down the rule to find the formula.

Term number   1   2   3   4

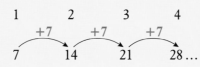

Look at the sequence: 7   14   21   28 ...

The rule is 'add 7'. Now look at the terms for: $m = 7n$

$m = 7n$ gives: $7 \times 1 = 7$, $7 \times 2 = 14$, $7 \times 3 = 21$, $7 \times 4 = 28$

$m = 7n$ gives the same sequence. So $m = 7n$ is the formula.

Exercise 10:12

1 **a** Copy the diagram for the sequence: 4, 8, 12, 16, ...

Term number   1   2   3   4

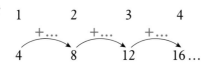

     4   8   12   16 ...

b Copy this. Fill it in.
The rule is **add** ... Now look at the terms for: $m = ...n$
$m = ...n$ gives $... \times 1 = ...$ $... \times 2 = ...$ $... \times 3 = ...$ $... \times 4 = ...$
$m = ...n$ gives the ... sequence. So $m = ...n$ is the formula.

2 a Copy the diagram for the sequence: 6, 12, 18, 24, …

Term number   1   2   3   4

+…   +…   +…

6   12   18   24 …

b Copy this. Fill it in.

The rule is **add** …   Now look at the terms for: $m = …n$

$m = …n$ gives   … × 1 = …   … × 2 = …   … × 3 = …   … × 4 = …

$m = …n$ gives the same sequence. So $m = …n$ is the formula.

For questions **3–6**:
a Draw a diagram.
b Write down the rule.
c Write down a formula for each sequence.

3 8, 16, 24, 32, …

5 20, 40, 60, 80, …

4 10, 20, 30, 40, …

6 11, 22, 33, 44, …

Formulas with two parts

Look at this sequence: 3, 5, 7, 9, …

+2   +2   +2   +2

3   5   7   9

The rule for this sequence is 'add 2'. It is not the 2 times table!
But it must have something to do with the 2 times table.

The formula for the 2 times table is: $m = 2n$
Write the terms for $m = 2n$ underneath. Compare the two sequences.
Because the rule is 'add 2' you can write 'related to $2n$' on your diagram.

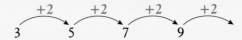

Term number   1   2   3   4

+2   +2   +2   +2   related to $2n$

Sequence in question   3   5   7   9

+1   +1   +1   +1   +1

Using formula $m = 2n$ 2   4   6   8 $2n$

You need to **add 1** to every term in $m = 2n$ to make the sequence in the question.
The formula for the sequence in the question is: $s = 2n + 1$

Exercise 10:13

1 **a** Copy the sequence diagram below. Fill in the missing numbers.

Term number   1   2   3   4

               +4   +4   +...   +...   related to ...n

Sequence in question   5   9   13   17

               $+1$ $+1$ $+...$ $+...$ $+...$

Using $m = ...n$ 4   8   ...   .n

   b Write down the formula for the sequence: 5, 9, 13, 17 ...

2 **a** Copy the sequence diagram below. Fill in the missing numbers.

Term number   1   2   3   4

               +4   +4   +...   +...   related to ...n

Sequence in question   2   6   10   14

               -2 $-...$ $-...$ $-...$ $-...$

Using $m = ...n$ 4   ...   .n

   b Write down the formula for the sequence: 2, 6, 10, 14 ...

3 For each of these sequences:
   (1) draw sequence diagrams   (2) find the formula
   a   7, 11, 15, 19, ...   **f**   3, 8, 13, 18, ...
   b   7, 10, 13, 16, ...   **g**   11, 17, 23, 29, ...
   c   7, 12, 17, 22, ...   **h**   9, 15, 21, 27, ...
   d   5, 7, 9, 11, ...   ● **i**   27, 29, 31, 33, ...
   e   3, 5, 7, 9, ...   ● **j**   5.5, 8, 10.5, 13, ...

If you know the formula for a sequence you can work out the value of each term.

Example   Here is a formula for a sequence: $s = 2n + 3$
           This is how you can work out the first four terms:

       Term 1 is when $n = 1$ so $s = 2n + 3$ is: $s = 2 \times 1 + 3 = 5$
       Term 2 is when $n = 2$ so $s = 2n + 3$ is: $s = 2 \times 2 + 3 = 7$
       Term 3 is when $n = 3$ so $s = 2n + 3$ is: $s = 2 \times 3 + 3 = 9$
       Term 4 is when $n = 4$ so $s = 2n + 3$ is: $s = 2 \times 4 + 3 = 11$

4   Copy these. Join each sequence to the correct formula with an arrow.

| 9   15   21   27   ... |

$s = 7n + 3$

| 3   8   13   18   ... |

$s = 5n - 2$

| 10   17   24   31   ... |

$s = 6n + 3$

Patterns with shapes

Look at these pillars.
Count the blocks for each pillar. This gives a sequence.

The sequence is: 3   4   5   6
You can work out the formula for the sequence.

Term number   1   2   3   4 n

            +1   +1   +1   +1   related to $1n$

Sequence in question   3   4   5   6

        +2   +2   +2   +2   +2

Sequence $1n$ 1   2   3   4 $1n$

So the formula is: $s = 1n + 2$. You write this as: $s = n + 2$

Exercise 10:14

1   **a**   Copy the diagrams.
    b   Fill in the sequence of numbers.
    c   Use a sequence diagram to work out the formula.

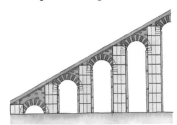

The sequence is: ...   .

2 **a** Copy the diagrams.
  b Fill in the sequence of numbers.
  c Use a sequence diagram to work out the formula.

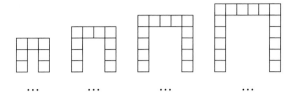

The sequence is ... ...

3 Luciana has some patterns on her wall made from tiles.
  a Work out the formula for the sequence.
  b How many tiles would you need for the 8th pattern?

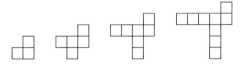

4 The aliens are flying by!
  a Write down how many are in the next group in the pattern.
  b Work out the formula for their flying formation.

5 These penguins were seen on an ice flow watching RAF aircraft.
  a How many are in the next group in the pattern?

  b Work out the formula for their formation.
  c Check your formula works.
      Find the first three terms.
      Do they match the numbers in your sequence?

1   **a**   Copy the diagram.
     b   Reflect the shape in the line $y = 2$.
       Label the new position A.
     c   Reflect the shape in the line $x = 1$.
       Label the new position B.
     d   Rotate the shape $180°$ anticlockwise
       about O.
       Label the new position C.
     e   Rotate the shape $90°$ clockwise
       about O.
       Label the new position D.

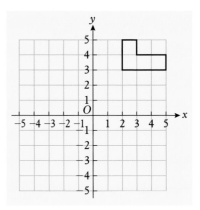

2   **a**   The rectangle ABCD is rotated through
       $90°$ clockwise about O.
       Write down the new
       co-ordinates of D.
     b   The rectangle ABCD is
       reflected in the line $x = 1$.
       Write down the new
       co-ordinates of D.

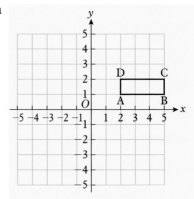

3   These are Penny's marks for tests in five subjects:

Maths (%)	65	53	57	71	60	72
English (%)	82	64	51	74	64	49
History (%)	64	50	58	63	59	66
Art (%)	58	64	78	56	71	66
French (%)	57	46	62	49	56	63

     a   Find the mean mark for each subject.
     b   Use the means to decide which are Penny's best and worst subjects.
     c   Find the median mark for each subject.

4   Find the median of each set of data:
     a   7, 5, 7, 3, 9, 2, 1, 6, 3   **c**   13, 18, 25, 20
     b   35, 38, 28, 31, 42, 30   **d**   3.4, 2.6, 4.8, 3.8, 1.9, 2.0, 1.5

5   Write down the mode of each set of data:
     a   2, 3, 5, 3, 2, 6, 3, 1, 8   **c**   18, 17, 12, 16, 17, 18, 17
     b   23, 27, 24, 28, 26, 25, 24, 21   **d**   2, 4, 7, 4, 3, 2, 6, 7, 2, 4, 7, 4

6 Write each of these diagrams as:
(1) a top heavy fraction   (2) a whole number and a fraction.

 a    **c**   **e**

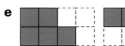 **b**    **d**    **f**

7 Make these fractions equivalent.
Copy these down. Fill them in.

  $\dfrac{}{8} = \dfrac{}{16}$ $\dfrac{}{16} = \dfrac{}{8}$

8 Work these out:

a $2\frac{1}{4} + 1\frac{1}{2}$ **c** $3\frac{5}{8} + 4\frac{3}{4}$ **e** $6\frac{5}{16} + 2\frac{7}{8}$ **g** $8\frac{1}{2} + 7\frac{9}{16}$

b $2\frac{3}{4} - 2\frac{1}{8}$ **d** $7\frac{1}{16} - 6\frac{3}{8}$ **f** $11\frac{3}{4} - 9\frac{13}{16}$ **h** $40\frac{3}{4} - 9\frac{15}{16}$

9 Write down a formula for each of these:
a 13, 26, 39, 52, 65, ...   **b** 15, 30, 45, 60, 75, ...

10 Find the 10th term in the sequence whose formula is:
a $m = 3n$ **b** $m = 5n$ **c** $m = 12n$

11 Write down a formula for each of these:
a 5, 7, 9, 11, 13, ...   **c** 12, 22, 32, 42, 52, ...
b 3, 8, 13, 18, 23, ...   **d** 10, 17, 24, 31, 38, ...

12 Work out the 3rd, 4th, 5th and 6th terms for each sequence:
a $s = 3n + 1$ **b** $s = 5n - 2$ **c** $s = 7n + 5$

13 **a** Write the pattern of shapes as a number sequence.
b Use a sequence diagram to work out the formula.

1 The diagram shows an equilateral triangle.
The triangle is rotated 180° anticlockwise about O.

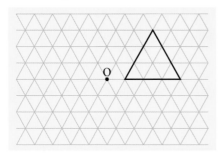

  a Copy the diagram onto triangular paper.
  b Draw the new position of the triangle on your diagram.

2 George has scored an average of 12 runs in the last four cricket matches.
  a What is his total number of runs in all four matches?
  b His mean score must be 15 or more for him to be picked for the school team.
    How many runs must he make in the next match to get into the school team?

3 The diagram shows the plan of the inside of a bus. The bus has 32 seats.
  a 24 passengers get on the bus.
    What fraction of the seats are used?
    Give your answer in its lowest terms.
  b Two more similar buses come along.
    One has 12 passengers.
    The other has 15 passengers.
    What fraction of the seats are used on each bus?
    Give your answers in their lowest terms.
  c Work out the total of the fractions in parts **a** and **b**.

4 Use a sequence diagram to work out the formula for the sequence
    5, 8, 11, 14 …

MINT SAUCE
WINGWALKERS
CLUB

1 **a** Write down the co-ordinates of A, B and C.
   b Copy the diagram.
       Reflect the shape in the *x* axis.
   c Write down the co-ordinates of point B after it has been reflected.

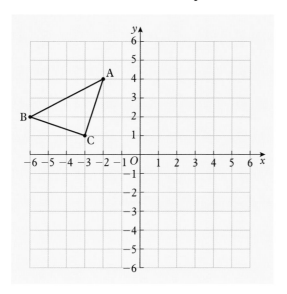

2 **a** Copy the diagram in question **1** again.
   b Rotate the triangle through 90° anticlockwise about (0, 0).
       Draw the triangle in its new position.

3 These are the number of interviews attended by a group of students
    before they got a job:

   8   12   3   7   10   13   2   6   1   8

    Find: **a** the mean   **b** the mode   **c** the median.

4 A local police station records the number of emergency calls it receives
    each day for 4 weeks.
    The table shows the data.

Number of calls	2	3	4	5	6	7	8
Number of days	2	6	1	8	3	4	4

Write down the modal number of calls.

5 Write each of these diagrams as:
(1) a top heavy fraction
(2) a whole number and a fraction

a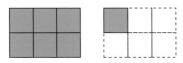

b

6 Work these out. Cancel the fraction in the answer if you can.

a $\frac{3}{8} + \frac{4}{8}$ **c** $\frac{1}{4} + \frac{5}{12}$ **e** $3\frac{1}{4} + 4\frac{3}{8}$

b $\frac{7}{12} - \frac{5}{12}$ **d** $\frac{1}{2} - \frac{1}{6}$ **f** $5\frac{3}{4} - 2\frac{1}{2}$

7 Look at this sequence:

12   19   26   33

a Draw a sequence diagram.
b Find the formula for the sequence.

8 **a** Draw the next pattern in this sequence.
b Write this pattern of stars as a number sequence.
c Use a sequence diagram to work out the formula.

11

1 Measurement
Using imperial units
- length
- weight
- capacity

2 Finding probabilities
Deciding if outcomes are equally likely
Using equally likely outcomes to find
probabilities
Using data from two-way tables to find
probabilities

CORE

3 BODMAS
Putting calculations in the right order
Using BODMAS
Dealing with brackets
Solving division problems

No Steven, it does NOT stand for boring old division, multiplication, addition and subtraction.
BODMAS

4 As a percentage of ...
Making one amount a percentage of another
Making sure both amounts have the same
units

Henman
Points won on first serve 82%
Points won on second serve 43%

QUESTIONS

EXTENSION

TEST YOURSELF

1 **Measurement**

Len is looking at some old sports records from 1941.
All the lengths were measured in miles, yards, feet and inches.

These are known as **imperial units**.

Imperial system	The **imperial system** of measurement is mainly used in the UK and the USA. It uses miles, yards, feet and inches for **length**.
Length	1 foot (ft) = 12 inches (in) 1 yard (yd) = 3 feet = 36 inches 1 mile = 1760 yards

1 inch

Example

Change each of these to the new units given:
a 4 yd to feet
b 3 ft to inches
c 6 ft 3 in to inches
d $2\frac{1}{2}$ miles to yards

a There are 3 ft in every yard.
So 4 yd = 4 × 3 ft = 12 ft

b There are 12 in in every foot.
So 3 ft = 3 × 12 = 36 in.

c 6 ft = 6 × 12 = 72 in.
So 6 ft 3 in = 72 + 3 = 75 in.

d There are 1760 yd in every mile.
So $2\frac{1}{2}$ miles = $2\frac{1}{2}$ × 1760 = 4400 yd.

Exercise 11:1

1 Change each of these to inches.
Remember: There are 12 inches in every foot.

   a 3 ft   **c** 7 ft   **e** 5 ft 9 in
   b 4 ft   **d** 6 ft 3 in   **f** $6\frac{1}{2}$ ft

2 Change each of these to feet.
Remember: There are 3 ft in every yard.

   a 4 yd   **c** 4 yd 2 ft   ● **e** $4\frac{1}{2}$ yd
   b 6 yd   **d** 3 yd   ● **f** $9\frac{1}{2}$ yd

3 Change each of these to yards.
Remember: There are 1760 yd in every mile.

   a 2 miles   **c** 3 miles   ● **e** $3\frac{1}{4}$ miles
   b 5 miles   **d** $6\frac{1}{2}$ miles   ● **f** $6\frac{3}{4}$ miles

---

Example

Change each of these to the new units shown:
   a 108 in to feet
   b 12 ft to yards
   c 9680 yd to miles

   a Every 12 inches make 1 ft.
      Find how many lots of 12 inches there are in 108 inches.
      $108 \div 12 = 9$, so 108 in = 9 ft.
   b Every 3 ft make 1 yd.
      Find how many lots of 3 ft there are in 12 ft.
      $12 \div 3 = 4$, so 12 ft = 4 yd.
   c Every 1760 yd make 1 mile.
      Find how many lots of 1760 yd there are in 9680 yd.
      $9680 \div 1760 = 5.5$, so 9680 yd = $5\frac{1}{2}$ miles.

---

4 Change each of these to feet.
Remember: Every 12 inches make 1 ft.

   a 36 in   **c** 120 in   **e** 51 in
   b 84 in   **d** 102 in   **f** 81 in

5 Change each of these to yards.
Remember: Every 3 ft make 1 yd.

    a 12 ft   **c** 39 ft   **e** $46\frac{1}{2}$ ft

    b 21 ft   **d** 42 ft   ● **f** 13 ft

6 Change each of these to miles.
Remember: Every 1760 yd make 1 mile.

    a 5280 yd   **c** 7920 yd   **e** 11 000 yd

    b 8800 yd   **d** 20 240 yd   ● **f** 16 060 yd

Exercise 11:2

1 Steve lives $1\frac{1}{2}$ miles from school.
How many yards is this?

2 Steve says he is 2 yd tall!
What is his height in feet?

3 Steve's armspan is 66 in.
What is his armspan in feet?

4 Steve runs 3 miles every day.
Each stride he takes is 1 yd.
How many strides does he take on his 3 mile run?

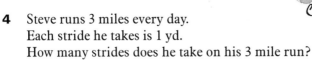

Weight	

The imperial units of **weight** are stones, pounds and ounces.

    16 ounces (oz) = 1 pound (lb)
    14 pounds   = 1 stone (st)

Example

Change each of these to the new units shown.
    a 8 st to pounds   **b** 72 oz to pounds

    a There are 14 lb in every stone.
       So 8 st = $8 \times 14 = 112$ lb.

    b Every 16 oz make 1 lb.
       Find how many lots of 16 oz there are in 72 oz.
       $72 \div 16 = 4.5$, so 72 oz = $4\frac{1}{2}$ lb.

Exercise 11:3

1 Change each of these to ounces.
Remember: There are 16 oz in every pound.
  a 3 lb   **b** 7 lb   **c** $4\frac{1}{2}$ lb   **d** 6 lb 3 oz

2 Change each of these to pounds.
Remember: There are 14 lb in every stone.
  a 3 st   **b** 8 st   **c** $9\frac{1}{2}$ st   **d** 8 st 12 lb

3 Change each of these to stones.
Remember: Every 14 lb make 1 st.
  a 98 lb   **b** 168 lb   **c** 115.5 lb   **d** 127.75 lb

4 Kathryn weighs 10 st 4 lb.
What is her weight in pounds?

5 Alan's grandmother sends him to the shops for $\frac{1}{2}$ st of potatoes.
How many pounds of potatoes should he buy?

6 Americans always give their weight in pounds.
Zak weighs 170 lb.
What is his weight in stones?

Capacity   The imperial units of **capacity** are pints, quarts and gallons.

       2 pints (pt) = 1 quart (qt)
       8 pints = 4 quarts = 1 gallon (gal)

Example   A milk churn holds 20 gal. How many pints is this?

       There are 8 pt in every gallon: $20 \times 8 = 160$.
       So 20 gal = 160 pt

Exercise 11:4

1 Alison buys 1 gal of milk.
How many pints is this?

2 An elephant drinks about 25 gal of
water each day. How many pints of
water does an elephant drink each
day?

3 An average person uses 160 pt of
water each day. How many gallons
is this?

4 Carsington reservoir in Derbyshire holds 7800 million gallons of water.
How many 1 pt bottles could you fill from the reservoir?

Converting length

Sometimes we want to swap between metric and imperial units. You
call this **converting units**.

	Conversion number
1 in is about 2.5 cm	2.5
1 ft is about 30 cm	30
1 yd is about 90 cm	90
1 mile is about 1.6 km	1.6

To change from imperial to metric **multiply** by the conversion number.
To change from metric to imperial **divide** by the conversion number.

Example   **a** Convert 4 yd to centimetres.
b Convert 56 km to miles.

a Every yard is about 90 cm.
Multiply by the conversion number.
4 yd is 4×90 cm $= 360$ cm

b There are about 1.6 km in every mile.
Divide by the conversion number.
$56 \div 1.6 = 35$, so 56 km is about 35 miles.

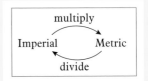

Exercise 11:5

1 Dave is 6 ft tall. What is his height in centimetres?

2 Helen lives 3 miles out of town. About how many kilometres is this?

3 A ruler is 12 in long. About how many centimetres is this?

4 The distance from Sheffield to Leeds is about 60 km.
About how many miles is this?

5 A holiday brochure says that a hotel is 300 yd from the beach.
   a Approximately what is this distance in centimetres?
   b Approximately what is this distance in metres?

6 Natalie uses the width of her thumb to make measurements on a map.
She says it is about half an inch wide.
How many centimetres is this?

		Conversion number
Converting weight	1 oz is about 30 g	30
	1 lb is about 450 g	450
	1 st is about 6.5 kg	6.5
Converting capacity	1 pt is about 600 ml	600
	1 gal is about $4\frac{1}{2}l$	4.5

7 A recipe asks for 4 oz of sugar. About how many grams is this?

8 An average person should drink 4 pt of liquid each day.
About how many millilitres is this?

9 George weighs about 9 st. About how many kilograms is this?

● **10** Mohammed weighs 154 lb. About how many kilograms is this?

Estimating

It is useful to be able to estimate lengths and weights.
You can do this in imperial or metric units.
To make good estimates, you need objects to compare things with.
These need to be familiar objects that you know the length or weight of.
Here are some examples.

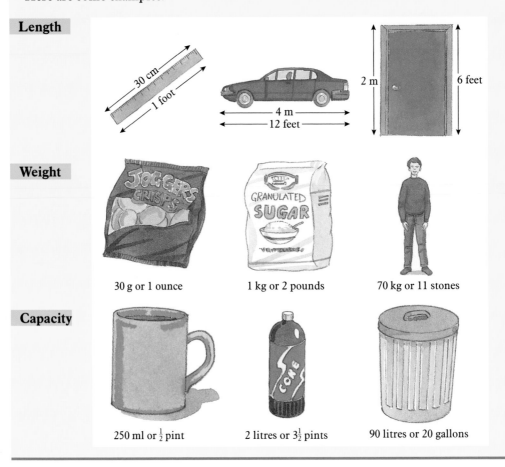

Length

30 cm / 1 foot

4 m / 12 feet

2 m / 6 feet

Weight

30 g or 1 ounce

1 kg or 2 pounds

70 kg or 11 stones

Capacity

250 ml or ½ pint

2 litres or 3½ pints

90 litres or 20 gallons

Exercise 11:6

1 Fill in Worksheet 11:1.

2 Fill in Worksheet 11:2.

3 Draw some pictures of your own.
Label them in imperial and metric units.

2 Finding probabilities

All the balls in the machine have an equal chance of being the first ball out.
The probability of one ticket matching the six numbers is 0.000 000 071 5

Equally likely

Two events are **equally likely** if they have the same chance of happening.

The chance of getting a red with this spinner is the same as the chance of getting a blue. Getting a red and getting a blue are equally likely.

You are more likely to get a red with this spinner than a blue. Getting a red and getting a blue are not equally likely with this spinner.

Exercise 11:7

1 Which of these spinners give equally likely events?

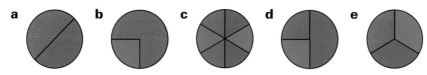

2 A person is chosen at random from a group of students.
It is equally likely that the person chosen will be male or female.
What does this tell you about the number of males and females in the group?

3 A gardener plants 200 bulbs. He knows that 1 bulb in 20 will not grow. He chooses a bulb at random. Are these two events equally likely?

'The bulb will grow.'   'The bulb will not grow.'

Explain your answer.

4 A box of chocolates contains 50% plain and 50% milk chocolates. Judy chooses a chocolate at random. Are the events 'She chooses a milk chocolate' and 'She chooses a plain chocolate' equally likely? Explain your answer.

● **5** John is given the choice of playing football or table tennis after school. Are the events 'He chooses football' and 'He chooses table tennis' equally likely? Explain your answer.

You can use equally likely events to work out probabilities.

Danny uses this spinner.
There are 5 equal sections.
They are green, red, yellow, blue and red.
Red has two sections.

Probability of an event A	The **probability of an event A** is:

$$\frac{\text{Number of ways that event A can happen}}{\text{Total number of things that can happen}}$$

The probability of getting a green $= \frac{1}{5}$ only 1 of the 5 sections is green.

The probability of getting a red $= \frac{2}{5}$ 2 of the 5 sections are red.

Exercise 11:8

1 George spins this spinner. Find the probability that the colour he gets is:
a yellow
b purple.

2 A bag holds 2 red balls and 3 blue balls.
A ball is chosen at random.
Find the probability that the ball is:
a blue **b** red.

3 John buys a box of 12 eggs. 2 of these are cracked.
John picks an egg at random from the box.
Find the probability that the egg is:
a cracked **b** not cracked.

4 This fair dice is rolled.

Find the probability of getting:
a a 2 **c** an even number **e** 3 or more
b a 6 **d** 2 or less **f** a prime number.

5 Jim asks his friends where they are spending their Easter holiday.
7 are staying at home, 5 are visiting relatives and 3 are going abroad.
Jim picks one of his friends at random.
Find the probability that, for Easter, they are:
a staying at home **c** not going abroad
b going abroad **d** not visiting relatives.

6 Joggers crisps have a special offer. 8 bags
in every 100 contain a voucher for a free
packet of crisps. Pranav buys a packet of
crisps at random. Find the probability that
his packet contains a voucher.

7 Look at these numbers: 4, 5, 7, 9, 10, 13, 15, 19, 20, 22, 27
A number is chosen from these at random.
Find the probability that the number is:
a even **d** a square number
b a multiple of 5 **e** a number greater than 10.
c a prime number

You can get data from tables to find probabilities.

Example   The table shows the type of person that took part in a survey.

	Male	Female
Child	12	15
Adult	5	8

a How many people took part in the survey?
b How many children took part in the survey?
A person is chosen at random.
Find the probability that the person is:
c a male adult
d a child.

a You add up all the numbers to find the total number of people.
　　Number of people = 12 + 15 + 5 + 8 = 40
b To find the number of children you look at the child row.
　　Number of children = 12 + 15 = 27
c 5 male adults took part in the survey.
　　The total number of people was 40.

$$\text{The probability that the person is a male adult} = \frac{5}{40}$$

d 27 children were asked. The total number of people was 40.

$$\text{The probability that the person is a child} = \frac{27}{40}$$

Exercise 11:9

1   The table gives the membership of a club.

	Male	Female
Child	14	19
Adult	46	55

a How many members does the club have?
b How many children are members?
c How many members are female?
A member is chosen at random.
Find the probability that this member is:

d a child **f** a male adult **h** a female adult
e female **g** a girl **i** male.

2 The table shows the shoe sizes of a class of 30 students.

Shoe size	3	4	5	6
Number of boys	1	3	7	5
Number of girls	2	5	6	1

A student is chosen at random from the class.
Find the probability that the student will be:
a a boy
b a girl
c a boy with shoe size 5
d a girl with shoe size 4.

3 A store sells duvet covers of different sizes and colours.
The table shows how many of each size and colour they have in stock.

	Single	Double	King size
white	5	11	3
blue	2	6	1
green	8	5	1

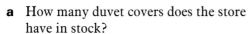

a How many duvet covers does the store have in stock?
A duvet cover is chosen at random.
Find the probability that it is:
b white
c double size
d blue king size
e green single size.

4 A machine fills bags of sugar. They should contain 2 kg of sugar.
Rosemary tests the machine by weighing 100 bags of sugar chosen at random. The table shows her results.

Weight of sugar	less than 2 kg	exactly 2 kg	more than 2 kg
Number of bags	5	64	31

Find the probability that a bag chosen at random will:
a contain exactly 2 kg
b be overweight
c be underweight
d not contain exactly 2 kg.

3 BODMAS

No Steven, it does NOT stand for boring old division, multiplication, addition and subtraction.

BODMAS

To use your calculator properly you need to know the rules of BODMAS.

Scientific calculators know the rules of BODMAS.
Basic calculators do not.

Exercise 11:10

Do these questions without a calculator.
Work out the **red** parts first.

1 **a** $3 \times 4 + 5$
$= \ldots \quad + 5$
$= \ldots$

b $3 \times 4 + 5$
$= 3 \times \ldots$
$= \ldots$

2 **a** $5 + 6 \times 3$
$= \ldots \quad \times 3$
$= \ldots$

b $5 + 6 \times 3$
$= 5 + \ldots$
$= \ldots$

3 **a** $6 + 4 \div 2$
$= \ldots \quad \div 2$
$= \ldots$

b $6 + 4 \div 2$
$= 6 + \ldots$
$= \ldots$

4 **a** $18 \div 6 - 3$
$= \ldots \quad - 3$
$= \ldots$

b $18 \div 6 - 3$
$= 18 \div \ldots$
$= \ldots$

5 Work out questions **1–4** using a scientific calculator.
Which of your two answers does the calculator get each time?
Write down either **a** or **b**.

You should have noticed that the calculator always worked out the × or the ÷ first.
This is part of the BODMAS rule.

BODMAS

First do	**B**rackets
then powers	**O**f
Next do	**D**ivision
and	**M**ultiplication
Then	**A**ddition
and	**S**ubtraction

Example

Work these out using the BODMAS rule.
a $8 + 6 × 4$ **b** $13 ÷ 2 + 6$ **c** $8 × 6 - 4$

a $8 + 6 × 4$ BOD**MA**S   × comes before +
   $= 8 + 24$
   $= 32$

b $13 ÷ 2 + 6$ BO**D**M**A**S   ÷ comes before +
   $= 6.5 + 6$
   $= 12.5$

c $8 × 6 - 4$ BOD**MA**S   × comes before −
   $= 48 - 4$
   $= 44$

Exercise 11:11

Work these out without using your calculator.

1
a $6 × 4 + 3$ **d** $15 + 7 × 3$ **g** $4.2 - 1.3 × 2$
b $8 - 8 ÷ 2$ **e** $16 ÷ 4 - 1$ **h** $5.6 ÷ 4 - 2$
c $13 - 3 ÷ 1$ **f** $100 - 10 × 10$ ● **i** $18.2 - 0.2 ÷ 0.1$

2 Hiring a car costs £30 plus £40 per day. How much does it cost for 5 days?

3 Charlotte buys an air freshener for £4.50 and 3 refills for 88 p each. How much does she pay altogether?

Brackets **always** come first. They overrule any other operation.

Example

Work these out using the BODMAS rule.

a $(8 + 4) \times 3$ **b** $14 \div (8 - 6)$ **c** $(8 + 4) \times (3 - 1)$

a $(8 + 4) \times 3$ BODMAS   ( ) comes before $\times$
    $= 12 \times 3$
    $= 36$

b $14 \div (8 - 6)$ BODMAS   ( ) comes before $\div$
    $= 14 \div 2$
    $= 7$

c $(8 + 4) \times (3 - 1)$ BODMAS   ( ) comes before $\times$
    $= 12 \times 2$
    $= 24$

Exercise 11:12

Work these out without using your calculator.

1
   a $6 \times (4 + 3)$ **d** $(15 + 7) \times 3$ **g** $(4.2 - 1.3) \times 2$
   b $(8 - 8) \div 2$ **e** $16 \div (5 - 1)$ **h** $5.6 \div (4 - 2)$
   c $(13 - 3) \div 1$ **f** $(100 - 10) \times 10$ ●   **i** $(18.2 - 0.2) \div 0.1$

2   Compare your answers to question **1** in this exercise with your answers
for question **1** in Exercise 11:11.
Are any of the answers the same?
Now compare the questions. They look very similar but the brackets
change the answers.

Powers (like squaring something) come before everything except
brackets.

Example

Work out $5 \times 6^2 - 7$ using the BODMAS rule.

    $5 \times 6^2 - 7$ BODMAS   power of then $\times$ then $-$
  $= 5 \times 36 - 7$
  $= 180 - 7$
  $= 173$

Exercise 11:13

Work these out without using your calculator.

1 **a** $6^2 \times 5$ **d** $8^2 \div 4$ **g** $(3 - 5) - 2^3$

     b $7 + 5^2$ **e** $(5^2 + 1) \div 2$ **h** $(6 + 4^2) + (7 \times 3^2)$

     c $3 + 4^2 \times 2$ **f** $4^2 + 5$ ● **i** $(18 - 3^2 \times 2) - (4^2 \div 4 - 4)$

2 A stone is dropped off the top of a cliff.

The formula for the distance it travels is $d = 5 \times t^2$.

t stands for the number of seconds it has been travelling.

Work out how far the stone has travelled after:

     a 2 s   **b** 3 s   **c** 10 s   ● **d** 12 s.

Some division problems can be written without brackets.

A calculation like $(6.3 - 2.1) \div (4.2 + 1.6)$ can be written as $\dfrac{6.3 - 2.1}{4.2 + 1.6}$

Notice that the brackets have gone.
If you use a calculator to work this out you have to put the brackets back in.

Example Work out: $\dfrac{23.7 - 5.2}{6.2 - 5.95}$

This is the same as $(23.7 - 5.2) \div (6.2 - 5.95)$
Put this into your calculator exactly as it is.
Don't forget the brackets.
The answer is 74.

Exercise 11:14

1 Work these out on your calculator.

     a $\dfrac{7.25}{3.6 + 1.4}$ **b** $\dfrac{15.3 - 7.8}{13.4 - 10.9}$ **c** $\dfrac{28.6 + 14.7}{5}$

2 Put brackets into these questions to make them correct.

     a $2 + 3 \times 4 = 20$ **c** $10 + 14 \times 6 = 144$

     b $6 - 4 \div 2 = 4$ **d** $60 \div 4 \times 5 - 2 = 1$

4   As a percentage of ...

These figures show that Henman is more likely to win a point if his first serve is in.

He is losing more than half the points when he has to play a second serve.

These figures are for the match so far. They change as the match carries on. They are worked out from the start of the match.

Henman
Points won on first serve 82%
Points won on second serve 43%

In the **first game** of a tennis match, Greg got 4 first serves in. He won 3 of these 4 points.

You can work out the percentage of points that Greg won on his first serve in this game. You need to work out 3 as a percentage of 4.

To do this:
(1) Write the numbers as a fraction.
(2) Turn the fraction into a decimal. Multiply by 100%.

For the first game:

Write 3 out of 4 as a fraction $\frac{3}{4}$

Multiply by 100% $= \frac{3}{4} \times 100\%$

Key in: $\boxed{3}$ $\boxed{\div}$ $\boxed{4}$ $\boxed{\times}$ $\boxed{1}$ $\boxed{0}$ $\boxed{0}$ $\boxed{=}$

                          $= 75\%$

So Greg has won 75% of his first serves in this game.

Exercise 11:15

1 **a** In the **third game** Greg got 5 first serves in.
          He won 4 of these 5 points.
          What percentage of points did Greg win on his first serve in this game?
     b In the **fifth game** Greg got 10 first serves in.
          He won 9 of these 10 points.
          What percentage of points did Greg win on his first serve in this game?

2 This table shows the number of first serves that Greg got in, in his next 2 service games. It also shows the number of these points that Greg won.

Game	Number of first serves in	Number of these points won
7th	8	5
9th	8	7

    a What percentage of points did Greg win on his first serve in the 7th game?
    b What percentage of points did Greg win on his first serve in the 9th game?

3 So far Greg has served for 5 games (see above).
    a How many first serves has he got in altogether?
    b How many of these points has he won?
    c What percentage of points has Greg won on his first serve so far?

4 In the whole match, Greg served 82 first serves in.
  He won 67 of these points.
    a What fraction of first serves did he win?
    b What percentage of first serves did he win?
       Write your answer to the nearest whole number.

5 In the whole match, Greg served 65 second serves in.
  He won 28 of these points.
    a What fraction of second serves did he win?
    b What percentage of second serves did he win?
       Write your answer to the nearest whole number.

You can use this method to write any number as a percentage of another number.

Example   Jill asks 200 people what their favourite breakfast cereal is.
           130 say cornflakes.
           What percentage of people in Jill's survey said cornflakes?

Write 130 as a fraction of 200. $\qquad \dfrac{130}{200}$

Multiply by 100%. $\qquad = \dfrac{130}{200} \times 100\%$

Key in: **1** **3** **0** **÷** **2** **0** **0** **×** **1** **0** **0** **=**

$$= 65\%$$

So 65% of the people in Jill's survey said cornflakes.

Exercise 11:16

1 Mrs Hamer spends £35 in Tesco's.
She spends £21 on food.
  a What fraction of the money
  does she spend on food?
  b What percentage of the money
  does she spend on food?

2 In 1 month, 60 people took their
driving test with FastPass.
45 passed first time.
  a What fraction of the people who
  took their test passed first time?
  b What percentage of the people who
  took their test passed first time?

3 John scores 24 out of 60 in a maths test.
  a Write John's mark as a fraction.
  b Work out John's percentage for the test.

4 Helen is doing a sponsored walk.
She will walk 75 miles in 4 days.
The table shows the number of miles
that she will walk each day.

Day	1	2	3	4
No. of miles	20	22	18	15

  a Write down the fraction of the walk
  that Helen will do each day.
  b Write down the percentage of the
  walk that Helen will do each day.
  Write your answers to 1 dp.

5 Gary and Samira have a meal in a restaurant.
The bill is £32.
They leave a tip of £3.
  a What fraction of the bill is the tip?
  b What percentage of the bill is the tip?
  Give your answer to 1 dp.

> You need to be careful with units.
> Both amounts must be in the same units.

Example

Work out 25 cm as a percentage of 4 m.

You need to change the metres to centimetres.

$$4 \text{ m} = 400 \text{ cm}$$

The fraction is $\frac{25}{400}$.   The percentage is $\frac{25}{400} \times 100\% = 6.25\%$

6 Find:
   a 45 cm as a percentage of 3 m
   b 60 g as a percentage of 2 kg
   c 30 min as a percentage of 2 h
   d 20 p as a percentage of £4

7 Lucy gets £6.80 pocket money.
   She spends £5.10
   a What percentage does she spend?
   Lucy has 34 p left at the end of the week.
   b What percentage of her pocket money is this?

Game – 100 pair cent

This is a game for two players.
You need a set of game cards from your teacher.
You both play the game at the same time.
Both of you pick two cards.
Write down the two numbers on your cards.
Work out what percentage the smaller number
is of the larger number.
This is your score.
Put the cards back and shuffle the cards. Now pick again.
Work out your score again.
Add this to your last score and keep your total score.
The winner is the first player to pass 100%.
You might both get there on the same turn.
If this happens the game is a draw.

| 4 | 40 |

$$\frac{4}{40} \times 100\% = 10\%$$

1 A bag holds 4 black and 6 white counters.
A counter is chosen at random. Find the probability that it is:
a black   **b** white

2 Look at these numbers: 5, 20, 25, 30, 35, 45, 70, 100
One of these numbers is chosen at random.
Find the probability that the number is:
a 70   **d** a multiple of 10
b an even number   **e** a multiple of 5
c a square number   **f** a number greater than 25

3 Pauline sells scarves of different shapes and colours.
The table shows how many of each shape and colour she has.

	Square	Rectangular
Blue	12	26
Red	7	13
Brown	20	16

a How many scarves does Pauline have?
A customer chooses a scarf at random.
Find the probability that the scarf is:
b blue and square
c red
d rectangular
e brown and rectangular

4 39 coach seats out of a total of 50 are sold.
What percentage are sold?

5 The top mark in a test is 68 out of 85.
What percentage is this?

6 Raaziya drives around the country on business.
In one week she travelled 800 miles.
The table shows how far she travelled on each day.

Day	Monday	Tuesday	Wednesday	Thursday	Friday
Miles	256	80	64	240	160

Find the percentage of the total that she travelled each day.

7 Work these out:

a 75 cm as a percentage of 3 m   **c** 150 g as a percentage of 5 kg

b 40 ml as a percentage of 3 l   **d** 7 p as a percentage of £3.50

8 Change each of these to inches.

Remember: There are 12 inches in every foot.

a 5 ft   **b** $6\frac{1}{2}$ ft   **c** 3 ft 9 in

9 Change each of these to yards.

Remember: Every 3 ft make 1 yd.

a 15 ft   **b** 45 ft   **c** $19\frac{1}{2}$ ft

10 Copy these. Fill them in.

a 1 m is just over … ft

b 1 kg is about … lb

c 1 pt is about … l

11 Copy these. Fill them in.

a 1 oz is about … g

b 1 lb is about … g

c 1 st is about … kg

12 Work these out without using your calculator.
Use the rules of BODMAS.

a $8 \times 3 + 3$ **c** $16 + 9 \times 2$ **e** $8.9 - 1.8 \times 2$

b $15 - 6 \div 2$ **d** $24 \div 5 - 3$ **f** $6.4 \div 4 - 1.5$

13 Work these out without using your calculator.
Use the rules of BODMAS.

a $(14 - 3) \div 2$ **b** $(16 + 10) \times 10$ **c** $(14.4 - 0.2) \div 0.2$

1 The number of children in each of 40 families is shown in the bar-chart.
A family is chosen at random. Find the probability that the family has:
  a 2 children
  b less than 2 children
  c more than 1 child.

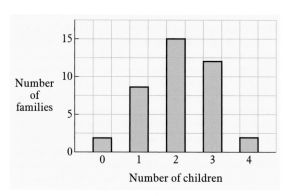

Number of families

Number of children

2 Cindy is taking part in a quiz show. So far she has won £90.
She has the choice of taking this money or opening a box.
If she opens a box she loses her £90.
There are 40 boxes containing different amounts of money.
The table shows the number of boxes with the amounts of money.
What should she do? Explain your answer.

Amount (£)	0	50	100	500
Number of boxes	10	6	14	10

3 1 litre of water weighs exactly 1 kg.
Work out the approximate weight of 1 pt of water.

4 Work these out using the rules of BODMAS.

  a $\dfrac{5.6 - 2.1}{9.1 - 5.6}$
  b $3.6 + \dfrac{5.4}{0.2}$
  c $\dfrac{5.2}{6.5} - 3.6$

5 The distance from Matlock to London is about 140 miles.
  a What distance is this in kilometres?
  b Ingrid travels from Matlock to London at 80 km per hour.
    How long will the journey take?

6 In a survey of 200 cats, 68 preferred Paws & Claws cat food.
  a What percentage of cats preferred Paws & Claws?
  b A similar survey is done with 350 cats.
    How many would you expect to prefer Paws & Claws?

1   Change each of these to the new units given.

    a 5 yd to feet

    b 36 in to feet

    c 2 lb to ounces

    d 7 gal to pints

2   **a** A bag contains 5 kg of potatoes.
        About how many pounds is this?

    b A curtain is 2 yards in length.
        (1) How many inches is this?
        (2) About how many centimetres is this?

    c A river is 56 miles long.
        About how many kilometres is this?

3   John is flying to Spain.
        He is allowed to take up to 18 kg of luggage.
        His bag weighs 42 pounds.
        Is this under 18 kg?
        Show your working.

4   Write down estimates for the amounts shown underneath each picture.

    a

        (1) Length is about … m
        (2) Length is about … yd

    c

        (1) Weight is about … kg
        (2) Weight is about … lb

    b

        (1) Capacity is about … *l*
        (2) Capacity is about … pt

    d

        (1) Weight is about … oz
        (2) Weight is about … g

5 A box contains 8 plain chocolates and 12 milk chocolates.
Aslan picks a chocolate at random.
Are the events 'He picks a plain chocolate' and 'He picks a milk chocolate' equally likely? Explain your answer.

6 Look at these numbers: 2, 3, 4, 6, 10, 18
A number is chosen from these at random.
Find the probability that the number is:

a odd

b a multiple of 6

c a triangle number

d a number less than 4

7 The table shows the favourite science of a group of pupils.

	Physics	Chemistry	Biology
Girls	7	11	12
Boys	13	8	9

a How many pupils are represented in the table?

A pupil is chosen at random. Write down the probability that this pupil is:

b a girl who prefers Physics

c a pupil who prefers Biology

d a boy who prefers Biology

e a girl

8 Work these out:

a $7 - 2 \times 3$

b $24 \div 4 + 2$

c $(7 + 5) \times 8$

d $18 - 2 \times 3^2$

9 Work these out:

a $\dfrac{53.6 - 11.8}{13.2 - 9.4}$

c $\dfrac{40^2}{16 \times 25}$

10 A company sends 950 letters in one week.
They send 703 of these by first class post.

a What fraction is sent first class?

b What percentage is sent first class?

12

CORE

1 Reading scales
Reading whole number scales
Reading decimal scales
Working out average speed

2 Grouped averages
Working out the mean from a table of data
Finding the mode from a table of data
Finding the mode for data that is in groups

3 Foreign currency
Changing £s to other currencies
Changing other currencies to £s
Using graphs to change currencies

4 Negative numbers
Using negative numbers in golf
Using negative numbers in games and puzzles
Working with negative numbers

LEADERBOARD

Player	Score
Barry Russell	–5
Andrew Mason	–2
Lloyd Beadle	–1
Roger Allnutt	0
Adrian Cheeseman	1
Andrew Lingham	3
Gary Myer	3
Jon Eves	5

QUESTIONS

EXTENSION

TEST YOURSELF

1 Reading scales

Police use signs to warn drivers that speed cameras are in use.
They do this to stop people speeding.

When a vehicle breaks the speed limit the camera takes two pictures, which show the vehicle in two positions.

Road markings are used as a scale to measure the speed of the vehicle.

Scales

A **scale** has marks on it with gaps in between. The gaps are called divisions.
You need to work out what each division stands for to be able to read the scale.

There are 5 divisions from 0 to 10 on this scale.
$5 \times 2 = 10$, so each division stands for 2 units.

The pointer is 3 divisions from the start.
$3 \times 2 = 6$
So the number shown by the pointer is 6.

Exercise 12:1

1 Write down what each division stands for in these diagrams.

a 0 ———— 12

b 16 ———— 46

c 24 ———— 74

d  0 ———— 18

e  30 ———— 70

2 Write down the numbers shown by the pointers.

a
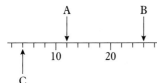

c
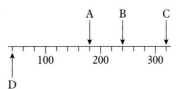

b
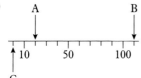

d
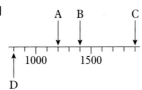

3 A computer game shows you the amount of energy that a player has left.
You start the game with a 100% energy level.
Write down the energy level of each of these players as a percentage.

a
Player A

c
Player C

b
Player B

d
Player D

Example This scale shows divisions in two different sizes.

What is the weight shown by the pointer?

Each large division stands for a weight of 250 g.
There are 10 small divisions between each large one.
Each small division stands for a weight of $250 \text{ g} \div 10 = 25 \text{ g}$

The pointer is 4 small divisions after 500 g.
So the weight is $500 \text{ g} + (4 \times 25 \text{ g})$
$= 500 \text{ g} + 100 \text{ g}$
$= 600 \text{ g}$

The weight shown by the pointer is 600 g.

4 Write down the weights shown by the pointers.

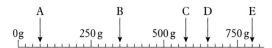

5 A measuring jug is marked with a scale in millilitres.

Some of the numbers have been rubbed off the scale.

Write down the volumes in millilitres shown by the pointers.

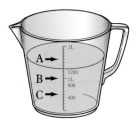

Examples **1** Each large division on this scale stands for 1 volt (V).
10 small divisions make 1 large division.
Each small division stands for $1 \div 10 = 0.1$ V
The pointer shows 1.3 V.

2 Each large division on this scale stands for 1 kg.
5 small divisions make 1 large division.
Each small division stands for $1 \div 5 = 0.2$ kg.
The pointer shows 0.8 kg.

---

6 Write down the values shown by these pointers.

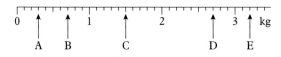

7 Write down the values shown by these pointers.

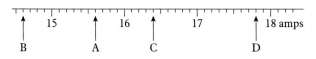

The dashboard of a sports car has lots of different dials.

8 Write down the reading shown on each of these dials.
Remember to include the units.

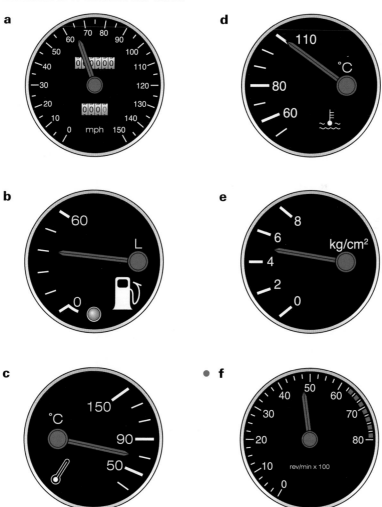

9 A car has broken the speed limit in a 40 mph area.
The speed of the car can be worked out using divisions marked on the road as a scale.
Each division stands for 9 mph.
There are 5 divisions shown for this car.

How fast was the car travelling?

Average speed	You can work out the **average speed** of an object if you know how far it has travelled and how long it has taken.

$$\text{Average speed} = \frac{\text{distance}}{\text{time}}$$

Example

Peter swam 100 m in 55 s.
What was his average speed?

The distance is in **metres** and the time is in **seconds** so his speed is in **metres** per **second** (**m/s**).

$$\text{Average speed} = \frac{100}{55} \text{ m/s} \quad \text{Key in:} \quad \boxed{1}\,\boxed{0}\,\boxed{0}\,\boxed{\div}\,\boxed{5}\,\boxed{5}\,\boxed{=}$$

$$= 1.818\,18\dots \text{ m/s}$$

Peter's average speed was 1.8 m/s to 1 dp.

Exercise 12:2

1 On sports day, Adam ran the 100 m race in 12.5 s.
What was his average speed?

2 A bobsled team completes a 1200 m course in 42 s.
Find the average speed of the sled.

3 A high-speed train called the *Bullet* runs from Tokyo to Osaka.
It can travel the 320 km route in $2\frac{1}{2}$ h. Find its average speed.

● **4** In one day the Earth travels 1 600 000 miles in orbit around the Sun.
  a Find the speed of the Earth in miles per hour.
  b Find the speed of the Earth in miles per second.

A lot of speed calculations are still done in miles per hour.
When the times are given in hours and minutes you have to change the minutes into a fraction of an hour.

Example   Write 3 hours 45 minutes in hours.

1 minute is $\frac{1}{60}$ of an hour.

This means that 45 minutes is $\frac{45}{60}$ of an hour.

Now change $\frac{45}{60}$ into a decimal.

Key in **4** **5** **÷** **6** **0** **=**

The answer is 0.75

So 3 hours 45 minutes is the same as 3.75 hours.

Exercise 12:3

1   Write each of these times in hours.
  a 2 hours 30 minutes
  b 4 hours 15 minutes
  c 3 hours 12 minutes
  d 1 hour 36 minutes
  e 3 hours 20 minutes
  f 40 minutes

2   A car travels 60 miles in 1 hour 30 minutes.
  a Write 1 hour 30 minutes in hours.
  b Work out the average speed of the car.

3   A ferry travels 32 miles across the English Channel in 1 hour 24 minutes.
  a Write 1 hour 24 minutes in hours.
  b Work out the average speed of the ferry.

4   A jet travels 800 miles in 2 hours 15 minutes.
  Work out the average speed of the jet.

5   It takes Ned 1 hour 20 minutes to walk 6 miles.
  a Write 1 hour 20 minutes in hours.
       Write your answer correct to 2 dp.
  b Work out Ned's average speed.
       Write your answer correct to 2 dp.

2 Grouped averages

Jim is the quality controller at Joggers crisps. He has to check the weight of the bags.

The average contents has to be 26 g.

Factory inspectors check that he has done his job properly.

Jim picks 30 bags from the production line. He weighs each one. He records his results in a table.

Weight (g)	Tally	Total
24					3
25						4
26	ⅢⅠ ⅢⅠ	10
27	ⅢⅠ |||	8
28	ⅢⅠ	5

Jim wants to work out the mean weight.
He needs to add up all the weights.
He adds two extra columns to his table.

Weight (g)	Tally	Total	Working	Total (g)
24	|||	3	3×24	72
25	||||	4	4×25	100
26	ⅢⅠ ⅢⅠ	10	10×26	260
27	ⅢⅠ |||	8	8×27	216
28	ⅢⅠ	5	5×28	140
Total		**30**		**788**

He has 3 bags that weigh 24 g. Their total weight is 72 g.
He has 4 bags that weigh 25 g. Their total weight is 100 g.

Jim works out all the other totals.
He adds up all the total weights: $72 + 100 + 260 + 216 + 140 = 788$ g
To find the mean weight, Jim works out $788 \div 30 = 26.266 \dots$ g

The mean weight is 26 g, to the nearest gram.
This means that the packing machine is working properly.

Exercise 12:4

1 These are Jim's results from another sample.

Weight (g)	Tally	Total
24	||	2
25	Ⅲ̶	5
26	Ⅲ̶ Ⅲ̶ ||	12
27	Ⅲ̶ |	6
28	Ⅲ̶	5
Total		**30**

  a Copy this table.
  b Add two extra columns for 'Working' and 'Total (g)'.
  c Fill in these two new columns.
  d Work out the mean weight of this sample of crisps.
  e Was the packaging machine working properly when this sample was taken? Explain your answer.

2 Another production line produces Family packets of crisps.
The weight of these bags should be 100 g.
Here are the weights of a sample of 50 bags.

Weight (g)	Tally	Total
98	Ⅲ̶ ||	7
99	Ⅲ̶ Ⅲ̶	10
100	Ⅲ̶ Ⅲ̶ |||	13
101	Ⅲ̶ Ⅲ̶ |	11
102	Ⅲ̶ ||||	9
Total		**50**

  a Copy this table.
  b Add two extra columns for 'Working' and 'Total (g)'.
  c Fill in these two new columns.
  d Work out the mean weight of this sample of crisps.
  e Was the packaging machine working properly when this sample was taken? Explain your answer.

3 Gurjeet throws a dice 100 times.
The scores he gets are shown in the table below.

Score	Number of times thrown	Working	Total
1	14		
2	17		
3	16		
4	18		
5	17		
6	18		
Total	**100**		

   a Copy this table.
   b Fill in the last two columns.
   c Work out the mean score on the dice.

4 Hayley is doing a survey into the number of
people travelling in cars.
She records the number of people in 60 cars
which pass her school.
Here are Hayley's results.

No. of people	No. of cars	Working	Total number of people
1	34		
2	12		
3	6		
4	4		
5	3		
6	1		
Total	**60**		

   a Copy this table.
   b Fill in the last two columns.
   c Work out the mean number of people in the cars.

It is easy to find the mode from a table of data.

| Mode | The **mode** is the most common or the most popular data value. It is sometimes called the **modal value**. |

Example Write down the modal weight of these packets of crisps.

Weight (g)	Tally	Total
24	||	2
25	⦀⦀	5
26	⦀⦀ ⦀⦀ ||	12
27	⦀⦀ |	6
28	⦀⦀	5

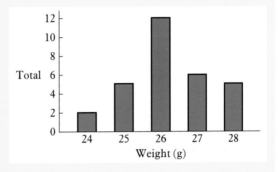

More packets weigh 26 g
than anything else.
The modal weight is 26 g.
You can also see the mode from a bar-chart.
It is always the highest bar.

Exercise 12:5

1 Here are the weights of a sample of 30 bags of Joggers crisps.

Weight (g)	Tally	Total
24	||||	4
25	⦀⦀ ⦀⦀	10
26	⦀⦀ ||||	9
27	||	2
28	⦀⦀	5

a Draw a bar-chart of this data.
b Write down the modal weight of this sample.

2 Vinny and Sarah do a dice experiment.
They throw 2 dice and record the
total score.
They do this 50 times.
Here are their results.

Score	Number of throws	Score	Number of throws
2	3	8	3
3	5	9	2
4	6	10	4
5	7	11	2
6	7	12	3
7	8		

a Draw a bar-chart of this data.
b Write down the modal score of this sample.

Modal group

You can also find the mode for grouped data. This is known as the **modal group**.

Example

This table shows the heights of 30 Year 11 students to the nearest centimetre.

Height (cm)	Number of students
130 up to 139	2
140 up to 149	5
150 up to 159	6
160 up to 169	8
170 up to 179	9

a Draw a bar-chart to show this data.
b Write down the modal group.

a

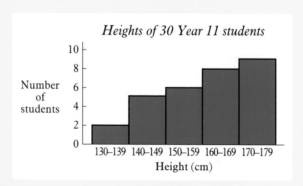

b The 170–179 cm group has the most people in it. This is the modal group.

Exercise 12:6

1 This table shows the heights of 30 Year 11 students.

Height (cm)	Number of students
130 up to 139	3
140 up to 149	6
150 up to 159	9
160 up to 169	7
170 up to 179	5

   a Draw a bar-chart to show this data.
   b Write down the modal group.

2 This table shows the amount of time 30 Year 11 students spent on their homework in one week.

Time (h)	Number of students
0–1	2
1–2	5
2–3	7
3–4	10
4–5	6

   a Draw a bar-chart to show this data.
   b Write down the modal time spent on homework.

3 50 people take part in a chocolate survey.
They record how many chocolate bars they eat in 1 month.
Here are their results.

```
12   15   16   30    8   24   28   12    9
 7   14   16   21   27   35   14    5    0
14   16   18   24   29   35   12   14   18
 1    0   19   18   14   18   17   21   28
 3    6   34   31   28   27   14   19   16
27   15   14   17    6
```

   a Tally this information in a table.
      Use groups 0–9, 10–19, 20–29, 30–39.
   b Draw a bar-chart to show this data.
   c Write down the modal group.

3   Foreign currency

When you travel abroad you need to change money from one currency to another.

The amount that you receive depends on the exchange rate.

Exchange rate

When you buy foreign currency the **exchange rate** tells you how much £1 is worth.

An exchange rate of £1 = 9.8 francs (F) means that every £1 is worth 9.8 F. £2 is worth 9.8 × 2 = 19.6 F.

Example

Juliette went to France when the exchange rate was £1 = 9.7 F. She changed £60 into francs. How much did she receive?

$$£1 = 9.7\,F$$
$$so\ \ £60 = 60 \times 9.7\,F$$
$$= 582\,F$$

Juliette received 582 F.

Exercise 12:7

1 The exchange rate for Japanese yen is £1 = 214 yen (Y).
Change these amounts into yen.

a	£70	**e**	£135
b	£450	**f**	£450
c	£85	**g**	£325
d	£180	**h**	£760

2 The exchange rate for Italian lira
is £1 = 2864 lira (L).
Change these amounts into Italian lira.
Give your answers to the nearest 100 L.
a	£35	**d**	£110
b	£80	**e**	£95
c	£235	**f**	£750

3 The exchange rate for US dollars
is £1 = $1.632
Change these amounts into US dollars.
Give your answers to 2 dp.
a	£55	**d**	£195
b	£325	**e**	£415
c	£75	**f**	£565

When shopping abroad you can use the exchange rate to work out the
price of goods in pounds.

Example A bottle of perfume costs 695 F in Paris.
The exchange rate is £1 = 9.7058 F
What is the equivalent price of the perfume in pounds?

Every 9.7058 F make £1.
Find how many lots of 9.7059 there are in 695.
    695 ÷ 9.7058 = 71.606…

The price is £71.61 to the nearest penny.

4 The exchange rate for German marks (DM)
is £1 = 2.9105 DM.
Find the missing values in this table.
Give your answers to the nearest penny.

Item	Cost in marks	Cost in pounds
television	1749	
jeans	57	
trainers	89.99	
car	22 950	

5 Emily went on a touring holiday in Europe.
She found the same CD on sale in each country.
  a Copy the table.
  b Fill in the missing values.
  c Where should she have bought the CD?

Country	Cost of CD	Exchange rate	Cost in pounds
Germany	32.95 DM	£1 = 2.9105 DM	
France	119.49 F	£1 = 9.7058 F	
Italy	34 400 L	£1 = 2864 L	
Spain	2189 pta	£1 = 243.25 pta	

You can use a conversion graph to change from one currency to another.

Example
To change **20 DM** into
US dollars:
Start at 20 on the marks
scale.
Go up to the graph and
across to the dollars scale.
  20 DM = $11

To change **$17** into marks:
Start from the dollars scale.
Go across to the graph and
down to the marks scale.
  $17 = 29 DM

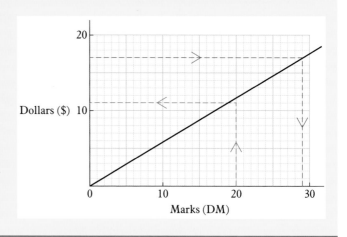

6 Copy these.
Use the conversion
graph to fill in the
missing values.
  a 2000 L = ... Y
  b 1600 L = ... Y
  c 2400 L = ... Y
  d 90 Y = ... L
  e 240 Y = ... L
  f 165 Y = ... L

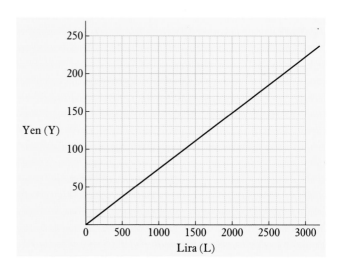

4 Negative numbers

LEADERBOARD

Player	Score
Barry Russell	−5
Andrew Mason	−2
Lloyd Beadle	−1
Roger Allnutt	0
Adrian Cheeseman	1
Andrew Lingham	3
Gary Myer	3
Jon Eves	5

This is the score board from a golf tournament.
The players in the lead are 'under par'.

This means that they have taken fewer shots than the standard set for the course.
Barry Russell is in the lead and is 5 shots under par. His score is shown as −5.

Golf uses lots of positive and negative numbers in its scoring.
Each hole has a par. This is the standard number of shots a good player should take to play the hole.
If you play the hole in less shots you are under par.
There are special names for some scores. They are shown in this table.

Albatross	3 under par	−3
Eagle	2 under par	−2
Birdie	1 under par	−1
Par		0
Bogey	1 over par	+1
Double	2 over par	+2

Example

A golf player plays the first five holes on a golf course.
She gets: Birdie, Birdie, Par, Par, Eagle.
What is her score?

Birdie	Birdie	Par	Par	Eagle
−1	−1	0	0	−2

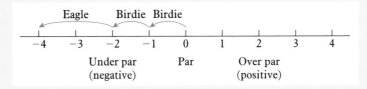

Her score is −4.

Exercise 12:8

W 1 Work out the scores of each of these players.
Use the scales on Worksheet 12:1 to help you.

Player	Hole 1	Hole 2	Hole 3	Hole 4	Hole 5
Duncan	Par	Par	Birdie	Par	Birdie
Fiona	Par	Birdie	Eagle	Par	Par
Lindsey	Eagle	Par	Par	Eagle	Birdie
Steve	Par	Par	Eagle	Birdie	Birdie

2 Work out the scores of each of these players.

Player	Hole 1	Hole 2	Hole 3	Hole 4	Hole 5
Anne	Bogey	Par	Eagle	Birdie	Par
Mohammed	Par	Bogey	Par	Birdie	Eagle
James	Bogey	Bogey	Birdie	Eagle	Eagle
Alison	Albatross	Eagle	Eagle	Birdie	Par

3 At the end of a round of golf, 5 friends had the following scores:

  Duncan   −4
  Alison   −5
  Dave   +2
  Pardeep   −2
  Tim   −3

a Who won the game?
b Who came last?
c Write the names and scores in order. Start with the winner.

4 In a tournament, competitors play 4 rounds of golf.
This table shows the scores for each round for the players.

Player	Round 1	Round 2	Round 3	Round 4	Total
Gary	−3	−4	−4	−1	
Tony	−4	−2	+1	+2	
Tiger	−4	−5	−1	+2	
Alan	−2	+2	+1	+3	
Brian	−3	−3	−3	+1	

a Copy the table. Fill in the Total column.
b Write the names and scores in order. Start with the winner.

Now that you have used negative numbers, you need to be able to write down calculations.

Example

Work out: **a** $-3 + 4$ **b** $4 - 6$ **c** $-3 + -5$

You can use a scale to help you.
Start at the first number. For +, move to the right.
For −, move to the left.

a

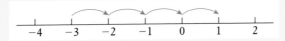

Start at -3 and move 4 to the right. $-3 + 4 = 1$

b

Start at 4 and move 6 to the left. $4 - 6 = -2$

c

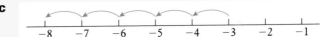

Adding a negative number is the same as taking away.
Start at -3 and move 5 to the left. $-3 + -5 = -8$

Exercise 12:9

1 Work these out. Use the scales on Worksheet 12:2 to help you.

a $3 - 5$	**g** $-6 - 3$	**m** $-12 + -12$
b $12 - 15$	**h** $-5 - 7$	**n** $-15 + -9$
c $6 - 15$	**i** $-6 - 8$	**o** $-15 + 32$
d $-4 + 6$	**j** $8 + -6$	**p** $-17 - 25$
e $-5 + 16$	**k** $15 + -7$	**q** $62 - 100$
f $-3 + 9$	**l** $16 + -16$	**r** $-100 - 100$

2 Copy this table of temperatures. Fill it in.

Starting temperature (°C)	Change	Warmer or colder?	New temperature (°C)
-15	$+6$		
4	-10		
-12	$+7$		
-6	$+6$		
-4	-5		

3 Copy each of these patterns.
Write down the next three numbers in each pattern.
  a 6, 4, 2, 0, −2, ..., ..., ...
  b 0, −3, −6, ..., ..., ...
  c 10, 5, 0, ..., ..., ...
  d −5, −8, −11, ..., ..., ...
  e 7, 4, 1, ..., ..., ...
  f −25, −20, −15, ..., ..., ...

4 Copy these pairs of numbers.
Put a circle around the *bigger* number.
  a 6   −4
  b −3   −5
  c −6   −4
  d −7   −8
  e 10   −24
  f −32   −35

5 *A negative maze*
  a Look at this maze.

−7	3	−6	4	Out
2	−2	7	−2	
7	−1	2	0	
−3	−4	2	−4	
In				

Move only up, down or across.
You must *not* move diagonally.

You can only visit each square *once*.

Start at 'In' and finish at 'Out'.

  b Read the rules next to the maze.
Your aim is to get the smallest total you can.
Try different routes through the maze, using copies of the maze on
Worksheet 12:3.

These are the scores given by 4 judges at an ice-skating contest.

If you add up the scores you get:
$$8 + 5 + 3 + -2 = 14$$

The judge who gave the negative score was taken out.
The total is now: $8 + 5 + 3 = 16$
It has gone up.

Taking away the negative score makes the total go up.
It is the same in maths calculations.
Taking away a negative number is the same as adding.

Example

Work out   **a** $3 - -6$ **b** $-5 - -2$ **c** $-4 - -10$

a Taking away -6 is the same as adding 6.
$$3 - -6 = 3 + 6 = 9$$

b Taking away -2 is the same as adding 2.
$$-5 - -2 = -5 + 2 = -3$$
Another way of looking at it is:

−1	−1	−1
−1	−1	−1
−1	−1	−1
−1	−1	
−1	−1	

Start with   Take away =   Leaves
-5 -2 -3

c Taking away -10 is the same as adding 10.
$$-4 - -10 = -4 + 10 = 6$$

Exercise 12:10

1 Work these out:

  a $5 - -7$ **c** $2 - -2$ **e** $-3 - -6$
  b $3 - -5$ **d** $5 - -5$ **f** $-6 - -10$

2 Work these out:

a $-6 - -7$ **c** $6 - 9$ **e** $-7 - 7$
b $-5 - -5$ **d** $6 - -9$ **f** $-35 - -25$

3 Look through these calculations.

(1) $6 + -5 = 1$
(2) $6 - 5 = 1$
(3) $6 - -2 = -8$
(4) $-3 - -5 = -8$
(5) $-4 - 4 = -8$
(6) $-6 - -9 = -3$

a Write down the numbers of the calculations that you think are wrong.
b Work out the correct answers to the ones that are wrong.

4 Copy down these questions.
Fill in the missing numbers.

a $4 - \ldots = 7$
b $7 - \ldots = 13$
c $-6 + \ldots = -11$
d $\ldots - -7 = 12$
e $\ldots - -8 = 20$
f $\ldots - -9 = 0$

5 These are magic squares.
The diagonal lines, rows and columns always add up to the same total.
Copy the magic squares. Fill them in.

a

-1		-3
	0	2
3		1

b

	5	-9
	-3	
3		

c

-6		
-11	-4	-9

1 Write down the numbers shown by the pointers.

a

A   B   C

90   120

b

A B   C

1000   2000

2 Members of the local youth club are trying to raise money to buy equipment.
Their target figure is £10 000.
The chart shows their progress since January.

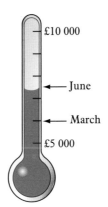

a How much had been raised by the end of March?
b How much had they raised by the end of June?
c How much more do they need now?

3 **a** Chris drove from London to Manchester in 4 hours.
The distance is 184 miles.
What was his average speed?
b Paul drove the same distance in 3 hours 20 minutes.
What was Paul's average speed?

4 Mandeep is doing a survey into the number of people travelling in cars.
She records the number of people in 50 cars which pass her school.

Number of people	Number of cars	Working	Total
1	27		
2	8		
3	4		
4	6		
5	4		
6	1		
Total	**50**		

a Copy the table.
b Fill in the last two columns.
c Work out the mean number of people in the cars.

5 The exchange rate for French francs is £1 = 9.7058 F.
Change these amounts into French francs. Give your answers to 2 dp.

    a £95   **c** £610   **e** £750
    b £140   **d** £245   **f** £2300

6 Copy these.
Use the conversion
graph to find the
missing values.

    a $80 = ... L
    b $125 = ... L
    c $140 = ... L
    d 50 000 L = $...
    e 150 000 L = $...
    f 280 000 L = $...

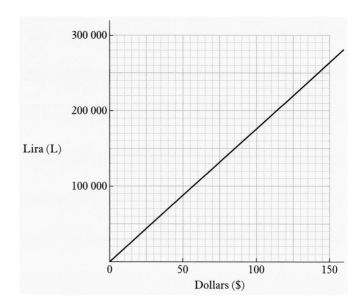

7 Temperatures are recorded in towns around Britain each day.
These are some of the temperatures for one day in January.

Aberdeen	−7 °C	Orkney	−8 °C
London	1 °C	Sheffield	−5 °C
Bristol	−2 °C	Exeter	3 °C

Write these temperatures in order.
Start with the smallest.

8 Write down the next three numbers in each of these patterns.

    a −12, −10, −8, ..., ..., ...
    b 6, 4, 2, ..., ..., ...
    c −10, −7, ..., ..., ...

9 Copy these. Fill in the gaps.

    a $6 - ... = -3$
    b $8 - ... = 10$
    c $-3 + ... = 4$
    d $-5 - ... = -9$
    e $-8 - ... = -1$
    f $... + -3 = 11$

1   The stopwatch shows the time that
    Barbara took to run 100 m.
    Write down the time in seconds
    to 1 dp.

2   **a** Peter drives 9 miles to work. Today, the journey took 15 min.
        What was his average speed in miles per hour?
    b Barbara took $1\frac{1}{2}$ h to drive between 2 service stations on the
        motorway.
        Her average speed was 60 mph.
        What is the distance between the service stations?

3   This table shows the amount of time 30 Year 11 students spent watching
    television one Saturday.

Time (h)	Number of students
0–1	4
1–2	8
2–3	15
3–4	2
4–5	1

    a Draw a bar-chart to show this data.
    b Write down the modal time spent watching TV.

4   Steve changed £150 into German marks when the exchange rate was
    £1 = 2.9105 DM. He didn't spend the money. He changed the marks
    back to pounds when the exchange rate was £1 = 3.1253 DM.
    How much did he lose?

5   Complete this magic square.

−4		−6
	−3	−1
0		−2

1   Write down the numbers shown by the pointers.

a

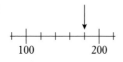

b

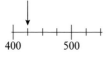

c

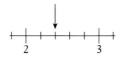

2   **a**   Arvind drives 102 miles in 3 hours.
Find his average speed in miles/hour.

     b   Donna walks 5 kilometres in 1 hour 40 minutes.
Find her average speed in km/hour.

3   Tom keeps a record of the number of planes that pass over his house each day. He does this for 15 days.

Number of planes	Number of days	Working	Total
3	4		
4	2		
5	6		
6	3		
Total			

Copy the table.
Work out the mean number of planes using the table.

4   Ken is opening an account in a Belgian bank.
The account is in euros. £1 = €1.67

     a   Ken transfers £1500 to his new account.
How many euros is this?

     b   The new total in the account is 3841 euros.
How much is this in £s?

5   Work these out:

     a $2 - 9$ **c** $10 + -7$

     b $-5 - 3$ **d** $8 - -6$

13

CORE

1 Area
Finding areas by counting squares
Estimating areas of irregular shapes

2 Range
Finding the range
Finding the mean
Using the range to compare two sets of data

GREECE - ATHENS						
	Jan	Feb	Mar	Apr	May	Jun
Daily Max temp °F	55	57	60	68	73	78
Daily Min temp °F	44	44	46	52	61	68
Average daily sunshine hours	4	5	5.5	7.5	9	10.5

3 Check it out!
Rounding to 1 sf to give an estimate
Solving problems and checking by estimating
Using inverses to check answers
Estimating square roots

4 Substitution
Substituting whole numbers into formulas
Substituting decimals and fractions into formulas

QUESTIONS

EXTENSION

TEST YOURSELF

1 Area

The Amazon is in South America.
It is one of the world's largest forests.
It covers an area of 2 million square miles.
Every year a large part of the forest is destroyed.

Area

The **area** of a shape is the amount of space it covers.
Area is measured using squares.

This square has sides of 1 cm.
The area of the square is 1 square centimetre.
You write this as 1 cm^2.

This rectangle covers 8 squares.
Area of the rectangle = 8 cm^2

Exercise 13:1

For each of the rectangles in questions **1–4**, write down:
a the number of squares
b the area of the rectangle in square centimetres.

1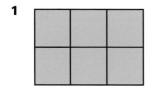

2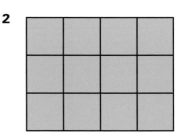

3

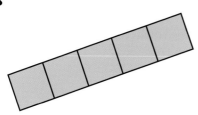

4

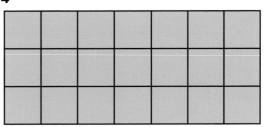

Write down the area of each of the shapes in questions **5–8**.

5

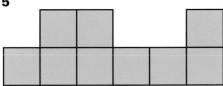

7

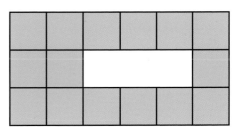

6

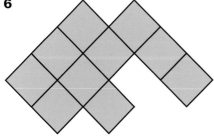

8

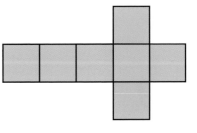

Some areas are more difficult to work out.
This is a drawing of the county of Cheshire.
You can only estimate the area of the drawing.
To estimate the area of a shape:
(1) Count the whole squares.
   There are 5 of these.
(2) Count the squares which have more than
   half inside the shape.
   There are 4 of these.
(3) Add the two numbers together.
   $5 + 4 = 9$

An estimate of the area is 9 squares.

Exercise 13:2

Estimate the area of each country by counting squares.

1

3

2

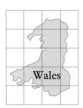

4

5 Write down the country in the British Isles with:
  a the largest area
  b the smallest area.

6 The squares in this diagram have sides that represent 1 km.
The area of 1 square represents 1 km².

The green area is a forest.
Estimate the area of the forest:
a in squares
b in square kilometres.

Look at this shape.
It is drawn on 1 cm squared paper.

It covers 6 whole squares and 4 half squares.
The 4 halves make 2 whole ones.
The area of the shape is $6 + 2 = 8$ cm²

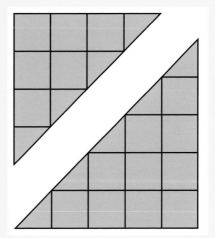

This shape covers 10 whole squares and 5 half squares.
The 5 halves make $2\frac{1}{2}$ whole ones.
The area of the shape is $10 + 2\frac{1}{2} = 12\frac{1}{2}$ cm²

Exercise 13:3

1 Work out the area of each of these shapes in square centimetres.
They are drawn on 1 cm² paper.

a

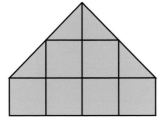

b

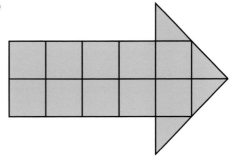

c

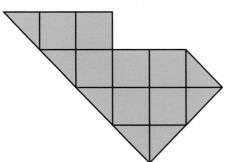

d

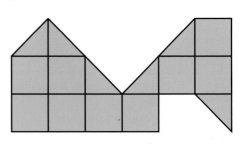

2 Samuel has drawn a plan of his wall on squared paper.
Each square has sides of 1 cm.
Find the area, in square centimetres, of:
a the poster
b the no smoking sign
c the flag.

Estimate the area, in square centimetres of:
d the dartboard
e the mirror.

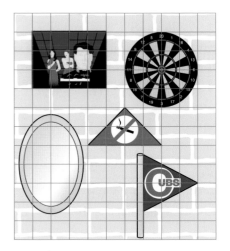

3 Kerry has drawn a floor plan of the village hall.
Part of the floor is marked out as a stage.
Each square has sides of 1 m.
a Write down the area of 1 square.
b Find the area of the whole floor.
c Estimate the area of the stage.

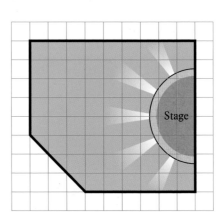

2 Range

GREECE - ATHENS						
	Jan	Feb	Mar	Apr	May	Jun
Daily Max temp °F	55	57	60	68	73	78
Daily Min temp °F	44	44	46	52	61	68
Average daily sunshine hours	4	5	5.5	7.5	9	10.5

John is planning a holiday in Greece for March.
He needs to know what clothes to pack.
This chart is from the holiday brochure.
It gives the maximum and minimum temperatures for the first six months of the year.
John can see that the temperature ranges from 46 °F to 60 °F in March.

Range

The **range** of a set of data is the biggest value take away the smallest value.

$$\text{The range of temperatures for March} = 60 - 46$$
$$= 14\,°F$$

The range must always be a single number.

Exercise 13:4

1 Use the chart at the top of the page to answer this question.
   a Write down the range of temperatures for each month.
   b Which month has the largest range?

2 The table shows the day and night temperatures for five days in February.

	Monday	Tuesday	Wednesday	Thursday	Friday
Day	11 °C	9 °C	6 °C	3 °C	5 °C
Night	3 °C	0 °C	−4 °C	−3 °C	1 °C

   a Write down the range of temperatures for each day.
   b Which day has the smallest range?

333

3 Rachel has six hamsters.
These are their ages in months:

   5   8   3   12   15   4

Write down the range of their ages.

4 These are the ages of six people in a quiz team:

   38   61   30   55   52   48

   a Find the range of their ages.
   b They are in a competition with another quiz team.
   The range of ages in this team is 5 years.
   What can you say about the ages of the people in this team?

5 Jack is looking at data on the heights of pupils at his school.
He has worked out the range of heights for his class and also for the whole school.
The two values he gets are 89 cm and 31 cm.
Which of these is the range for the whole school?
Explain your answer.

6 Tina is entering the village competition to grow the longest cucumber.
She needs to decide which type of cucumber to grow.
Tina grew two types of seed last year: Growmor and Morcrop.
She measured the lengths of all the cucumbers grown.
Growmor seed gave a range of 14 cm.
The smallest Growmor cucumber was 30 cm.
Morcrop gave a range of 39 cm.
The smallest Morcrop cucumber was 20 cm.
Which type of seed should Tina use to try and grow the longest cucumber?
Explain your answer.

The range can help you to compare two sets of data.
Two sets of data may have the same mean but their ranges can be different.

These are the marks scored by Alan and Robert in their last six tests:

Alan	15	6	12	17	8	14
Robert	11	14	13	13	9	12

Alan's mean is $\dfrac{15 + 6 + 12 + 17 + 8 + 14}{6} = 12$

His range is $\quad 17 - 6 = 11$ marks

Robert's mean is $\dfrac{11 + 14 + 13 + 13 + 9 + 12}{6} = 12$

His range is $\quad 14 - 9 = 5$ marks

Their means are the same but Alan's range is much bigger.
The bigger range shows that Alan has scored both some high marks and some low marks.

Robert's smaller range shows that his marks are always about the same.
The smaller range shows that he is more consistent.

Exercise 13:5

1 The table gives the marks that Angela and Hannah got in the summer exams.

	English	Maths	Science	Art	History	French	Geography
Angela	65	71	59	47	52	39	55
Hannah	52	49	56	61	54	50	51

a Find the range of Angela's marks.
b Find the range of Hannah's marks.
c Who is more consistent in the exams?
Explain your answer.

2 Pupils take a test in each subject every half term in Luke's school.

These are Luke's results for one year.

English	56	49	62	63	58	52
Maths	61	54	63	59	60	57
Science	68	70	53	61	73	48
History	75	56	63	72	69	59
French	71	67	58	45	60	42
Geography	85	72	88	79	73	80
Art	72	76	37	83	79	75

a Find the range for each subject.

b Write down the subject where Luke is most consistent.

c Write down Luke's best subject.

3 The table shows the runs scored by Tom and Ian in their last six innings.

Tom	53	67	40	54	21	95
Ian	51	60	67	56	50	60

a Find Tom's mean score.

b Find Ian's mean score.

c Find the range of Tom's scores.

d Find the range of Ian's scores.

e Comment on the differences between the two players.

f Which of the two players would you choose if you needed 55 runs to win the match?
Explain your answer.

4 Lisa and Ria are trying to get into the school quiz team.

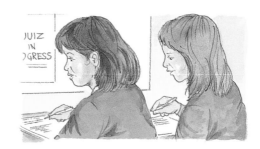

These are their scores in the last seven practice quizzes.

Lisa	70	76	80	78	71	73	77
Ria	85	66	69	79	76	91	59

a Find Lisa's mean score.
b Find Ria's mean score.
c Find the range of Lisa's scores.
d Find the range of Ria's scores.
e Who would you choose for the quiz team? Explain your answer.

5 Jenny is doing a survey on the number of people in each car passing the school gate.

These are her results for the period 8.30 a.m. to 9.00 a.m.

Number of people per car	1	2	3	4	5	6
Number of cars	12	26	31	19	3	13

a What is the range of the number of people per car?

These are her results for the period 10.30 a.m. to 11.00 a.m.

Number of people per car	1	2	3	4
Number of cars	33	15	5	1

b What is the new range of the number of people per car?
c Give a reason for the difference between the two ranges.

3 Check it out!

This is a picture of the Channel Tunnel.

The original estimate of the cost was £3 billion.
The tunnel actually cost £10 billion.

Some estimates are very difficult to do!

You often work things out on a calculator.
One way to check your answers is by estimating.
To get an estimate, round each number to one significant figure.

You saw this at the end of Unit 7.

Example   Work out: 3.9×5.2

Calculation:　**3** . **9** × **5** . **2** =　Answer: 20.28

Estimate:　3.9 is 4 to 1 sf
5.2 is 5 to 1 sf
3.9×5.2 is about $4 \times 5 = 20$
20 is near to 20.28
So the answer is probably right.

Exercise 13:6

1 Work these out. Write down the answer and an estimate for each one.

　a 2.7×6.1　**c** 3.4×7.7　**e** 5.5×4.5　**g** 1.9×7.32
　b 6.3×2.7　**d** 3×8.5　**f** 5×7.1　**h** 0.7×4.42

Example   Work out: 67×32

Calculation:　**6** **7** × **3** **2** =　Answer: 2144

Estimate:　67 is 70 to 1 sf
32 is 30 to 1 sf
67×32 is about $70 \times 30 = 2100$
2100 is near to 2144
So the answer is probably right.

---

2 Work these out. Write down the answer and an estimate for each one.

a 46×24 **c** 28×71 **e** 55×22 **g** 30×71

b 37×13 **d** 57×32 **f** 60×57 **h** 80×65

Example   Work out: 232×286

Calculation: **2** **3** **2** **×** **2** **8** **6** **=**   Answer: 66 352

Estimate: 232 is 200 to 1 sf
286 is 300 to 1 sf
232×286 is about $200 \times 300 = 60\,000$
60 000 is near to 66 352
So the answer is probably right.

---

3 Work these out. Write down the answer and an estimate for each one.

a 324×176 **c** 568×212 **e** 398×623 **g** 200×652

b 273×513 **d** 434×897 **f** 300×525 **h** 800×233

4 Work these out. Write down the answer and an estimate for each one.

a 7.3×26 **c** 3.9×58 **e** 21×34.9 **g** 1.9×435

b 325×58 **d** 153×76.8 **f** 26.1×24 **h** 20.89×338

5 Work these out. Write down the answer and an estimate for each one.

a $6.2 + 2.6$ **d** $2.4 + 7.5$ **g** $5.7 - 2.1$ **j** $8.923 - 2.731$

b $31.5 \div 4.2$ **e** $18 \div 4.8$ **h** $234 + 567$ **k** $315 - 189$

c $437 - 95$ **f** $4.8 \div 1.2$ **i** $248 \div 49.6$ **l** $499.2 \div 9.6$

6 Seema is doing this calculation.
She writes the answer 4599.
How can you tell that this is wrong
without doing the calculation?

87×47

Exercise 13:7

When you answer questions you should always do an estimate to check your answer. In this exercise:

a Work out the answers using a calculator. You may have to round your answer.
b Write down an estimate to check that each answer is about right.

1 The height of a television stand is 53 cm.
The television is 65 cm high.
How high are the television and the stand together?

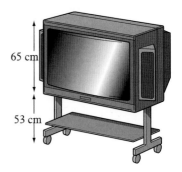

2 The height of a fridge-freezer is 210 cm.
The freezer is 57 cm high.
How high is the fridge?

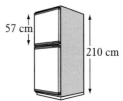

3 Phil buys 13 packets of crisps.
Each packet costs 23 p.
How much does he pay?

4 A bag of fun-size Mars Bars costs £2.19
There are 18 bars in the bag.
How much is 1 fun-size bar?

5 A bag of chicken pieces costs £4.89
The bag contains 8 pieces of chicken.
What is the cost of 1 piece?

6 A chart CD costs £13.99
Find the cost of 11 chart CDs.

● **7** First-class stamps cost 27 p. Sharon has £8.
How many stamps can Sharon buy?

• **8** 164 pupils go on a school trip by coach.
Each coach can carry 46 pupils.
How many coaches are used?

You know that you can use an estimate to check an answer.

You can also check your answers by reversing the problem.
This is a different way of checking.

Example Work out: 234 × 45

Calculation: **2** **3** **4** **×** **4** **5** **=** Answer: 10 530

The reverse of multiplying is dividing.
So you can check your answer by
doing a division question.
You can work out 10 530 ÷ 45
You should get 234.

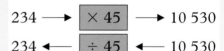

234 ⟶ × 45 ⟶ 10 530
234 ⟵ ÷ 45 ⟵ 10 530

Exercise 13:8

For each question:
a Work out the answer on your calculator.
b Write down a question that you can use to check your answer.

1 24 × 367

2 45 × 167

3 365 × 289

4 683 × 289

5 23 × 28.98

6 39.39 × 1987

7 573 + 2998

8 387 ÷ 3

9 19 875 − 2876

Estimating square roots

You need to round the numbers to the nearest square number.

Square numbers 1, 4, 9, 16, 25, … are the **square numbers**.
1 × 1 2 × 2 3 × 3 4 × 4 5 × 5

Example Estimate $\sqrt{23}$
$\sqrt{23} \approx \sqrt{25} = 5$

If you round $\sqrt{23}$ to one significant figure you get $\sqrt{20}$
This is just as difficult to work out as the question!

Exercise 13:9

For each question:
a Estimate the answer.
b Work out the answer using your calculator.
Give your calculator answer to three significant figures.

1 $\sqrt{34}$ **3** $\sqrt{5}$ **5** $\sqrt{46}$ **7** $\sqrt{103}$

2 $\sqrt{14}$ **4** $\sqrt{10}$ **6** $\sqrt{67}$ **8** $\sqrt{120}$

Sometimes you have to estimate in stages.

Example

Estimate the answer to:

$$\sqrt{\frac{23 \times 489}{35}}$$

To do this start by rounding the numbers to one significant figure.

$$\approx \sqrt{\frac{20 \times 500}{40}}$$

Work this out:

$$= \sqrt{\frac{10\,000}{40}}$$

$$= \sqrt{250}$$

Now look for the nearest square number
Square root to get the answer

$$\approx \sqrt{256}$$
$$= 16$$

Exercise 13:10

For each question:
a Estimate the answer.
b Work out the answer using your calculator.
Give your calculator answer to three significant figures.

1 $\sqrt{\dfrac{197 \times 24}{38}}$ **3** $\sqrt{\dfrac{212 \times 64}{310}}$ **5** $\sqrt{\dfrac{48 \times 68}{47}}$ **7** $\sqrt{\dfrac{189 \times 97}{22 \times 564}}$

2 $\sqrt{\dfrac{134 \times 46}{52}}$ **4** $\sqrt{\dfrac{86 \times 47}{153}}$ **6** $\sqrt{\dfrac{184 \times 43}{82 \times 31}}$ **8** $\sqrt{\dfrac{16^2 \times 13}{167}}$

4 Substitution

You see substitutions a lot in sport.

When a manager makes a substitution, one player on the pitch is replaced with another player.

Substitution works the same way in maths.

When you substitute in maths you usually replace a letter with a number.

You have seen substitution before in Units 5, 8 and 10. This shows you how important it is. The substitution that you have seen before has involved whole numbers as in the following example.

Example Find the value of $2a + 6$ when $a = 5$.

To do this question you need to replace the a with the number 5.

You need to remember that $2a$ means $2 \times a$.

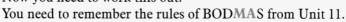

So you get: $2 \times 5 + 6$
You have replaced the a with 5.
Now you need to work this out.
You need to remember the rules of BODMAS from Unit 11.
You do the **M**ultiply before the **A**dd.

$$2 \times 5 + 6 = 10 + 6$$
$$= 16$$

So the value of $2a + 6$ when $a = 5$ is 16.

Exercise 13:11

1 Find the value of $2a + 6$ when a is:
   a 3 　　　　**b** 4 　　　　**c** 6 　　　　**d** 10

2 Find the value of $3a + 2$ when a is:
   a 2 　　　　**b** 3 　　　　**c** 5 　　　　**d** 6

3 Find the value of $4a + 1$ when a is:
   a 1   **b** 2   **c** 3   **d** 5

4 Find the value of $5a + 3$ when a is:
   a 2   **b** 3   **c** 5   **d** 6

5 Find the value of $2a - 3$ when a is:
   a 3   **b** 4   **c** 6   **d** 10

6 Find the value of $4a - 5$ when a is:
   a 4   **b** 5   **c** 7   **d** 9

7 Find the value of $3b + 2$ when b is:
   a 1   **b** 3   **c** 8   **d** 10

8 Find the value of $3c - 5$ when c is:
   a 2   **b** 3   **c** 5   **d** 8

9 Work out the value of each of these expressions when $p = 3$
   a $2p + 3$ **c** $3p + 4$ **e** $5 + 3p$ **g** $14 - p$
   b $2p - 1$ **d** $5p - 2$ **f** $30 - 4p$ ● **h** $43 + p^2$

Now you can use negative numbers too.
The method is just the same.

Example   Find the value of $2a + 4$ when $a = -3$.

To do this question you need to
replace the a with the number -3.

$2a$ means $2 \times a$

So you get: $2 \times -3 + 4$
You have replaced the a with -3.
Now you work this out.
   $2 \times -3 + 4 = -6 + 4$
              $= -2$
So when $a = -3$, the value of $2a + 4$ is -2.

Exercise 13:12

1 Find the value of $2a + 6$ when a is:

   a -1 **b** -2 **c** -3 **d** -4

2 Find the value of $3b + 2$ when b is:

   a -2 **b** -3 **c** -5 **d** -6

3 Find the value of $4r + 1$ when r is:

   a -1 **b** -2 **c** -3 **d** -5

4 Find the value of $5q + 3$ when q is:

   a -2 **b** -3 **c** -5 **d** -6

5 Find the value of $2a - 3$ when a is:

   a -1 **b** -4 **c** -6 **d** -10

6 Find the value of $3c - 5$ when c is:

   a -2 **b** -3 **c** -5 **d** -8

7 Work out the value of each of these expressions when $p = -2$

   a $2p + 3$ **c** $3p + 4$ **e** $5 + 3p$ ● **g** $14 - p$

   b $2p - 1$ **d** $5p - 2$ ● **f** $30 - 4p$ ● **h** $43 + p^2$

You can also use decimals.

Example $P = 3s - 4$

Find the value of P when $s = 2.5$

To do this question you need to replace the s with the number 2.5

$3s$ means $3 \times s$

So you get: $3 \times 2.5 - 4$
You have replaced the s with 2.5
Now you work this out.
    $3 \times 2.5 - 4 = 7.5 - 4$
                  $= 3.5$
So when $s = 2.5$, the value of P is 3.5

Exercise 13:13

1 $P = 2a + 6$ Find the value of P when a is:
   a 3.5   **b** 2.5   **c** 4.5   **d** 5.5

2 $Q = 3b + 2$ Find the value of Q when b is:
   a 4.5   **b** 3.5   **c** 5.5   **d** 6.5

3 $G = 4c + 1$ Find the value of G when c is:
   a 0.25   **b** 2.25   **c** 3.25   **d** 5.25

4 $T = 5s + 3$ Find the value of T when s is:
   a 0.2   **b** 3.2   **c** 5.6   **d** 6.4

5 $r = 2a - 3$ Find the value of r when a is:
   a 3.3   **b** 4.7   **c** 6.2   **d** 10.3

6 $j = 2g + 3$ Find the value of j when g is:
   a 1.3   **b** 2.6   **c** 3.7   **d** 8.4

7 $k = 2d - 5$ Find the value of k when d is:
   a 3.1   **b** 5.8   **c** 12.2   **d** 23.1

8 $w = 3m + 1$ Find the value of w when m is:
   a -1.3 **b** -3.7 **c** -4.2 **d** -5.3

9 Work out the value of each of these expressions when $p = -3.2$
   a $2p + 3$ **c** $3p + 4$ **e** $5 + 3p$ **g** $14 - p$
   b $2p - 1$ **d** $5p - 2$ **f** $30 - 4p$ ● **h** $43 + p^2$

You can also use fractions.
You can also have more complicated equations.
The method is still exactly the same.

Example $T = 3r^2 - 7$

Find the value of T when $r = \frac{1}{3}$.

To do this question you need to
replace the r with the number $\frac{1}{3}$.

You need to remember that $3r^2$
means $3 \times r \times r$.

So you get: $3 \times \frac{1}{3} \times \frac{1}{3} - 7$
You have replaced the r with $\frac{1}{3}$.
Now you work this out.

Key in:

$$3 \times \frac{1}{3} \times \frac{1}{3} - 7 = \frac{1}{3} - 7$$

$$= -6\frac{2}{3}$$

So when $r = \frac{1}{3}$, the value of T is $-6\frac{2}{3}$.

---

10 $F = 4a - 3$ Find the value of F when a is:

   a $\frac{1}{2}$ **b** $\frac{1}{4}$ **c** $1\frac{1}{2}$ **d** $2\frac{1}{4}$

11 $s = 3b + 2$ Find the value of s when b is:

   a $\frac{1}{3}$ **b** $\frac{2}{3}$ **c** $2\frac{1}{3}$ **d** $3\frac{1}{3}$

12 $y = 4c + 5$ Find the value of y when c is:

   a $\frac{1}{2}$ **b** $\frac{1}{3}$ **c** $\frac{1}{5}$ **d** $2\frac{1}{3}$

13 $r = 4h - 5$ Find the value of r when h is:

   a $\frac{1}{2}$ **b** $\frac{1}{3}$ **c** $\frac{1}{5}$ **d** $2\frac{1}{3}$

14 $y = 3x^2 + 2$ Find the value of y when x is:

   a $\frac{1}{2}$ **b** $\frac{1}{3}$ **c** $\frac{1}{5}$ **d** $\frac{1}{6}$

15 $q = 2p^2 + 4$ Find the value of q when p is:

   a $\frac{1}{2}$ **b** $\frac{1}{4}$ **c** $2\frac{1}{5}$ **d** $3\frac{1}{6}$

1 Write down the area of each of these shapes.
Each square represents 1 cm².

a   **b**   **c**

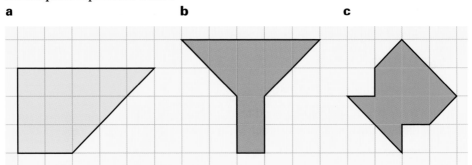

2 Estimate the area of each of these shapes.
They are drawn on 1 cm squared paper.

a   **b**   **c**

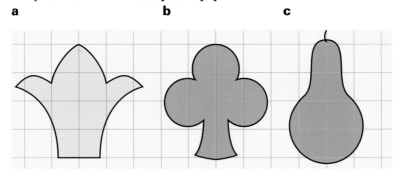

3 The weights of bags of seed should be 500 g.
Sally has two machines to fill the bags.
She tests each machine by weighing a sample of 8 bags of seed.
These are her results.

Machine A	498	501	505	500	521	500	503	510
Machine B	506	510	500	498	507	505	508	500

a Find the range for each machine.
b Which machine is more consistent?
Explain your answer.

4 Work these out. Write down the answer and an estimate for each one.
  a $2.3 + 5.1 + 7.8$ **c** $12.2 - 4.9$ **e** 2.8×41 **g** $36 \div 9.1$
  b $457 + 326$ **d** $792 - 309$ **f** 672×10.4 **h** $892 \div 20.3$

5 Jessica and Sylvester are estimating the answers to an exam question.
  a Jessica says that 31×21 is about 600.
    Show how she did this estimate.
  b Sylvester says that $3380 \div 49$ is about 60.
    Show how he did this estimate.

6 Joe is working at his local supermarket.
  The supermarket sells about 8200 cans of beans each week.
  The cans are packed in boxes. Each box contains 42 cans.
  Joe's boss asks him how many boxes they need each week.
  Show how Joe can give his boss a quick estimate.

7 For each part:
  (1) Work out the answer on a calculator.
  (2) Write down a calculation that you can use to check your answer.
  a 23×562 **b** $8298 + 564$ **c** $684 \div 4$ **d** $28\,973 - 7629$

8 For each part:
  (1) Estimate the answer.
  (2) Work out the answer using a calculator.
    Give your answer to three significant figures.

  a $\dfrac{279 \times 84}{24}$ **b** $\sqrt{79}$ **c** $\sqrt{\dfrac{7 \times 834}{222}}$ **d** $\sqrt{\dfrac{8 \times 812}{328}}$

9 **a** This is a simple formula for changing from degrees Celsius to
    degrees Fahrenheit:

$$F = 2C + 30$$

  Find the value of F when C is:

  (1) 5   (2) 100   (3) -20 (4) -40 (5) 0

  b This is the most accurate formula for changing from degrees Celsius
    to degrees Fahrenheit:

$$F = \frac{9}{5}C + 32$$

  Find the value of F when C is:

  (1) 5   (2) 100   (3) -20 (4) -40 (5) 0

1 **a** Write down the area of
this rectangle.
   b Write down the perimeter
of the rectangle.

You should notice that the
answers to parts **a** and **b**
are equal.

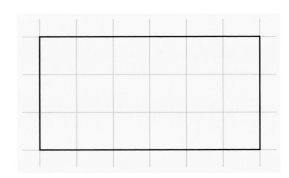

   c Find three other rectangles
that have the same area and
perimeter.
A square is a special kind of rectangle, so a square is one possible
answer.

2 The range of the heights of some plants is 30 cm.
The smallest plant is 64 cm high.
A new plant is included and the range increases to 40 cm.
How big is the new plant? There are two possible answers.

3 Indira is using the formula: $s = \dfrac{d \times n}{k}$

She knows that $d = 293.25$, $n = 9.8711$ and $k = 588.6942$
   a Substitute the numbers into the formula.
   b Work out the exact value of s using your calculator.
Give your answer to three significant figures.
   c Write down the values of d, n and k that Indira could use to work out
an estimate of s.
   d Estimate the value of s.

4 **a** Use your calculator to work out the value of:

$$\sqrt{\dfrac{6.982^2 \times 38.719}{8197 + 7774 - 5186}}$$

Give your answer to three significant figures.
You will need to use the rules of BODMAS.
   b Estimate the value of the expression.
Show all your working.

5 David is using the formula $v = u + at$ in his physics lesson.
   a In one experiment he finds that $u = 40$, $a = -5$ and $t = 4$.
Use the formula to find v.
   b In another experiment he finds that $v = 130$, $a = 10$ and $t = 9$.
Use the formula to find u.

1 Work out the area of each of these shapes.
Give your answers in square centimetres.
Each square represents 1 cm².

a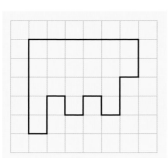

b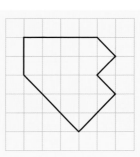

c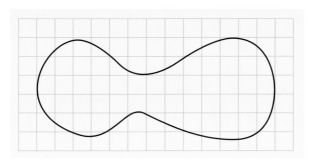

2 This is a scale drawing of an island.
Each square represents an area of 30 square miles.
Estimate the area of the island.

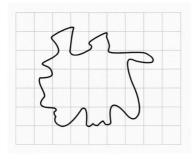

3 Julia and Norma each recorded their scores in their last 8 rounds of golf.
These are Norma's scores: 53, 47, 60, 59, 62, 49, 58, 60
   a Find the range of Norma's scores.
   b The range of Julia's scores is 7.
   Use the ranges to compare the two golfers.

4 The table shows the range of temperatures and the maximum temperature for two cities during March.

City	Chester	Eilat
Range of temperatures	13°C	9°C
Maximum temperature	15°C	26°C

Use the information given in the table to compare the temperatures in the two cities.

5 Estimate an answer for each of these.
Show clearly how you get your estimate.

a $\dfrac{102 - 57}{19.35}$

c $\sqrt{\dfrac{5.83 \times 6.7}{2.95}}$

b $\sqrt{78}$

6 Find the value of $4d - 3$ when d is:
a 5
b 12
c -8
d 3.5

7 $y = 2x^2 + 13$
Find the value of y when x is:
a 6
b 11
c -5
d -1

8 The perimeter of a rectangle is found by using the formula

$$P = 2(l + b)$$

Find the value of P when $l = 13$ and $b = 9$.

14

1 Measuring shapes

Finding the area of a rectangle
Finding the area of a triangle
Finding the area of a parallelogram
Finding the area of more complicated shapes
Finding the surface area of a solid
Converting between units of area

2 Fractions

Finding a fraction of an amount
Multiplying fractions
Dividing fractions

CORE

3 Misleading graphs

Changing the vertical scale
Making pictograms misleading
Using diagrams without a scale

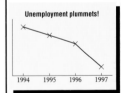

Unemployment plummets!

1994   1995   1996   1997

4 Ratio

Writing down simple ratios
Using ratios to compare objects
Simplifying ratios
Dividing into two parts
Dividing into more than two parts

QUESTIONS

EXTENSION

TEST YOURSELF

1   **Measuring shapes**

The Pentagon in Arlington, USA, is the office building with the largest ground floor area in the world.

29 000 people work in the Pentagon.

There are 7748 windows to be cleaned. Can you estimate the total area of windows to be cleaned?

Finding the area of a rectangle

You have counted squares to find the area of a rectangle.
There is a quicker method using the formula:

> Area of a rectangle = length × width

The area of this rectangle = 9 × 7 cm²
                   = 63 cm²

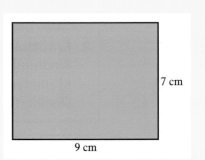

Exercise 14:1

1   Find the area of these rectangles.
Make sure you use the correct units in your answer.

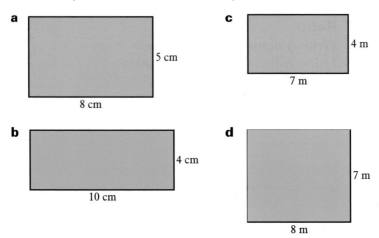

a   5 cm, 8 cm

b   4 cm, 10 cm

c   4 m, 7 m

d   7 m, 8 m

2 Find the area of a rectangle with these measurements.
   a length = 12 cm; width = 8 cm
   b length = 30 m; width = 15 m
   c length = 8.5 cm; width = 11 cm

3 Find the area of each of these squares.

a  5 cm
5 cm

b 2 cm

c
7 m

4 Find the area of a square with side:
   a 6 cm
   b 12 m
   c 8 km

5 Both of these rectangles have an area of 120 cm².
   a Find the length of this rectangle.

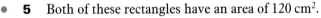
10 cm

   b Find the width of this rectangle.

15 cm

Finding the area of a triangle

Look at the triangle.
You can draw a rectangle around it.

The **length** of the rectangle is the **base** of the triangle.
The **width** of the rectangle is the **height** of the triangle.
The area of the rectangle = length × width
$$= \text{base} \times \text{height}$$

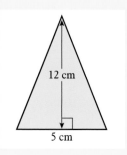

The triangle is half the area of the rectangle.
The area of the triangle = area of the rectangle ÷ 2
$$= (\text{base} \times \text{height}) \div 2$$

Examples **1** The area of this triangle = (5 × 12) ÷ 2
$$= 60 \div 2$$
$$= 30 \text{ cm}^2$$

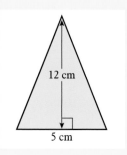

2 This triangle is upside down.
The height must be at right angles to the base.
The area of this triangle = (7 × 8) ÷ 2
$$= 56 \div 2$$
$$= 28 \text{ cm}^2$$

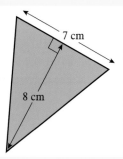

Exercise 14:2

1 Find the area of each of these triangles:

a

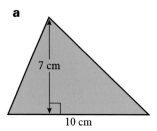

7 cm

10 cm

b

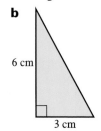

6 cm

3 cm

c

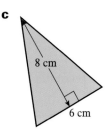

8 cm

6 cm

The triangles in questions **2–5** are drawn on 1 cm squared paper.
For each triangle:
a Write down the base.
b Write down the height.
c Work out the area.

2

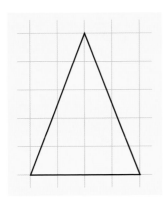

4

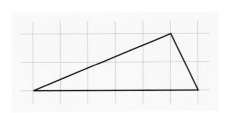

3

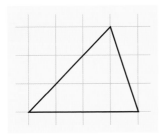

5

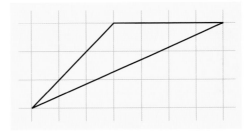

6 Natasha has designed this flag.
  a Find the area of the red triangle.
  b Find the area of the blue triangle.
  c Find the total area of the two triangles.
  d Find the total area of the flag.
  e Use your answers to parts **c** and **d** to work out the area of the white section.

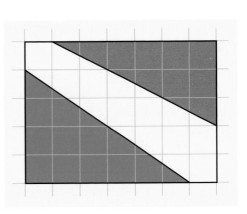

Finding the area of a parallelogram

This is a parallelogram.

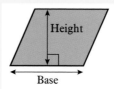

You can change a parallelogram into a rectangle by moving a triangle like this:

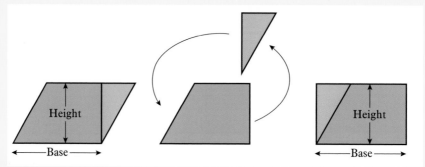

This shows that the area of a parallelogram is the same as the area of a rectangle with the same base and height.

Area of a parallelogram	**Area of a parallelogram** = base × height

Example   Find the area of this parallelogram.

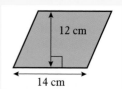

Area = base × height
= 14 × 12
= 168 cm²

Exercise 14:3

Find the area of each of these parallelograms.

1   8 m, 9 m

2   15.8 m, 3.2 m

3   4.7 mm, 12.7 mm

4   62 cm, 94 cm

Finding the areas of more complicated shapes

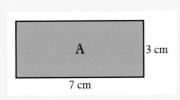

Area of rectangle A is 7 × 3
$$= 21 \text{ cm}^2$$

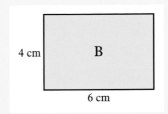

Area of rectangle B is 6 × 4
$$= 24 \text{ cm}^2$$

The two rectangles are
joined together.
The dashed line shows the join.

Area of new shape:

= area of A + area of B
= 21 + 24
= 45 cm²

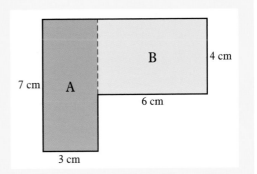

Exercise 14:4

1 Two rectangles have been joined to
make this shape.
  a Find the area of C.
  b Find the area of D.
  c Find the total area of the shape.

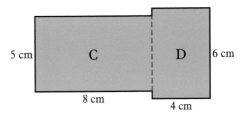

2 Find the total area of each of these shapes.

  a

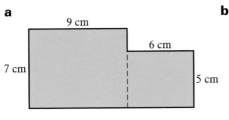

  b

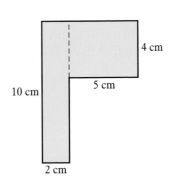

c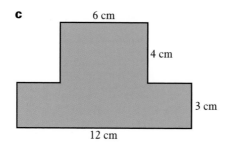

6 cm

4 cm

3 cm

12 cm

d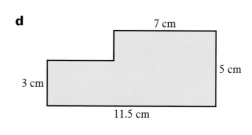

7 cm

5 cm

3 cm

11.5 cm

3 A rectangle and a triangle have been joined to make this shape.
  a Find the area of the rectangle.
  b Find the area of the triangle.
  c Find the total area of the shape.

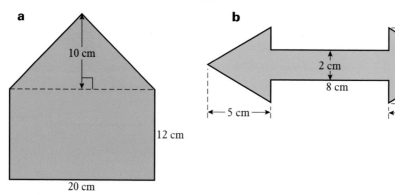

5 cm ← 8 cm

6 cm

4 Find the area of each of these shapes.

a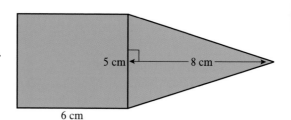

10 cm

12 cm

20 cm

b

2 cm

8 cm

5 cm

5 cm

5 cm

5 This door has 3 glass panels.
  a Find the total area of the glass panels.
  b Find the area of the whole door.
  c Use your answers to parts **a** and **b** to find the area of wood in the door.

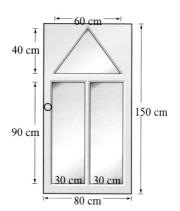

60 cm

40 cm

150 cm

90 cm

30 cm 30 cm

80 cm

6 This shape is made from a rectangle and two triangles.
  a Find the area of rectangle A.
  b Find the area of triangle B.
  c Find the area of triangle C.
  d Find the total area of the shape.

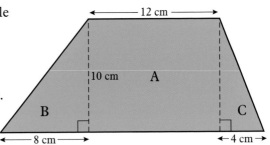

The shape in question **6** is called a trapezium. It has one pair of parallel sides. There is a formula for finding the area of a trapezium.

You need to be told the lengths of the two parallel sides, a and b.
You also need the distance between the parallel sides. This is the height h.

The area of a parallelogram is

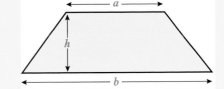

$$\frac{1}{2}(a + b)h$$

You do not have to learn this formula! It will be given to you on your exam paper. It is the **only** formula that you will be given in your exam.

---

7 Copy this. Fill it in.

Area of trapezium $= \dfrac{1}{2}(6 + 8)4$

$$= \frac{1}{2} \times \ldots \times 4$$

$$= 7 \times 4$$

$$= \ldots \text{ cm}^2$$

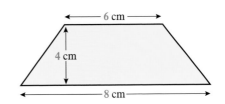

8 Find the area of each trapezium.

  a

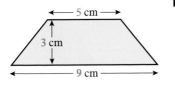

  b

  c

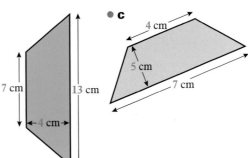

Finding the surface area of a solid

A simple way to do this is to sketch the net.
Then you will not miss any faces.

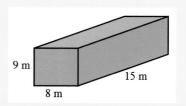

9 m
15 m
8 m

To find the surface area of a solid:
(1) Sketch the net.
(2) Work out the areas of the different faces.
(3) Find the total of all the areas.

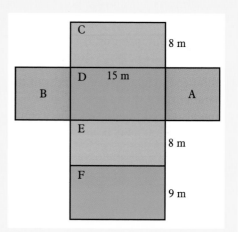

C
8 m
D   15 m
B
A
E
8 m
F
9 m

In this cuboid, there are 3 pairs of faces
the same size.
They are **A** and **B**, **C** and **E** and **D** and **F**.

Area of rectangles **A** and **B** $= 2 \times 8 \times 9$ $= 144 \text{ m}^2$
Area of rectangles **C** and **E** $= 2 \times 15 \times 8$ $= 240 \text{ m}^2$
Area of rectangles **D** and **F** $= 2 \times 15 \times 9$ $= \underline{270 \text{ m}^2}$
Total surface area $= \underline{\underline{654 \text{ m}^2}}$

Exercise 14:5

Work out the surface areas of the solids in questions **1–3**.

1

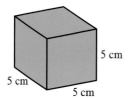

5 cm
5 cm
5 cm

3 This is a square-based pyramid.
All of the triangular sides are the
same size.

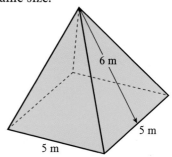

6 m
5 m
5 m

2

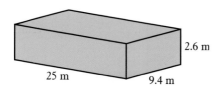

2.6 m
25 m
9.4 m

This is a square millimetre.

This is a square centimetre.

There are 10 mm in every 1 cm.
So the square centimetre
   is   10 mm across
   and 10 mm down.
So there are $10 \times 10 = 100$ mm² in 1 cm².

A square metre is too big to draw here!
This is a diagram of one.
There are 100 cm in every 1 m.
So the square metre
   is   100 cm across
   and 100 cm down.
So there are $100 \times 100 = 10\,000$ cm² in 1 m².

There are 1000 m in every 1 km.
So there are $1000 \times 1000 = 1\,000\,000$ m² in 1 km².

This diagram shows you how to convert square units.

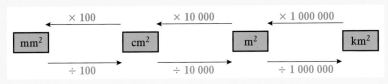

Exercise 14:6

1 Draw a square 2 cm by 2 cm. Find the area in square millimetres.

2 Change each of these areas into square centimetres.
    a 2 m²   **c** 12 m²   **e** 0.43 m²   **g** 128 mm²   **i** 2050 mm²
    b 8 m²   **d** 0.9 m²   **f** 400 mm²   **h** 672 mm²   **j** 25 mm²

3 Change each of these areas into square metres.
    a 40 000 cm²   **b** 7900 cm²   **c** 0.4 km²   **d** 8.95 km²

4 Change each of these areas into square kilometres.
    a 10 000 m²   **b** 7 500 000 m²   **c** 4 230 000 m²   **d** 8 161 000 m²

2   Fractions

Alf is a chef.

He often deals with fractions.

If he is using a recipe that is designed for 4 people he has to be able to work out fractions of amounts to make a meal for a different number of people.

A recipe for 4 people tells Alf to use 240 g flour.
He wants to know how much flour to use for 3 people.

He writes 3 as a fraction of 4 to get $\frac{3}{4}$.

Then he works out $\frac{3}{4} \times 240$ g.

He works out $\frac{1}{4}$ first. $240 \div 4 = 60$

Then he multiplies by 3. $60 \times 3 = 180$ g

So he needs 180 g of flour for 3 people.

Exercise 14:7

1   The amounts given are needed in recipes for meals for 4 people.
Work out the amounts you need for 3 people.
    a   360 g of flour   **c**   8 g of salt   **e**   4 eggs
    b   600 ml of milk   **d**   500 g of butter   **f**   460 g of sugar

---

You can use a calculator to work out the amounts.
This is very useful when the answer needs to be left as a fraction.

Example   A recipe for 6 people needs 200 g of flour.
How much flour would you need for 5 people?

You need to work out $\frac{5}{6} \times 200$ g.

Key in   **5**   **aᵇ/c**   **6**   **×**   **2**   **0**   **0**   **=**

to get this display $166 \; r \, 2 \, r \, 3$ or $166 \, \lrcorner \, 2 \, \lrcorner \, 3$

This means $166\frac{2}{3}$ g.

This is the exact answer.

You would not try to measure out exactly $166\frac{2}{3}$.

You would probably measure 167 grams to the nearest gram.

---

2 The amounts given are needed in recipes for meals for 6 people.
Work out the amounts you need for 5 people.

    a 400 g of flour   **c** 1 g of salt   **e** 350 g of water
    b 700 ml of milk   **d** 310 g of butter   **f** 440 g of sugar

3 Look at your answers to question **2**.
These amounts would be very difficult to measure.
How much would you actually use in each part?

Alf is using half a carton of soup.

A carton is a quarter of a pack.
Alf wants to know what fraction of the pack he is using.
On the diagram you can see that half of a quarter is an eighth.
So Alf is using one eighth of a pack.

You can also see this by multiplying the fractions $\frac{1}{2} \times \frac{1}{4} = \frac{1}{8}$

You get $1 \times 1 = 1$ on the top
and $2 \times 4 = 8$ on the bottom.
You can multiply other fractions together like this.

Example   Work these out.

    a $\frac{1}{4} \times \frac{1}{3}$ **b** $\frac{2}{5}$ of $\frac{1}{7}$ **c** $\frac{1}{7} \times 5$

    a $\frac{1}{4} \times \frac{1}{3} = \frac{1 \times 1}{4 \times 3} = \frac{1}{12}$

    b $\frac{2}{5}$ of $\frac{1}{7} = \frac{2 \times 1}{5 \times 7} = \frac{2}{35}$ of tells you to multiply

    c $\frac{1}{7} \times 5 = \frac{1}{7} \times \frac{5}{1}$ write the whole number 5 as $\frac{5}{1}$

          $= \frac{1 \times 5}{7 \times 1} = \frac{5}{7}$ then multiply like before.

Exercise 14:8

1 Work these out.

   a $\frac{1}{3} \times \frac{1}{5}$ **c** $\frac{1}{2} \times \frac{1}{3}$ **e** $\frac{1}{3} \times \frac{1}{3}$ **g** $\frac{1}{5} \times 4$

   b $\frac{1}{5} \times \frac{1}{2}$ **d** $\frac{1}{5} \times \frac{1}{6}$ **f** $\frac{1}{4} \times 3$ **h** $\frac{1}{7} \times 6$

2 Work these out.

   a $\frac{3}{4} \times \frac{1}{2}$ **c** $\frac{3}{4} \times \frac{1}{7}$ **e** $\frac{3}{8} \times \frac{1}{4}$ **g** $\frac{3}{5} \times \frac{1}{3}$

   b $\frac{2}{5} \times \frac{1}{3}$ **d** $\frac{4}{7} \times \frac{1}{5}$ **f** $\frac{2}{5} \times \frac{1}{4}$ **h** $\frac{4}{7} \times \frac{1}{2}$

3 **a** Work out 20×4.
    b Multiply your answer to **a** by $\frac{1}{4}$.
    c What do you notice about your answer to **b**?

4 Write down the answer to each of these questions.

   a $18 \times 4 \times \frac{1}{4}$ **c** $120 \times 3 \times \frac{1}{3}$ **e** $11 \times 20 \times \frac{1}{20}$ **g** $\frac{1}{5} \times 6 \times \frac{1}{6}$

   b $17 \times 5 \times \frac{1}{5}$ **d** $20 \times 12 \times \frac{1}{12}$ **f** $\frac{1}{3} \times 4 \times \frac{1}{4}$ **h** $\frac{1}{12} \times 14 \times \frac{1}{14}$

Alf has $\frac{1}{2}$ a carton of concentrated tomato paste.

He wants to use this to make 3 pizzas.

He wants to divide the $\frac{1}{2}$ into three equal parts.

Each part is $\frac{1}{6}$ of the whole carton.

So $\frac{1}{2} \div 3 = \frac{1}{6}$

You can do this more quickly by multiplying the denominator of the fraction by the number that you are dividing by to get your answer.

This is the same as doing $\frac{1}{2} \div 3 = \frac{1}{2} \times \frac{1}{3} = \frac{1}{6}$.

---

5 Work these out.

   a $\frac{1}{4} \div 5$ **c** $\frac{1}{4} \div 6$ **e** $\frac{1}{8} \div 5$ **g** $\frac{1}{8} \div 8$

   b $\frac{1}{3} \div 4$ **d** $\frac{1}{6} \div 3$ **f** $\frac{1}{7} \div 7$ **h** $\frac{1}{12} \div 6$

3 Misleading graphs

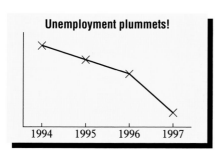

Unemployment plummets!

1994 1995 1996 1997

This graph shows that the number of people that are unemployed has fallen very sharply. Or does it?

It has no scale or labels.
Every 1 cm on the graph could stand for 1 person or 10 000 people

It makes a big difference!

When you are reading a statistical diagram, you should look at it very carefully. You should read the scale and not just go on first impressions.

This section shows how some people use diagrams to give a false impression. Look out for this type of diagram in adverts and on political broadcasts.

Weldham Motors sell second-hand cars. The Sales Manager is looking at the sales figures for the first 3 months of the year.

Month	Jan	Feb	Mar
Cars sold	65	72	79

She wants to make the sales look good.
She decides to draw some bar-charts of the figures.

All three bar-charts show the same information but the vertical scales are different. Look at the scales very carefully.

On the chart on the left, it looks as if the number of cars sold is hardly changing. The chart on the right makes the sales figures look as if they are increasing very sharply.

Exercise 14:9

1 Here are the sales figures for Weldham Motors for the second 3 months of the year.

Month	Apr	May	June
Cars sold	76	72	65

    a Draw a bar-chart to show these figures.
       Draw your vertical axis from 0 to 100.
    b Draw another bar-chart of the same figures.
       This time, draw your vertical axis from 60 to 80.
    c You will have noticed that the sales are falling.
       If you were the Sales Manager, which graph would you use for this period? Explain your answer.

2 Bill owns an ice-cream van.
He is about to retire and wants to sell his van.
He draws a bar-chart to show his profits.
He wants to show potential buyers how well he is doing.
Here is the bar-chart that Bill drew.

    a Copy this table.
       Fill in the rest of Bill's profits.

Year	1994	1995	1996	1997
Profit (£)	8000			

    b Draw another chart.
       Draw a vertical scale from £7000 to £10 000
    c Which chart do you think Bill should use? Explain your answer.

3 This table shows the percentage of people in different countries who own a TV.

Country	Austria	Denmark	Germany	Netherlands
Percentage with a TV	48	53	55	49

a Imagine that you live in Germany.
You want to make your country look wealthier than all of the others.
Draw a bar-chart with a scale that will help you to make your point.

b Now imagine you live in Austria.
You want to make your country look as wealthy as possible.
Draw a bar-chart with a scale that will help you to make your point.

You can change other types of diagram to make your point.
Pictograms can be drawn out of scale.
You can even draw diagrams without a scale at all!

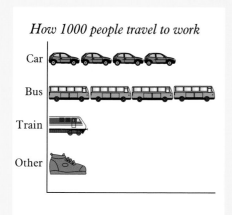

How 1000 people travel to work

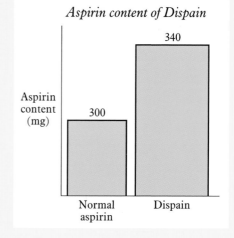

Aspirin content of Dispain

This pictogram is misleading

The symbols are all different sizes. There is no key to say what each symbol stands for.

This bar-chart is misleading.

The bars are not drawn to scale. There is 13% more aspirin in Dispain than normal aspirin. The Dispain bar is 250% of the area of the other bar!

Exercise 14:10

1 1000 people were asked how they travel to work.
The results are shown in this table.

Method	Car	Bus	Train	Walk
Number of people	300	200	150	350

a Draw a pictogram to show these results.
Make sure that all the symbols are the same size and that it has a key.
b The bus companies want to show that they are doing well.
Draw a pictogram that they might use.
You are allowed to bend the rules!

2 This computer advert compares the speed of computer processors.

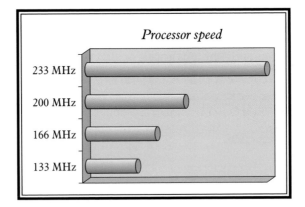

a Explain what is wrong with this diagram.
b Why has the advertiser chosen to use this type of diagram?

3 This diagram was used in an advert for Woodhouse Tea.

The second box is 4 times as high, 4 times as wide and 4 times the length of the first box.

The sales in 1998 were 4 times more than 5 years ago.

Explain why this diagram is misleading.

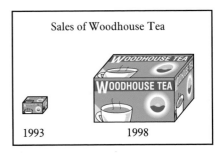

4 Ratio

Blackpool Tower was opened in 1893 and was the second tallest building in the world. It is a copy of the Eiffel Tower in Paris which was then the tallest structure in the world.

The Blackpool Tower is not an exact copy and it is only 0.53 of the height of the Eiffel Tower.

Ratio

Ratios can be used to compare two measurements.

The first building is twice the height of the second one.
The ratio of their heights is **2 : 1** (said 'two *to* one').

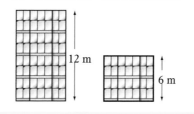

Exercise 14:11

1 Look at each of these pairs of pictures.
For each one, write down the ratio of the lengths marked.

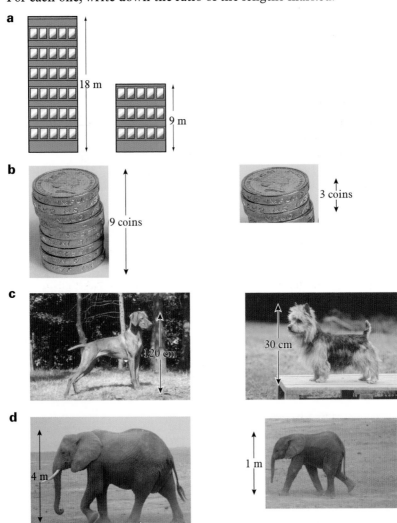

a 18 m   9 m

b 9 coins   3 coins

c 120 cm   30 cm

d 4 m   1 m

2 Look at the weights of each of these objects.
Write down the ratio of their weights.

a  Pasta 500g   Pasta 100g

b

The order that you write the numbers down *is* important.

The ratio of the volumes of
these Coke bottles is **2 : 1**
The one on the left has **twice**
as much Coke as the one on the right.

The ratio of the volumes of
these Coke bottles is **1 : 2**
The one on the left has **half**
as much Coke as the one on the right.

Example

Write down the ratio of the number of pages in a writing pad
with 100 pages compared with one of 300 pages.

The ratio is **1 : 3**.
The second pad has 3 times the number of pages.

Exercise 14:12

1 Steve is half the weight of his father.
Copy and complete:
    The ratio of Steve's weight to his father's is … : …

2 Dfer the Dalmatian eats twice as much food as Spanner the Spaniel.
Copy and complete:
    The ratio of the amount Dfer eats to the amount Spanner eats is … : …

3 A large tin of paint contains $5\,l$. A small tin holds $\frac{1}{2}\,l$.
What is the ratio of their contents?

4 A mouse weighs about 30 g. A cat weighs about 900 g.
What is the ratio of their weights?

Simplifying ratios

Ratios that look different can be the same. Ratios will simplify like fractions.
Tom has three packs of tapes. There are three tapes in each pack.
Mike has two packs of the tapes.
If you look at the ratio of *tapes* they have it is 9:6.
If you look at the ratio of *packs* they have it is 3:2.
These two ratios **must be the same**.
If you can find a number that divides exactly into both parts of a ratio then you can simplify it.

Example   Simplify these ratios if possible.

    a   9:6   **b**   20:15   **c**   9:2

a   3 divides into 9 and 6 exactly.
    $9 \div 3 = 3$ and $6 \div 3 = 2$
    so $9:6 = 3:2$

c   No whole number divides exactly into 9 and 2.
    $9:2$ can't be simplified.

b   5 divides into 20 and 15 exactly.
    $20:15 = 4:3$

Exercise 14:13

1   Simplify these ratios if possible.
    a $10:5$ **c** $3:9$ **e** $16:12$ **g** $18:6$ **i** $9:15$
    b $12:4$ **d** $12:6$ **f** $21:14$ **h** $17:2$ **j** $7:28$

2   Simplify these ratios if possible.
    a $100:25$ **b** $36:10$ **c** $35:24$ **d** $21:10$ **e** $18:72$ • **f** $\frac{1}{2}:\frac{1}{4}$

Because simplifying ratios is very similar to fractions, you can use the fraction button on your calculator.

Example   Simplify the ratio $72:24$.

Because of the way the calculator works, you must enter the **smaller** number first.
You can swap them over later!

Enter: **2**   **4**   **a^b/c**   **7**   **2**   **=**

You should see $1{\llcorner}3$ or $1{\lrcorner}3$

Remember to write the ratio around the other way. So $72:24 = \mathbf{3:1}$.

---

3   Simplify these ratios if possible.
    a $52:39$ **b** $28:21$ **c** $34:85$ **d** $45:54$ **e** $42:75$ **f** $28:39$

• **4**   Simplify these ratios. Make sure they are in the same units first.
    a $5\,\text{kg}:100\,\text{g}$ **c** $4\,\text{h}:30\,\text{min}$ **e** $50\,\text{ml}:6\,l$
    b $2.5\,\text{m}:50\,\text{cm}$ **d** $500\,\text{kg}:3\,\text{tonnes}$ • **f** $750\,\text{ml}:7\,l$

Splitting up

Sharon is painting her lounge.
She wants a specific shade of green.
She is having the paint specially
mixed at a DIY store.

Blue and yellow are mixed in the
ratio 4 : 3.

The machine puts 400 ml of blue
paint and 300 ml of yellow paint in
the mixture.

Ratios are used to describe how something is divided up.

Example

Tullis wants 1 *l* of green paint.
For the shade of green he wants he needs to mix blue and yellow
in the ratio 3 : 1.
How much of each type of paint does he need?

1 *l* is the same as 1000 ml.
The ratio 3 : 1 means 3 parts blue to 1 part yellow.
This is 4 parts altogether.

Divide 1000 by 4: $1000 \div 4 = 250$
So 1 part is 250 ml.

Tullis needs $3 \times 250 = 750$ ml of blue paint
and $1 \times 250 = 250$ ml of yellow paint.

Check: 750 ml + 250 ml = 1000 ml.

Exercise 14:14

1   Orange paint is made by mixing red and yellow paint.
Sunburst Orange is red and yellow in the ratio 4 : 2.
How much red and yellow paint is needed to make these amounts of
Sunburst Orange?
a   600 ml   **b**   1200 ml   • **c**   3 *l*

2 Midnight Orange is red and yellow in the ratio 4 : 3.
How much red and yellow paint is needed to make these amounts of
Midnight Orange?
  a 700 ml
  b 1400 ml
  c 350 ml

3 A builder needs strong mortar for his
bricklaying.
He mixes sand and cement in the ratio 3 : 1.
How much sand and cement does he need
to make these amounts of mortar?
  a 40 kg
  b 100 kg
  c 500 kg

4 ALT lemon drink is made by mixing lemonade and lemon juice in the
ratio 7 : 3.
How much lemonade and lemon juice is needed to make these amounts
of ALT?
  a 1 *l*
  b 3 *l*
  c 500 ml

5 Linden and Alex are partners in a T-shirt company.
To set up the company, they invested money in the ratio 7 : 3.
The company makes £13 000 profit in its first year.
Linden and Alex split the profit in the same ratio as their investments.
How much does each person get?

6 Banana milkshake is made by
mixing milk and flavouring in
the ratio 14 : 1.
How much milk and flavouring
is needed to make these amounts
of milkshake?
  a 300 ml
  b 900 ml
  c 3 *l*

It is possible to divide things up into more than two parts.

Example

A metal alloy is made from iron, copper and nickel in the ratio 7 : 4 : 1.
How much of each metal is needed to produce 300 kg of the alloy?

Find the total number of parts:
  7 parts iron + 4 parts copper + 1 part nickel = 12 parts.

Divide the total by 12 to find the size of 1 part:
  300 ÷ 12 = 25, so 1 part = 25 kg.

Metals needed   7 × 25 = 175 kg of iron
         4 × 25 = 100 kg of copper
         1 × 25 = 25 kg of nickel.

Check: 175 + 100 + 25 = 300 kg.

Exercise 14:15

1 The £10 000 profits of a company are shared out among the three owners.
They are shared in the ratio 3 : 2 : 5.
Calculate how much each person gets.

2 Ned, Ben and Mary are in a lottery syndicate.
Each week, Ned pays £3, Ben pays £1 and Mary pays £4.
They agree to split any winnings in the same ratio.
Calculate how much each person receives if they win:
  a £10   **b** £66   **c** £120 000

3 The 3 angles of a triangle are in the ratio 1 : 2 : 3.
Calculate the size of each angle.

4 St Aiden's school is ordering *Key Maths GCSE* books.
They order Foundation, Intermediate and Higher levels in the ratio 4 : 5 : 2.
They order 176 books altogether.
How many of each type of book do they order?

1 Find the area of each of these shapes:

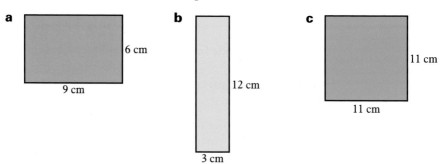

a 6 cm, 9 cm

b 12 cm, 3 cm

c 11 cm, 11 cm

2 Find the area of each of these shapes:

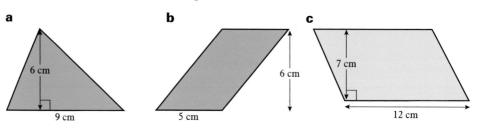

a 6 cm, 9 cm

b 6 cm, 5 cm

c 7 cm, 12 cm

3 Find the total area of each of these shapes:

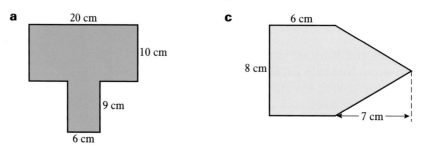

a 20 cm, 10 cm, 9 cm, 6 cm

c 6 cm, 8 cm, 7 cm

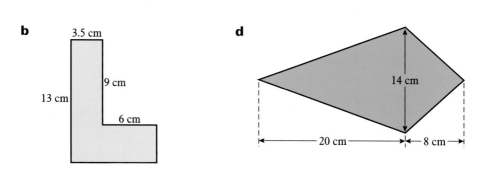

b 3.5 cm, 9 cm, 13 cm, 6 cm

d 14 cm, 20 cm, 8 cm

4 Find the area of each of these shapes.

a

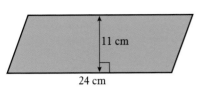

11 cm

24 cm

b

8 cm

3 cm

5 Find the area of each of these shapes:

a

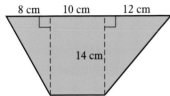

8 cm 10 cm 12 cm

14 cm

b

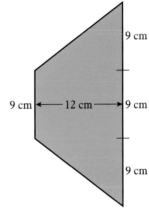

9 cm

9 cm ←— 12 cm —→ 9 cm

9 cm

6 Work out the surface area of each of these solids:

a

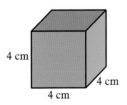

4 cm

4 cm

4 cm

4 cm

c

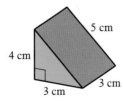

5 cm

4 cm

3 cm 3 cm

b

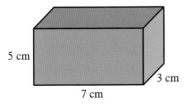

5 cm

7 cm

3 cm

d

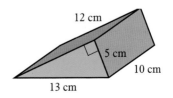

12 cm

5 cm

10 cm

13 cm

7 The amounts given are needed in recipes for meals for 6 people.
Work out the amounts you need for 5 people.

    a 300 g of flour   **d** 180 g of margarine

    b 900 ml of water   **e** 12 eggs

    c 6 g of salt   **f** 660 g of sugar

8 Work these out.

    a $\frac{1}{4} \times \frac{1}{5}$ **e** $\frac{1}{4} \times \frac{1}{4}$

    b $\frac{2}{7} \times \frac{1}{3}$ **f** $\frac{3}{7} \times \frac{1}{4}$

    c $\frac{1}{5} \times \frac{1}{3}$ **g** $\frac{1}{4} \times 3$

    d $\frac{2}{9} \times \frac{1}{5}$ **h** $\frac{4}{9} \times \frac{1}{3}$

9 Work these out.

    a $\frac{1}{6} \div 2$ **e** $\frac{1}{9} \div 8$

    b $\frac{1}{2} \div 3$ **f** $\frac{1}{5} \div 5$

    c $\frac{1}{5} \div 6$ **g** $\frac{1}{10} \div 7$

    d $\frac{1}{7} \div 4$ **h** $\frac{1}{11} \div 5$

10 Here are the sales figures for Jolly Hollys for the first 3 months of the year.

Month	Jan	Feb	Mar
No. of holidays sold	130	142	156

    a Draw a bar-chart to show these figures.
Draw your vertical axis from 0 to 200.

    b Draw another bar-chart of the same figures.
This time, draw your vertical axis from 120 to 160.

    c If you were the Sales Manager, which graph would you use?
Explain your answer.

11 Super Cereals are producing a new type of corn flakes.
Their flakes contain 2.6 g of fibre per 100 g.
Their rival's brand only contains 2.3 g of fibre per 100 g.
Imagine that you are producing an advert for Super Cereals.
Draw a diagram to show how much fibre your flakes contain.

12 A large tin of paint contains 6 *l*. A small tin holds 2 *l*.
What is the ratio of their contents?

13 Simplify these ratios.
  a 3 : 15   **c** 21 : 35   **e** 225 : 50
  b 22 : 10   **d** 48 : 64   **f** 1800 : 200

14 Joanne and Sherene are partners
in a birthday card company.
To set up the company, they invest
money in the ratio 6 : 4.
The company makes £23 000
profit in its first year.
Joanne and Sherene split the
profit in the same ratio as their
investments.
How much does each person get?

15 Graham makes mortar by mixing
5 parts of sand with 1 part of
cement.
  a How much cement will he need
    to make 12 kg of mortar?
  b How much sand will he need to
    make 18 kg of mortar?
  c How much sand will he need if
    he uses 4 kg of cement?

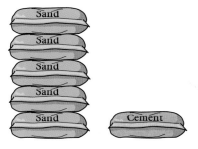

16 A tin of paint is made by mixing blue, yellow and white paints. The
3 colours are mixed in the ratio 1 : 3 : 4.
900 ml of yellow paint is used.
Calculate how much of the other 2 colours is used.

1   These letters fit between the red parallel lines. Find the area of each letter. All measurements are in centimetres.

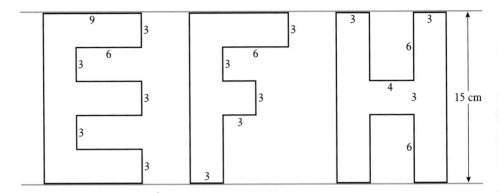

2   This diagram shows the increase in sales of Sunny Spread. All measurements are in centimetres.

Sales of Sunny Spread double in 6 months!!

a   Find the volume of the small box.

b   Find the volume of the larger box.

c   How many times bigger than the small box is the larger box?

d   Explain why this advert is misleading.

3   The 4 angles of a quadrilateral are in the ratio 2 : 3 : 4 : 9. Calculate the size of each angle.

4   A prize of £6500 is to be shared between 4 people in the ratio of their ages. Amandeep, Maggie, Andrew and Katy share the prize in the ratio 40 : 38 : 10 : 6. Work out the amount each person receives to the nearest penny.

5   A piece of string is cut into 2 pieces in the ratio 3 : 1. The shorter piece is 15 cm long. Work out the length of the original piece of string.

1 Find the area of each of these shapes.

a

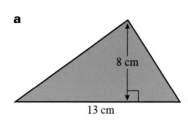

c

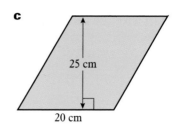

b

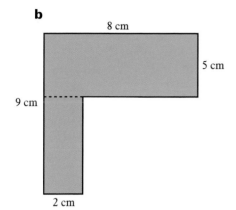

d

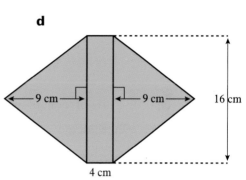

2 Find the surface area of this cuboid.

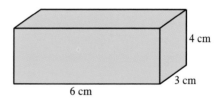

3 Work these out:

   a $\frac{3}{4} \times \frac{1}{5}$ **b** $\frac{1}{3} \times 4$ **c** $\frac{1}{4} \div 3$

4 Sara wants to sell her shop.
She drew this chart to show
the profits made by the
shop during the last 4 years.
Why is the graph misleading?

5 Look at the heights of these trees.
Write down the ratio of the heights.
Start with the smaller tree.

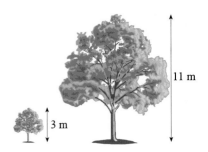

3 m

11 m

6 Simplify these ratios.

a 21 : 14 **b** 16 : 24 **c** 250 : 375

7 A recipe for 1 litre of 'orange surprise' is:

300 ml orange juice
450 ml lemonade
250 ml grapefruit juice.

a How much grapefruit juice would you need to make 5 litres of 'orange surprise'?
b How much orange juice is needed if 1350 ml of lemonade is used?
c How much lemonade is needed if 150 ml of orange juice is used?

8 The areas of two triangles are in the ratio 1 : 8.
The smaller triangle has an area of 25 cm².
What is the area of the larger triangle?

9 Pele gets £40 birthday money. He spends some and saves the rest.
The ratio of money spent to money saved is 5 : 3.
a How much money does he save?
b What fraction of his money does he spend?

10 The three angles of a triangle are in the ratio 2 : 3 : 5.
Find the size of each angle.
(The angles of a triangle add up to 180°.)

15

1 Transformations
Moving shapes in straight lines
Making shapes bigger

2 Time
Adding times
Taking times
Reading timetables

CORE

3 Rounding
Rounding to 1 decimal place
Rounding to 2 decimal places
Rounding to any number of decimal places
Rounding to 1 significant figure
Rounding to any number of significant figures

4 Solving equations
Solving 1 step equations
Solving 2 step equations

QUESTIONS

EXTENSION

TEST YOURSELF

1 **Transformations**

Tom knew how the bucket would move.

A transformation can change the size or position of an object.

Object	The shape that you start with is called the **object**.
Image	The transformed shape is called the **image**. A transformation maps the object onto the image.
Translation	A **translation** is a movement in a straight line.

You can map shape A onto shape B using a translation. You need to move it **3** places right and **2** places up.

You can't map shape A or B onto shape C by translation. This is because shape C points in a different direction.

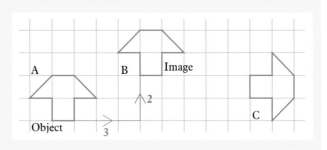

Exercise 15:1

1 **a** Copy the diagram.
   b Complete shape B to make it a translation of shape A.
   c Copy this and fill in the gaps to describe the translation:
      Shape A maps to shape B using a translation of … places right and … places …

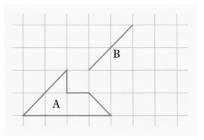

2 **a** Copy the diagram.
b Show the image of the shape after a translation of 4 places left and 1 place down.

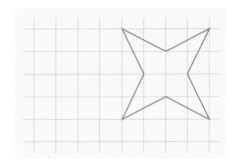

3 **a** Which of these shapes could **T** map to after a translation?
b Describe each translation.

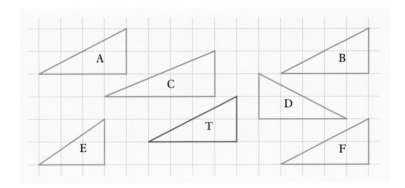

- **4** **a** Draw x and y axes from -6 to 6
  b Plot the points A(-5, -1), B(-3, 1) and C(0, -2).
  c Write down the co-ordinates of the point D so that ABCD is a rectangle.
  d Draw the rectangle ABCD.
  e The rectangle is given a translation so that A is moved to (1, 3). Draw the rectangle in its new position.
  f Describe the translation.

5 **a** Copy the diagram.
b Complete shapes A and B so that B is a translation of A.
c Describe the translation.

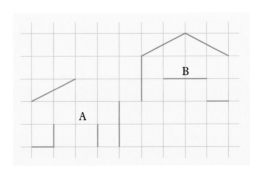

Enlargement	An **enlargement** changes the size of an object. The change is the same in all directions.
Scale factor	The **scale factor** tells you how many times bigger the enlargement is.

Triangle A has been enlarged using a scale factor of 2 to make triangle B. Each side of triangle B is 2 times as long as the matching side of triangle A.

The triangles are the same shape but they are not congruent because they are *not* the same size. The shapes are similar.

Exercise 15:2

1 Copy these shapes on to squared paper.
Enlarge each shape using a scale factor of 2.

   a 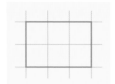   **b** 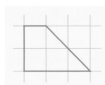   **c**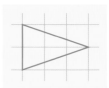

2 Enlarge the shapes in question **1** using a scale factor of 3.

3 Copy these shapes on to squared paper.
Enlarge each shape using a scale factor of 2.

   a 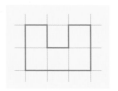   **b** 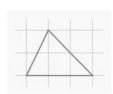   **c**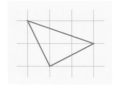

4 a Copy the diagram on to squared
paper. Leave room to draw the
enlargement.

b Shape A maps to shape B using an
enlargement. Complete shape B.

c Write down the scale factor of the
enlargement.

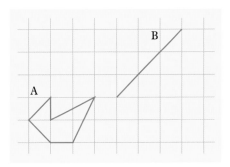

5 a Which of these shapes could **T** map to using an enlargement?

b Write down the scale factor of each enlargement.

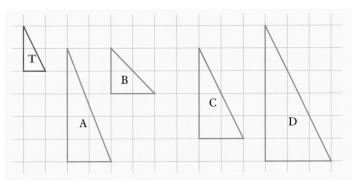

| **Centre of enlargement** | You can enlarge an object by measuring from a point called the **centre of enlargement**. |

Example   Enlarge shape A using a
scale factor of 3 and centre C.

Start with one corner of
shape A and find its image.

Look at the corner marked ●

To get from C to ● you
move 2 squares to the right
and 1 square down.

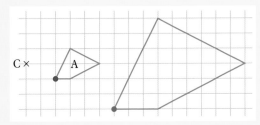

Now start again from C but go 3 times as far in each direction.
You need to move 6 squares to the right and 3 squares down.

The image of ● is marked ●

Check: The three points C, ● and ● lie on a straight line.
Draw the enlargement of shape A starting from ●

Exercise 15:3

1 Copy the diagram on to squared paper.
Leave room to draw the enlargement.
Enlarge shape A using a scale factor
of 3 and centre C.

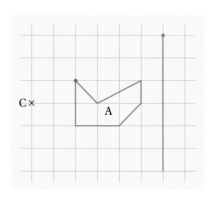

2 Copy these shapes on to squared paper.
Enlarge each shape using a scale factor of 3.
Use C as the centre of enlargement.

a

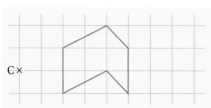

b

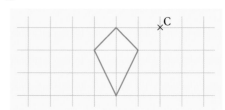

The centre of enlargement can be inside the object.

3 Copy this shape on to squared paper.
Enlarge the shape using a scale factor
of 2.
Use C as the centre of enlargement.

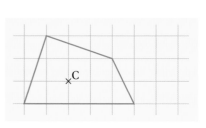

The centre of enlargement can even be on the object.

4 Copy this shape on to squared paper.
Enlarge the shape using a scale factor of 2.
Use C as the centre of enlargement.

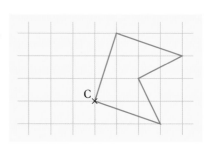

5 **a** Copy this shape onto squared paper.
  b Work out the perimeter of the shape.
  c Enlarge the shape using a scale factor 2. Use C as the centre of enlargement.
  d Work out the perimeter of the new shape.
  e Write down what has happened to the perimeter of the shape when it has been enlarged.

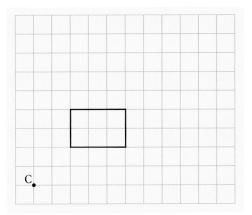

6 **a** Copy this shape onto squared paper.
  b Work out the perimeter of the shape.
  c Enlarge the shape using a scale factor 3. Use C as the centre of enlargement.
  d Work out the perimeter of the new shape.
  e Write down what has happened to the perimeter of the shape when it has been enlarged.

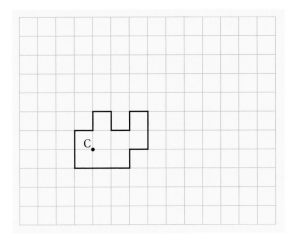

7 A shape has a perimeter of 12 cm.
  The shape is enlarged by a scale factor of 4.
  Write down the perimeter of the new shape.

2 **Time**

Do you have time on your hands?

Example	Peter has booked three visits to the dentist.
	His first visit is on 14 July.
	His second visit is 5 days later.
	His third visit is 22 days after the first one.
	a What is the date of his second visit?
	b What is the date of his third visit?
	a Add 5 onto the 14.
	$14 + 5 = 19$
	So his second visit is on 19 July.
	b Add 22 onto the 14.
	$14 + 22 = 36$
	But there are only 31 days in July.

July	29	30	31	32	33	34	35	36
			August	1	2	3	4	5

$36 - 31 = 5$

So his third visit is on 5 August.

Exercise 15:4

1 James went on holiday for 15 days. He left on 24 July.
Copy the working. Fill in the gaps to find when James returned.

$$24 + \ldots = \ldots$$
$$\ldots - 31 = \ldots$$

James returned from holiday on … August.

2 Saadiya's birthday is on 17 July. Ellen's birthday is 40 days after Saadiya's. Copy the working. Fill in the gaps to find when Ellen's birthday is.

$17 + \ldots = \ldots$
$\ldots - 31 = \ldots$

Ellen's birthday is on …

3 On 10 June 1799, John Brown and 5 British deserters set off across the Atlantic Ocean in a rowing boat.
They crossed the Atlantic in 28 days.
No one has ever rowed it faster.
When did they finish their journey?
Remember that there are 30 days in June.

Terry is a taxi driver.
He sets off for the station at 9.32 a.m. The journey takes 45 min.
When does Terry arrive at the station?

Add up the minutes.
$32 + 45 = 77$
There are only **60** min in 1 h.
$77 - 60 = 17$

So Terry arrives at **17** min past the *next* hour.
Terry arrives at 10.17 a.m.

Exercise 15:5

1 Terry sets off to collect Huw at 3.41 p.m. The journey takes 48 min. Copy the working. Fill in the gaps to find when Terry reaches Huw.

$41 + 48 = \ldots$
$\ldots - 60 = \ldots$

Terry reaches Huw at …

2 Terry has to fill in a time-sheet as a record of his work.
Copy the table. Fill in the gaps.

Set off at:	Time taken	Arrived at:
8.15 a.m.	22 min	
8.46 a.m.	43 min	
9.38 a.m.	51 min	

Example

Chris started his maths exam at 9.47 a.m.
The exam lasted for 2 h and 30 min.
Chris finished the paper after 1 h and 12 min.
a What time did Chris finish?
b What time did the exam finish?

a Add on the hours first. $9 + 1 = 10$
Now add up the minutes. $47 + 12 = 59$
Chris finished at **10.59** a.m.

b Add on the hours first. $9 + 2 = 11$
Now add up the minutes. $47 + 30 = 77$
This is more than **60**. $77 - 60 = 17$
This is **17** min past the *next* hour ($11 + 1 = 12$).
The exam finished at **12.17** p.m.

---

3 Dave is in charge of exams at his school.
He keeps a record of when the exams start and finish.
Copy the table. Fill it in.

Start	Length of exam	Finish
9.20 a.m.	2 h 25 min	
9.20 a.m.	$2\frac{1}{4}$ h	
9.35 a.m.	2 h 40 min	
1.43 p.m.	1 h 45 min	
1.45 p.m.	$2\frac{1}{2}$ h	
1.48 p.m.	2 h 35 min	

4 Jaswinder finishes one exam at 3.17 p.m. He is allowed a 30 min break.
He then starts another exam which lasts for 2 h and 40 min.
What time should Jaswinder finish his second exam?

You need to use 24-hour clock time to understand bus and train timetables.

All 24-hour clock times have
4 figures.
Put an extra **0** at the start if you
need to.
Add 12 h to p.m. times to get the
24-hour clock times.

a.m./p.m.	24-hour clock
9.30 a.m.	09:30
1.25 p.m.	13:25
10.48 p.m.	22:48

Exercise 15:6

1 Write these times using the 24-hour clock.
   a 7.43 a.m.   **b** 7.43 p.m.   **c** 8.15 p.m.   **d** 10.20 p.m.   **e** 11.05 p.m.

2 Write these times as a.m. or p.m. times.
   a 09:34   **b** 11:21   **c** 16:30   **d** 14:25   **e** 19:41

Example

Tom arrives at the station at 14:32.
Find how long he will have to wait for the trains at these times.
   a 15:39   **b** 16:08

a Look at the hours first. $15 - 14 = 1$ h
Now look at the minutes. $39 - 32 = 7$ min
Tom has to wait **1** h **7** min.

b Look at the hours first. $16 - 14 = 2$ h
Now look at the minutes. $8 - 32$ (you can't do this)
Change **1** of the hours to minutes. $+60$ ($68 - 32 = 36$ min
Tom has to wait **1** h **36** min.

3 Peter wants to travel from Stafford to
Newcastle-upon-Tyne.
He has to change trains at Crewe,
Manchester and York.
Find the time it takes to get from:
   a Stafford to York
   b Stafford to Crewe
   c Crewe to York
   d York to Newcastle
   e Stafford to Newcastle.

Station	Arrive	Depart
Stafford		14:40
Crewe	15:05	15:20
Manchester	16:02	16:12
York	17:42	17:50
Newcastle	18:48	

4 What is the longest time that Peter has to wait for a train?

3   Rounding

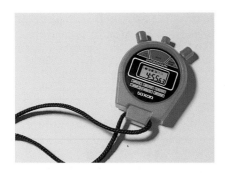

Athletes use stop watches to record their times, because they are more accurate than watches showing minutes and seconds. This watch display shows hundredths of seconds as well.

Can you work out what time is shown?

Rounding to one decimal place (1 dp)

On part of the sports field, Darren is measuring discus throws.
His PE teacher says he should take the readings in metres to one decimal place.

The first throw lands. Darren looks at the tape.

It reads 28.44 m. This is nearer to 28.4 m than 28.5 m.
Numbers that are less than half-way are always rounded down.
So Darren rounds it to 28.4 m to 1 dp.

The second throw lands. Darren looks at the tape again.

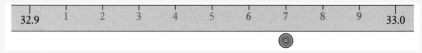

It reads 32.97 m. This is nearer to 33.0 m than 32.9 m.
Numbers that are more than half-way are always rounded up.
So Darren rounds it to 33.0 m to 1 dp.

The third throw lands. Darren looks at the tape again.

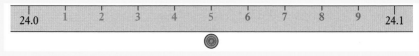

It reads 24.05 m. This is half-way between 24.0 m and 24.1 m.
Numbers that are exactly half-way are always rounded up.
So Darren rounds it to 24.1 m to 1 dp.

Exercise 15:7

1 Round these discus throws to 1 dp.

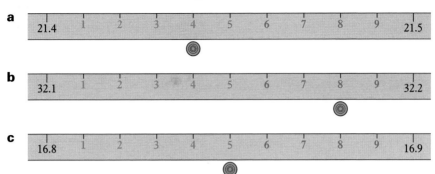

a
21.4 | 1 | 2 | 3 | 4 | 5 | 6 | 7 | 8 | 9 | 21.5

b
32.1 | 1 | 2 | 3 | 4 | 5 | 6 | 7 | 8 | 9 | 32.2

c
16.8 | 1 | 2 | 3 | 4 | 5 | 6 | 7 | 8 | 9 | 16.9

2 Round these discus throws to 1 dp.

a	29.41 m	**d**	42.48 m	**g**	45.25 m
b	12.32 m	**e**	27.18 m	● **h**	19.04 m
c	38.44 m	**f**	23.66 m	● **i**	29.96 m

When you work out questions with your calculator you sometimes get lots of numbers after the decimal point.

Susan wants to work out her daily use of electricity to the nearest 0.1 of a unit.
She has used 53 units in the last week.
She needs to do 53 ÷ 7 to find the average number of units used per day.
Susan keys in: **5** **3** **÷** **7** **=**

This is the calculator display ⨽.5ᒥ|ᔈᒭᔈ5ᒥ|

She draws a line after 1 dp 7.5|7   7.5|7⬭⟨⟩   ⟨
The next number is 7.

She takes no notice of the numbers after the 7. She covers them with her finger.

7.57 is between 7.5 and 7.6

7.57 is nearer to 7.6 than 7.5

7.5 ———————————↑————— 7.6
                7.57

So Susan uses an average of 7.6 units per day.

3 These are the amounts of electricity used by college students in a week.
Work out their average daily use.
Round your answers to 1 dp.

   a Rajiv   41 units   **d** Wayne   64 units
   b Emma   45 units   **e** Jaqui   51 units
   c Trevor   96 units   **f** Tara   73 units

Prices in shops usually have 2 decimal places, e.g. £24.99, £2.25, £6.72
If you work out questions with money, you round to 2 dp.

Hugh goes into a sports shop.
He buys 6 tennis balls for £7.49
He wants to work out the cost of 1 tennis ball.

He keys in: **7** **.** **4** **9** **÷** **6** **=**

The calculator display shows 1.248333333

He draws a line after 2 decimal places 1.24|8

1.24|8

The next number is an 8.
He takes no notice of the numbers after the 8. He covers them with his finger.

   1.248 is between 1.24 and 1.25

   1.248 is nearer to 1.25 than 1.24

So each tennis ball costs £1.25 to the nearest penny.

---

4 Work out the price per item in these multi-packs.
Round your answers to 2 dp.

Item	Cost
a golf ball	6 for £8.49
b orange juice	4 for £5.22

Item	Cost
c roller-ball pen	5 for £5.99
d tie	3 for £22

5 Roger and Kirsty go on holiday to
Australia. They go with 7 other friends.
The cost of the air fares is £12 479
The cost of hotels is £2344.62
The cost of car hire is £1786.71
The cost of day trips is £4138.07
Find the cost per person of the holiday.
Give your answer to the nearest penny.

Rounding to any number of decimal places

To round to any number of decimal places:
(1) Count out the number of decimal places that you want, then draw a line.
(2) Look at the next digit:
    If it is 5, 6, 7, 8 or 9, add 1 on to the digit that you are keeping.
    If it is 0, 1, 2, 3 or 4, ignore it.

2.349 234   to 3 dp is 2.349
0.007 624 16   to 5 dp is 0.007 62

Exercise 15:8

1 Round each of these numbers to the number of decimal places shown:

a 2.7842   3 dp
b 0.6757   3 dp
c 22.906 76   4 dp
d 3327.491   1 dp
e 0.008 224 6   4 dp

f 0.000 456 7   5 dp
g 27.490 054 78   4 dp
h 2.474 747 59   5 dp
● **i** 1.980 056   1 dp
● **j** 0.099 500 1   3 dp

2 A metre is 39.37 in. How many inches are there in 8 m?
Give your answer to 1 dp.

Significant figures

Significant figure

In any number the first **significant figure** is the first digit which isn't a 0. For most numbers this is the first digit.

The first significant figure is the digit in red:

21.4   312   45.78   0.081

3 Copy these numbers.
Put a circle round the first significant figure in each.

a 23.5
b 467
c 75.89
d 3500

e 6.9876
f 42 897
● **g** 4000.0987
● **h** 72 980 006

i 0.5
j 0.07
k 2.07
l 0.040 06

m 0.0007
n 0.009 000 2
● **o** 0.000 030 7
● **p** 360°

Rounding to one significant figure (1 sf)

If you want to round to one significant figure (1 sf):
(1) Look at the next digit after the first significant one:
> If it is 5, 6, 7, 8 or 9 add 1 on to the digit that you are keeping.
> If it is 0, 1, 2, 3 or 4, ignore it.

(2) Be careful to keep the number about the right size.

23 is 20 to 1 sf. It is *not* 2!
312 is 300 to 1 sf. It is not 3.
45.78 is 50 to 1 sf.
0.81 is 0.8 to 1 sf.

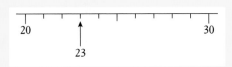

Exercise 15:9

1 Round these numbers to 1 sf.

a 12	**d** 317	**g** 3529	**j** 0.462
b 59	**e** 550	**h** 7878	**k** 0.356
c 15	**f** 4218	**i** 32 034	**l** 0.077

Rounding to any number of significant figures

To round to any number of significant figures:
(1) Look at the first unwanted digit.
(2) Use the normal rules of rounding.
(3) Be careful to keep the number about the right size.

341.4 to 2 sf is 340, *not* 34
42 312 to 3 sf is 42 300
7845.78 to 1 sf is 8000
0.003 154 2 to 2 sf is 0.0032
0.000 203 45 to 3 sf is 0.000 203

Here the 0 after the 2 is significant because it is *after* the first significant figure. A 0 is only significant when it is on the right of the first significant figure.

2 Round these numbers.

a 3.7824 to 3 sf	**c** 273 to 1 sf	**e** 0.034 892 to 2 sf
b 58.344 to 3 sf	**d** 255 643 to 2 sf	**f** 0.000 354 6 to 3 sf

3 Round these calculator displays to 2 sf.

a 14.87625 **b** 3.9586287 **c** 0.4652357

4 Solving equations

Alan, Andrew and Katie are brothers and sister.

Alan is the youngest.
Andrew is 3 years older than Alan.
Katie is 3 years older than Andrew.

Their ages add up to 39.
How old are Alan, Andrew and Katie?

Problems like this can be solved using linear equations.

Linear equations	Equations with simple letters and numbers are called **linear equations.**

Linear equations must not have any terms like x^2 in them.

When you solve an equation, you are trying to work out the value of a letter.
You solve them by getting the letter by itself on one side of the equation.

Example

Solve these equations:

a $p + 3 = 8$ **b** $p - 4 = 7$

a You could think of this equation as:
'The number of pounds in a money tin plus 3 = 8'

$p + 3 = 8$

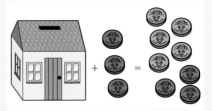

To solve $p + 3 = 8$, notice that p has 3 *added* to it.
To leave p by itself, *take 3* from each side of the equation.

$p + 3 - 3 = 8 - 3$
$p = 5$

b $p - 4 = 7$

You could think of this equation as: 'The number of pounds in a money tin minus 4 = 7'

$$p - 4 = 7$$

To solve $p - 4 = 7$, notice that p has 4 *taken* from it.
To leave p by itself, *add* 4 to each side of the equation.

$$p - 4 + 4 = 7 + 4$$
$$p = 11$$

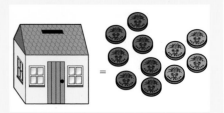

Exercise 15:10

Solve these equations. Show your working out.
You can draw pictures if you want.

1 **a** $p + 3 = 10$ **c** $p + 5 = 9$ **e** $p + 6 = 8$
   b $p + 1 = 6$ **d** $p + 3 = 11$ **f** $p + 9 = 14$

2 **a** $p - 4 = 2$ **c** $p - 5 = 5$ **e** $p - 8 = 3$
   b $p - 1 = 3$ **d** $p - 2 = 9$ **f** $p - 11 = 4$

3 **a** $x + 2 = 10$ **c** $x + 9 = 12$ **e** $x - 12 = 8$
   b $x - 7 = 5$ **d** $x - 8 = 9$ ● **f** $x + 7 = 19$

4 **a** $a + 7 = 18$ **c** $q + 6 = 19$ ● **e** $s + 11 = 9$
   b $h - 3 = 15$ **d** $z - 5 = 12$ ● **f** $x - 2 = -5$

Example   Solve these equations:

a $2a = 8$ **b** $\dfrac{a}{4} = 2$

a In the equation $2a = 8$, the a has been *multiplied* by 2.
To solve this equation, *divide* both sides by 2.

$$\frac{2a}{2} = \frac{8}{2}$$
$$a = 4$$

b $\dfrac{a}{4} = 2$ This means 'one quarter of a equals 2'.

The a has been *divided* by 4.
So to solve this, *multiply* both sides by 4.

$$\dfrac{a}{4} \times 4 = 2 \times 4 \quad \text{Remember that 4 quarters make a whole.}$$
$$a = 8$$

Exercise 15:11

Solve these equations. Show your working out.

1 **a** $2a = 10$ **c** $4a = 20$ **e** $10a = 20$
   b $3a = 6$ **d** $5a = 15$ **f** $8a = 32$

2 **a** $5c = 25$ **c** $6k = 36$ ● **e** $10x = 25$
   b $7h = 49$ **d** $4x = 36$ ● **f** $8p = 3$

3 **a** $\dfrac{a}{4} = 2$ **c** $\dfrac{a}{5} = 4$ ● **e** $\dfrac{t}{6} = 7$

   b $\dfrac{a}{2} = 5$ **d** $\dfrac{x}{3} = 7$ ● **f** $\dfrac{x}{9} = 8$

Equations that need two steps

Sometimes you need to do two things to solve an equation.
Look at this equation: $2x + 1 = 7$

The x has been *multiplied* by 2 and then had 1 *added*.
To solve the equation, do the opposite in the reverse order,
so *subtract* 1 then *divide* by 2:

$$2x + 1 - 1 = 7 - 1$$
so $\qquad\qquad 2x = 6$

then $\qquad \dfrac{2x}{2} = \dfrac{6}{2}$

so $\qquad\qquad x = 3$

Exercise 15:12

Solve these equations. Show your working out.

1 **a** $2x + 3 = 7$ **c** $4x + 1 = 21$ **e** $6p + 2 = 8$
     b $3x + 5 = 11$ **d** $5t + 4 = 19$ **f** $8s + 9 = 65$

Example   Solve the equation: $3x - 2 = 4$
The x has been *multiplied* by 3 and then had 2 *taken away*.
To solve the equation, do the opposite in the reverse order,
so *add* 2 then *divide* by 3:

$$3x - 2 + 2 = 4 + 2$$
$$\text{So} \qquad 3x = 6$$
$$\text{then} \qquad \frac{3x}{3} = \frac{6}{3}$$
$$\text{so} \qquad x = 2$$

---

2 **a** $2x - 3 = 7$ **c** $4b - 1 = 23$ **e** $6j - 4 = 8$
     b $3x - 5 = 7$ **d** $6c - 5 = 13$ **f** $8h - 3 = 69$

3 **a** $2x - 8 = 32$ **c** $8b + 9 = 41$ **e** $11j - 3 = 96$
     b $7x + 5 = 33$ **d** $7c - 9 = 47$ ● **f** $6h - 4 = 11$

You need to do two things to solve: $\dfrac{x}{2} + 3 = 9$

The x has been *divided* by 2 and then had 3 *added*.
To solve this, *subtract* the 3 then *multiply* by the 2.

$$\frac{x}{2} + 3 - 3 = 9 - 3$$
$$\text{so} \qquad \frac{x}{2} = 6$$
$$\text{then} \qquad \frac{x}{2} \times 2 = 6 \times 2$$
$$\text{so} \qquad x = 12$$

---

4 **a** $\dfrac{x}{4} + 5 = 8$ **b** $\dfrac{x}{5} - 3 = 17$ **c** $\dfrac{t}{6} - 4 = 7$

Some equations have letters on both sides.
To solve them, you need to change them so that they only have
the letter on one side.

Example

Solve: $3x = 2x + 4$

Look to see which side has *the smaller number* of xs.
In this example, the right-hand side has only $2x$.

Subtract $2x$ from each side. $3x - 2x = 2x - 2x + 4$

You now have x on its own: $x = 4$

Exercise 15:13

1 Solve these equations.
- **a** $3x = 2x + 5$
- **b** $7x = 2x + 10$
- **c** $4x = 2x + 8$
- **d** $3x = x + 6$
- **e** $9x = 3x + 24$
- **f** $10x = 5x + 20$
- **g** $11x = 6 + 8x$
- **h** $15x = 8x + 147$
- **i** $9x - 8 = 7x$
- **j** $5x = 2x - 12$

Sometimes, the side with the smaller number of xs will be the
left-hand side. You can still solve these equations in the same
way.

Example

Solve: $4x + 9 = 7x$

Take $4x$ from both sides. $4x + 9 - 4x = 7x - 4x$
You now have x on the right-hand side: $9 = 3x$
Divide by 3 to give: $3 = x$

You can write this the
other way around. $x = 3$

2 Solve these equations.
- **a** $6x + 4 = 7x$
- **b** $4x + 7 = 11x$
- **c** $2x + 13 = 4x$
- **d** $3x + 9 = 6x$
- **e** $4x - 2 = 5x$
- **f** $3x = 7x - 4$

3 Solve these equations.

a $3x = 7x - 4$

● **b** $1.5x + 9 = 3.5x$

c $3x - 6 = 5x$

d $2x + 4.5 = 4x$

e $5x - 3 = 7x$

● **f** $4x - 6 = 6x$

g $23x = 29x + 6$

● **h** $45x = 75x + 60$

Some equations have letters and numbers on both sides.
To solve these, change the equation so it has x on only one side.

Example

Solve: $11x - 20 = 6x + 5$

The right-hand side has the smaller number of xs.
Take $6x$ from each side. $11x - 6x - 20 = 6x - 6x + 5$

$$5x - 20 = 5$$

Now remove the numbers from the side with the x.

Add 20 to each side $5x - 20 + 20 = 5 + 20$

$$5x = 25$$

Divide both sides by 5 $x = 5$

Exercise 15:14

1 Solve these equations.

a $4x + 4 = 2x + 10$

b $2x - 7 = x + 3$

c $6x - 13 = 4x + 5$

d $8x + 9 = 4x + 13$

e $4x + 6 = 6x + 2$

f $7x - 21 = 3x - 5$

2 Solve these equations.

a $3x - 15 = x - 4$

b $5x + 2 = x + 14$

c $9x - 1 = 5x + 7$

d $12x + 7 = 12 + 2x$

e $2x - 15 = x - 3$

f $5x + 25 = 3x + 25$

3 Solve these equations.

a $2x - 12 = x - 2$

● **b** $6x + 2 = 17 + x$

c $14x + 2 = 20 + 5x$

d $7x + 7 = 12 + 2x$

● **e** $3.5x - 15 = x + 5$

● **f** $7.5x + 10 = 2.5x + 50$

1 **a** Copy the diagram.
   b Complete shapes A and B so
         that B is a translation of A.
   c Describe the translation.

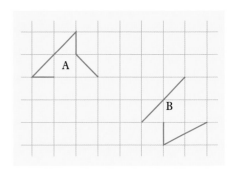

2 Copy these shapes onto squared paper.
   Enlarge each shape using a scale factor of 3. Use C as the centre of enlargement.

a

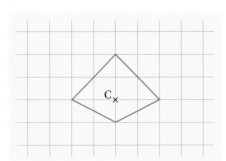

b

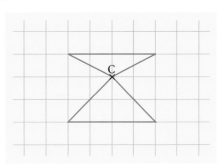

3 **a** Draw x and y axes from -6 to 6.
   b Plot the points P($-2, -1$), Q($-2, 2$), R($1, 2$) and S($3, -3$).
   c Join the points to make the kite PQRS.
   d Draw an enlargement of PQRS using a scale factor of 2 and centre
         the origin.

4 Kath started school after half term on 3 March.
   Her term ends 36 days later. What is the date of the end of term?

5 Write these times using the 24-hour clock.
   a 8.25 p.m.   **b** 9.45 a.m.   **c** 1.18 p.m.   **d** 12.23 p.m.   **e** 12.23 a.m.

6 Write these times as a.m. or p.m. times.
   a 10:28   **b** 04:30   **c** 14:10   **d** 23:35   **e** 00:01

7 This is part of a bus timetable between Stafford and Stoke.
   Copy the table. Fill in the gaps. The journeys always take the same time.

Stafford		10:35	11:05	
Stone			11:32	
Stoke			12:17	13:52

407

8 Round these discus throws to 1 dp.

a

| 11.3 | 1 | 2 | 3 | 4 | 5 | 6 | 7 | 8 | 9 | 11.4 |

b

| 9.8 | 1 | 2 | 3 | 4 | 5 | 6 | 7 | 8 | 9 | 9.9 |

9 Round these calculator displays to 2 sf.

a 2.4367866 **c** 325347 **e** 0.7465379

b 24.887912 **d** 188656 **f** 75.977513

10 Joe goes into a shop to buy some canvas.
It costs £4.09 per metre. He buys 2.4 m.
How much does it cost him?
Give your answer to a sensible degree of accuracy.

11 Work out:
     a 2.37×4.96 **b** $21.97 \div 6.21$ **c** $\sqrt{19}$
     Give your answers to 3 sf.

Solve the equations in questions **12–17**. Show all your working out.

12   **a** $p + 2 = 8$ **c** $x + 7 = 9$ **e** $y + 12 = 28$
       b $p - 1 = 6$ **d** $x - 3 = 11$ **f** $y - 9 = 14$

13   **a** $2a = 8$ **c** $7t = 14$ **e** $4f = 28$
       b $3d = 15$ **d** $5h = 45$ **f** $12x = 84$

14   **a** $\dfrac{a}{2} = 6$ **b** $\dfrac{x}{6} = 2$ **c** $\dfrac{s}{15} = 4$

15   **a** $4x + 5 = 17$ **b** $2d - 1 = 15$ **c** $9k - 4 = 68$

16   **a** $5x = 2x + 15$ **c** $4x + 4 = 8x$
       b $10x = 5x + 20$ **d** $2x + 42 = 4x$

17   **a** $3x - 8 = 2x + 2$ **c** $2x + 6 = 4 + x$
       b $7x - 15 = 4x + 6$ **d** $4x + 3 = 21 + 2x$

1 **a** Copy the diagram.
  b Complete shape B to make it an enlargement of shape A.
  c Write down the scale factor of the enlargement.
  d Write down the co-ordinates of the centre of the enlargement.

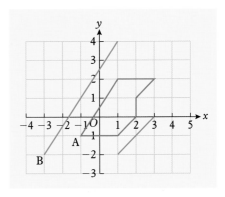

2 Dai left Bridlington at 3.45 a.m. and arrived at Watford $4\frac{1}{2}$ h later. He left Watford at 9.05 a.m. and returned to Bridlington.
  a What time did Dai arrive in Watford?
  b How long did he stay there?
  c It took Dai 55 min longer to return to Bridlington. What time did he arrive?

3 Roger is building an extension. He is working out some costs. Copy his list. Fill it in.

Item	Amount	Cost	Total price to nearest penny
Electrical cable	25.3 m	£1.14 per metre	
Copper piping	15.62 m	£2.99 per metre	
Wood (50 mm × 50 mm)	10.8 m	£1.07 per metre	
		Grand total	

4 This is the problem you saw at the start of Section 4.
  Alan, Andrew and Katie are brothers and sister.
  Alan is the youngest. Andrew is 3 years older than Alan.
  Katie is 3 years older than Andrew.
  Their ages add up to 39.
  How old are Alan, Andrew and Katie?
  Call Alan's age y.
  So Andrew's age is $y + 3$.
  a Write down Katie's age in terms of y.
  b Add their ages together and put this equal to 39.
  c Solve this equation to find y. This is Alan's age.
  d Work out the ages of Andrew and Katie.

1   Write down the transformation that maps T onto T′.

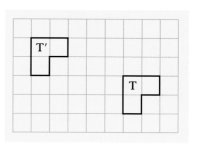

2   Copy the diagram onto squared paper. Leave room to draw the enlargement. Enlarge shape A using a scale factor of 3 and centre C.

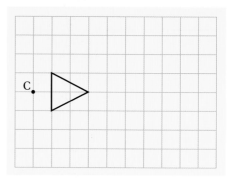

3   **a**   A TV programme starts at 21:30 hours and finishes at 22:50 hours. How long does it last?

   b   The next programme starts at 22:50 hours and lasts 2 hours 35 minutes. What time does it finish?

4   Mark leaves his old job on 21 August. He starts his new job 19 days later. On what date does he start his new job?

5   Round these numbers.

   a   2.746 to 1 dp   **c**   0.0609 to 2 dp   **e**   0.38592 to 3 sf
   b   6.3774 to 2 dp   **d**   0.00731 to 1 sf   **f**   0.0047523 to 4 sf

6   Jan buys a pack of 48 balloons for £1.99
Find the cost of one balloon.
Give your answer to the nearest penny.

7   Solve these equations.

   a $3x - 7 = 17$ **c** $2a + 12 = 5a$

   b $\dfrac{x}{3} + 8 = 11$ **d** $7m - 3 = 4m + 12$

16

CORE

QUESTIONS

EXTENSION

TEST YOURSELF

1 Volume

Jim is building a garage.
He needs to make a solid base to put the garage on.
This is called the 'footings' for the garage.
He digs out a cuboid shape and fills it with concrete.
He needs to know how much concrete to order.
He needs to be able to work out the volume of the footings.

Volume

The amount of space than an object takes up is called its **volume**.

Volume is measured in cubic units.
These can be millimetres cubed (**mm³**), centimetres cubed (**cm³**) or metres cubed (**m³**).

1 cm³

1 cm³ is the space taken up by a cube with all its edges 1 cm long.

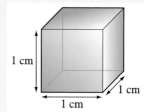

Capacity

The **capacity** of a hollow object is the volume of space inside it.

1 ml

This cube has been filled with water.
The volume of liquid inside is **1 millilitre**.
This is written **1 ml**.

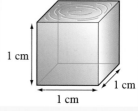

1 *l*

Large volumes are measured in **litres**.
  1 litre = 1000 ml   1 litre is written **1 *l***.

A capacity of **1 ml** is the same as a volume of **1 cm³**.
1000 **ml** is the same as 1 *l*

Exercise 16:1

1 Draw a diagram of a cube that has a volume of:
     a 1 cm³   **b** 1 mm³   **c** 1 m³   ● **d** 8 cm³

2 The capacity of a normal can of Pepsi is 330 ml.

Estimate the capacity in millilitres of each of these:

a **b**  **c** **d**

3 The capacity of this bottle of lemonade is 2 *l*.

Estimate the capacity in litres of each of these:

a **b**  **c**  **d**

4 a Write down the volume of each drink in centimetres cubed.
  b Calculate the volume of Coca-Cola that you get for 1 p for each container.
  Give your answers to 2 dp.
  c Which container gives the best value for money?

---

1 cm³ A cube that has sides of 1 cm is called a 1 cm cube.
It has a volume of 1 cm cubed.
This is written as **1 cm³**.

This cuboid has 12 cubes in each layer.
Each cube has a volume of 1 cm³.
It has 2 layers.
The volume of the cuboid is:
  $12 \times 2 = 24 \text{ cm}^3$

Exercise 16:2

For each of these cuboids, write down:
a the number of cubes in one layer
b the number of layers
c the volume of the cuboid

1

2

3

4

5

6

7

8

9

10

● **11** Look at this solid.
 The yellow cubes go right through
 the shape.
 a Find the volume of the red cubes.
 b Find the volume of the yellow
  cubes.
 c Find the total volume of the
  shape.

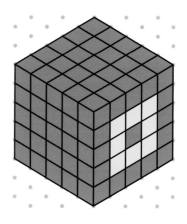

Volume of a cuboid

There is a faster way to find the volume of a block of cubes.
(1) Multiply the length by the width.
  This tells you how many cubes there are in one layer.
(2) Multiply your answer by the height.
  This tells you how many cubes there are altogether.

Volume of a cuboid

You can do this all at once:
  Volume of a cuboid = length × width × height

Example

Work out the volume of this block of cubes.

 Volume = length × width × height
    = 6 × 3 × 4
    = 72 cm³

Exercise 16:3

In questions **1–8**, find the volume of each of the blocks. Write your
answers in cm³.

1

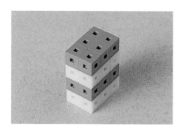

2

3

4

5

6

7

8 cm

3 cm

2.5 cm

8

3.5 cm

3.5 cm

3.5 cm

9 A 750 g cereal box has sides of length
7 cm, 19 cm and 29 cm.
Find the volume of the box.

10 A 1 *l* carton of orange juice is in the
shape of a cuboid.
It measures 5.9 cm by 9 cm by
19.5 cm.
  a Find the volume of the box.
  b How much space is there in the
box if it contains exactly 1 *l* of
orange juice?

In this exercise you need to use the right units in your answers.
So far you have only used cm³ for volume.
In this exercise you will need to use m³ and mm³ too.
Look carefully at the units in the question to help you give the right
units in your answer.

Exercise 16:4

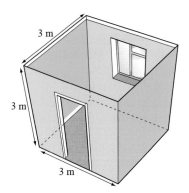

1 Work out the volume of
   this boxroom.
   It is a cube of side 3 m.

2 a Jim dug a hole for his garage
      footings.
      The hole was 5 m long, 3 m
      wide and 1.5 m deep.
      Find the volume of earth
      that he removed.
   b He had to buy the concrete
      in litres.
         $1 \text{ m}^3 = 1000\,l$.
      How many litres of concrete
      did Jim have to buy?

3 A box of computer disks is a cuboid.
   The width of the box is 92 mm.
   The height is 96 mm.
   The depth is 38 mm.
   Find the volume of the box.

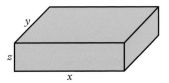

4 a Measure the length, the width and the depth of your *Key Maths*
      GCSE book in millimetres to the nearest millimetre.
      Write down your answers.
   b Work out the volume of paper in the book.

5 This cuboid has length x cm, width
   y cm and height z cm.
   Write down the volume of the cuboid
   in terms of x, y and z.

This is a cubic millimetre.
All the sides are 1 mm.

This is a cubic centimetre.

There are 10 mm in every 1 cm.
  So in the cubic centimetre
  the width is 10 mm
  the length is 10 mm
  the height is 10 mm.
  So there are $10 \times 10 \times 10 = 1000 \text{ mm}^3$ in 1 cm³.

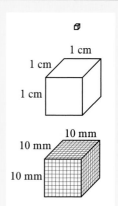

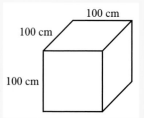

A cubic metre is too big to draw here!
This is a diagram of one.
There are 100 cm in every 1 m.
  So in the cubic metre
  the dimensions are 100 cm × 100 cm × 100 cm.
So there are $100 \times 100 \times 100 = 1\,000\,000 \text{ cm}^3$ in 1 m³.

This diagram shows you
how to convert cubic units.

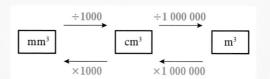

Exercise 16:5

1 Draw a sketch of a cube 2 cm by 2 cm by 2 cm. Find the volume in mm³.

2 Change each of these volumes into cm³.

 a 6 m³   **c** 12.36 m³   **e** 672 mm³
 b 0.4 m³   **d** 2050 mm³   **f** 401 mm³

3 Change each of these volumes into m³.

 a 40 000 000 cm³   **b** 7 900 000 cm³   **c** 459 000 cm³

2 Relative frequency

Belinda is fed up with her relatives coming to her house.

Her Mum says that she is being unfair. She thinks that Belinda's friends come to the house just as often.

Belinda wants to find the probability that a visitor is a relative.

She needs to work out the relative frequency!

This terrible mathematical joke tells you something important about probability. If you don't have equally likely outcomes that you saw in Unit 11 you cannot write down the probability that something will happen.
You have to do an experiment to estimate the probability.

Laura has made a tetrahedral dice. Its sides are numbered 1, 2, 3 and 4.

The score is the side that is face down when she rolls the dice.

She rolls the dice 100 times and records the score each time.

This table shows her results.

If the dice is fair then she should get each score equally.

The probability of getting each score would be $\frac{1}{4}$.

Number	Tally	Frequency
1	IIII IIII IIII III	18
2	IIII IIII IIII IIII	20
3	IIII IIII IIII IIII IIII IIII IIII III	38
4	IIII IIII IIII IIII IIII	24

So she should get each score 25 times.
This dice does not look as though it is fair.
The 3 has come up 38 times which is a lot more than 25.
Laura can use her results to estimate the probability of getting each score.

Event   An **event** is something that happens in a probability experiment.

Frequency	The **frequency** of an event is the number of times that it happens.

Relative frequency	The **relative frequency** of an event is the number of times that it happens divided by the total number of events that happen.

$$\textbf{Relative frequency} = \frac{\text{frequency}}{\text{total frequency}}$$

The relative frequency gives an estimate of the probability. Relative frequency gives you a better estimate of probability the more times you do the experiment.

So Laura can estimate the probability of getting each score.
Here are her results from before.

She has thrown the dice
$18 + 20 + 38 + 24 = 100$ times

Score	Frequency
1	18
2	20
3	38
4	24

She has worked out the relative frequency for each score.

These are estimates for the probabilities of each score.
She could get better estimates by doing the experiment more times.

Score	Relative frequency
1	$\frac{18}{100} = 0.18$
2	$\frac{20}{100} = 0.2$
3	$\frac{38}{100} = 0.38$
4	$\frac{24}{100} = 0.24$

Exercise 16:6

1 Darren tossed a coin 50 times. These are his results.
   a Find the relative frequency of:
      (1) a head   (2) a tail
   b Do you think his coin is fair? Explain your answer.
   c How could Darren be more sure about whether his coin is fair?

Outcome	Tally	Frequency
Head	∦ ∦ ∦ ∦	20
Tail	∦ ∦ ∦ ∦ ∦ ∦	30

2 Jasmine throws a 6-sided dice 100 times.
   She gets a 6 forty times.
   a Find the relative frequency of getting a 6.
   b Do you think Jasmine's dice is fair? Explain your answer.

3 Balraj thinks that he has a biased dice.
He has thrown it 12 times.
This table shows his results.

Score	1	2	3	4	5	6
Frequency	1	1	6	1	2	1

    a Is Balraj right to think that his dice is biased?
    b What would you tell Balraj to do to be more sure about whether or
       not his dice is biased?

4 Greg is playing in a tennis tournament.
His coach is recording the points that he wins and loses on his first
serve when his first serve is in.
Here are his results.

	Points won	Points lost
First serve in	35	15

    a How many first serves has Greg served in?

Greg gets his next first serve in.
    b Estimate the probability that Greg wins the point.
    c Estimate the probability that Greg loses the point.

5 Gemma is testing a biased spinner.
She has spun it 100 times.
The table shows her results.
Gemma is going to spin the spinner again.
Estimate the probability that Gemma
will get:
    a blue   **b** green   **c** yellow.

Colour	Frequency
blue	20
green	45
yellow	35

6 A factory makes skirts.
The waist sizes of 200 skirts were measured.
35 were smaller than they should have been.
62 were bigger than they should have been.
    a How many skirts were the right size?
The next skirt off the production line is
tested.

Estimate the probability that it will be:
    b bigger than it should be
    c smaller than it should be
    d the right size.

Methods of finding probability

There are three ways of finding probability.

Method 1   Use equally likely outcomes.

You use this method to find the probability of getting a six on a fair dice. You saw this in Unit 11.

The probability of getting a six is $\frac{1}{6}$.

Method 2   Do a survey or do an experiment.

This will tell you the relative frequency of an event.
For example, do this to find the probability that a drawing pin would land point up when you drop it onto the floor.

Method 3   Look back at data that someone else has collected.

For example, use this method to find the probability that it will snow in London on Christmas Day next year.

Exercise 16:7

For each of the questions in this exercise.
a Write down which method you would use to find the probability.
b Say whether your answer would be the actual probability or an estimate.
If your answer is Method 2, say what survey or experiment you would do and how many people you would ask or how many times you would repeat the experiment.

1 The probability that the next car to pass your school will be white.

2 The probability that a blue cube will be chosen at random from a box containing 20 cubes.

3 The probability that there will be a flu epidemic next winter.

4 The probability that a fair coin will show heads.

5 The probability that a person chosen at random will vote Labour in the next election.

6 The probability that a biased 6-sided dice numbered from 1 to 6 will land on 5.

7 The probability that a kitten chosen at random will live to be 18.

Game: win or lose?

This is a game for two players.
You need two dice.
Take it in turns to roll both the dice.
Multiply the scores on the two dice together.
Player 1 scores a point if the result is even.
Player 2 scores a point if the result is odd.
The first player to get to a score of 10 wins.

Investigating the game
Who wins the game? Why?
Investigate whether the game is fair.
You need to work out the relative frequency of getting an even result and getting an odd result.
Can you change the game to make it fair?

3 BIG numbers

Pluto is the furthest planet from the Sun in our solar system.

The distance from the Sun to Pluto is 5 907 000 000 miles correct to the nearest million miles!

This is the most digits that most calculators can fit in their display.
You may find that your calculator cannot fit all the digits into its display.

There is a way of putting numbers like this and bigger ones into your calculator. Before you see it you need to remember about powers.

Power	The number 5^3 is 5 to the **power** of 3. This means $5 \times 5 \times 5$. The power tells you how many 5s to multiply together. $5^3 = 5 \times 5 \times 5 = 125$

Exercise 16:8

1 Copy these. Fill them in.

a $2^3 = \ldots \times \ldots \times \ldots$
$= \ldots$

b $4^2 = \ldots \times \ldots$
$= \ldots$

c $7^3 = \ldots \times \ldots \times \ldots$
$= \ldots$

d $4^3 = \ldots \times \ldots \times \ldots$
$= \ldots$

e $10^3 = \ldots \times \ldots \times \ldots$
$= \ldots$

f $10^5 = \ldots \times \ldots \times \ldots \times \ldots \times \ldots$
$= \ldots$

2 Work these out.

a 3^2
b 5^2
c 3^3
d 5^3

e 4^4
f 5^4
g 6^2
h 7^3

i 2^5
j 3^5
k 4^5
l 8^3

m 10^3
n 10^4
o 10^5
p 10^6

3 Write each of these using a power.

  a 3×3 **c** $5 \times 5 \times 5$ **e** $2 \times 2 \times 2 \times 2$
  b $4 \times 4 \times 4$ **d** $4 \times 4 \times 4 \times 4$ **f** $5 \times 5 \times 5 \times 5 \times 5$

4 Copy these. Fill them in.

  a $2 \times 2 \times 2 \times 3 \times 3 = 2^{\cdots} \times 3^{\cdots}$ **c** $3 \times 3 \times 3 \times 4 \times 4 \times 4 = 3^{\cdots} \times 4^{\cdots}$
  b $2 \times 2 \times 3 \times 3 \times 3 = 2^{\cdots} \times 3^{\cdots}$ **d** $5 \times 5 \times 4 \times 4 \times 4 \times 4 = 4^{\cdots} \times 5^{\cdots}$

Square

Square is a special name for a power of 2.
You can read 4^2 as 'the square of 4' or '4 squared'.

Cube

Cube is a special name for a power of 3.
You can read 4^3 as 'the cube of 4' or '4 cubed'.
You need to remember the values of 2^3, 3^3, 4^3, 5^3 and 10^3.

---

5 Work out the value of each of these.

  a 2^2 **d** 5^2 **g** 10^2 **j** 4^3
  b 3^2 **e** 6^2 **h** 2^3 **k** 5^3
  c 4^2 **f** 7^2 **i** 3^3 **l** 10^3

Square root

To find the **square root** you have to do the opposite of squaring.
You know that $4^2 = 4 \times 4 = 16$.
The square root of 16 is 4.
The square root has a symbol of its own.
$\sqrt{}$ means 'the square root of'.
So $\sqrt{16} = 4$.

---

6 Work out the value of each of these.

  a $\sqrt{4}$ **d** $\sqrt{36}$ **g** $\sqrt{144}$
  b $\sqrt{9}$ **e** $\sqrt{100}$ **h** $\sqrt{10\,000}$
  c $\sqrt{25}$ **f** $\sqrt{81}$ **i** $\sqrt{1\,000\,000}$

7 Find the square root key, , on your calculator.
Use the key to check your answers to question **6**.

For part **a**, key in: $\sqrt{}$ 4 =

As well as a $\sqrt{}$ key you have other keys on your calculator that you can use for doing powers.

x^2 key

The x^2 **key** is for squaring.

Key in: [calculator] **3** x^2 **=**

to work out that $3^2 = 9$.

x^y key or y^x key

The x^y **key** or y^x **key** is for working out any power.

Key in: [calculator] **5** y^x **3** **=**   [calculator] **5** x^y **3** **=**

to work out that $5^3 = 125$.

8   Use your calculator to check your answers to question **2**.

9   Use your calculator to work these out.
   a 7.1^2 e 2.8^4 i 2.2^5 m 9.2^3
   b 8.5^2 f 5.1^4 j 8.3^5 n 23.1^4
   c 4.1^3 g 7.6^2 k 4.3^5 o 1.01^5
   d 9.3^3 h 7.1^3 l 1.62^3 p 12.92^6

10   a   Use your calculator to work these out.
       (1) 10^2 (2) 10^3 (3) 10^4 (4) 10^5 (5) 10^6 (6) 10^7
     b   Look at your answers to part **a**.
         Write down the answers to these questions.
         (1) 10^8 (2) 10^9 (3) 10^{10} (4) 10^{11} (5) 10^{12} (6) 10^{13}
     c   Now do part **b** using x^y or y^x on your calculator.
         Write down exactly what you get on your calculator next to your answers to part **b**.
     d   Your answers to part **c** should give you a clue how your calculator deals with really big numbers.
         Write a sentence or a short paragraph to explain what it is doing.

Standard form

Very large numbers are written down using **standard form**. Standard form is like a code that you need to use when numbers get so big that they won't fit on a calculator. You can use standard form for smaller numbers too if you want to! A number is in standard form if it has two parts:

   a number between 1 and 10 multiplied by **10 to a power**.

This is a number in standard form: 2×10^{12}

When your calculator gets a big answer it will give you the answer in standard form. New calculators are really helpful.

2×10^{12} will appear as $2.^{\times 10\, 12}$

You must write your answer as 2×10^{12} and not use the strange sizes that the calculator does.

If you have an older calculator your display will look like this $2.^{12}$ or 2^{12}

If you have a calculator like this you must not write down the calculator display as your answer. You must still write your answer as 2×10^{12} and you have to remember to put the $\times 10$ part in.

To see what sort of calculator you have, key in:

2 0 0 0 0 0 0 × 1 0 0 0 0 0 0 =

Exercise 16:9

1 Write these calculator displays as numbers in standard form.

a $3.^{\times 10\, 11}$

d $7.1^{\times 10\, 06}$

g 7.1^{06}

b $4.^{\times 10\, 6}$

e $4.^{13}$

h 2.51^{16}

c $2.4^{\times 10\, 12}$

f $5.^{08}$

i 6.04^{15}

2 Work these out. Give your answers in standard form.
  a $1\,000\,000 \times 3\,000\,000$
  b $4\,000\,000 \times 3\,000\,000$
  c $6\,000\,000 \times 4\,000\,000$
  d $12\,000\,000 \times 3\,000\,000$
  e $200\,000 \times 300\,000$
  f $180\,000 \times 450\,000$

| Exp, EXP, EE keys | You can enter numbers that are written in standard form into your calculator. You need to use the **Exp** or **EXP** or **EE** key. |

The **Exp** or **EXP** or **EE** key means 'times 10 to the power of'.

You use it to enter numbers into your calculator that are in standard form. Find the key that your calculator has and use it from now on wherever you see **Exp**.

To enter the number 2×10^9:

all you have to press is **2** **Exp** **9**

and you will get the right display for 2×10^9.

Example

Work out $(3 \times 10^7) \times (2.5 \times 10^8)$
Key in:

$$\boxed{3} \ \boxed{\text{Exp}} \ \boxed{7} \ \boxed{\times} \ \boxed{2} \ \boxed{.} \ \boxed{5} \ \boxed{\text{Exp}} \ \boxed{8} \ \boxed{=}$$

The answer is 7.5×10^{15}.

---

3 Work these out. Give your answers in standard form.
   a $(7.1 \times 10^5) \ \times (2.8 \times 10^8)$ **e** $(2.2 \times 10^{25}) \ \div (2 \times 10^3)$
   b $(8.5 \times 10^{12}) \times (5.1 \times 10^{14})$ **f** $(8.4 \times 10^{15}) \ \div (2.1 \times 10^4)$
   c $(4.1 \times 10^3) \ \times (7.6 \times 10^{12})$ **g** $(4.8 \times 10^{25}) \ \div (1.2 \times 10^5)$
   d $(9.3 \times 10^3) \ \times (7.1 \times 10^{13})$ **h** $(1.62 \times 10^{23}) \div (8.1 \times 10^6)$

4 The capacity of a computer is
   measured in bytes.
   One kilobyte is 1.024×10^3 bytes.
   One gigabyte is 1 000 000 kilobytes.
   How many bytes are in a gigabyte?
   Give your answer in standard form.

5 The table gives the masses of
   4 planets.
   a Which planet has the largest mass?
   b How much heavier is the Earth than Venus?
      (You need to work out $5.98 \times 10^{24} - 4.87 \times 10^{24}$)
   c How much heavier is Jupiter than Venus?
      (You need to work out $1.25 \times 10^{27} - 4.87 \times 10^{24}$)
   d How many *times* heavier than the Earth is Saturn?
      (You need to work out $5.69 \times 10^{26} \div 5.98 \times 10^{24}$)
      Give your answer to the nearest whole number.
   e How many times heavier than Venus is Jupiter?
      (You need to work out $1.25 \times 10^{27} \div 4.87 \times 10^{24}$)
      Give your answer to the nearest whole number.

Planet	Mass (kg)
Earth	5.98×10^{24}
Jupiter	1.25×10^{27}
Saturn	5.69×10^{26}
Venus	4.87×10^{24}

6 You have 4.7×10^{12} blood cells in every litre of your blood.
   Your body contains about $4.9\,l$ of blood.
   About how many blood cells do you have in your body?

1 Estimate the volume of these containers.
You need to choose millilitres or litres.

a

b

c

2 Find the volume of each of these blocks of cubes.
Write your answers in cm³.

a

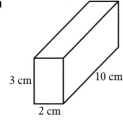

b

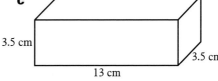

3 Find the volume of these cuboids.

a

3 cm   10 cm

2 cm

c

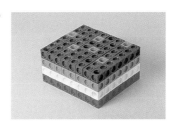

3.5 cm   3.5 cm

13 cm

b

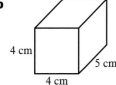

4 cm   5 cm

4 cm

d

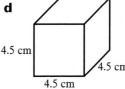

4.5 cm   4.5 cm

4.5 cm

4 John rolls a biased dice 100 times. He gets a 6 forty-five times.
Work out the relative frequency of getting a 6 for John's dice.

5 **a** Ellen is given the choice of having chips or mashed potato with her
    sausages at lunchtime. Are the events 'she chooses chips' and 'she
    chooses mashed potato' equally likely? Explain your answer.
   b How would you find out the probability that Ellen will choose chips?

6 In the last 40 matches the school chess team has won 26, lost 8 and drawn the rest.
Estimate the probability that in their next game the team will:
a win **b** lose **c** draw.

7 **a** How would you work out the probability that a battery chosen at random from its production line will be faulty?
b Will your method give you the exact probability or an estimate?

8 Use your calculator to work these out:
a	5.1^2	**e**	6.9^4	**i**	$\sqrt{2500}$	**m**	8.1^3
b	8.9^2	**f**	2.5^4	**j**	7.3^5	**n**	81.4^4
c	6.1^3	**g**	$\sqrt{256}$	**k**	4.9^5	**o**	1.01^8
d	12.3^3	**h**	$\sqrt{121}$	**l**	7.32^3	**p**	10.01^9

9 These numbers are written in standard form.
Give your answers in standard form.

$$A = 4.5 \times 10^{11} \quad B = 1.3 \times 10^{17} \quad C = 4.2 \times 10^{10} \quad D = 9.5 \times 10^{4}$$

a Write down the biggest of these numbers.
b Write down the smallest of these numbers.
c Work out the value of:
(1) $A + C$ (2) AB (3) BC (4) CD

10 Give your answers in standard form.
The speed of light is about $3 \times 10^8 \, \text{m s}^{-1}$.
How far will light travel in:
a 1 s
b 1 min
c 1 h
d 1 week
e 1 year?
This distance is called a light year.

11 Work these out. Give your answers in standard form.
a $(5.9 \times 10^5) \times (2.9 \times 10^8)$ **c** $(6 \times 10^{19}) \div (3 \times 10^8)$
b $(7.24 \times 10^3) \times (9.12 \times 10^7)$ **d** $(8.2 \times 10^{12}) \div (4.1 \times 10^{10})$

1 Work out the volume of each of these shapes.
You need to split the shapes into cuboids.

a

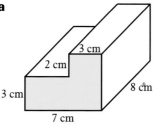

c

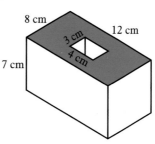

b

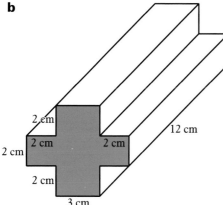

d

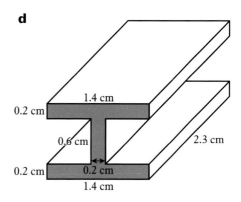

2 Gary has done a survey of cars in
a supermarket car-park.
He has drawn this bar-chart
to show his results.
If a car is chosen at random from
the survey, find the probability
that the make will be:

a Nissan   **b** Ford   **c** Peugeot.

The next day, Gary chooses a car at
random from the same car-park.
Estimate the probability that the
make of the car will be:

d Vauxhall   **e** Honda   **f** Rover.

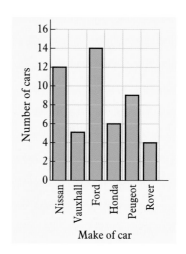

3 An estimate for the volume, V, of a cylinder is given by the formula:

$$V = \frac{3d^2h}{4}$$

Find the value of V when:

a $d = 3.4 \times 10^5$ and $h = 7.2 \times 10^9$
b $d = 9.2 \times 10^4$ and $h = 1.2 \times 10^6$

1   This shape is made from 1 cm cubes.
Write down the volume of the shape.

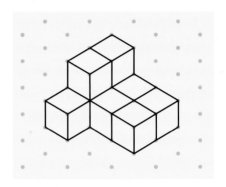

2   Find the volume of this cuboid.

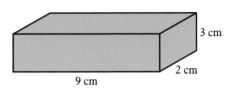

3 cm

2 cm

9 cm

3   Nick recorded the number of times his football team won, drew or lost matches during the first half of the season.

	Tally	Frequency
Won	卌 ‖	
Drew	卌	
Lost	‖‖	

   a   Copy the tally-table. Fill in the last column.
   b   Estimate the probability that Nick's team will win their next match.

4   How would you estimate the probability that:
   a   you would get a 5 with a biased dice
   b   there will be a flu epidemic this winter.

5   Work these out.
   a 8^2 **c** $\sqrt{36}$ **e** $\sqrt{10\ 000}$
   b 5^3 **d** 4^3 **f** 10^5

6   These numbers are written in standard form.
Give your answers to **b** in standard form.

     $P = 7.2 \times 10^7$ $Q = 4.6 \times 10^8$ $R = 5.6 \times 10^6$

   a   Which number is:
      (1) the biggest   (2) the smallest.
   b   Work out the value of:
      (1) $P \times R$ (2) $Q \div 0.02$

17

1 Scatter graphs
Drawing scatter graphs
Describing correlation
Estimating values – lines of best fit

2 Value for money?
Comparing prices
Using direct proportion

CORE

3 Collecting terms
Collecting simple letters
Collecting powers
Multiplying out brackets and equations
Factorising

4 Circles
Drawing circles
Finding the circumference of a circle
Finding the area of a circle

QUESTIONS

EXTENSION

TEST YOURSELF

1 Scatter graphs

Anne is the Head of the Maths department at Adhamup School.

She is looking at the test results of some of her pupils.

She is comparing them with their results in other subjects.

She decides to draw some scatter graphs to help her compare the results.

Anne starts by comparing the Maths results with the Science results. She thinks these should be similar.

| Scatter graph | A **scatter graph** is a diagram that is used to see if there is a connection between two sets of data. One value goes on the x axis and the other goes on the y axis. It doesn't matter which way round they go. |

This is the scatter graph that Anne produced. One pupil scored 35 in Maths and 40 in Science. She plotted a point at (**35, 40**).

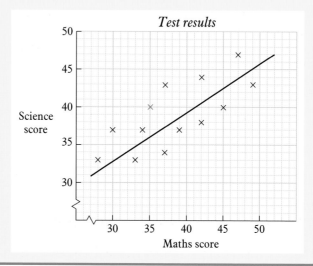

Exercise 17:1

1 Here are some of the results for class 10P in Maths and Science

Maths	27	34	26	28	34	27	40	21	35	27	29
Science	29	38	22	29	27	32	43	20	32	25	31

a Copy these axes on to graph paper.

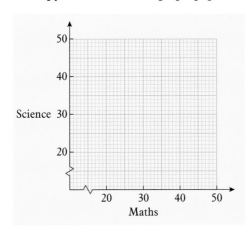

b The first column in the table shows that a pupil scored 27 in Maths and 29 in Science. Plot a point at (27, 29) on your graph.
c The second pupil scored 34 in Maths and 38 in Science. Plot a point at (34, 38).
d Plot the rest of the points on your graph.
e Notice how the points are roughly in a line going from the bottom left to the top right of your graph.
Do you think that pupils who did well in the Maths exam also did well in the Science exam?

2 These are the English results for the same pupils in 10P.

English	35	40	20	22	28	21	35	29	30	26	40

a Draw some axes like you did in question **1**.
b Draw a scatter graph of the Maths scores against the English scores.

3 **a** Draw a scatter graph of the Science and English scores.
b What do you notice about your graph?

Correlation	**Correlation** is a measurement of how strongly connected two sets of data are.
	There are different types of correlation.

Positive correlation	This scatter graph shows the weights and heights of people. As the weight increases so does the height. This is **positive correlation**.	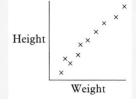

Negative correlation	This graph shows the values of cars and their ages. As age increases, value decreases. This is **negative correlation**.	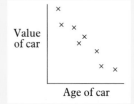

Zero correlation	This graph shows the height of some students against their maths scores. There is no connection between these two things. There is **zero correlation**.	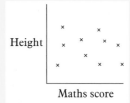

Correlation can be strong or weak.

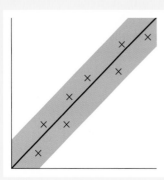

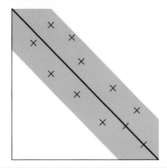

Strong correlation
The points all lie close to the line.

Weak correlation
The points are well spread out from the line but still follow the trend.

Exercise 17:2

1 The ages of 10 Ford Escorts and their sale values are shown in this table.

Age (years)	3	6	5	4	2	6	5	3	6	5
Value (£)	6000	2500	2900	3500	6500	2300	3100	5800	2100	3300

   a Plot a scatter graph to show this data.
   b Describe the type of correlation that this data shows.
      Choose from strong/weak and positive/negative.

2 Two judges awarded marks in an art competition.
  Judge A scored out of 20. Judge B scored out of 15.
  Here are their results for 10 paintings.

Judge A	15	12	8	19	7	6	17	8	15	16
Judge B	12	9	7	13	8	3	12	5	12	14

   a Plot a scatter graph to show these data.
   b Describe the type of correlation that this data shows.

Estimating values

If two sets of data show correlation, you can use your scatter graph to estimate missing values. You can draw a line that goes through the middle of the points. This is called a line of best fit.
This line is used to estimate other data values.
To do this, draw from one axis to the line and then to the other axis.
This is similar to a conversion graph.

Example
Ben scored 32 in Maths but missed the Science test.
Work out an estimate for his Science score.
(1) Find 32 on the Maths axis.
(2) Draw a line up to the line.
(3) Draw across to the Science axis.
(4) Read off the Science score.

The estimate is shown by the red lines on the graph.
The estimate for Ben's Science mark is 34.

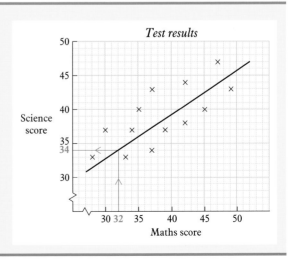

3 Look back at the scatter graph you did in question **1**.
  a Draw a line of best fit on your graph.
  b Estimate the age of a car that is worth £5500.
  c Estimate the value of a $3\frac{1}{2}$ year old car.

4 Look back at the scatter graph you did in question **2**.
  a Draw a line of best fit on your graph.
  b Judge A gives a piece of work 14 marks. Estimate the score Judge B would give.

5 LoPrice supermarkets are doing a survey of their customers.
They asked how many visits people made to the supermarket during a 3 month period.
They also asked how far away from the store the people lived.
Here are the results for 14 customers.

Number of visits	9	7	12	11	14	12	6
Length of journey (miles)	7	5	5	8	3	4	8

Number of visits	8	15	13	5	12	2	9
Length of journey (miles)	5	3	6	10	1	7	6

  a Plot a scatter graph to show this data.
  b Draw a line of best fit through your points.
  c Describe the type of correlation that this data shows.
  d Estimate the number of visits made by a shopper living 9 miles away.
  e Say how reliable you think this estimate is.
     What other factors could affect your answer?

2   Value for money?

Washing powder is sold in lots of different sized containers.

It is often difficult to spot which is the best value for money.

Some shops put extra information on the ticket to help you.

To compare the value for money you need to work out the price for a fixed amount.

Example

Brazen washing powder costs £4.30 for a 500 g box or £2.52 for a 300 g box. Which is better value?

It is easy to work out how much 100 g costs in each box.

    500 g box: £4.30 ÷ 5 = 86 p per 100 g
    300 g box: £2.52 ÷ 3 = 84 p per 100 g

The 300 g box is better value.
You pay less for each 100 g.

Exercise 17:3

1   Wizzo milkshake costs 66 p for a 300 ml bottle or 90 p for a 500 ml bottle.
   a   Work out 66 p ÷ 3.
      This is the cost per 100 ml in the small bottle.
   b   Work out 90 p ÷ 5.
      This is the cost per 100 ml in the large bottle.
   c   Which size of bottle is better value?

2 Paws & Claws cat food costs 45 p for a 300 g tin or 70 p for a 500 g tin.
Which size of tin is better value for money?
   a Work out the cost per 100 g in the 300 g tin.
   b Work out the cost per 100 g in the 500 g tin.
   c Which size of tin is better value for money?

3 Woodhouse tea costs £1.56 for 80 bags and £1.98 for 120 bags.
   a Work out the cost of 10 bags in the 80 bag box.
   b Work out the cost of 10 bags in the 120 bag box.
   c Which is better value?

4 Choc Pops breakfast cereal is sold in
three sizes.
The sizes and prices are:
   300 g   £1.26
   500 g   £1.95
   800 g   £3.20
   a Work out the price of 100 g in each
   size of box.
   b Which size of box is the best value?

5 Sprinters crisps are sold in 3 ways.
Single bags cost 22 p
A 6 pack costs £1.26
An 8 pack costs £1.80 but has a special offer of 1 extra bag free.
   a Work out the cost of each bag in the 6 pack.
   b Work out the cost of each bag in the 8 pack.
   (It's *not* 22.5 p.)
   c Which pack is the best value?

Sometimes sizes are not so easy to compare.

Example   Panine shampoo is sold in two sizes.
The 325 ml bottle costs £2.40 and the 412 ml bottle costs £3.16
Which is the better value?

This time it's not so easy to work out the cost of 100 ml in each bottle.
So, work out the amount of shampoo per £1 in each bottle.
To do this divide the volume by the price.

325 ml bottle: 325 ÷ £2.40 = 135 ml for £1
412 ml bottle: 412 ÷ £3.16 = 130 ml for £1

The smaller bottle is slightly better value for money.
You get slightly more shampoo for each £1.

Exercise 17:4

1 Goblin washing-up liquid comes in 2 sizes:

525 ml costs £1.58 and 740 ml costs £2.12

a Work out the amount of liquid you get for £1 in the small bottle (525 ÷ 1.58).

b Work out the amount of liquid you get for £1 in the large bottle (740 ÷ 2.12).

c Which bottle is better value?

2 Columbo Coffee costs £3.45 for 175 g and £4.58 for 260 g.

a Work out the amount of coffee you get for £1 in the small jar (175 ÷ 3.45).

b Work out the amount of coffee you get for £1 in the large jar.

c Which jar is better value?

3 Tomato ketchup comes in 3 sizes.
The sizes and costs are shown in this table:

Size	Cost
125 ml	£1.24
263 ml	£2.51
415 ml	£3.99

Which size is the best value for money?

4 Satellite washing powder comes in lots of different sizes.
Look at the following offers.
Decide which is the best value for money.
Show all your working.

Size	Cost	Offers
1.5 kg	£2.54	
2.3 kg	£3.67	Buy 2 get 50 p off.
3.7 kg	£5.68	
4.2 kg	£7.45	Extra 200 g free.

Direct proportion

Some products are sold in a way that makes it easy to compare.
For example, if you buy bananas, you would pay by the kilogram.
If 1 kg costs £1.20, you can be sure that 2 kg would cost twice as much, £2.40
Petrol is the same. $2\,l$ will cost twice as much as $1\,l$ and $3\,l$ will cost 3 times as much.

This is called **direct proportion**.

Example

Copy this table showing petrol prices.
Fill in the gaps marked with letters.

Amount	1 l	2 l	6 l	**c**	**d**
Cost	70 p	**a**	**b**	£4.90	£6.30

a $2\,l$ will cost twice as much as $1\,l$.
   $2 \times 70\,\text{p} = £1.40$

b $6\,l$ will cost 6 times as much as $1\,l$.
   $6 \times 70\,\text{p} = £4.20$

c Divide the price by the price for $1\,l$.
   $£4.90 \div 70\,\text{p} = 7$
   $7\,l$ cost £4.90

d Divide the cost by the price for $1\,l$.
   $£6.30 \div 70\,\text{p} = 9$
   $9\,l$ cost £6.30

Exercise 17:5

1 a Copy this table. Leave spaces for your answers for parts (1)–(4).
   It shows the prices of different amounts of apples.

Amount	1 kg	2 kg	5 kg	(3)	(4)
Price	38 p	(1)	(2)	£3.04	£5.32

b Work out the cost of 2 kg (38 p × 2).
   Put your answer in space (1).
c Work out the cost of 5 kg.
   Put your answer in space (2).
d Work out how many kilograms of apples you can
   buy for £3.04 (304 ÷ 38).
   Put your answer in space (3).
e Work out how many kilograms of apples you can
   buy for £5.32
   Put your answer in space (4).

2 a Copy this table.
   It shows the prices for different amounts of carpet.

Amount	2 m²	6 m²	11 m²	(3)	(4)
Price	£35	(1)	(2)	£245	£472.50

b Fill in the gaps marked with numbers.
   Show your working.

3 Pic 'n' Mix sweets cost 74 p per 100 g.
   a Work out the cost for 300 g.
   b Work out the cost of 450 g.
   c What weight of sweets could you buy for £4.81?
   d What weight of sweets could you buy for £1.11?

3 Collecting terms

Graham is adding his bottles to the bottle bank.

He must make sure that the different coloured bottles are all collected together.

There is a different collecting bin for each colour.

In algebra, you can collect terms together as long as they are the same type.

Term	A **term** is the name given to one part of an equation or formula. In the formula $y = kv + 3q$, **kv** and **$3q$** are terms.
Collecting terms	**Collecting terms** means adding or subtracting terms in an equation or formula to make it simpler. To collect terms together they must have exactly the same letters in them.

Example	Simplify these by collecting terms. **a** $t + t + t + t + t$ **b** $b + b + b + c + c$
	
	 a Adding five ts together gives 5 lots of t.
	     $t + t + t + t + t = 5 \times t = 5t$
	 b You can collect together the 3 bs and the 2 cs. You can't add the bs to the cs.
	     $b + b + b + c + c = 3b + 2c$

Exercise 17:6

1 Simplify these by collecting terms.

   a $g + g + g + g + g$ **d** $r + r + r + r + r + r$

   b $k + k + k + k + k + k$ **e** $y + y$

   c $t + t + t$ **f** $a + a + a + a$

2 Simplify these by collecting terms.

a $g + g + h + h + h$

b $m + m + m + k + k + k$

c $t + t + s + s + s - s$

d $r + r + r + r + w + w$

e $y + y + h + h + h + h + h$

● **f** $a + a + a - b - b + c + c$

The letters are sometimes already in groups.
Remember that $5t$ means $5 \times t$ or 5 lots of t.

Example

Simplify these by collecting terms.

a $5a + 3a + 2a$

b $3a + 6bc + 2a - 4bc$

a All the terms involve just a so they can all be added together.

$$5a + 3a + 2a = 10a$$

b The terms involving a can be collected together.
So can the terms with bc in them.
You can't collect the as and the bcs together.

$$3a + 6bc + 2a - 4bc = 5a + 2bc$$

---

3 Simplify these by collecting terms.

a $3g + 3g + 2g + 5g$

b $5m + 2m + 5m + 3k + 5k$

c $3t + 2t + 5s + 4s + 3s$

d $3r - 6r + 5w + 8w$

e $3y - 6y + 7h + 4h + y$

● **f** $5a + 9a + 7b + 11b + 10c + 4c$

4 Simplify these by collecting terms.

a $3ab + 5ab$

b $5mn - 2mn + 4mn$

● **c** $3ts + 2st$

d $3pr - 6pr + 5kw - 10kw$

e $5xy - 12xy + 9z - 4z + y$

● **f** $6ad - 9da + 8bc - 6cb + 15c - 24c$

Power

$k^4 = k \times k \times k \times k$

The **power** 4 tells you how many ks are multiplied together.

Example

Write $t \times t \times t$ as a power of t.

There are 3 ts multiplied together.
The power is 3.

$$t \times t \times t = t^3$$

Exercise 17:7

1 Write each of these as powers.

   a $t \times t$

   b $y \times y \times y$

   c $p \times p \times p \times p$

   d $k \times k \times k \times k \times k \times k$

   e $b \times b \times b \times b \times b \times b \times b \times b$

   ● **f** $2a \times 2a \times 2a$

You can only collect terms with powers when they are:
- the same letter or groups of letters
- exactly the same power.

Example

Simplify these by collecting terms where possible.

   a $x^2 + 3x^2 + 5x^2$

   b $3ab^2 + 5ab^2 - 2ab^2$

   c $3x^2 + 5x$

   d $3a^2b + 5ab^2$

   a All the letters and all the powers are the same, so these can be collected.
$$x^2 + 3x^2 + 5x^2 = 9x^2$$

   b The terms all have ab^2 in them, so these can be collected.
$$3ab^2 + 5ab^2 - 2ab^2 = 6ab^2$$

   c Both terms have just x in them, but they are *different powers*. These terms *cannot* be collected.

   d Both terms involve a and b and squared, but the power 2 is on a different letter in each term. These terms *cannot* be collected.

---

2 Simplify these by collecting terms where possible.
When it is not possible to collect terms, give a reason.

   a $6x^2 + 5x^2$

   b $9x^2 - 3x^2$

   c $3t^2 + 2t^3$

   d $3r^2s - 6r^2s$

   e $3y^3 + 6y^3 - y^3$

   f $5a^2 - 3a^2 + 7a^4$

3 Simplify these by collecting terms where possible.
When it is not possible to collect terms, give a reason.

   a $3x^2 + 2x^2 + 6y^2 - 3y^2$

   b $9x^2 - 3x^2 - 7z^2 - 2y^2$

   c $3t^2 - 5h^2 + 6t^3 + 6h^3$

   d $6a^2b + 5a^2b - 3a^2b$

   ● **e** $4xy^2 + 7xy - 8x^2y$

   ● **f** $7ab^2 - 4ab^2 + 5b^2a$

4 Simplify these as far as possible by collecting terms.

a $5x + 4x^2 + 6x - 3y$

b $7x^2 - 3x - 4x^2 - 2x$

c $5t^2y - 8h + 6t^2y + 6h$

d $7a + 9a^2b - 4ab^2$

e $4y^2 + 4x^2y - 9x^2y$

● **f** $4x^2yz + 3yx^2z - zyx^2$

Equations or formulas often have brackets in them.
You need to multiply out the brackets before you can simplify them.
Before you multiply out brackets, here is a reminder of how to
multiply terms together.

Example

Simplify these.

a $f \times g$

b $3z \times y$

c $4g \times 7h$

d $3y \times 2y$

a When 2 letters are multiplied together you should miss out
the $\times$ sign.
This is because the $\times$ sign can get confused with the letter x.
$$f \times g = fg$$

b Numbers always come before letters.
Letters should be in alphabetical order.
$$3z \times y = 3yz$$

c When you have 2 numbers, multiply them together as well.
$$4g \times 7h = 28gh$$

d When the letters are the same, they should be written as
powers.
$$3y \times 2y = 6 \times y \times y = 6y^2$$

Exercise 17:8

1 Simplify these.

a $t \times s$

b $3 \times 5c$

c $7r \times 5$

d $6w \times 3y$

e $3a \times 5b$

f $5y \times 2y$

2 Simplify these.

a $3p \times 5p$

b $6t \times 8t$

● **c** $4z \times 2z$

d $(3h)^2$

e $4c \times 2c \times 3c$

f $2a \times 3b \times 6c$

● **3** Simplify these.

a $3t \times 5s$

b $8p \times 6p \times 2q$

c $3c \times 4d \times 6e$

d $3t \times 8t \times 4s$

e $p \times t \times r \times p \times t \times r$

f $(2p)^3$

Multiplying out brackets

It is easiest to start with numbers before looking at letters.
To work out $2(3 + 6)$ you need to use **BODMAS**.

First you do **B**rackets
then powers **O**f.
Next you do **D**ivision
and **M**ultiplication.
Then you do **A**ddition
and **S**ubtraction.

So, to work out $2(3 + 6)$ you need to work out the bracket: $3 + 6 = 9$
Then multiply by the 2: $2 \times 9 = 18$

Another way to work this out is to **multiply out** the bracket.
To do this you multiply everything inside the bracket by the number outside.

$$2(3 + 6) = 2 \times 3 + 2 \times 6$$
$$= 6 + 12$$
$$= 18$$

Exactly the same method works with letters.

Example Multiply out these brackets.
  a $2(3 + x)$ **b** $-6(x^2 - 4)$

a To work out $2(3 + x)$ multiply the 3 and the x by the 2.
$$2(3 + x) = 2 \times 3 + 2 \times x$$
$$= 6 + 2x$$

b $-6(x^2 - 4) = -6 \times x^2 + (-6) \times (-4)$
$$= -6x^2 + 24$$

Exercise 17:9

Multiply out these brackets.

1 $4(x + 1)$ **4** $9(2x + 3)$ **7** $6(y^2 - 3y)$

2 $2(b + 3)$ **5** $5(3x - 5)$ **● 8** $8(f^2 - 3f - 4)$

3 $4(c - 8)$ **6** $4(x^2 + x)$ **9** $9(4x - x^3)$

Multiply out these brackets.
Watch the minus signs!

10 $-3(x + 4)$ **13** $-2(2x + 3)$ **16** $-4(2 - 3x)$

11 $-6(x^2 + 5)$ **14** $-3(4x - 2)$ ● **17** $-5(-x - 3)$

12 $-4(x - y)$ **15** $-6(5 - x)$ ● **18** $-(3x^2 - x)$

You can also have a letter outside a bracket.
The bracket can be multiplied out in the same way.

Example   Multiply out these brackets.
     a $x(x + 3)$ **b** $x(3x - 2y)$

     a To work out $x(x + 3)$ multiply the x and the 3 by the x.
$$x(x + 3) = x \times x + x \times 3$$
$$= x^2 + 3x$$
     b To work out $x(3x - 2y)$ multiply the $3x$ and the $-2y$ by the x.
$$x(3x - 2y) = x \times 3x - x \times 2y$$
$$= 3x^2 - 2xy$$

---

19 $x(x + 1)$ **22** $x(x - 6)$ ● **25** $y(x + 2y)$

20 $x(3x - 2)$ **23** $x(y + 5)$ ● **26** $2y(y - 3)$

21 $p(2p + 6)$ **24** $y(x + 5)$ ● **27** $-3y(y - x)$

You also get brackets in some equations.
The best way to deal with these is to get rid of them!

Example   Solve the equation $3(2x + 1) = 27$

     Multiply the bracket out: $3 \times 2x + 3 \times 1 = 27$
$$6x + 3 = 27$$
     Take 3 from each side: $6x = 24$
     Divide both sides by 6: $x = 4$

Exercise 17:10

Solve these equations.
Multiply the brackets out first.

1 $3(2x + 1) = 21$

2 $4(7x - 4) = 40$

3 $6(2x - 7) = 42$

4 $5(8x - 1) = 35$

5 $10(2x - 10) = 40$

6 $9(3x - 5) = -18$

7 $6(3x - 2) = 42$

8 $4(2x - 1) = -8$

9 $5(3x + 1) = -10$

● **10** $2(2x - 1) = x + 7$

● **11** $3(x + 5) = 5x + 13$

● **12** $10(3x - 4) = 5(6 - x)$

Factorising

Factorising is the opposite of multiplying out brackets.
You are trying to work out what number or letter was outside the bracket before it was multiplied out.
You have to try to find common factors.

Example   Factorise $6x + 10y$.
The numbers 6 and 10 both have a factor of 2.
2 is the biggest number that divides exactly into 6 and 10.
You take a 2 outside the bracket as a factor:
$6x + 10y = 2(\quad)$

Next, you work out what goes inside the bracket.
$2 \times 3x = 6x$ and $2 \times 5y = 10y$.
So you put $3x$ and $5y$ inside the bracket.

This means that $6x + 10y = 2(3x + 5y)$.
This is now factorised.

Exercise 17:11

Factorise each of these.
Use the hints to help you in questions **1–4**.

1 $4x + 18 = 2($ $)$ **5** $6x - 36$

2 $3x - 27 = 3($ $)$ **6** $8x^2 - 16y$

3 $12y - 16 = 4($ $)$ **7** $30t - 40s - 50r$

4 $35x - 25 = 5($ $)$ **8** $21y - 49z$

You can also take letters outside brackets as common factors.

The expression $xy + xz$ has a common factor of x.
$xy + xz$ has an x in both terms.
So $xy + xz = x(y + z)$.

The expression $y^2 + y$ has a common factor of y.
$y^2 + y$ has a y in both terms.
So $y^2 + y = y(y + 1)$

Notice the 1 at the end of the bracket. It is very important.
If you multiply the bracket out you must get back to where you started.
$y(y + 1) = y \times y + y \times 1$
$\qquad\quad = \quad y^2 \quad + \quad y$

If you missed the 1 out, you would not get the y term at the end.

Exercise 17:12

Factorise each of these. Use the hints to help you in questions **1–4**.

1 $ax + bx = x($ $)$ **5** $6x^2 - 11x$

2 $5xy - 6xz = x($ $)$ **6** $t^3 + t^2$

3 $5bc - 8bd = b($ $)$ **7** $3x^3 + 5x^2 + 7x$

4 $7x - 9xy = x($ $)$ **8** $12xy^2 - 13x^2y$

Exercise 17:13

Sharon has been learning about collecting terms.
Sadly, she has not been using *Key Maths*!
This is a copy of her last piece of work.
Look carefully through the work and spot all the errors.
Some of her answers are correct!
Re-write all the questions that Sharon has got wrong.

1 $t + t + t + t + t = t^5$

2 $3p + 2p + 4y + 5y = 5p + 9y = 14py$

3 $3ab + 5ab + 6ab = 14ab$

4 $6ad + 7da$ Can't be collected because the terms are different.

5 $x^2 + 3x^2 - 5x^2 = 9x^2$

6 $3t^2 - 5h^2 + 6t^3 + 6h^3$ Can't be collected because the terms are different.

7 $3p \times 5q = 15qp$

8 $2(x + 3) = 2x + 3$

9 $4(x^2 - 5) = 4x^2 + 20$

10 $3(x - 1) = 12$
  $3x - 1 = 12$
    $3x = 13$
      $x = 13 \div 3 = 4.33 \ (2 \ dp)$

11 $9x + 3 = 3(6x + 0)$

12 $x^2 + 3x = x(x + 3)$

4   Circles

This is the circular maze at Doddington Hall.

There are special names for the different parts of a circle.

You also need to learn some formulas to work out the distance around a circle and its area.

Radius	The **radius** of a circle is the distance from the centre to the edge.
Diameter	The **diameter** of a circle is the distance from one side to the other through the centre.

Exercise 17:14

1   Write down (1) the radius and (2) the diameter of each of these circles.

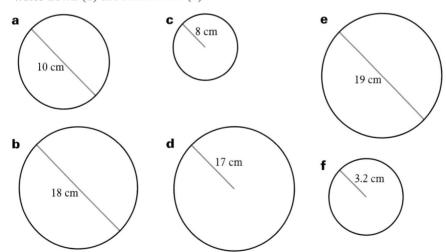

a   10 cm

b   18 cm

c   8 cm

d   17 cm

e   19 cm

f   3.2 cm

2   a   Use a pair of compasses to draw a circle with a radius of 4 cm.
   b   Mark a radius and a diameter on your circle.

3 a Use a pair of compasses to draw a circle with a *diameter* of 10 cm.
   b Mark a radius and a diameter on your circle.

4 a Draw a line 7 cm long.
   b Draw a circle with this line as a diameter.

| Circumference | The distance around the outside of a circle is called its **circumference**. This is the same as the perimeter of the circle. |  |

5 a Draw a circle with a radius of 6 cm.

   b Keep your compasses set to 6 cm. Put the point of your compasses anywhere on the circumference of the circle.
Make a mark with your pencil on the circumference of the circle.

   c Move the point of your compasses to the mark you have just made. Make another mark further around the circle.

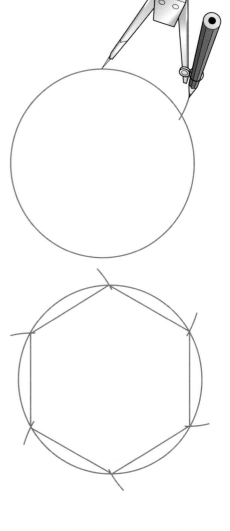

   d Repeat part **c** 5 times. Your last mark should be the point where you started.
   e Join each mark on the circumference to the next one. You should have a hexagon.

6 **a** Draw a circle with a radius of 5 cm.
   b Copy this diagram using your compasses.

You have already seen the words **radius, diameter** and **circumference**.
There are other parts of the circle which have special names.

Chord

A **chord** is a line going from one side
of a circle to the other but **not** through
the middle.
A chord is always a straight line.

Arc

An **arc** is a part of the circumference.
An arc is always a curved line.

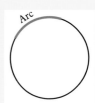

Tangent

A **tangent** to a circle is a straight
line that just touches the circle.

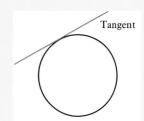

7 Look at each of these diagrams.
For each part look at the line in red and say if it is an **arc**, a **tangent** or a
chord.

  a   **c**   **e**

  b   **d**   **f**

Finding the length of the circumference

To find the length of the circumference you need a special number.
The special number is π (spelt *pi* and said like 'pie').

$$\pi = 3.142 \text{ (3 dp)}$$

In fact, π is a decimal number that carries on forever without any pattern.
You can buy a book with π printed to five million decimal places!
You don't need this many. 1 dp or 2 dp will usually be enough and you
can use the π button on your calculator.

The formula for the circumference is:

Circumference = π × diameter

In algebra this is written as:

$$C = \pi \times d \text{ or just } C = \pi d$$

Example Find the circumference of a circle with a diameter of 8 cm.

$$\text{Circumference} = \pi \times \text{diameter}$$
$$= \pi \times 8$$

Key in: $\boxed{\pi}$ $\boxed{\times}$ $\boxed{8}$ $\boxed{=}$

$$= 25.14 \text{ cm (2 dp)}$$

Exercise 17:15

In this exercise, round your answers to 2 dp.

1 Find the circumference of a circle with diameter 12 cm.
Copy this. Fill in the gaps.

$$\text{Circumference} = \pi \times \text{diameter}$$
$$= \pi \times \ldots$$

Key in: $\boxed{\pi}$ $\boxed{\times}$ $\boxed{1}$ $\boxed{2}$ $\boxed{=}$

$$= \ldots \text{ cm (2 dp)}$$

2 Find the circumference of a circle with diameter 18 cm.
Copy this. Fill in the gaps.

$$\text{Circumference} = \pi \times \ldots$$
$$= \pi \times \ldots$$
$$= \ldots \text{ cm (2 dp)}$$

3 Find the circumference of a circle with radius 24 cm.
Copy this. Fill in the gaps.

   Diameter $= 2 \times$ radius
                  $= 2 \times 24$
                  $= 48$ cm

   Circumference $= \pi \times \ldots$
                 $= \pi \times \ldots$
                 $= \ldots$ cm (2 dp)

4 Find the circumference of these circles:
   a diameter $= 6$ cm   **b** diameter $= 13$ cm   **c** diameter $= 15$ cm

5 Find the circumference of these circles:
   a radius $= 7$ cm   **b** radius $= 19$ cm   **● c** radius $= 2.7$ cm

6 Find the **red** circumference of this
semi-circle.
It is half of the circumference of the
full circle. Give your answer to 2 dp

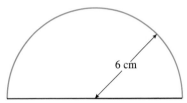

6 cm

● 7 Find the perimeter of these shapes.

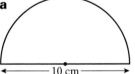

a

10 cm

b

8 cm

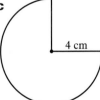

c

4 cm

The formula for the area of a circle also has π in it.
The area formula uses the **radius** of the circle instead of the diameter.
The formula is:

Area $= \pi \times$ radius $\times$ radius

In algebra this is
$$A = \pi \times r \times r \quad \text{or} \quad A = \pi r^2$$

Example   Find the area of a circle with a radius of 9 cm.

   Area $= \pi \times$ radius $\times$ radius
        $= \pi \times 9 \times 9$

   Key in: [π] [$\times$] [9] [$\times$] [9] [$=$]

        $= 254.5$ cm^2 (1 dp)

Exercise 17:16

In this exercise, round your answers to 1 dp.

1 Find the area of a circle with radius 10 cm.
Copy this. Fill in the gaps.

$$\text{Area} = \pi \times \text{radius} \times \text{radius}$$
$$= \pi \times 10 \times 10$$
$$= \dots \text{ cm}^2 \text{ (1 dp)}$$

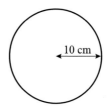

10 cm

2 Find the area of a circle with radius 17 cm.
Copy this. Fill in the gaps.

$$\text{Area} = \pi \times \text{radius} \times \text{radius}$$
$$= \pi \times \dots \times \dots$$
$$= \dots \text{ cm}^2 \text{ (1 dp)}$$

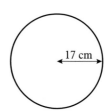

17 cm

3 Find the area of a circle with diameter 24 cm.
Copy this. Fill in the gaps.

$$\text{Radius} = \text{diameter} \div 2$$
$$= 24 \div 2$$
$$= 12 \text{ cm}$$

$$\text{Area} = \pi \times \dots \times \dots$$
$$= \pi \times \dots \times \dots$$
$$= \dots \text{ cm}^2$$

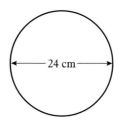

24 cm

4 Find the area of these circles.

a

8 cm

b

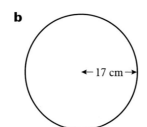

17 cm

c

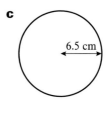

6.5 cm

5 Find the area of these circles.
You will need to find the radius first.

a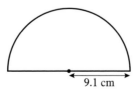
40 cm

b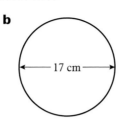
17 cm

c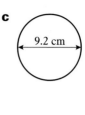
9.2 cm

6 Find the area of a circle with radius:
a 7 cm   **b** 19 cm   **c** 2.7 cm

7 Find the area of a circle with diameter:
a 6 cm   **b** 13 cm   **c** 6.3 cm

You can find the area of parts of a circle.

Example   Find the area of this semi-circle.

Area of the whole circle $= \pi \times$ radius $\times$ radius
$$= \pi \times 9 \times 9$$
$$= 254.47 \text{ cm}^2 \text{ (2 dp)}$$

Area of the semi-circle $= 254.47 \div 2$
$$= 127.2 \text{ cm}^2 \text{ (1 dp)}$$

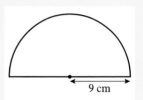
9 cm

---

8 Find the area of these semi-circles.

a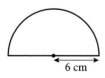
6 cm

b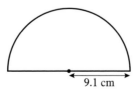
9.1 cm

c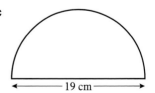
19 cm

9 Find the area of these shapes.

a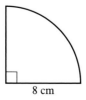
8 cm

b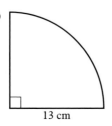
13 cm

c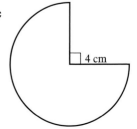
4 cm

1 Stripes toothpaste is sold in 2 sizes:

    The small size contains 85 ml and costs 74 p
    The large size contains 140 ml and costs £1.38

Which size gives better value for money?

2 Lisper washing-up liquid comes in 2 sizes:

    550 ml costs £1.63 and 850 ml costs £2.24

  a Work out the amount of liquid you get for £1 in the small bottle.
  b Work out the amount of liquid you get for £1 in the large bottle.
  c Which bottle is better value?

3 It takes 150 g of flour to make 4 scones.
  a How many scones could you make with 900 g?
  b Calculate the weight of flour needed to make 22 scones.

4 Collect these terms where possible.
  a $t + t + t$ **c** $s + s + t + t$ **e** $d + c + d + c - d + c$
  b $f^2 + 2f$ **d** $3g^2 + 2g^2$

5 Simplify these by multiplying.
  a $4x \times 8x$ **d** $(2y)^2$
  b $7t \times 3t$ **e** $6b \times b \times 2b$
  c $4t \times -3t$ **f** $3z \times 2z \times \frac{1}{2}z$

6 Multiply out these brackets.
  a $2(x + 3)$ **b** $-3(2x + 6)$ **c** $-4(3y - 2)$

7 Multiply out these brackets.
  a $x(x + 2)$ **b** $y(y^2 - 3)$ **c** $3y(2y + x)$

8 Find the circumference of a circle with:
  a diameter = 12 cm   **b** diameter = 6.3 cm   **c** radius = 8 cm

9 Find the circumference of this semi-circle.
It is half of the circumference of the full circle.

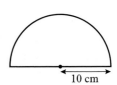

10 cm

10 Find the area of these circles.

a

12 cm

b

19 cm

c

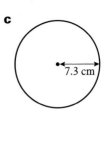
7.3 cm

11 The ages of 10 houses and their sale values are shown in this table.

Age (years)	10	25	30	8	2	40	30	25	5	1
Value (£000)	50	80	35	105	45	65	80	100	120	95

a Plot a scatter graph to show this data.
b Describe the type of correlation that this data shows.

12 A form tutor asked her form to say how many hours a week they spent playing sport and how many they spent watching TV.
These are the results of her survey.

Hours playing sport	2	0	5	8	4	3	9	2	5
Hours watching TV	15	19	10	5	9	20	5	4	16

a Plot a scatter graph to show this data.
b Describe the type of correlation that this data shows.
c Put a circle around the value that does not follow the trend of the rest of the data.
d Pete spends 13 hours a week playing sport.
By drawing a suitable line on your diagram, estimate how many hours he spends watching TV.

13 Multiply out these brackets.

   a $-4(x + 2)$ **c** $-6(x - 9)$ **e** $-(2 - 3y)$

   b $-3(x - 1)$ **d** $-8(d + 1)$ **f** $-3(s + t)$

14 Multiply out these brackets.

   a $x(x + 2)$ **c** $x(x - 9)$ **e** $y(x - 3y)$

   b $x(2x - 1)$ **d** $x(p - 3)$ **f** $y(y + z)$

15 Solve these equations.

   a $3(2x + 1) = 30$ **d** $5(2x - 2) = -10$

   b $4(7x - 6) = 32$ **e** $4(2x - 1) = -8$

   c $6(2x - 1) = -36$ **f** $5(3x - 4) = -35$

16 Factorise these.

   a $5x + 15$ **c** $6y - 18$ **e** $x^2 + 3x$

   b $4x - 12$ **d** $15x - 20$ **f** $3y + y^2$

17 Look at each of these diagrams.
For each part look at the line in red and say if it is an **arc**, a **tangent** or a **chord**.

   a   **c**   **e**

   b   **d**    **f**

1 Simplify these by collecting terms where possible.
When it is not possible to collect terms, give a reason.

a $5x^2 + 3x^2 + 4y^2 - 3y^2$ **d** $5a^2b + 8a^2b - 6a^2b$

b $11x^2 - 13x^2 - 5z^2 - 2z^2$ **e** $6xy^2 - 4xy - 9xy^2$

c $6t^2 - 2h^2 - 6t^3 + 2h^3$ **f** $12ab^2 - 8ab^2 + 3b^2a$

2 Popster Popcorn is sold in 4 sizes:

> Small bags cost 28 p and contain 100 g.
> Medium bags cost 65 p and contain 250 g.
> Large bags cost £1.25 and contain 450 g.
> Family bags cost £2.70 and contain 1 kg.

Which bag is the best value?

3 This table shows the marks scored by students in a French test and a Spanish test.

French	30	25	18	21	32	27	19	28	26
Spanish	56	49	35	40	60	54	37	51	47

a Draw a scatter graph to show this data.

b Describe the relationship between the 2 sets of marks.

c Francesca scored 29 in the French test.
Use your graph to estimate her score in the Spanish test.

4 This diagram shows a circular
running track.
The diameter of the track is 100 m.
Steve runs backwards and
forwards along the diameter.
Seb runs at the same speed round
the circumference of the track.
How many times will Steve have
run along the diameter while Seb
runs round the track once?

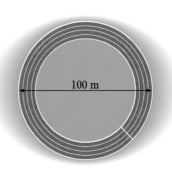

100 m

1 Arum is looking at widths and lengths of pebbles for a science project. The table shows his data for 10 pebbles.

Length (mm)	23	50	15	33	58	10	43	23	55	35
Width (mm)	19	34	13	22	40	13	30	16	35	27

     a Plot a scatter graph to show this data.
     b What type of correlation does your graph show?
     c Draw a line of best fit on your graph.
     d Use your line to estimate the length of a pebble with width 21 mm.

2 Shinerite shampoo comes in two sizes: 250 ml for £1.80
                                               400 ml for £2.45

     a Work out the price of 10 ml for each size of bottle.
     b Which size is the better value?

3 Simplify these.
     a $2f + 6f - 7f$ **b** $4x + 3x^2 - x + 5x^2$ **c** $4t \times 2t$

4 Solve these equations.
     a $4(3x + 5) = 68$ **b** $14 = 7(2x - 8)$

5 For each circle find: (1) the circumference   (2) the area.
     a   **b**

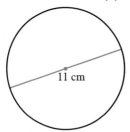

11 cm

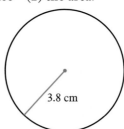

3.8 cm

6 Write down the name of each **red** part marked with a letter.

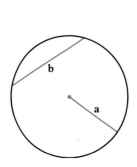

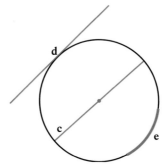

18

1 Forming equations
Writing down formulas from sentences
Solving problems using formulas

2 Sample space diagrams
Using sample space diagrams in probability

3 Angles and polygons
Remembering angle facts
Looking at angles in polygons
Working with interior and exterior angles

4 Trial and improvement
Solving equations with whole number answers
Solving equations with answers to 1 dp
Finding an answer for a non-linear equation
Solving equations giving answers to 1 dp
accuracy
Solving worded problems

CORE

QUESTIONS

EXTENSION

TEST YOURSELF

1 **Forming equations**

In Science and Maths, you often have to work out equations for yourself.

Some equations and formulas become very famous like $E = mc^2$ and $A = \pi r^2$.

In this final algebra section, you are going to write some equations to help you solve problems.

Formulas are just a shorthand way of writing down sentences.
One letter is used instead of a whole word.

Example

Read this sentence:
'The perimeter of a square is four times the length of one of its sides.'
Write down a formula for the perimeter of a square.

Pick out the important words and numbers in the sentence:
'The **perimeter** of a square is **four times** the **length** of one of its sides.'

Choose letters to stand for the important words:
    perimeter = p length = l

Write down a formula:
    $p = 4 \times l$ or just $p = 4l$

Exercise 18:1

Read each of these sentences in questions **1–9** carefully.
The important words and numbers are highlighted.
Each one has a word in **red**.
Write down a formula for the **red** word.
Don't forget to say what each letter in your formula stands for.

1 The total cost of some carpet that costs £24 for each square metre.

2 Simon's total wages if he earns £6 per hour.

3 The perimeter of a rectangle if you know its length and its width.

4 The distance left on a 500 mile journey if you know how many miles you have already travelled.

5 The number of 4 metre pieces that can be cut from a length of material.

6 The sale price of a CD player with £20 off the normal price.

7 The total cost of a set of magazines that cost £2.75 per week and £12 for a set of binders.

8 The total cost of a class trip which includes a £3 entrance fee for each pupil and £120 for a coach.

9 The average speed for a journey when you know the total distance and the time taken.

10 Read this sentence:

'To estimate the circumference of a circle, multiply the diameter by 3.'

Write down a formula to estimate the circumference of a circle.

Once you have written a formula, you can use it to solve problems.

Example

The perimeter of a square is 56 cm.
Find the length of one of the sides.

The formula for the perimeter of a square is $p = 4l$.
You know that the perimeter is 56,
so $56 = 4l$.

Now solve the equation. $\qquad 4l = 56$
Divide by 4. $\qquad\qquad\qquad l = 14$
The length of a side is 14 cm.

Exercise 18:2

1 Alan pays £432 for some carpet that costs £24 per square metre.
  a Write a formula for the **total cost** of some carpet at **£24** per square **metre**.
  b Re-write the formula, putting in the cost of Alan's carpet.
  c Solve your equation to find how many square metres of carpet Alan buys.

2 Simon earns £6 per hour. This week he has earned £252.
  a Write a formula for Simon's **total wages** if he earns **£6** per **hour**.
  b Re-write the formula, putting in Simon's wages for this week.
  c Solve your equation to find how many hours Simon has worked this week.

3 The perimeter of a rectangular field is 84 m. The length of the field is 22 m.
  a Write a formula for the **perimeter** of a rectangle if you know its **length** and its **width**.
  b Re-write the formula, putting in the perimeter of the field and its length.
  c Solve your equation to find the width of the field.

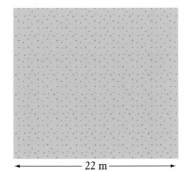

◄——————— 22 m ———————►

4 Lindsey is driving from London to Glasgow, which is about 500 miles. She has travelled 240 miles so far.
  a Write a formula for the **distance** left on a **500** mile journey if you know how many **miles** you have already travelled.
  b Re-write the formula, putting in the distance Lindsey has travelled so far.
  c Solve your equation to find how far Lindsey has left to go.

Some problems have slightly more complicated equations.

Example   These two rectangles have the
same area.
  a Write down a formula for the
area of each rectangle.
  b Write down an equation in
terms of x.
  c Solve your equation to find the
area of the rectangles.

4

$x + 1$ **A**

$x + 5$

2   **B**

  a Area of rectangle **A** is $4(x + 1)$.
Area of rectangle **B** is $2(x + 5)$.

  b If the two areas are equal then:
$$4(x + 1) = 2(x + 5)$$
This is called an equation in x because x is the only letter.

  c Now solve the equation.
First remove the brackets: $4x + 4 = 2x + 10$
Now solve it: $2x + 4 = 10$
$$2x = 6$$
$$x = 3$$

Putting this value of x into the formulas for the areas gives:
$$4(x + 1) = 4(3 + 1) = 16$$
and $2(x + 5) = 2(3 + 5) = 16.$

The area of each of the rectangles is 16.

Exercise 18:3

1 These two rectangles have the same
area.
  a Write down a formula for the area
of each rectangle.
  b Write down an equation in terms
of x.
  c Solve your equation to find the
area of the rectangles.

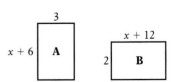

3

$x + 6$ **A**

$x + 12$

2   **B**

2 Read these 2 sentences:
   (1) Ned is 10 years older than his sister.
   (2) Ned is twice as old as his sister.

   a Call the age of Ned's sister n.
   Use sentence (1) to write down a formula for Ned's age.
   b Use sentence (2) to write down another formula for Ned's age.
   c Write down an equation in terms of n.
   d Solve your equation to find the age of Ned's sister.
   e How old is Ned?

3 Mr Short's lawn has a perimeter of 90 m.
   It is twice as long as it is wide.
   a Call the width of the lawn w.
   Write down a formula for the length
   of the lawn.
   b Write down a formula for the
   perimeter of the lawn.
   c Write down an equation in terms
   of w.
   d Solve your equation to find the
   width of the lawn.
   e How long is the lawn?

4 Karen is asked to think of a number.
   She is then told to double it and add 7.
   She says that her answer is 55.
   a Call Karen's number n.
   Write down a formula for what Karen has done to the number.
   b Write down an equation in terms of n.
   c Solve your equation.
   d What number did Karen think of?

5 Joe thinks of a number, multiplies it by 9 and takes away 6.
   He gets 129.
   a Write down an equation to show what Joe does.
   b Solve your equation to find the number Joe thought of.

6 I am 13 years older than my sister.
   In a year's time I will be 3 times her age.
   How old am I?

2 Sample space diagrams

Sharon and her father are buying paint. They are trying to find the best colour to use for redecorating her bedroom. They have to decide which paint colours to mix. They are using a paint chart to help them.
It shows all the possible colours.

You can use diagrams to help in probability.

Sample space	A **sample space** is a list of all the things that can happen in a probability experiment.
Outcome	Each thing that can happen in an experiment is called an **outcome**.
Sample space diagram	A table which shows all of the possible outcomes is called a **sample space diagram**.

Example　Toby rolls a dice and spins a coin.

　a Draw a sample space diagram to show all the possible outcomes.
　b Write down the probability that Toby gets a head and a 5.

　a Draw a table. Put all the numbers for the dice along the top.
　　Put head and tail down the side.
　　Fill in each possible outcome.

	1	2	3	4	5	6
Head	H,1	H,2	H,3	H,4	H,5	H,6
Tail	T,1	T,2	T,3	T,4	T,5	T,6

　b There are 12 possible outcomes. They are equally likely.
　　A head and a 5 appears once.
　　The probability of getting a head and a 5 is $\frac{1}{12}$.

Exercise 18:4

1 Ben rolls an 8-sided dice and spins a coin.
He draws a sample space diagram to show all the possible outcomes.

a Copy this table.

	1	2	3	4	5	6	7	8
Head								
Tail								

b Fill in all the possible outcomes in your table.
c How many outcomes are there altogether?
d Write down the probability of getting a head and a 5.

2 Saleem is doing a probability experiment with 2 dice.
He has 1 red and 1 blue dice.
He draws a sample space diagram to show all the possible outcomes.

a Copy this table.

Red dice

		1	2	3	4	5	6
	1	1, 1	1, 2	1, 3			
	2	2, 1	2, 2	2, 3			
Blue	3	3, 1					
dice	4						
	5						
	6						

b Fill in all the possible outcomes in your table.
The first few have been done for you.
c How many outcomes are there altogether?
d What is the probability of throwing a 4 on both dice?
e What is the probability of throwing a double?

3 Jenny is doing the same experiment as Saleem.
She decides to draw her sample space diagram slightly differently.
Her diagram shows the *total* score on the 2 dice.
  a Copy this table.

Red dice

		1	2	3	4	5	6
	1	2	3	4			
	2	3	4	5			
Blue	3	4	5				
dice	4						
	5						
	6						

  b Fill in the rest of the totals.
  c Write down the probability of getting a total of 2.
  d Write down the probability of getting a total of 3.
  e Write down the probability of getting a total of 4.
  f Copy this table. Fill in the probabilities.

Total	2	3	4	5	6	7	8	9	10	11	12
Probability											

  g Which total has the highest probability?

4 Robbie plays in the school football team.
They have 2 important matches coming up.
They are equally likely to win, lose or draw each match.
  a Copy this table.

Match 2

		Win	Lose	Draw
	Win			
Match 1	Lose			
	Draw		D, L	

  b Fill in the table.
  c What is the probability that the team will win both matches?

5 Mrs Jones has decided to change the flowers in one of her garden tubs.
She has 2 bags of tulips.
Each bag contains 1 bulb of each of these colours:

    Red   Yellow   Pink   Orange   Violet   White

She takes a bulb at random from each bag.
a Draw a sample space diagram to show all the possible outcomes.
Write down the probability that the tulips that Mrs Jones chooses are:
b both red
c both the same colour
d different colours

6 Louise has made these 2 spinners to
use in a game at the school fair.
To play the game, you spin both
spinners.
You win a prize if they both land on
the same colour.
a Draw a sample space diagram for
this game.
b Write down the probability that
a player will win.
c Louise charges 20 p to play the game.
How much will she collect for 16 games?
d 16 people play Louise's game.
How many prizes would Louise expect to give out?
e Suggest how much Louise should give out as a prize.

7 Make the spinners used in Louise's game.
Do an experiment to check the theory of question **6**.
Write a short report on your results.

3 Angles and polygons

This building is called the Pentagon.

The reason is fairly obvious!
It houses the defence department in America.

To draw a regular pentagon, you need to know about angles.

Here are some angle rules that you might remember.

Full turn	There are 360° in a **full turn**.
Half turn	There are 180° in a **half turn**.
Quarter turn	A **quarter turn** is 90°. This is known as a **right angle**.
Acute angle	An acute **angle** is an angle less than 90°.
Obtuse angle	An **obtuse angle** is between 90° and 180°.
Reflex angle	A **reflex angle** is bigger than 180°.

Exercise 18:5

1 Look at each of these angles.
Write down whether they are acute, right, obtuse or reflex angles.

a

c

e

b

d

f
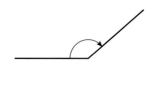

2 Use an angle measurer or protractor to draw each of these angles.
Write under each one whether it is an acute, right, obtuse or reflex angle.
a 30°   **b** 135°   **c** 210°   **d** 342°   **e** 193°

3 Use an angle measurer or protractor to measure each of these angles.

a
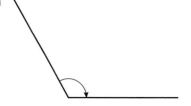

c
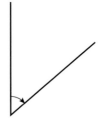

b
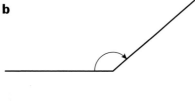

d
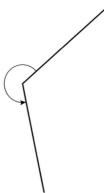

4 Estimate the size of each of these angles.
Measure them afterwards to check your answers.

a   **b**    **c**

Angles on a straight line add up to 180°.
This is because a half turn makes a
straight line.

You can use this rule to calculate angles.

Example   Work out the angle marked $a°$.

The angles add up to 180°.
So $a° = 180° - 70°$
$\quad\quad = 110°$

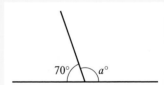

Exercise 18:6

For each question, calculate the angle marked with a letter.

1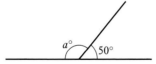

4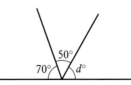

2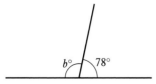

5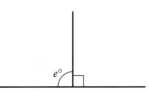

3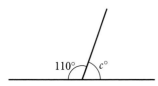

6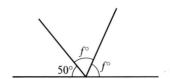

Angles around a point add up to 360°.
This is because they make up a full turn.

Example Work out the angle marked $b°$.

The angles add up to 360°.
So $b° = 360° − 70° − 120°$
$= 170°$

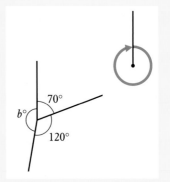

For each question, calculate the angle marked with a letter.

7

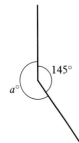

8

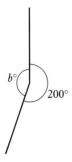

9

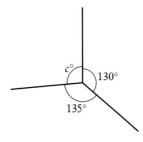

10

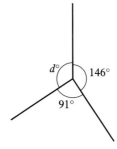

● **11**

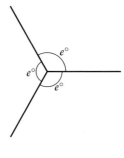

● **12**

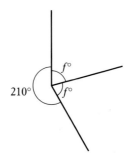

Opposite angles　Angles that are opposite each other in
a cross are equal.
They are known as **opposite angles**!

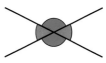

Example　Find the angles marked with letters.

$b°$ is opposite $a°$ and so it is the same angle:
$b° = 56$

$c°$ makes a straight line with $a°$.
This means that $a° + c° = 180°$.
$c° = 180° - 56° = 124°$

$d°$ is opposite $c°$ and so it is the same angle:
$d° = 124°$

Exercise 18:7

For each question, calculate the angle marked with a letter.

1

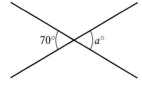

4

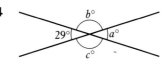

2

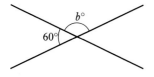

5

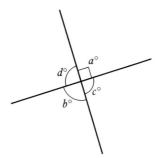

3

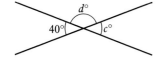

6

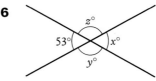

Angles in a triangle	**Angles in a triangle** add up to 180°.
Example	Find the angle marked $x°$. The angles add up to 180°. So $x° = 180° - 73° - 46°$ $\qquad x° = 61°$

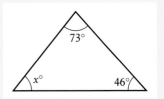

Exercise 18:8

For each question, calculate the angle marked with a letter.

1

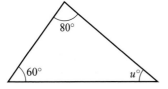

2

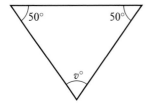

3

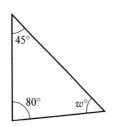

4

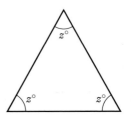

● **5**

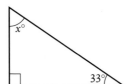

● **6**

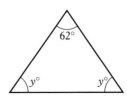

You can use the opposite angles rules to work out **angles on parallel lines**.

$a°$ and $b°$ are equal because they are opposite angles.

The sloping line crosses the bottom line at the same angle that it crosses the top line. This means that $p°$ and $q°$ are the same as $a°$ and $b°$.

$c°, d°, r°$ and $s°$ are all equal in the same way.

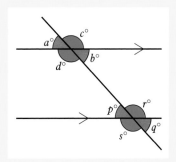

Exercise 18:9

1 a Copy this diagram. The angles do not need to be exact.
  b Colour all the angles **red** that are equal to $a°$.
  c Colour all the angles **blue** that are equal to $b°$.

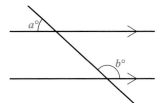

2 a Write down the letters of all the angles that are 70°.
  b Write down the letters of all the angles that are 110°.

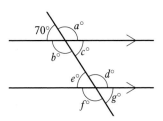

3 Work out all the angles marked with letters.

a

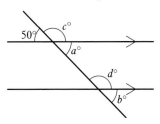

c

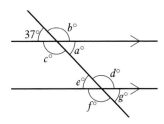

b

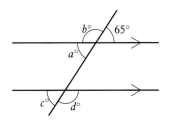

d

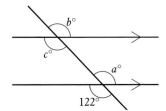

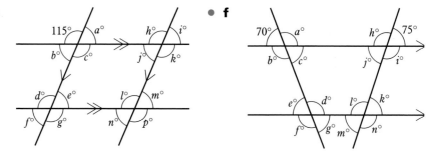

• e

• f

Polygon	A **polygon** is a shape with straight sides.
Regular polygon	All the sides of a **regular polygon** are the same length. All the angles are also equal.

Exercise 18:10

1 Copy this table. Fill it in. The first letters are given as a hint.

Number of sides	Name of polygon
3	t...
4	q...
5	p...
6	h...
7	h...
8	o...
9	n...
10	d...
11	h...
12	d...

2 **a** Draw a horizontal line 10 cm long with 5 cm solid and 5 cm dotted. Leave some space above it.
  b Put your angle measurer on the end of the solid line. Measure 72° from the dotted line.
  c Draw another line. Draw 5 cm solid and 5 cm dotted.
  d Repeat parts **b** and **c** at the end of your new line.
  e Keep going until you complete a pentagon.

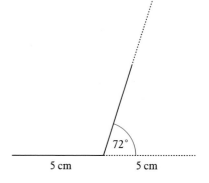

5 cm   5 cm

72°

3 Draw a regular hexagon.
You can do this in the same way, but use an angle of 60°.

4 Draw a regular octagon. The angle you will need is 45°.

Exterior angle	The angle that you used to draw the shapes is called an **exterior angle**. It is outside the shape.

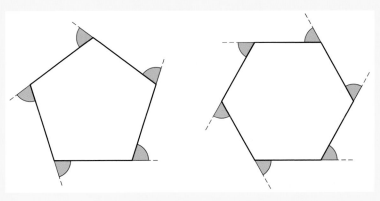

The exterior angles of any polygon add up to 360°.

Example   Work out the size of the exterior angle of a regular hexagon.

The angles add up to 360°.
If the hexagon is regular, all the angles will be equal.

$$\text{Exterior angle} = \frac{360°}{6} = 60°$$

Exercise 18:11

1 Work out the exterior angle of:
  a a regular octagon
  b a regular nonagon
  c a regular decagon
  ● **d** a regular heptagon (round your answer to 2 dp)

2 Work out the exterior angles for regular polygons with the following numbers of sides:
  a 12
  b 15
  c 11
  d 18

3 4 of the exterior angles of a pentagon are 56°, 47°, 103° and 67°. What is the size of the fifth angle?

4 The exterior angle of a regular polygon is 36°. How many sides has it got?

Interior angle	The angles inside a polygon are called **interior angles**. They always make a straight line with the exterior angle. This means that:

Exterior angle + interior angle = 180°
Interior angle = 180° − exterior angle

Example Work out the size of the interior angle of a regular hexagon.

$$\text{Exterior angle} = \frac{360°}{6} = 60°$$

$$\text{Interior angle} = 180° − 60° = 120°$$

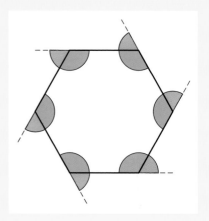

Exercise 18:12

1 Copy this table. Fill it in.

Number of sides	Name of polygon	Exterior angle	Interior angle
3	equilateral triangle		
4	square		
5	regular pentagon		
6	regular hexagon		
7	regular heptagon		
8	regular octagon		

Of course, not all polygons are regular.

This is a pentagon because it has five sides,
but is not a regular pentagon.
All of its sides are not the same length.

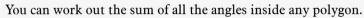

You can work out the sum of all the angles inside any polygon.
This is called **the sum of the interior angles**.
This is how you do it.

Draw lines from one corner of the polygon
so that you split it into triangles.

Count the number of triangles: there are 3 here.

There are 180° in each triangle so multiply 3 by 180.

$3 \times 180° = 540°$.

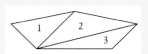

The sum of the interior angles of a pentagon is 540°.

2   **a** Draw any hexagon.
    b Split the hexagon into triangles by drawing lines from one corner.
    c Write down how many triangles you have made.
    d Work out the sum of the interior angles in a hexagon.

3   **a** Draw any octagon.
    b Split the octagon into triangles by drawing lines from one corner.
    c Write down how many triangles you have made.
    d Work out the sum of the interior angles in an octagon.

4   **a** Work out the sum of the interior angles of a heptagon.
    b Divide your answer to part **a** by 7.
    c Check that this matches with the value you worked out in your table
         in question **1**.

5   The sum of the interior angles in a polygon is 1440°.
    a How many triangles has it been split into?
    b How many sides does the polygon have?

4 Trial and improvement

Fred is trying to fence off a rectangular area to keep his sheep in.
He has 30 m of fencing.
He wants to make sure that each sheep has 1 m² of grass to graze in.
He has 50 sheep.
He wants to use the hedge as one side of the rectangle.
How would you build the fence?

Fred knows that he needs to solve a problem.
He can solve problems by guessing different answers.
He keeps trying different answers until he thinks he has found the best one.

This method is called **trial and improvement**.
You can use this method to solve lots of problems in Maths.
The method works for the equations that you solved in section 1 of this Unit.
You would usually only do it this way if you were told to!

Example   Solve $12x - 35 = 163$

Value of x	Value of $12x - 35$		
10	$12 \times 10 - 35 = 85$	too small	
20	$12 \times 20 - 35 = 205$	too big	x is between 10 and 20
16	157	too small	x is between 16 and 20
17	169	too big	x is between 16 and 17
16.5	163	correct	

Answer: $x = 16.5$

Exercise 18:13

Solve these equations by trial and improvement.
For each question:
- copy the table
- fill it in
- add more rows until you find the answer.

1 $2x - 3 = 31$

Value of x	Value of $2x - 3$	
10	$2 \times 10 - 3 = \ldots$	…
20	…	…
17	…	…

2 $3x + 5 = 47$

Value of x	Value of $3x + 5$	
10	$3 \times 10 + 5 = \ldots$	…
20	…	…
15	…	…
…	…	…

3 $4x + 5 = 73$

Value of x	Value of $4x + 5$	
10	…	…
20	…	…
15	…	…
…	…	…

4 $4x - 5 = 45$

Value of x	Value of $4x - 5$	
10	…	…
20	…	…
12	…	…
13	…	…
12.5	…	…

5 $4x - 13 = 33$

Value of x	Value of $4x - 13$	
10	…	…
20	…	…
11	…	…
12	…	…
…	…	…

6 $5p + 23 = 221$

Value of p	Value of $5p + 23$	
20	...	...
...	...	...
...	...	...

7 $12y - 14 = 156.4$

Value of y	Value of $12y - 14$	
...	...	...

Usually this method is used for harder equations.
This is where it becomes even more useful.

Example   Solve $x^2 = 1444$ *Remember:* $x^2 = x \times x$

Value of x	Value of x^2	
30	$30 \times 30 = 900$	too small
40	$40 \times 40 = 1600$	too big
38	1444	correct

x is between 30 and 40

Answer: $x = 38$

Exercise 18:14

Solve these equations by trial and improvement.
For questions **1–9**:
- copy the table
- fill it in
- add more rows until you find the answer.

1 $x^2 + 45 = 270$

Value of x	Value of $x^2 + 45$	
10	...	...
20	...	...
15	...	...

2 $x^2 - 41 = 155$

Value of x	Value of $x^2 - 41$	
10	...	...
20	...	...
14	...	...

3 $x^2 - 54 = 622$

Value of x	Value of $x^2 - 54$	
20	...	...
30	...	...
...	...	...

4 $x^2 + 63 = 504$

Value of x	Value of $x^2 + 63$	
10	...	...
20	...	...
...	...	...

5 $r^2 - 250 = 906$

Value of r	Value of $r^2 - 250$	
20	...	...
30	...	...
...	...	...

6 $p^2 - 50 = 311$

Value of p	Value of $p^2 - 50$	
...	...	...

7 $x^2 + x = 812$

Value of x	Value of $x^2 + x$	
...	...	...

You can also solve number problems using trial and improvement.

Example   A number cubed is 1728. What is the number?

Trial number	Number cubed	
10	1000	too small
15	3375	too big
12	1728	correct

So $12^3 = 1728$ and the number you need is 12.

Use trial and improvement to solve these problems.

8   A number cubed is 216. What is the number?

9   A number cubed is 12 167. What is the number?

10   A square has an area of 289 cm². How long are its sides?

11   The length of a picture is 6 inches more
than its width.
The area of the picture is 40 in².
Find the width and length of the picture.
Use this table to help you.

Width	Length	Area	
1	7	7	too small
2	8	16	too small

• 12   Howard is buying some cassettes and some CDs.
The CDs cost £12.50 each and the tapes cost £9.50 each.
Howard has £66 birthday money to spend.
He wants to spend all the money – not a penny more and not a penny
less!
Work out what combination of tapes and CDs he can buy.

Sometimes answers do not work out exactly.
When this happens, you may have to give your answer correct to 1 dp.
Start by trapping the answer between two consecutive whole numbers.
Then look at values to 1 dp.
When your answer is trapped between two 1 dp values you check the value half-way
between them.
If this number gives you an answer that is too big then the smaller 1 dp value is
correct to 1 dp.
If this number gives you an answer that is too small then the bigger 1 dp value is
correct to 1 dp.

Example   Solve $x^3 = 135$

Value of x	Value of x^3		
5	125	too small	
6	216	too big	x is between 5 and 6
5.5	166.375	too big	x is between 5 and 5.5
5.1	132.651	too small	x is between 5.1 and 5.5
5.2	140.608	too big	x is between 5.1 and 5.2
5.15	136.590 875	too big	x is between 5.1 and 5.15

This value is half-way between 5.1 and 5.2

x must be somewhere in the **green** part
of the number line.

Any number in the **green** part rounds
down to 5.1 to 1 dp.

Answer: $x = 5.1$ to 1 dp.

Exercise 18:15

1 Solve these equations by trial and improvement.
Draw a table to help you find each answer.
Give all of your answers to 1 dp.

    a $x^2 = 160$ **c** $x^3 = 250$ **e** $x^3 + x = 45$
    b $x^2 - 50 = 30$ **d** $x^2 + x = 900$ **f** $x^3 + 4x = 70$

2 This is a square rug.
The area of the rug is 10 m².

    a Write down the equation that you need
to solve to find the length of a side.
    b Solve the equation to find the length
of the side of the rug.
Give your answer in metres to 1 dp.

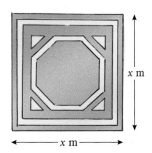

x m

x m

1 The perimeter of a rectangular school field is 140 m.

The width of the field is 38 m.

a Write a formula for the **perimeter** of a rectangle if you know its **length** and its **width**

b Re-write the formula, putting in the perimeter of the field and its width.

c Solve your equation to find the length of the field.

38 m

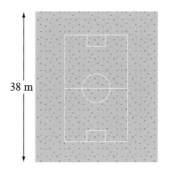

2 Nathan is asked to think of a number.

He is then told to treble it and add 15. He says that the answer is 69.

a Call Nathan's number n.

Write down a formula for what Nathan has done to the number.

b Write down an equation in terms of n.

c Solve your equation.

d What number did Nathan think of?

3 Elliott rolls a 10-sided dice and spins a coin.

He draws a sample space diagram to show all the possible outcomes.

a Copy this table.

	1	2	3	4	5	6	7	8	9	10
Head										
Tail										

b Fill in all the possible outcomes in your table.

c How many outcomes are there altogether?

d Write down the probability of getting a tail and a 7.

e Work out the probability of getting a head and an even number.

4 Estimate the size of each of these angles.

Measure them afterwards to check your answers.

a   **b** 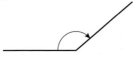   **c**

5 For each question, calculate the angle marked with a letter.

a
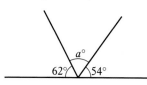

d
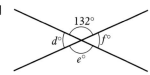

b
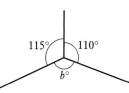

e
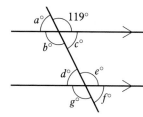

c
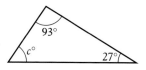

f
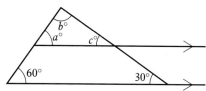

6 The exterior angle of a regular polygon is 18°.
  a How many sides has it got?
  b Write down the size of the interior angle.

7 Solve these equations by trial and improvement.
For each part:
- copy the table
- fill it in
- add more rows until you find the answer.

  a $x^2 + 56 = 681$

Value of x	Value of $x^2 + 56$	
20	...	...
30	...	...
...	...	...

  b $x^2 - 51 = 2350$

Value of x	Value of $x^2 - 51$	
40	...	...
50	...	...
...	...	...

8 Solve these equations by trial and improvement.
Draw a table to help you find each solution.
Give all of your answers 1 dp.
  a $x^2 = 190$ **b** $x^3 - 26 = 37$ **c** $x^2 + x = 440$

1 Tina buys 6 m of fencing to make a run for her rabbit.
She wants to make the run 0.75 m wide.

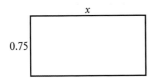

   a Write down an equation for the perimeter of the run.
   b Solve the equation to find the length of the run.

2 Ian spins a 5-sided spinner numbered from 1 to 5 at the same time as he
rolls a normal dice numbered from 1 to 6.
   a Copy this sample space diagram to show the two numbers that he
gets. Fill it in.

Spinner

		1	2	3	4	5
	1	1, 1	1, 2			
	2					
Dice	3					
	4		4, 2		4, 4	
	5	5, 1				
	6					

Use the sample space diagram to write down the probability that:
   b the total score is 7
   c the score is the same on the spinner and the dice
   d the total score is less than 5
   e the score on the spinner and the dice is the same and the total score
      is less than 5.

3 The interior angle of a regular
polygon is 160°.
How many sides does the polygon have?

160°

4 Solve these equations using trial and improvement.
You need to rearrange the equations to get all the xs on the same side.
Part **a** has been rearranged for you.
Give your answers to 1 dp.

   a $x^2 + 1 = \dfrac{1}{x}$ This is the same as $x^2 + 1 - \dfrac{1}{x} = 0$

   b $x^2 = \dfrac{1}{x} + 5$

   c $x^3 = \dfrac{1}{x}$

1 **a** Write down a formula for the perimeter of each rectangle, P = ...

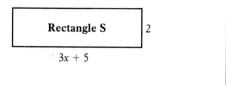

Rectangle S   2

3x + 5

Rectangle T   x

4x − 3

b The two perimeters are equal.
Write down an equation in terms of x.
c Solve the equation.
d Use the value of x to find the length of each rectangle.

2 Keanu spins these two spinners.
Draw a sample space diagram to
show all the possible outcomes.

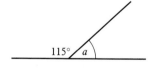
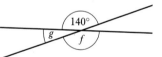

3 Calculate the angles marked with letters.

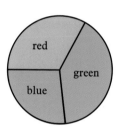
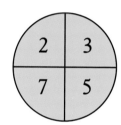
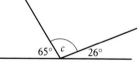
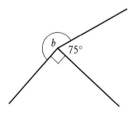
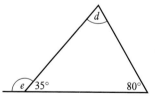
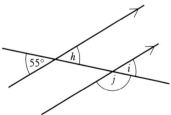

4 This is a regular hexagon.
a Find the size of each exterior angle.
b Find the sum of the interior angles
by drawing triangles.

UNIT 1

1　**a**　cuboid

　　b　(1) 8　　(2) 6　　(3) 12

　　c

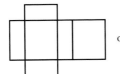 or similar

2　**a**　any angle bigger than 180°, e.g. 210°

　　b　any angle less than 90°, e.g. 58°

　　c　any angle between 90° and 180°, e.g. 104°

3　1.45, 1.37, 1.30, 1.29, 1.21, 1.08

4　**a**　square based pyramid 　　**b**　triangular prism

5　**a, b**

Number of calls	Tally	Total
1	|	1
2	|||	3
3	||||	4
4	⦀|	6
5	⦀ |||	8
6	|||	3
7	⦀ ||	7
8	||||	4

6　**a**　(1) 140 709　　(2) 141 000

　　b　(1) Ninety five thousand and eighty two　　(2) 95 100

7　**a**

Car	Price in £	Price to the nearest £100
Ford Ka	9595	9600
Nissan Micra	9550	9600
Peugeot 106	9070	9100
Rover Mini Cooper	9630	9600
Vauxhall Corsa	9295	9300
Fiat Punto	9995	10 000

　　b　Peugeot 106, Vauxhall Corsa, Nissan Micra, Ford Ka, Rover Mini Cooper, Fiat Punto

1 a front side   **b** front side

2 a

Time (minutes)	Tally	Total
0 to 20	|||	3
21 to 40	|||| ||||	9
41 to 60	|||| ||||	10
61 to 80	|||| ||||	10
81 to 100	|||| |||	8

b $10 + 10 + 8 = 28$

3 a $420 \div 3 = 140$
   b $\frac{1}{4}$ is $420 \div 4 = 105$ $\frac{3}{4}$ is $3 \times 105 = 315$

4 a £1 = 100 p $100 \div 4 = 25$ p
   b 3×25 p $= 75$ p
   c $\frac{1}{5}$ is $100 \div 5 = 20$ p, $\frac{3}{5}$ is $3 \times 20 = 60$ p
   d $\frac{1}{10}$ is $300 \div 10 = 30$ p, $\frac{7}{10}$ is $7 \times 30 = 210$ p
   e $\frac{1}{6}$ is $900 \div 6 = 150$ p
   f $\frac{1}{7}$ is $140 \div 7 = 20$ p, $\frac{2}{7}$ is $2 \times 20 = 40$ p

5 a $3 \times 12 = 36$ **b** $\frac{1}{5}$ is $24 \div 2 = 12$, $\frac{5}{5} = 5 \times 12 = 60$
6 a 27, 33 (add 6 each time)   **b** 162, 486 (multiply by 3 each time)
7 a $4 \times 10 - 20 = 40 - 20 = 20$ Second term is 20
       $20 \times 10 - 20 = 200 - 20 = 180$ Third term is 180
   b 1, 3, 6, 10, 15

8 a

   b

Pattern number	1	2	3	4	5
Number of dots	8	11	14	17	20

   c Start with 8 and add 3 each time

1 a $2.35 \times 10 = \mathbf{235}$ **d** $21.5 \times 1000 = \mathbf{21\,500}$ **g** $762 + 509 = \mathbf{1271}$
   b $45 \times \mathbf{100} = 4500$ **e** $0.04 \times 10 = \mathbf{0.4}$ **h** $407 - 267 = \mathbf{140}$
   c $0.3 \times \mathbf{10} = 3$ **f** $40.625 \times 100 = \mathbf{4062.5}$

2 a isosceles triangle   **c** hexagon
   b quadrilateral   **d** pentagon

3   **a** $18.7 + 25.4 + 13.9 + 16 + 22.1 = 96.1$ km

     b $25.4 - 8.7 = 16.7$

     c $18.7 + 25.4 + 13.9 + 16 = 74$

        $74 - 64 = 10$ km

4   £20.40

5   **a**   pictogram   **b**   50   **c** $50 + 125 + 25 = 200$

6   **a**   21

     b $12 + 25 + 21 + 16 + 29 + 48 + 32 = 183$

     c $32 \times £89.99 = £2879.68$

     d   Saturday. More people go shopping on a Saturday.

UNIT 4

1   The rectangles are the same size and shape.

2   **a**   rhombus   **c**   square   **e**   parallelogram

     b   trapezium   **d**   rectangle   **f**   kite

3

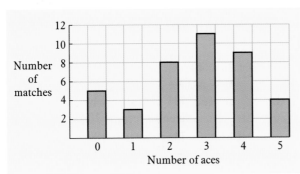

4   **a**   33 lb (approximately)   **b**   22 kg (approximately)

5   **a**   8 km   **c**   6 km   **e**   5 km

     b   10 min   **d**   15 min   **f**   13:20 (or 1.20 p.m.)

UNIT 5

1

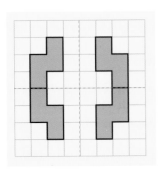

2   No. There are 5 multiples of 4 (4, 16, 24, 40, 8) and only 3 numbers that are not multiples of 4. Sam is therefore more likely to walk the dog.

3 **a** 33% **c** 0.6 **e** 35%

   b 64% **d** $\frac{57}{100}$ **f** 0.81

4 **a** overtime pay = $4.75 \times 7 = £33.25$

   b total pay = $145 + 33.25 = £178.25$

5 **a** $C = 30 + 0.25 \times 50 = 30 + 12.5 = 42.5$ so cost = £42.50

   b $30 + 0.25 \times ? = 35$ so $0.25 \times ? = 5$

    the visit was $5 \div 0.25$ minutes = 20 minutes

UNIT 6

1 **a**
$$\begin{array}{r} 7.91 \\ \times \quad 4 \\ \hline 31.64 \\ 3 \end{array}$$

  b
$$\begin{array}{r} 2.47 \\ \times \quad 31 \\ \hline 2.47 \\ {}_17_24.10 \\ \hline 76.57 \end{array}$$

  c $5 \times 8 = 40$
    $0.040 = 0.04$

  d
$$\begin{array}{r} 1.78 \\ 4\overline{)7\,.^31^32} \end{array}$$

2 **a** $£15.98 \div 2 = £7.99$ **b** $£7.99 + £15.98 = £23.97$

3 **a** $(395 \div 51)$; $7 \times 51 = 357$, $8 \times 51 = 408$ 8 coaches are needed.

  b
$$\begin{array}{r} 395 \\ \times \quad 17 \\ \hline 2_67_365 \\ 3950 \\ \hline 6715 \\ {}_1_1 \end{array}$$
    So the trip will cost £6715.

4
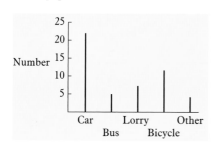

5 **a** (1) 5 (2) 5

  b (1) none (2) 2

  c (1) 8 (2) 8

  d (1) 1 (2) none

UNIT 7

1 **a** P(3, 2)   Q(4, 6)   R(0, 5)

  b, c
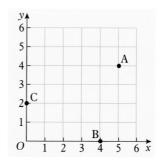

2 **a** 12 m   **b** 11 m   **c** 2 cm   **d** 1.5 cm (or $1\frac{1}{2}$)

3 **a**

b

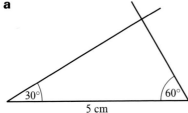

4 $1 - 0.55 = 0.45$ **5** $100 - 67 = 33\%$ **6** $8 + 5 = 13$; $\frac{8}{13}$

7 **a** 420   **c** 1150   **e** 40

b 1100   **d** 24 000   **f** 200

8

Stem	Leaf
2	7 8 9
3	0 1 2 5 6 8 9
4	0 1 2 4

Key: 3|2 means 32 seconds

9 **a** 174 cm   **b** 165 cm

UNIT 8

1 **a** NE   **b** S   **c** SW   **d** SW

2 **a** 110°   **b** 315° (135° + 180°)

3 Numbers using cars and taxis have increased a lot.
Numbers using trains are about the same.
Numbers using buses and coaches have gone down by about half.
Numbers using pedal cycles have gone down and are now very close to zero.

4 **a** Davies Electricals   Buyrite   Discount TVs

5% of £268 = £13.40 $\frac{1}{3}$ of £390 = £130   25% of £350 = £87.50

£268 − £13.4 = £254.60   £390 − £130 = £260   £350 − £87.50 = £262.50

b Davies Electricals

5 3% of 864 = 25.92 ≈ 26

6 **a**

s	1	2	3	4
t	2	7	12	17

b, c, d, e

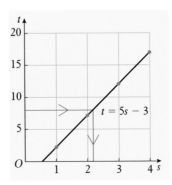

$t = 5s - 3$

f 2.2 (using green lines shown)

7 a

x	1	2	3	4
y	7	6	5	4

b, c, d

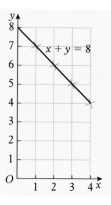

UNIT 9

1 a 1270 cm   **c** 3200 g   **e** 2500 ml
   b 5.9 cm   **d** 4.7 g   **f** 670 l
2 $4 + 6.2 + 3.5 + 12 = 25.7$ cm
3 a 25%   **b** $465 \div 3 = 155$ **c** $\frac{107}{360}$ $(360 - 120 - 90 - 43 = 107)$
4 factors of 48 are   1, 2, 3, 4, **6**, 8, 12, 16, 24, 48
   factors of 90 are   1, 2, 3, 5, **6**, 9, 10, 15, 18, 30, 45, 90
   Highest common factor is **6**
5 a $7 \times 7 = 49$ **b** 9
6 2, 3, 5, 7, 11, 13
7 loss = £282.89 − £215 = £67.89
   percentage loss $= \dfrac{67.89}{282.89} \times 100 = 23.9987\ldots = 24\%$ (2 sf)
8 17.5% of £178 $= 17.5 \div 100 \times 178 = £31.15$
   total bill = £178 + £31.15 = £209.15

UNIT 10

1 a A(−2, 4)   B(−6, 2)   C(−3, 1)   **c** (−6, −2)
   b

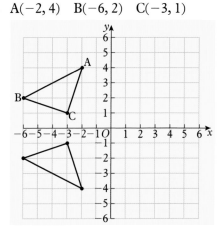

2 **a, b**

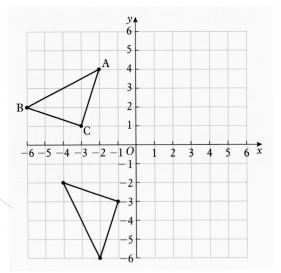

3 **a** $8 + 12 + 3 + 7 + 10 + 13 + 2 + 6 + 1 + 8 = 70$
    $70 \div 10 = 7$ mean $= 7$
  b mode $= 8$
  c $1, 2, 3, 6, 7, 8, 8, 10, 12, 13$ $(7 + 8) \div 2 = 7.5$
    median $= 7.5$

4 5 calls

5 **a** (1) $\frac{7}{6}$ (2) $1\frac{1}{6}$ **b** (1) $\frac{11}{8}$ (2) $1\frac{3}{8}$

6 **a** $\frac{7}{8}$ **d** $\frac{1}{2} - \frac{1}{6} = \frac{3}{6} - \frac{1}{6} = \frac{2}{6} = \frac{1}{3}$
  b $\frac{2}{12} = \frac{1}{6}$ **e** $3 + 4 = 7$ $\frac{1}{4} + \frac{3}{8} = \frac{2}{8} + \frac{3}{8} = \frac{5}{8}$ $3\frac{1}{4} + 4\frac{3}{8} = 7\frac{5}{8}$
  c $\frac{1}{4} + \frac{5}{12} = \frac{3}{12} + \frac{5}{12} = \frac{8}{12} = \frac{2}{3}$ **f** $\frac{23}{4} - \frac{5}{2} = \frac{23}{4} - \frac{10}{4} = \frac{13}{4} = 3\frac{1}{4}$

7 **a**

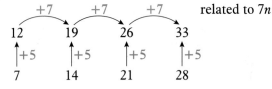

  using $m = 7n$

  b formula is $s = 7n + 5$

8 **a**

  b 5, 8, 11, 14
  c

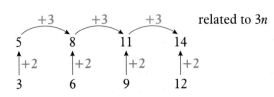

  using $m = 3n$

  formula is $s = 3n + 2$

502

1 **a** $5 \times 3 = 15$ feet   **c** $2 \times 16 = 32$ ounces

   b $36 \div 12 = 3$ feet   **d** $7 \times 8 = 56$ pints

2 **a** 5 kg $= 5000$ kg

       $5000 \div 450 = 11.1$ (3 sf)

       so 5 kg is about 11 lb.

   b (1) 1 yd is 36 in

          $2 \times 36 = 72$ in

      (2) 1 inch is about 2.5 cm

          $72 \times 2.5 = 180$ cm

   c 1 mile is about 1.6 km

      $56 \times 1.6 = 89.6$ km ≈ 90 km

3 1 pound is about 450 g

   so 42 pounds is about 18 900 g $= 18.9$ kg

   John's bag is over 18 kg

4 **a** (1) 3 m   **c** (1) 100 kg

      (2) 3 yards   (2) 220 lb

   b (1) $\frac{1}{3}$ litre   **d** (1) 5 oz

      (2) $\frac{1}{2}$ pint   (2) 150 g

5 No. Because there are more milk chocolates than plain chocolates.

6 **a** (3 is the only odd number) $\frac{1}{6}$

   b (6 and 18 are multiples of 6) $\frac{2}{6} = \frac{1}{3}$

   c (3, 6, 10 are triangle numbers) $\frac{3}{6} = \frac{1}{2}$

   d (2 and 3 are less than 4) $\frac{2}{6} = \frac{1}{3}$

7 **a** $7 + 11 + 12 + 13 + 8 + 9 = 60$ **d** $\frac{9}{60} = \frac{3}{20}$

   b $\frac{7}{60}$ **e** $(7 + 11 + 12 = 30)$ $\frac{30}{60} = \frac{1}{2}$

   c $(12 + 9 = 21)$ $\frac{21}{60} = \frac{7}{20}$

8 **a** $7 - 2 \times 3 = 7 - 6 = 1$ BODMAS $\times$ comes before $-$

   b $24 \div 4 + 2 = 6 + 2 = 8$ BODMAS $\div$ comes before $+$

   c $(7 + 5) \times 8 = 12 \times 8 = 96$ BODMAS ( ) comes before $\times$

   d $18 - 2 \times 3^2 = 18 - 2 \times 9 = 18 - 18 = 0$

                      BODMAS Powers of first, then $\times$ and then $-$

9 **a** 11   **b** 4

10 **a** $\frac{703}{950}$ $(= \frac{37}{50})$ **b** $\frac{703}{950} \times 100 = 74\%$

1 **a** 180   **b** 425   **c** 2.4

2 **a** $102 \div 3 = 34$ miles/hour

   b 40 minutes $= 40 \div 60$ hour $= 0.6666\ldots$

      so 1 hour 40 minutes $= 1.6666\ldots$

      $5 \div 1.6666 = 3$ km/hour

3

Number of planes	Number of days	Working	Total
3	4	3×4	12
4	2	4×2	8
5	6	5×6	30
6	3	6×3	18
Total	15		68

Mean number of planes $= 68 \div 15$
$= 4.53$
≈ 4.5

4 a $1500 \times 1.67 = 2505$ euros **b** $3841 \div 1.67 = £2300$
5 a $2 - 9 = -7$ **c** $10 + -7 = 3$
 b $-5 - 3 = -8$ **d** $8 - -6 = 8 + 6 = 14$

UNIT 13

1 a **b**

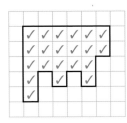 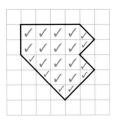

(21 squares) 21 cm² (13 whole squares + 8 half squares = 17 squares)
17 cm²

c

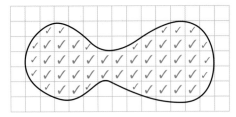

(35 whole squares + 16 squares over half = 51 squares) 51 cm²

2

(9 whole squares + 9 squares over half = 18 squares)
$18 \times 30 = 540$ square miles

3   **a** $62 - 47 = 15$

  b   Julia is more consistent than Norma as her range is much smaller.

4   The temperatures are more consistent in Eilat (i.e. less variation in temperature than in Chester).

  Also the temperatures are higher in Eilat.

5   **a** $\dfrac{100 - 60}{20} = \dfrac{40}{20} = 2$ **c** $\sqrt{\dfrac{6 \times 7}{3}} = \sqrt{\dfrac{42}{3}} = \sqrt{14} \approx \sqrt{16} = 4$

  b $\sqrt{78} \approx \sqrt{81} = 9$

6   **a** $4 \times 5 - 3 = 20 - 3 = 17$ **c** $4 \times -8 - 3 = -32 - 3 = -35$

  b $4 \times 12 - 3 = 48 - 3 = 45$ **d** $4 \times 3.5 - 3 = 14 - 3 = 11$

7   **a** $2 \times 6^2 + 13 = 2 \times 36 + 13 = 72 + 13 = 85$

  b $2 \times 11^2 + 13 = 2 \times 121 + 13 = 242 + 13 = 255$

  c $2 \times (-5)^2 + 13 = 2 \times 25 + 13 = 50 + 13 = 63$

  d $2 \times (-1)^2 + 13 = 2 \times 1 + 13 = 2 + 13 = 15$

8 $P = 2(13 + 9) = 2 \times 22 = 44$

UNIT 14

1   **a** $(13 \times 8) \div 2 = 104 \div 2 = 52 \text{ cm}^2$

  b $5 \times 8 = 40; \quad 2 \times (9 - 5) = 8; \quad 40 + 8 = 48 \text{ cm}^2$

  c $20 \times 25 = 500 \text{ cm}^2$

  d $4 \times 16 = 64 \qquad (9 \times 16) \div 2 = 144 \div 2 = 72$

   $64 + 72 + 72 = 208 \text{ cm}^2$

2 $4 \times 6 = 24; \quad 3 \times 4 = 12; \quad 3 \times 6 = 18$

  $24 + 24 + 12 + 12 + 18 + 18 = 108 \text{ cm}^2$

3   **a** $\frac{3}{20}$ **b** $\frac{4}{3} \ (= 1\frac{1}{3})$ **c** $\frac{1}{4} \div 3 = \frac{1}{4} \times \frac{1}{3} = \frac{1}{12}$

4   The vertical scale does not start at zero

5 $3 : 11$

6   **a** $3 : 2$ **b** $2 : 3$ **c** $2 : 3$

7   **a** $5 \times 250 = 1250 \text{ ml}$

  b $1350 = 3 \times 450; \quad 3 \times 300 = 900 \text{ ml}$

  c $150 = 300 \div 2; \quad 450 \div 2 = 225 \text{ ml}$

8 $25 \times 8 = 200 \text{ cm}^2$

9   total number of parts $= 5 + 3 = 8$

  size of one part $= £40 \div 8 = £5$

  a $3 \times £5 = £15$

  b   5 parts out of 8 parts so fraction is $\frac{5}{8}$

10   total number of parts $= 2 + 3 + 5 = 10$

  size of one part $= 180 \div 10 = 18°$

  angles are $2 \times 18 = 36°; \quad 3 \times 18 = 54°; \quad 5 \times 18 = 90°$

1 5 squares left and 2 squares up

2
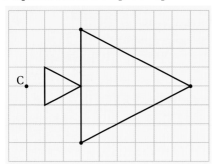

3 **a** 1 hour 20 minutes   **b** 01:25
4 9 September
5 **a** 2.7   **c** 0.06   **e** 0.386
       b 6.38   **d** 0.007   **f** 0.004 752
6 £1.99 = 199 p;   199 ÷ 48 = 4.145...
                        = 4 p to the nearest penny
7 **a** $3x - 7 = 17$ **c** $2a + 12 = 5a$
            $3x = 24$ $12 = 3a$
             $x = 8$ $4 = a$
                                            $a = 4$

       b $\dfrac{x}{3} + 8 = 11$ **d** $7m - 3 = 4m + 12$
            $\dfrac{x}{3} = 3$ $3m - 3 = 12$
             $x = 9$ $3m = 15$
                                              $m = 5$

1 $9\,\text{cm}^3$ (9 cubes each of $1\,\text{cm}^3$)
2 $9 \times 2 \times 3 = 54\,\text{cm}^3$
3 **a**

	Tally	Frequency
Won	||||| ||	7
Drew	|||||	5
Lost	|||	3

b $7 + 5 + 3 = 15$
estimate of probability $= \frac{7}{15}$

4 **a** carry out an experiment
       b look at data recorded for previous winters
5 **a** $64\ (8 \times 8)$ **c** 6   **e** 100
       b $125\ (5 \times 5 \times 5)$ **d** $64\ (4 \times 4 \times 4)$ **f** 100 000
6 **a** (1) Q   **b** (1) 4.032×10^{14}
            (2) R   (2) 2.3×10^{10}

1 **a, c**

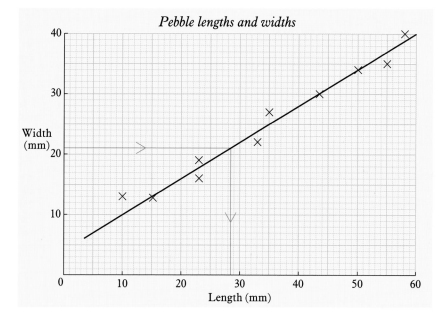

b (strong) positive correlation.

d 28.5 mm using the red lines shown.

2 **a** 250 ml for £1.80   180 p ÷ 25 = 7.2 p
    400 ml for £2.45   245 p ÷ 40 = 6.125 p

 b 400 ml for £2.45

3 **a** $2f + 6f - 7f = 8f - 7f = 1f = f$

 b $(4x - x = 3x; 3x^2 + 5x^2 = 8x^2)$ $3x + 8x^2$

 c $(4 \times 2 = 8;\ t \times t = t^2)$ $8t^2$

4 **a** $12x + 20 = 68$ **b** $14 = 14x - 56$
        $12x = 48$ $70 = 14x$
         $x = 4$ $5 = x$
                            $x = 5$

5 **a** (1) circumference $= \pi \times 11 = 34.56$ cm (2 dp)

   (2) radius $= 11 \div 2 = 5.5$ cm so area $= \pi \times 5.5^2 = \pi \times 5.5 \times 5.5$
                            $= 95.03$ cm^2 (2 dp)

 b (1) diameter $= 2 \times 3.8 = 7.6$ cm spaces so circumference $= \pi \times 7.6$
                            $= 23.88$ cm (2 dp)

   (2) area $= \pi \times 3.8^2 = \pi \times 3.8 \times 3.8$
                $= 45.36$ cm^2 (2 dp)

6 **a** radius   **c** diameter   **e** arc
   b chord   **d** tangent

1 **a** S: $P = 3x + 5 + 2 + 3x + 5 + 2 = 6x + 14$
        T: $P = 4x - 3 + x + 4x - 3 + x = 10x - 6$
   b $6x + 14 = 10x - 6$
   c $14 = 4x - 6$
        $20 = 4x$
        $5 = x$
        $x = 5$
   d S: $3x + 5 = 3 \times 5 + 5 = 20$
        T: $4x - 3 = 4 \times 5 - 3 = 17$

2

	2	3	5	7
red, R	R, 2	R, 3	R,5	R, 7
blue, B	B, 2	B, 3	B,5	B, 7
green, G	G, 2	G, 3	G,5	G, 7

3 **a** $180° - 115° = 65°$ angles on a straight line
   b $360° - (75° + 90°) = 360° - 165° = 195°$ angles at a point
   c $180° - (65° + 26°) = 180° - 91° = 89°$ angles on a straight line
   d $180° - (35° + 80°) = 180° - 115° = 65°$ angles in a triangle
   e $180° - 35° = 145°$ angles on a straight line
   f $140°$ opposite angles
   g $180° - 140° = 40°$ angles on a straight line
   h $55°$ opposite angles
   i $55°$ corresponding angles
   j $180° - 55° = 125°$ angles on a straight line

4 **a** exterior angle $= \dfrac{360°}{6} = 60°$

   b sum of interior angles $= 4 \times 180° = 720°$ (4 triangles)

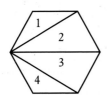